THE PEOPLE'S GALLERIES

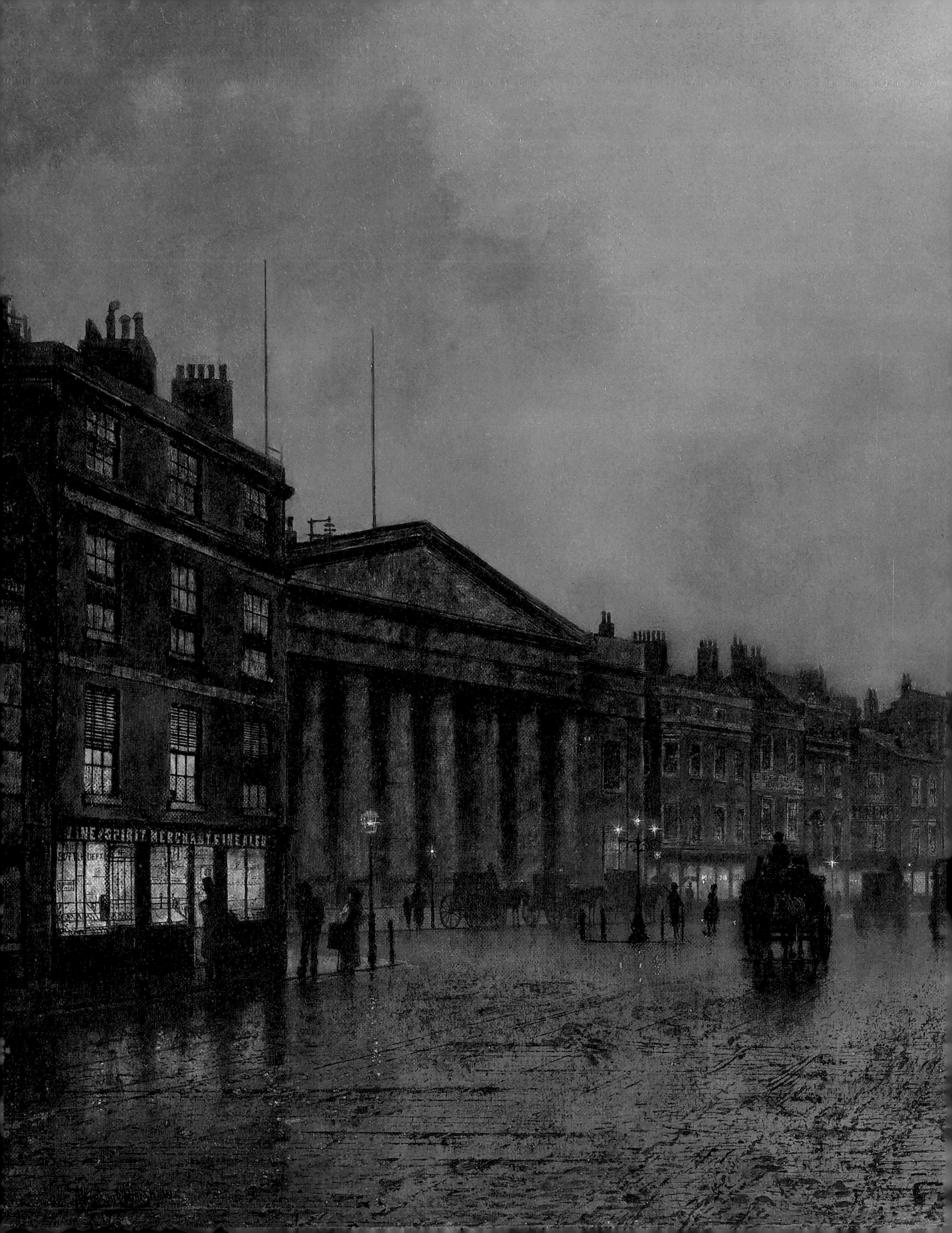

THE PEOPLE'S GALLERIES

ART MUSEUMS AND EXHIBITIONS IN BRITAIN, 1800–1914

Giles Waterfield

Published for
THE PAUL MELLON CENTRE
FOR STUDIES IN BRITISH ART
by
YALE UNIVERSITY PRESS
New Haven and London

Designed by Charlotte Grievson.
Printed in China.

Library of Congress Cataloging-in-Publication Data

Waterfield, Giles.
The people's galleries : art museums and exhibitions in Britain, 1800-1914 / Giles Waterfield.
pages cm
ISBN 978-0-300-20984-6 (cloth : alkaline paper)
1. Art museums--Great Britain--History--19th century. 2. Art museums--Great Britain--History--20th century. 3.
Art--Great Britain--Exhibitions--History. 4. Art museums--Social aspects--Great Britain--History. 5. Art and state-
-Great Britain--History. 6. Art and society--Great Britain--History. 7. City and town life--Great Britain--History. 8.
Great Britain--Intellectual life--19th century. 9. Great Britain--Intellectual life--20th century. 10. Great Britain--Social
conditions. I. Title.
N1020.W28 2015
708.209--dc23
2014041638

Frontispiece: *The Custom House, Liverpool, Looking South*, John Atkinson Grimshaw (detail of Fig. 38).
Page vi: The opening of the Walker Art Gallery, as illustrated in the *Graphic*, 15 September 1877 (detail of Fig. 104).
Page ix: *A Street in Brittany*, Stanhope Forbes (detail of Fig. 194).

For Peter Mandler

CONTENTS

ACKNOWLEDGEMENTS

This book began, rather longer ago than I care to remember, as a history of museums and art galleries in Britain, from their earliest days to the present. Further research made me realise what a huge subject I had undertaken. At the same time I became intrigued by the history of the great art galleries of Victorian Britain, a subject that has been well treated in terms of individual institutions but not much considered holistically. The book is therefore less wide-ranging than originally intended, but I hope that it illuminates a style of gallery that to this day remains contentious and often under threat, and in greater depth than was originally intended.

A number of people have read all or part of the text, and their comments have been extremely helpful: notably Simon Bradley, Peter Funnell, Charlotte Gere, Tanya Harrod, Jonathan King, Peter Mandler, Bernadette Sulgit and my copyeditor Michael Hall. The insights of the anonymous readers for Yale University Press were notably valuable.

I am indebted to a large number of people for detailed comments and assistance, as well as for generous hospitality. They include John Agnew, Julian Agnew, David Alexander, Adriano Aymonino, Sean Baggaley, Sara Basquill, Stella Beddoe, David Beevers, Susan Bennett, the late Victoria Bethell, Oliver Bradbury, Xanthe Brooke, Julius Bryant, Christina Cadogan, Marie Collier, Michael Conforti, Jonathan Conlin, Alan Crookham, Francis Graham, Melanie Hall, Kate Hill, Jeannie Hobhouse, James Holloway, Holger Hoock, Sara Knelman, Michael Ledger-Lomas, Philippa Lewis, James Lomax, Arthur Macgregor, Jan Marsh, Andrew McClellan, Edward Morris, Mark O'Neill, Sarah Nichols, Sandra Penketh, Philippa Lewis, Robert Maniura, Jan Piggott, Mark Pomeroy, Helen Rees Leahy, Michael Ripps, Nick Savage, David Scrase, John and Imogen Sheeran, Ruth Shrigley, Gavin Stamp, 'The Gentle Author', Hugh Stevenson, Tim Knox, Hugh Torrens, Julian Treuherz, Helen Valentine, Malcolm Warner, Andrew Wilton and Bridget Wright. My apologies to anyone inadvertently omitted.

For their help in sourcing illustrations, I would especially thank Ruth Solomons and the indefatigable and imaginative Mia Jackson. Obtaining illustrations has been an interesting process. I am much indebted to the generosity of institutions that have provided images free of charge or at very low cost, or that have given much time and effort to helping us with research. Notable in this respect were Brighton Museum and Art Gallery, the British Museum, the Getty Research Institute, the National Portrait Gallery, National Museums Liverpool, Gallery Oldham, The Atkinson at Southport, the Victoria and Albert Museum, and the Yale Centre for British Art.

I have been fortunate enough to spend some time as a visiting scholar in the United States. At the Yale Center for British Art I would like especially to thank Elizabeth Fairman, Amy Meyers, Maria Singer, Angus Trumble and Adrianna Bates. The Clark Art Institute in Williamsburg awarded me a summer fellowship and my thanks go to Michael Ann Holly and her colleagues.

Two periods as a scholar at the Getty Research Institute were of inestimable value even though the great cities of industrial Britain often seemed far away from Los Angeles, physically and mentally. I especially appreciate the kindness and advice of Thomas Gaehtgens, Peter Bonfitto, Elliott Kai-Kee, Rachel Longaker, Louis Marchesano, Alexa Sekyra, Rebecca Zamora and other members of the staff. Discussions with other visiting scholars benefitted my work, in particular those with Olivier Bonfait, Petra Chu, Isabelle Flour and Michael Marrinan.

I am very grateful to the Paul Mellon Centre for British Art for their generous support for this publication, and notably to Brian Allen, Mark Hallett and Martin Postle. It is a great privilege to be published by Yale University Press, where I have enjoyed the stimulus and pleasure of working with Hannah Jenner and above all Gillian Malpass and Charlotte Grievson.

INTRODUCTION

This book studies art museums in Britain, and especially in the regions, from their early days to the onset of the First World War. It was in these years, and particularly after 1865, that the majority of the country's public art galleries outside London were created. The book does not attempt to recount the entire history of art museums in nineteenth-century Britain, and, equally, avoids individual institutional histories. Rather, it considers the inspiration for and the nature of these Victorian galleries, changing attitudes to them, and the intimate, fruitful and often fraught relationship between the art gallery and the temporary exhibition (Fig. 1).

The first section of the book looks at the cultural and social context in which art museums developed in Britain. It posits a continuity of cultural attitudes from early in the eighteenth century through to late in the nineteenth century, a continuity that shaped the civic museum and art gallery. Much of the discussion concentrates on the development of national institutions and the difficulties that faced anyone attempting to create or nourish a public art museum. The second, and much the longest, section examines art galleries in Victorian Britain, focusing on municipal ones: their patrons and publics, the art they collected and its display, the role of temporary exhibitions and educational programmes, the buildings that housed them. The six civic galleries that were generally regarded as notably important – Bir-

mingham, Glasgow, Leeds, Liverpool, Manchester and Nottingham – receive particular attention that also (it is hoped) illuminates a broader argument.[1] The final section suggests that these art museums represented a bold experiment, which passed with the changing of social attitudes, and briefly examines their later history up to the tumultuous present. The book asks how far these Victorian museums succeeded, and argues that after many short-term victories their success was partial and fleeting. It is a particularly British story of pragmatism, opportunism, energy and shortsightedness (Fig. 2).

While concentrating on British art museums, the book seeks to put their history into an international context, the museum being a peculiarly international phenomenon. In some respects, the early history of art museums in Britain – the development of the princely or noble collection, the opening of state institutions early in the nineteenth century, the spread of museums and galleries across the burgeoning provincial cities of the late Victorian period – resembles their development in France and Germany. But the differences are as evident as the similarities. In France the closure of convents and the confiscation of aristocratic collections during the revolution of the 1790s, as well as the development under Napoleon and his successors of a centralised system of art and museum patronage, produced a network of museums and collections wholly unlike

1

their British equivalents. Museums in Lyon and Bordeaux developed quite differently from those in Manchester and Glasgow, notably in their collections: they were annually fed by the state with works of art, a procedure inconceivable on the other side of the Channel. In Germany, relatively few museums resembled the type of bourgeois civic enterprise that triumphed in Britain: much more prominent, in Berlin, Munich, Dresden and other cities, was the model of the princely collection, rich and multifaceted, transformed after 1815 into a semi-public, semi-royal network of museums open to the public but remaining under princely supervision. A pattern of civic patronage closer to Britain can be found in Basel, where in 1661 the city bought the astonishing Amerbach Cabinet, which includes works by Hans Holbein and very much else, creating the earliest civic collection in Europe, now proudly displayed in the Basel Kunstmuseum and the Basel Historisches Museum. And although the history of new museums in the fast-developing cities of the United States

later in the nineteenth century initially resembles the pattern in Britain, styles of collecting and educating were soon to diverge.

No claim is made here for British superiority. But the British history exerted a powerful influence on developments overseas. In particular, the pedagogic approach of the South Kensington Museum shaped the early development in American museums of collections of industrial art, while the concept of a museum of applied arts inspired comparable museums all over Europe, from Vienna onwards.[2] Closely related to South Kensington, the invention of the large-scale trade exhibition was always ascribed in the nineteenth century to France but it reached its initial apogee in the Great Exhibition of 1851, an event that sparked – in Paris, New York, Dublin and many other cities – a succession of competitive manifestations of international friendship. A more straightforward relationship can be posited between Britain and the development of art museums in the Anglophone colonies, notably Australia and New

Zealand: collections formed around 1900 in such cities as Sydney closely resembled their British prototypes and were often guided by British experts.

Conversely, the history of British museums and collecting was shaped by successive waves of inspiration from overseas. This inspiration included a fascination with classical antiquity, Renaissance art and Italian picture galleries from the seventeenth century into the nineteenth; the overwhelming impact of the Musée du Louvre, which early in the nineteenth century became a model for the British; in the mid-nineteenth century a powerful impetus from Germany, identified as a land of learning, whose scholars chronicled British collections and advised on new museums; and by 1900 a new interest in the United States, seen at the time as far ahead of Britain in its creation of new museums, whether scientific or artistic. These influences made a major impact in London and in the cosmopolitan cities of Liverpool and Glasgow.

At the same time, British municipal galleries differed from art museums in France, Germany or Italy. They offered a novel experience, valuable in its own time, though – as it turned out – not for very long. They did not rely on any familiar canon, but espoused industrial and contemporary art. They did not place their collections at the centre of their existence, nor strive for eternity, as museums regularly and vainly do. Instead, they provided a popular resource, based on what was wanted and what was readily available. They were internationally unique in uniting the enthusiasms of civic leaders, wealthy individuals and the mass of the population to create galleries of popular art. They illustrate the results, both lasting and limited, of non-statist cultural initiative (Fig. 3).

These were hugely visited museums, and much loved. They emerged within an innovative and contentious society – indeed, they were the earliest art museums to respond to a new public making its

3 The Royal Albert Memorial Museum, Exeter: the principal staircase with Prince Albert surrounded by antlers, shortly after the initial opening in 1869.

living in, and often suffering from, the cities of the Industrial Revolution. That revolution is central to their development, whether in the early form of the learned society or in the ambitious public monuments of late Victorian Britain. Above all they were intended by a powerful new bourgeoisie primarily to serve not the educated or the fashionable but the people in general: this was a new interpretation of an Enlightenment concept. In their heyday they appear to have provided exactly what this public required (Fig. 4).

Art museums have had a bad press since the 1980s. Historians influenced by the compelling ideas of the social and political philosophers Antonio Gramsci, Theodor Adorno, Michel Foucault and Pierre Bourdieu have delineated museums in a number of disturbing ways: as agents (intellectual and physical) of social control of the poor and the uneducated by the ruling classes; as devices for demarcating the possession of social capital and for manipulating modes of knowledge; as mausolea for the vanities of the wealthy; as repositories for the possessions

of manically obsessive collectors; and as agents of colonial oppression. World exhibitions have received an equally unfavourable press. The literature inspired by these approaches has often been rich and vigorous.[3]

In recent years reservations have, however, emerged about this theoretical approach, reservations shared by the present writer. In *Culture and Class in English Public Museums, 1850–1914* (2005), Kate Hill questions the influential Foucault-inspired idea that the nineteenth-century museum was constructed, like a prison, to provide an effective site for visual supervision of the public. Steven Conn's *Museums and American Intellectual Life* (1998) points out that 'the intellectual foundations of museums' have often not been investigated since the Foucauldian analysis 'tends to deal only in terms of power'. This 'leaves the historian careening from a conspiratorial view of this history on one side (who is doing what oppressive thing to whom in these museums), to an almost catachismic view of power on the other (where is power? power is everywhere)'.[4] For Conn, 'Critics in the Foucauldian vein, have only attended to one half of the over-simplified equation: they have analyzed power without understanding the knowledge that produces and is produced by it.'[5] In contrast, he identifies the essential conflict facing museums late in the nineteenth century as the loss of belief in the value of object-based epistemology, with a resulting shift in intellectual power from the museum to the increasingly professionalised and research-based university.

The premise that nineteenth-century museums were agents of oppression is not supported in this book. Though many of the strictures applied to Victorian and later museums are no doubt justified, notably their role as vehicles for the display of wealth and social position and their intimate association with social hierarchy, they are not seen here as fundamentally oppressive institutions, any more than their creators are viewed as necessarily members or agents of a power-hungry ruling class. This book attempts, rather, to address the complex motives that led to the foundation of these galleries, and notably the powerful philanthropic movements, private and public, that believed that they were transforming British cities from hideous chaos into models of civic virtue – even though the motives

behind this movement were complex and by no means always pure.

As a matter of nomenclature, several factors should be mentioned. Firstly, there is the tendency of nineteenth century, and later, writers to use the terms 'British' and 'English' interchangeably, particularly when attempting to define national art. The word 'English' tends to predominate, at least among English writers and overseas critics, who seemed unable to accord Scotland an individual identity. In neo-colonial fashion, 'English' sometimes absorbed Scots, such as David Wilkie, who were greatly admired and who practised primarily in London, but the two schools remained distinct. Secondly, while the terms 'provinces' and 'provincial' nowadays are loaded expressions, such negative associations did not apply in the nineteenth century – indeed, the usage often conveyed a sense of local identity and pride. The words are regularly used here in a positive, or at least neutral, Victorian sense.

A Victorian audience would have been familiar with the dualism of 'museum and art gallery'. Although the development of the 'scientific museum' and scientific curatorship is a recurring theme, this book concentrates on the art gallery, a term used alongside the more generally American term 'art museum'. 'Scientific museum' is used as a form of shorthand to denote museums beyond the field of fine art (itself a loaded term), industrial art and historical collections, even though municipal museums contained a range of archaeological and historical material that can only in the broadest sense be described as 'scientific'.[6]

A consideration of the period requires some mental adjustments. To start with, the narrative is shot through with issues of class. Though boundaries between classes were evidently permeable and indistinct, it is impossible to read nineteenth-century discussions of museums and galleries without being

aware of this preoccupation. Whether it is Thomas Carlyle thundering against the idle aristocracy, or the newly rich defining their status through the acquisition of works of art, or contemporary commentators' perennial division of 'the lower orders' into the deserving poor and the savage (though sometimes *apprivoisable*) others, an individual in nineteenth-century Britain could more recognisably be defined by class than they would today. For the modern student of the period the language, and the attitudes, associated with the acceptance of this class system can be hard to stomach: the idea that 'The rich man in his castle, The poor man at his gate' had had their estate divinely ordered is so inimical to modern ways of thinking that what seemed at the time quite radical social programmes and ideas may appear to us unacceptable condescension by the privileged. But the effort of adjustment is worth making.

❖

Seen from the early twenty-first century, the history of these museums has additional significance for those interested in their current state – firstly, because during the last generation there has been a full-blooded return to aspects of the educational approach taken by Victorian museums, and secondly, because the future of institutions created between 1860 and 1914 has become so uncertain. This history is, I hope, intrinsically interesting as a study of how the established mode of the art museum responded to the possibilities and limitations of a new society. But it is also intended to emphasise that they constituted, almost without knowing it, a radical experiment, and one that deserves reassessment in the light of today (Figs. 5 and 6).

6

6 *Little Girl Asleep at Whitechapel Art Gallery*, photographed by Horace Warner around 1900.

PART ONE

BRITAIN AND THE
VISUAL ARTS

BRITAIN AND THE VISUAL ARTS

To flourish, museums need at least one of these: an absolute ruler, government patronage, a society in which encouraging cultural institutions is a public obligation or a means of social advancement, or an exceptionally driven individual. In eighteenth and nineteenth-century Britain the first agent was lacking, the second and third only intermittently effective, the fourth rare. For the many foreign visitors who published their views on Britain, the administration of the arts and the limitations of state provision were sources of constant puzzlement, just as the private collections aroused wonder. This chapter addresses the achievements and failures of institutions representing the state, that is to say the Crown and national government, as well as Parliamentary Select Committees; the art-owning aristocracy; the Royal Academy of Arts, the closest to a state institution for the visual arts in Britain until the mid-twentieth century; and the emerging art museum curator. All of these contributed to the development of Victorian museums in the provinces, but their contributions were overshadowed by the local energy that inspired libraries, educational institutions, parks, choirs and orchestras, as well as museums and galleries.

OPPOSITE J. Elwood, *A Crowd Outside a Print-Shop* (detail of Fig. 8).

Princely galleries were established throughout Europe during the eighteenth century as popes, emperors and kings deposited their collections in galleries while retaining ownership and overall supervision: the Oberes Belvedere in Vienna, the Museo Pio-Clementino in the Vatican, the Galleria degli Uffizi in Florence, the picture galleries in Dresden, Düsseldorf and other German cities, the Nationalmuseum in Stockholm. In the German states, the princely galleries were converted into more public institutions after the fall of Napoleon, with public art museums being established in the 1820s and 1830s by reigning princes, notably the Altes Museum in Berlin, the Alte Pinakothek in Munich and the Gemäldegalerie in Dresden.[1] In the home of art-historical studies, these museums were established in purpose-built edifices combining paintings, sculptures and works on paper, with standards of display, cataloguing and scholarship that made many nineteenth-century public collections in Britain appear amateurish. The princes remained nominal owners, and often remained strongly involved, influencing acquisitions and senior appointments up to 1918.[2]

France and Britain were the exceptions to this pattern. In 1793 a new form of state-controlled museum outside princely control emerged when the former collection of the kings of France, confiscated by the state, was opened as the Musée Français in the Palais du Louvre.[3] In its various manifestations this museum became a symbol of the new government's power and sense of responsibility: in nineteenth-century France, as under Louis XIV, museums reflected a powerful centralist tradition and a faith in art as an expression of national glory.[4] By contrast, the public galleries of Britain expressed, variously, a thirst for economy, a belief in the utility of the fine arts, a sense of national pride, an educational mission, and – from time to time – passionate enthusiasm. With some remarkable exceptions, the governing class showed a lack of interest in the visual arts and was reluctant to support them. The difficulties faced by museums in London were reflected in the regions and in Scotland and Ireland. In the light of generations of precedent and prejudice, it would be hard to imagine a less promising public sphere for the creation of art museums than the United Kingdom. In spite of this, the years between 1850 and 1914 saw the blooming of museums and galleries all over England and Scotland (and to a lesser extent Ireland and Wales), and the creation of a whole range of new museum types.

THE ROLE OF MONARCHY AND ARISTOCRACY

The uniquely unhelpful role of the monarchy in European terms was largely a result of parliamentary control of national finances, which prevented British sovereigns from following Continental examples. The British monarchy was poor in comparison to its French or Austrian equivalents: the British Crown was the only sizeable European monarchy not to maintain a state opera or theatre.[5] Whereas the *Académie Royale de peinture et de sculpture*, founded in Paris in 1648, was funded by the Crown, George III's most enduring act of artistic patronage – the foundation of the Royal Academy of Arts in 1768 – could receive only temporary underwriting from his private purse. Even the extravagant George IV maintained this tradition. Although on the foundation of the National Gallery he wrote to the Earl of Liverpool, the First Lord of

the Treasury, that he was 'much gratified, that the Country is become possessed, by the Bargain you have made, of Mr Angerstein's most valuable Collection of Pictures',[6] the only picture he donated to the new gallery was a *Last Supper* by Benjamin West, which he may not much have regretted.[7]

The idea of the Royal Collection as a private possession extended to its care. By the late eighteenth century the princely collections in Düsseldorf and Dresden were housed in purpose-built galleries that were physically independent of the princely palace, regularly open to polite visitors and entrusted to experts.[8] No such professionalism applied at the English court, where the Hanoverian Surveyors of the King's Pictures tended to be painters of middling abilities, such as George Knapton, or artistically minded entrepreneurs, such as Richard Dalton.[9] The collections remained largely unpublished, apart from a series of engravings issued from 1795 onwards, and no printed catalogues appeared until the mid-nineteenth century.[10] Not until 1881 did Ernest Law publish his *Historical Catalogue of the Pictures in the Royal Collection at Hampton Court*, stating that the want of such a catalogue had 'long been felt by visitors to Hampton Court, and often been the subject of complaint in the public press'.[11] Given that a printed (and still more, illustrated) catalogue symbolised the transfer of intellectual capital from the private to the public realm, this long-standing reticence epitomised the royal family's resolution that their works of art should remain, legally and intellectually, private.[12]

On the other hand, a spirit of public responsibility did exist at court. Windsor Castle and Hampton Court could be visited by the public from the mid-eighteenth century onwards, with the earliest commercial guidebooks to Windsor issued in the 1740s, and artists were permitted to copy the Raphaels at Hampton Court.[13] An amateur tradition persisted, with visits dependent on the good will of servants, and a low pedagogical standard. The Victorian historian of Hampton Court described what was on offer late in the eighteenth century: 'the public were then admitted in batches, and walked round the rooms attended by the housekeeper, who pointed out the pictures with a long stick, calling out, at the same time, the roll of names in a loud voice to the awe-stricken visitors.'[14] But at least, providing access was always considered a royal duty.

The monarchy also played a role in philanthropy and exhibition loans. As Frank Prochaska has shown, from late in the eighteenth century onwards the Crown's declining political power was counterbalanced by increasing charitable involvement.[15] The king acted as patron not only of the Royal Academy but also of such bodies as the Royal Society and the British Institution. The royal family regularly visited the Royal Academy, occasions that were commemorated in prints. These events provided the institution with one of its most popular styles of self-presentation: the art exhibition as a site of royal condescension, with the Crown-appointed Academicians elevated into courtiers.[16] Some twenty academicians or courtiers, led by Benjamin West, Thomas Lawrence and Joseph Wilton as (respectively) Surveyor of the Pictures, Principal Portrait Painter and Statuary, held positions in the royal household.[17] But as we shall see, it was through repeated and generous loans to exhibitions that the Crown made its most marked contribution to public encouragement of the visual arts.

The monarchy's reticence was mirrored by successive governments. The National Gallery's reliance on the energy of individuals resulted from the British convention of minimal government. Eighteenth and early nineteenth-century national administrations – responsible only for raising taxes, conducting war, transporting mail, and enforcing justice and order – were not equipped to run novel institutions such as public museums. Staffing was on a modest scale: in the early 1820s the Home Office employed seventeen people, the Colonial Office fourteen.[18] After the defeat of Napoleon the government was under constant pressure to reduce taxation since 'Cheapness…was a mark of efficiency; the best government was that which administered least.'[19] Excessive public expenditure would lead, it was thought, to corruption and waste. A fear of state involvement in educational and social enterprises persisted through the nineteenth century, based on the idea that education provided by the state could be manipulated by interest groups for their own ends.[20]

In terms of museums, this shortage of public funding could have dismal results: the innovative founding of the British Museum in 1753 was succeeded by financial meanness, conservatism, unfriendliness to the public and lack of professionalism. Foreign visitors were scandalised by the ineptitude with which visits were organised, while British commentators deplored the indifference of government. In 1782 the mezzotinter Valentine Green, pointing out the many advantages, moral and intellectual, offered by the visual arts, lamented that in Britain 'yet shall the ignorant presume to arraign their expediency, and the illiterate decry their utility, to the disgrace of the enlightened state of modern manners, and the intelligence of present times!'[21] The 'want of national policy' (a constant theme) had made England 'a bye-word among the nations'.[22] This line of attack was maintained in successive books and pamphlets, particularly before the National Gallery's foundation. Prince Hoare, champion of the British school, satirised in 1813 the propensity of politicians faced by demands for a national gallery of art, to declare 'that "it was not then the time for such an expenditure on the encouragement of the Arts"'.[23] It is not surprising that, as Janet Minihan has noted, in the period between 1800 and 1820 the purchase of the Elgin Marbles for the nation was Parliament's only major expression of interest in the visual arts.[24]

After the National Gallery's foundation in 1824, the record hardly improved. As at the new British Museum in the 1750s, a town house was forced into service and abandoned only when its dangerous condition made it necessary, according to the advisory architect Robert Smirke, to move the paintings 'with the least possible delay'.[25] The German art historian J.D. Passavant was startled 'that in a country like England, where all is to be found that wealth can purchase, or luxury desire, such an important institution should bear so recent a date',[26] while the new building by William Wilkins, severely limited in ornament to satisfy critics of public expenditure, was widely criticised for its feebleness and smallness.[27] Attacks on the lack of funding for national museums were repeatedly launched, often using the theme of national honour as an argument for greater expenditure. To the artist Benjamin Robert Haydon the National Gallery was 'a disgrace to the nation', too small to accommodate the Raphael Cartoons or the Rubens ceiling from the Whitehall Banqueting House.[28] In Select Committees the Gallery was found to be 'too small for the National Gallery of England',[29] or 'a series of bandbox rooms', whereas 'a gallery fit for the nation

ought to be on a much larger scale than the present gallery'.[30] In 1840 Edward Edwards, champion of public libraries, criticised the inadequate building and collection (Fig. 7), the 'utterly wanting' arrangement of the paintings,[31] the unprofessional trustees and staff. Even during the tenure of its first (and brilliant) director, Sir Charles Eastlake, his colleague Ralph Wornum lamented in 1861 that Turner's bequest of his paintings to the nation could not be properly accommodated, since

the pictures in Trafalgar Square are more crowded than ever…the building is so inadequate, that half the National Collection is still forced to be lodged elsewhere than in the National

Gallery…many good pictures are placed virtually out of sight, as they cannot be properly seen, yet the six rooms together contain some four hundred pictures only, showing that five times the present accommodation would be but a moderate provision, even for the actual collection.[32]

The effect of the political turbulence in Continental Europe between 1789 and 1815 had diametrically opposite effects on France and Italy, on the one hand, and on Britain on the other. In France, the art collections of religious houses and churches were confiscated in the 1790s and put into museums. This approach was extended in the following decade to Italy, as at the Pinacoteca di Brera in Milan, which

14

was filled with spoils from the Church. The possessions of the French aristocracy were similarly confiscated, while in years of extreme peril works of art were frequently sold by traditional owners in France as well as in Spain and Italy. Museums became not only repositories but also statements of a new order, symbols of an age that rejected Church and nobility. Not so in Britain. Instead, the country became the principal recipient of these works of art, as the eighteenth-century practice of buying paintings and sculpture on the Grand Tour was transformed by vast importations organised by art dealers: as Francis Haskell noted, 'for many years it was very difficult for anyone with enough money not to be able to buy some celebrated masterpiece'.[33] By the early nineteenth century Britain possessed the richest private art collections in the world, to the amazement and often outrage of foreign connoisseurs. J.J. Volkmann, who toured England in 1761, expressed his astonishment in *Neueste Reisen durch England* that 'half Italy' was now held in Britain, and Rome 'is robbed of its finest treasures'.[34] At the same time, their accessibility was generally acknowledged: Louis Simond, a French-born American touring England in 1810–11, was impressed by 'those innumerable fine houses, scattered all over this country, which are allowed to be shewn to strangers'.[35] These private collections remained famous throughout the century, with Passavant listing the 'Collections of Art belonging to the different country seats in England',[36] and in the 1850s Dr Gustav Waagen, director of the picture collection at the Royal Picture Gallery in Berlin, describing with wonder the *Treasures of Art in Great Britain*.

Given the strength of private holdings, it might be expected that they would eventually enrich public museums. In actuality, most aristocratic owners showed little interest in giving them away, with a few exceptions, such as the National Gallery's champion, Sir George Beaumont, and some donors to the British Museum. Rubens's *Minerva Protects Pax from Mars*, was presented to the National Gallery by the first Duke of Sutherland in 1828, but this was a rare example of noble patronage. Noble donations tended to go to the two old universities,[37] notably the founding collection of the Fitzwilliam Museum, and to have a didactic quality, like William Fox-Strangways' donation of forty early Italian paintings to the Ashmolean Galleries.[38] In contemporary patronage, the aristocracy was equally uninvolved, W.M. Thackeray writing in 1843, 'I am sure the people of England are likely to be better patrons of art than the English aristocracy ever were, and that the aristocracy have been tried and *didn't* patronise it…No, no; *they* are not the friends of genius'.[39] What applied in London applied even more strongly in the regions. The precedent of the 1851 bequest by the thirteenth Earl of Derby of his vast natural history collections to the city of Liverpool was seldom followed. Many of the major donors to the National Gallery and the British Museum were not the aristocracy but members of the minor gentry, professional men, clergy and bankers.

Nevertheless, private collections and their owners came to occupy a dual public role. Unwilling to give objects, the aristocracy was happy to give advice, and played an important role in the governance of national art museums and sometimes of local learned societies and artists' societies. The traditional owners' main contribution was through loans to exhibitions, which – as with the Crown – came to be regarded as a duty. The loan exhibitions drawn largely from noble collections and organised under aristocratic patronage at the British Institution from 1806 onwards initiated a long tradition that was maintained in innumerable exhibitions.[40]

As we shall see, the idea that the owners of private collections had a duty to make them available to a broader public by opening their houses to visitors or lending works of art to temporary exhibitions was prevalent in the nineteenth century. The notion that private collections could somehow be seen to belong to the nation has been viewed with scepticism by historians, with Linda Colley positing that 'Only in Great Britain did it prove possible to float the idea that aristocratic property was in some magical and strictly intangible way *the people's property also*.'[41] Specious though this idea of shared ownership may appear to the modern eye, it was promulgated not by aristocratic apologists but by writers of a more radical tendency, who believed that works of art in the possession of old owners did have a national role, and ought ultimately to pass into the ownership of the people through the museums. This line of thinking runs from John Wilkes (in the 1760s, in relation to the Raphael Cartoons, which George III proposed to remove from public view) to the nineteenth-century historian and critic Anna Jameson and, at the end of the century, the German sculpture historian Adolf Michaelis. If it is conceded that regular access to a work of art, and the ability to study it, constitute – in a moral or para-legal sense – a sharing of intellectual possession, validity may be allowed to the idea that the extended availability of these works of art, and of the historic buildings that contained them, bestowed on them an aura of shared public ownership. That was certainly the belief that informed the outcry late in the nineteenth century over the disappearance of works of art overseas and especially to the United States: the paintings of the Duke of Marlborough, as a notable example, were seen as belonging to the nation.[42]

This notion of common 'moral' ownership was reinforced by the idea of the art museum as a refuge for vulnerable works of art. In *A Letter to the Dilettanti Society...*(1799), James Barry, painter and aggressive polemicist, excoriated 'those miscreant picture-cleaners, or rather defacers, who, like a pestilential blast, sweep away every vestige of the pristine health and vigour of well-nourished tints; leaving nothing to remain but a hoary meagreness and decrepitude'.[43] Citing privately owned paintings that he saw as the victims of such treatment, including Titian's *Cornaro Family* at Northumberland House and Van Dyck's *Pembroke Family* at Wilton, he proposed that such major works of art in private collections belonged to 'the public stock', since 'the mere purchase or possession does not give a title to the liberty of destroying it'.[44] The danger of restoration remained a recurring theme, reinforcing the notion that works of art did not morally belong to their legal owners. In 1823 Sir George Beaumont wrote that having been mortified to see 'the number of pictures which are annually destroyed by injudicious and unnecessary cleaning', he was 'anxious to deposit the few pictures [he had] been able to collect in a place of security for the use of the Public'.[45] Developing this idea much as Barry had done, he advocated removing works of art from private ownership to the public domain. In a letter later quoted by Anna Jameson, he wrote:

> I would rather see [works of art] in the Museum [he refers to the British Museum] than in the possession of any individual...because taste is not inherited, and there are few families in which it succeeds for three generations. My idea, therfore,

is, that the few examples which remain perfect can never be so safe as under the guardianship of a body which never dies; and I see every year such proofs of the carelessness with which people suffer these inestimable relics to be rubbed, scraped, and polished, as if they were their family plate, that I verily believe, if they do not find some safe asylum, in another half-century little more will be left than the bare canvases.[46]

In the absence of leadership from St James's or Westminster, public responsibility for fostering the fine arts devolved on the Royal Academy of Arts, a body that enjoyed a quasi-official status and huge public esteem. The development of nineteenth-century art galleries is intimately bound up with the Academy's pedagogic brief and prestigious summer exhibitions. It served as a forum for discussion of the arts: before 1824 many of the proposals made for establishing a national gallery were put forward in Academy circles.[47] Its instructional brief was sustained by several of its members, who possessed private collections that assumed a semi-public function and in some cases eventually became museums. These included its first President (PRA), Joshua Reynolds, whose house in Leicester Fields contained a picture gallery from which he lent works to be copied by Academy students; William Hunter, professor of anatomy, founder of Glasgow's Hunterian Museum; the Royal Academicians (RA) Francis Bourgeois, whose paintings established Dulwich College Picture Gallery, and John Soane, professor of architecture from 1806 to 1837; and Thomas Lawrence PRA, owner of a notable collection of drawings.[48] Pedagogy was central to these collections, as it had been to the Ashmolean Museum. Dulwich Picture Gallery, Sir John Soane's Museum and the Glasgow Hunterian were all envisaged as teaching collections.[49] This characterisation of early galleries and museums as sites of visual and intellectual instruction was intrinsic to their character, even if the intellectual framework for implementing schemes of instruction was lacking. The Academy acted throughout the century as a nursemaid and governess to the museum movement.

THE EMERGENCE OF
THE CURATOR

In spite of this extended tradition of public parsimony, the history of museums in nineteenth-century Britain is marked by successful innovation. The Ashmolean Museum, which opened in 1684 as part of the University of Oxford, was one of the earliest European cabinets to gain a permanent status as a university museum. The British Museum, founded in 1753, was chronologically the first national museum in the world, with the arguable exception of the Capitoline Museum in Rome.[50] And the mid-nineteenth century was a time of notable cultural activity. The National Portrait Gallery, created in 1856, constituted a wholly innovatory style of institution, widely imitated in the English-speaking world and in Scandinavia, while the South Kensington Museum, founded in 1852, was the earliest museum of applied arts worldwide. In spite of the general conservatism of the political establishment, the history of Victorian museums overall is one of intellectual creativity, and the development of the people's galleries belongs in this tradition.

This history did not emerge from the contributions of a trained body of museum professionals. The hazy boundaries between professional and amateur, commercial and academic, applied to the curatorship of collections.[51] The role of the art curator exhibited many curiosities until late in the nineteenth century, in contrast to the scientific museum, where the curator's function was clearer. The first keeper of the Ashmolean Museum in 1683 was Robert Plot, author of *The Natural History of Oxford* and *The Natural History of Staffordshire*, wide-ranging works in the spirit of Pliny the Elder's *Naturalis Historiae*. He was also the university's first professor of chemistry, and was expected to act as an upholder of the Baconian empirical approach to knowledge. He and such colleagues as Robert Hooke, curator at the Royal Society of London, initiated a succession of academically trained experts within the disciplines of the natural sciences, natural history and archaeology. Such men, responsible for the care and expansion of collections, were expected to be active researchers. The scientifically trained 'conservators' (as they were known) at the Hunterian Museum in London maintained this tradition through the nineteenth century, including

such notable figures as William Clift, the first to hold the office, Richard Owen, later the driving force behind the creation of the Natural History Museum, and W.H. Flower, subsequently Director of that museum.

Comparable professionalism did not apply to the visual arts. The usual person appointed as a curator for a private or public collection was an artist, expected to apply his expertise to the care of works of art through their display, reproduction as prints, cataloguing and restoration. He (it was always a man) played a role not dissimilar to that of the housekeeper in a great house or palace, responsible for keeping the rooms (and often the works of art) clean, and for providing elementary exposition. This flexibility reflects a concept of the status of a work of art that is quite different from our own: not as a sacrosanct and even fetishised offering to eternity, but as an object with an evolving physicality and purpose, to be altered according to need. The artist-curator belonged to a continuum of creativity that was not deemed to have ceased when the work of art was designated as 'finished' by its ostensible creator.

Even in the most established institutions, standards of knowledge and application remained haphazard. The creation of an independent department of prints and drawings at the British Museum in 1808 led *faute de mieux* to the appointment of only moderately suitable candidates. The lowly status of curatorial positions is evident in J.T. Smith's application to become keeper in 1816: to a lady who had written in Smith's support, the Archbishop of Canterbury, one of the three 'principal Trustees' responsible for the appointment, replied 'With such interest as Mr. J.T. Smith possesses, I am astonished he should think it worth while to waste his strength in pursuit of such a trifling office as that which is now vacant in the Museum.'[52] Smith was succeeded by William Young Ottley, a notable connoisseur but at the time of his appointment, aged sixty-two, suffering from financial problems and needing employment.

The epitome of this situation was William Seguier, from 1805 superintendent of the British Institution, from 1820 'Surveyor, Cleaner and Repairer of the King's Pictures' (the title is significant), and from 1824 Keeper of the National Gallery. In addition, he served as Curator (and restorer) to the Duke of Wellington and the Marquess of Westminster. He was evidently a man of great charm and in the view of an obituarist, 'His sound judgment and high character procured for him the intimate friendship of those far above him in rank and fortune, by whom he was ever esteemed a welcome guest.'[53] At the same time, he was ill educated – as a less friendly writer, reflecting the increased professionalisation of the museum, remarked on his death, 'The late director's knowledge of art was chiefly, or altogether, anecdotal and traditional; he could cite a pleasant tale about Claude when a pastrycook or tell what Cromwell said about his warts to the portraitist...he could descant upon the grace of Raffaele, and the airs of Guido, &c.&c., but a deeper vein of criticism, is, we trust, now in demand.'[54] Seguier was essentially seen as an upper servant, and the style of his subordination to the National Gallery board continued after his death, even with better qualified keepers: describing himself as a 'servant to the trustees', Thomas Uwins RA wrote that in this 'uncertain and dependent position...I must obey their orders.'[55] Evidently, the position of curator was despised; there was a shortage of appropriate candidates; the responsibilities largely consisted of carrying out orders and routine administration, as well as the care of the pictures. This approach was intimately linked to the old-fashioned style of connoisseurial gallery for which these curators cared. On the other hand, a major change in attitude to the role of director/ curator did take place after Seguier's death. When the *Athenaeum* remarked that 'a deeper vein of criticism' was expected, and that Seguier's having 'obtained the sovereign chair of connoisseurship...can be accounted for only by the despicable nature of the "aesthetics" then prevalent', it was time for a professional director such as Eastlake.[56]

THE RISE OF THE ART MUSEUM

The factors that stimulated the rise of art museums in the provinces as well as in London were, it is suggested, threefold: the links between the art museum and commerce; the intimate association between the new museums and temporary exhibitions; and the influence of the Parliamentary Select Committees that from the 1820s to at least the 1860s

developed a remarkable agenda for the diffusion of art and learning. The civic consolidation of the great industrial cities of England and Scotland from 1850 onwards encouraged a sense of civic pride that embraced art galleries and museums.

The relation of the art world to that of commerce is a constant underlying theme in the development of galleries in nineteenth-century Britain. In a country where official encouragement of the visual arts was at best spasmodic, trade offered an alternative artistic culture. In contrast to the old world of art, dominated by the connoisseur and the artist, the commercial art world encouraged mass consumption, vigorous publicity and artistic experiences based on spectacle and open to anyone with modest resources, all factors in the phenomenon of the universal exhibition. Commerce was often veiled. Since the public art gallery hardly existed early in nineteenth-century London, that increasingly brilliant city became the site of a shadow world of commercial galleries, fuelled by the growing public desire for spectacle and entertainment.[57] In this world, the art market used the vocabulary of the museum and the display techniques of the private collection to present its wares as objects transmogrified to a realm beyond financial transaction.[58]

The influence of this commercial art world was strikingly visible on the streets of London. Print shops exhibiting their wares, notably caricatures, in their windows had for a long time been seen as a people's gallery in 'the centre of the European print trade' (Fig. 8).[59] The frivolity of these prints aroused criticism: James Barry complained how little had been done 'towards the intellectual entertainment of the public or of posterity' so that 'our poor neglected public are left to form their hearts and their understandings upon those lessons, not of morality and philanthropy, but of envy, malignity, and horrible disorder, which everywhere stare them in the face, in the profligate caricatura furniture of print-shop windows, from Hyde-Park Corner to Whitechapel.'[60] The crude art available to the 'poor neglected public' through the agency of the public media contrasts strikingly with the blameless fare put on offer by public galleries a century later.

Even the print shop, however, could be elevated into a place of instruction and elegant sociability. Thus the Shakespeare Gallery, founded in 1786 by the print seller John Boydell, sold prints in a building

8 *A Crowd Outside a Print-Shop*,
1790. This watercolour, by
J. Elwood, demonstrates the appeal
exercised by the constantly
changing and topical displays of
print shops.

ACKERMANN'S REPOSITORY OF ARTS, 101 STRAND

9 Ackermann's Repository, 101 Strand. The Repository was established by the German-born Rudolph Ackermann in 1796, and flourished until the 1850s. Visitors could buy paintings and miniatures and study prints of fashionable clothing and interiors in an elegant setting. Ackermann also published *The Microcosm of London* (1808–10) and a monthly magazine, *The Repository of Arts*.

filled with paintings commissioned from British artists, and aimed to stimulate elevated history painting.[61] High-minded though it may have been, this was a commercial venture, which ultimately failed. A generation later, the print dealer Rudolph Ackermann, publisher of *The Microcosm of London* and many other series, determined to make his London establishment into a polite setting for the diffusion of artistic, scientific and topographical information. His 'Repository' (another word redolent of the early museum) or gallery was situated at various addresses in the Strand, close to the Royal Academy and at the centre of London's art world (Fig. 9). It included 'a fine and spacious gallery' as though in a private town house.[62] In the expansion of the world of art as entertainment, the signifiers that indicated an altruistic institution, display space or publication were freely appropriated by what were essentially commercial attractions. Boydell's Gallery and many others used the vocabulary and the styles of display

of the high art museum; Boydell presented himself as the champion of historical painting; 'Great Rooms' were a regular feature of these neo-galleries. The boundaries between commerce and artistic altruism were permeable: even sites such as the Leverian Museum in London, which contained important natural history and ethnographical collections including many items assembled by Captain Cook on his voyages, operated (late in the eighteenth century) as money-making ventures.[63]

It was, however, in the context of the temporary exhibitions that 'pure' fine art most nearly met the marketplace. In 1769 the Royal Academy launched its summer exhibitions of work by living artists, developing a function initiated by other societies a decade earlier. By the early nineteenth century, the temporary exhibition had become a favourite form of entertainment: in 1818 *The New Picture of London* remarked that exhibitions 'are uncommonly numerous; the mention of each almost impossible'.[64] Exhibitions represented an increasingly powerful, almost monstrous, influence as the nineteenth century passed. Often viewed with suspicion on account of their dangerous closeness to commerce (as Patricia Mainardi has discussed in her accounts of exhibition history in France), in the entrepreneurial world of the British industrial city, as in London, they assumed an importance at least equivalent to that of the high-minded art museum.[65] Before the advent around 1900 of the art-historical display, the temporary exhibition was generally an expression of modern art and of modernity, the themes that sustained the new provincial galleries.

Given that commerce and the associated temporary exhibition were seen to distort the noble values that should be associated with artistic practice, this disjunction exercised a converse influence on the few museums and galleries that, established and funded by the state or by universities, rejected the financial imperatives of the marketplace and by implication the richness of setting associated with commercial and private galleries. These more austere institutions included the British Museum (a Western art collection in that it contained the nation's holdings of classical sculpture as well as prints and drawings), the National Gallery, the university museums in Oxford, Glasgow, Cambridge and Edinburgh, along with a group of privately inspired galleries, including Dulwich College Picture Gallery and Sir John Soane's Museum.[66] Although their collections were varied, these were primarily 'high art' museums, dedicated to the display of historic paintings and classical sculpture. They made themselves available to artists and did not charge for admission. They made no concession to comfort. They seldom held temporary exhibitions or showed contemporary work. This concentration on the preservation and display of works of art, undiluted by other considerations, was to persist into the 1970s and beyond. Within living memory the British Museum and the National Gallery, under public patronage, resolutely contrasted the grandeur of their collections with the sobriety, indeed near-squalor, of spaces intended for retail or refreshment, with the British Museum's refreshment room resembling, at one period, a prison canteen. In total contrast, a bridge between pleasing the public and offering instruction emerged in the South Kensington Museum, and by extension in the regional museums.

PARLIAMENTARY SELECT COMMITTEES

One of the most important influences in the creation of civic museums, as of libraries, emerged from Westminster through the Parliamentary Select Committees convened for a limited period to investigate a particular theme. After 1815 perceptions of the role of national government began to shift. In a country where population and wealth were expanding rapidly, and economic power was shifting away from the traditional oligarchy, public opinion became dissatisfied with unreformed suffrage and the ramshackle system of local government, the ill administered and exclusive universities, public schools and other charitable foundations, mostly based on the established Church, which unrealistically claimed to represent the whole of England; and the exclusion from public office of Catholics and Nonconformists. Further pressure was applied by the old system's inability to deal with urban expansion, economic depression and starvation or the lack of urban sanitation, which led to the first major cholera epidemic, in 1831–2. The Select Committees in session from the 1820s onwards assumed an intensity of purpose unseen in British public life since the Cromwellian revolution of the seventeenth century. Though the reformers were frequently frustrated in realising plans that were sometimes more extreme than the aristocracy or the mercantile lobby could tolerate, the 1830s and 1840s were a period of public self-scrutiny. Many of the ideas that shaped the development of provincial museums – notably the interest in democratic access and their status as training places for artisans – were vigorously enunciated.

During these years Select Committees addressed popular education in the arts, the problem of design in relation to British manufactures, the provision of libraries, access to historic buildings (notably cathedrals), and the management of the national museums. In 1835 a committee enquired 'into the best means of extending a knowledge of the Arts, and of the Principles of Design among the People (especially the Manufacturing Population) of the Country', while also considering the 'Constitution, Management and Effects of Institutions connected with the Arts'. It returned to the subject the following year. In 1840 another committee examined Tra-

Support for public museums and libraries came from men of varying political affiliations. Dedicated members of the Select Committees included such prominent Tories as Robert Peel, Prime Minister and passionate collector and enthusiast for the arts, and Henry Thomas Hope, son of the designer and collector Thomas Hope, a vigorous, conservative politician and a supporter of the Great Exhibition. The main thrust, however, derived from the Radical party, a loosely knit group associated with such causes as extending parliamentary reform (the Reform Act of 1832 being considered insufficient) and Catholic emancipation. Certain individuals stand out. Radical Members of Parliament who appeared repeatedly on the committees included William Ewart, a member of a prominent Liverpool family and for a time MP for Liverpool, who regularly served as chairman. He proved an indefatigable and acute questioner eager to improve education for the working classes, notably through the creation of public libraries (Fig. 10). He worked closely with Joseph Hume, another tireless Select Committee member and an ardent supporter of museums.[67] B.R. Haydon, to whom Hume sat for a portrait in 1833, described him as 'an extraordinary man certainly, has enlarged views & original ones, and in moral feeling of what is truly great, is in advance of his Contemporaries. He must be in the House like a bit of granite' (Fig. 11).[68] For both Ewart and Hume, support for libraries and museums ran alongside advocacy of the abolition of colonial slavery and the death penalty – a duality of interest that was to be paralleled by Victorian philanthropists.

A leading force behind this reforming movement was the group known as the philosophical radicals, followers of Jeremy Bentham. In such publications as *An Introduction to the Principles of Morals and Legislation* (1789) Bentham had expressed his doctrine of utility, a distillation of ideas enunciated by David Hume and John Locke. His famous creed that 'the right and proper end of government in every political community, is the greatest happiness of all the individuals of which it is composed' posited the need for a society which through universal education, and the provision of professional security and a minimum wage, would ultimately free its members from the need to battle for survival, allowing them to pursue a rational planned existence in pursuit of

falgar Square and its impact on the National Gallery. A year later the possibility was considered of national monuments, especially Westminster Abbey and St Paul's, 'affording Facilities to the Public for their Inspection, as a means of moral and intellectual Improvement for the People', while another commission investigated the 'Promotion of the Fine Arts of this Country, in connection with the Rebuilding of the New Houses of Parliament'. Successive committees discussed, in 1847, how to accommodate the British paintings presented to the nation by Robert Vernon; in 1850 the accommodation available in the National Gallery; in 1853 the National Gallery's management; in 1860 provision of 'Facilities for promoting the Healthful Recreation and Improvement of the People'. Witnesses from artist to manufacturer, from scholar to artisan, were invited to speak – even Waagen travelled to London to be cross-examined. The proceedings and final reports constitute the most important corpus of thinking on museums and libraries in nineteenth-century Britain.

pleasure. Pleasure was to be defined not in hedonistic terms, but as the ability freely to follow the dictates of one's own will, as long as these did not conflict with the well-being of society. Both pleasure and pain could, according to Bentham, be quantitatively measured – the moral quality of an action could be assessed from the degree of pleasure it brought to the members of the community. In spite of the difficulty of interpreting Bentham's thoughts, his ideas about the proper conduct of government shaped much political thinking in the first half of the century and beyond. With the establishment of the *Westminster Review* in 1824 and the reforming Whig government of 1830, his followers influenced ministerial decisions and often dominated Select Committees. Bentham's emphasis on general education and on the obligation on the state to provide appropriate educational institutions underlay the huge development of the public museum, library and gallery later in the nineteenth century.

CULTURE IN THE PROVINCES

Important though the parliamentary Select Committees were to the development of cultural life in the regions, the greatest impetus came from the towns themselves. Many of the towns that were expanding in the eighteenth century into centres of industry, as well as some that remained market towns, enjoyed a rich cultural life. The impetus for this movement came from private individuals, whether antiquaries or businessmen treating museums as a business. The leaders of society in these towns, often men of great wealth and increasingly so as the nineteenth century advanced, saw themselves as heading a civic hierarchy separate from, and even opposed to, the established hierarchy of prince or church. A parallel might be made with late medieval cities where the merchant-classes' sense of civic identity stood in opposition to the established authority proclaimed by the ruling prince or bishop: not only a town hall but also a town church was often erected to proclaim the power of civic identity. This pose of defiant self-reliance, based on an urban élite in opposition to the landed aristocracy, was maintained in the eighteenth and nineteenth centuries in secular form, in town halls and in cultural institutions such as museums and galleries.

Up to the nineteenth century, most public art collections in provincial towns took the form of commemorative collections: portraits of dignitaries and founders commissioned by such old-established cities as Norwich, Bristol, Gloucester and Glasgow, by livery companies in the City of London and elsewhere, and by the colleges of the old universities for their halls and libraries (Fig. 12). The antiquarian tradition was strong, and these portraits were esteemed as documents rather than works of art.[69] Private antiquarianism also flourished. Already in the 1680s Ralph Thoresby had assembled in his museum-house in Leeds a rich collection containing 'the Curiosities natural and artificial, and the antiquities; particularly the Roman, British, Saxon, Danish, Norman, and Scotch Coins, with Modern Medals. Also – A Catalogue of the Manuscripts: The Various Editions of the Bible, and of Books published in the Infancy of the Art of Printing' (Fig. 13).[70] He was in communication with such leading collectors and antiquaries as John Ray, John Evelyn, Hans Sloane and John Woodward, and his collection attracted so much attention that Thoresby complained of 'the Influx of Visitors to his Museum'.[71] An alternative impetus came from

12 St Andrew's Hall, Norwich.
This fifteenth-century hall,
formerly part of the Blackfriars
convent, became the property of
the city and was used from the
1730s for the display of portraits
of civic dignitaries.

frankly commercial enterprises. As the tourist industry expanded in the Lake District in the 1770s and 1780s, museums containing a miscellany of objects such as natural history specimens, antiquities and modern scientific instruments and organised on a frankly commercial basis were set up in much-visited towns such as Keswick, where they could be expected to attract visitors willing to pay an admission charge and to buy the curiosities on sale.[72]

An unusual note of academic rigour was added to this miscellaneous group of museum types by the city of Liverpool. In 1816 the Royal Institution was given thirty-seven examples of the historically conceived collection of early Italian and Northern pictures belonging to the Liverpool banker and historian

William Roscoe, which had been purchased by his friends on his bankruptcy.[73] This was 'the first time in Britain [that] a group of important old master paintings had been bought and placed on permanent exhibition with the avowed intention of improving public taste' (Fig. 14).[74] The Royal Institution's collection predated Dulwich Picture Gallery and the National Gallery, which in their early days both contained sixteenth- and seventeenth-century paintings in the aristocratic tradition rather than instructive earlier works. As Edward Morris has noted, the Liverpool collection was also remarkable for the support it received from private subscribers and the Town Council. These subscribers were 'Radical, Nonconformist, and mercantile' to a man, and their

13 'Table of Antiquities', from 'A Catalogue and Description of the Natural and Artificial Rarities in this Musaeum', in Ralph Thoresby's *Ducatus Leodiensis* (2nd ed., 1816). The table illustrates Roman, ancient British and Druid relics.

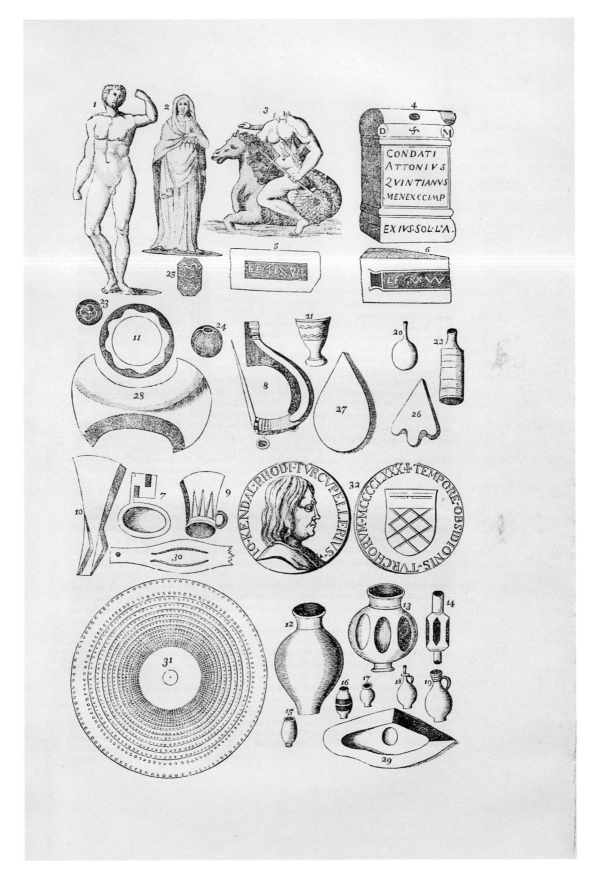

14 *The Entombment* by the Master of the Virgo inter Virgines, *c.* 1486. Oil and tempera on panel, 55.2 × 56 cm. This and the other paintings from the collection of William Roscoe were officially transferred from the Liverpool Royal Institution to the Walker Art Gallery in 1948 (National Museums Liverpool).

names, notably Ewart and Rathbone, would reappear prominently a generation or two later in the history of English regional museums.[75] In combining private and public funding and in its didactic purpose the Liverpool Royal Institution foreshadowed the patronage of Victorian cities.

CONCLUSION

The influence of the forward-looking politicians who motivated Parliamentary Select Committees between the 1830s and the 1850s cannot be over-emphasised as an expression of the vigorous tradition of radical thinking in Britain. Just as the libraries and museums Acts of Parliament emerged from this source, so the resulting institutions came to reflect the ideals of the Liberal Party, into which the Radicals were absorbed. It was their belief in the scope for improvement of the human condition that inspired the creation of popular museums. In the 1860s and later, the Liberal associations of the new museums gave many of them a political character in their educational programmes and their public imagery. It is no coincidence that the passage of the second Reform Bill in 1867 and the election

15 Herbert Gladstone addressing the Great Liberal Meeting at the Mixed Cloth Hall Yard in Leeds – a demonstration of the excitement generated by a Liberal Party meeting. Gladstone was the youngest son of the Prime Minister and his private secretary from 1880, the year Herbert became a Leeds MP.

of Gladstone's first reforming Liberal Government the following year coincided with the establishment of the earliest version of the first municipal art museum, in Nottingham. No less than the contemporary municipal reforms, the libraries, museums and art galleries of late Victorian England were the children of Liberalism (Fig. 15).

On the one hand, the new Victorian galleries were evidently powerfully shaped by their predeces-sors and by the capital. But in the face of a new society and a new style of living and wealth, the provincial cities developed their own policies and their own style of art gallery. Respectful though they were towards such symbols of authority as the Royal Academy, the creators of late Victorian provincial culture were motivated by moral, religious and educational values to create, through a modified utilitarianism, their own systems.

The Pantheon.
Rome

2

JUSTIFYING THE MUSEUM

Given the shortage of royal or noble patronage and the apathy of most governments, powerful justifications had to be found in Britain – more so than elsewhere – for the public funding of museums and galleries. In the eighteenth century and early in the nineteenth, arguments were successively proposed for the creation of a Royal Academy of Arts with an attendant teaching collection, for the establishment of a national gallery, for its expansion, and finally for a network of regional art museums. These arguments show remarkable consistency, from the writings of Jonathan Richardson early in the eighteenth century to Parliamentary Select Committees and civic discussions in the nineteenth. This chapter aims to set the Victorian development in the context of this earlier discourse. For those interested in early twenty-first-century discussions around museums, many of these arguments will seem disturbingly familiar.

There was no shortage of literature on the subject. Readers in eighteenth- and early nineteenth-century Britain had access to numerous publications on the fine arts,[1] including the anonymous *An Essay Towards an English School of Painting* (1706), the first publication of its kind in English, which presented a series of biographies and advocated the creation

of a native school.[2] British artistic theory was shaped by Continental writers, notably by Roger de Piles, whose *L'idée du peintre parfait* of 1699 was translated into English, as was the work of many later writers. The native theoretical tradition developed with the third Earl of Shaftesbury's *Characteristicks of Men, Manners, Opinions and Times* (1711) and the writings of the portraitist, collector and critic Jonathan Richardson the Elder, notably *An Essay on the Theory of Painting* (1715) and *Two Discourses* (1719). Their continuing validity is evident from the extensive quotations from Richardson made by Anna Jameson, who explained in 1842 that though Richardson's books were 'little known and I believe out of print…with all their faults of style, bad grammar, and quaint expression, they are written with an earnestness and elevation of feeling, a fullness of conviction, which would win toleration for greater faults'.[3] The discourses of successive Presidents of the Royal Academy to the Academy students contributed to the corpus of artistic theory, notably those of Joshua Reynolds, the first President, whose discourses have been described as 'one of the most eloquent, as well as one of the last, presentations of the ideas that dominated European art criticism and theory from the mid-fifteenth to the mid-eighteenth century.'[4]

Among the most vocal commentators early in the nineteenth century were such well-informed popularisers as William Hazlitt and Jameson, who both wrote eloquent surveys of English galleries open to the public, and that passionate advocate of history painting, the artist Benjamin Robert Haydon.

A number of themes recur: the importance of the academic tradition, the dignity of the artistic profession as distinct from the craftsman's trade, and the desirability of nurturing a school of native art. By the early nineteenth century, the academic tradition, with its emphasis on history painting as the finest of the painterly genres, was losing force. Reynolds's later discourses already showed a willingness to modify the strictly academic approach, a modification extended by such Romantic writers as Hazlitt, who emphasised the value of individual artistic creativity and self-expression and believed that nature, rather than the study of precedent, was the only true guide. History painting was not, however, vanquished. In France it maintained a tenacious life, its end symbolised by the death of Ingres in 1867, and in Britain historical paintings executed for the Houses of Parliament and Manchester Town Hall upheld the ideal.[5] The desirability of a healthy British school, advocated by numerous writers and collectors, was to be energetically fulfilled in the new art museums. Equally, the idea of two tiers of artistic activity – the learned artist above, the manually skilled but uneducated craftsman below – prevailed through the nineteenth century. It was this notion that inspired the Victorian concept of the museum of industrial and popular art in contrast to the gallery of high art.

DOUBTS OVER A NATIONAL GALLERY

Only in the 1860s did the creation of an art museum in Britain become a relatively straightforward and defensible proposition. Although retrospectively the establishment of the National Gallery in London may appear part of an ineluctable enlargement of cultural provision by the state, its foundation and subsequent funding were far from inevitable. It was regularly criticised by advocates of national economy targeting public spending on the arts: support for the Gallery 'took place under relentless parliametary

and public scrutiny'.[6] When the erection of a new building was discussed in Parliament in the 1830s the arguments of sentimental materialism were deployed, arguments that were to be heard again and again. It was urged that 'they [Members of Parliament] should not be called upon to erect palaces for the exhibition of works of the Fine Arts, when a famishing population was crying for bread'.[7] As Jameson recorded, Lord Liverpool 'and other ministers were absolutely intimidated by the fierce attacks of the economists, and scarcely dared to propose such a measure themselves, dreading the apathy of some and the animosity of others'.[8] Some of the arguments presented in favour of public art galleries may today seem pragmatic and limited but they should be seen through the prism of this hostility, a hostility that still has not disappeared.

This situation was peculiarly British, resembling only the developing culture of the United States. In nineteenth-century France, establishing the cultural credentials of a government was one of the most potent ways of asserting intellectual and political legitimacy. Successive regimes from Napoleon I through Louis Philippe to Napoleon III organised major exhibitions of French art, commissioned works of art for churches and museums, and fostered national and provincial museums. The public encouragement of art was loaded with significance – an approach that survives to this day, accounting for the stupefying size of the Musée du Louvre. In Germany, a belief in the value of the visual arts was inspired by writers from Immanuel Kant and Wilhelm Wackenroder to the architect Karl Friedrich Schinkel, who believed in the sacredness of art, and in the museum as a place distinct from and superior to the outside world, where the initiated could enjoy an epiphanic experience.[9] In Schinkel's Altes Museum in Berlin, the design is calculated to reconcile 'a secular exterior and a sacred interior'.[10] In Italy, the greatness of Italian culture was seen as a mark of national distinction, a point of view symbolised by the Pantheon in Rome, filled with the graves and memorials of Italian artists (Fig. 16).

In spite of cultural differences, France and Germany did inspire Britain's new museums. Germany, at least in aspiration, shaped the character of national and university museums. For such people as Charles and Elizabeth Eastlake, friends of Waagen and strongly Germanophile (she translated

16 The Pantheon, Rome, photographed by Francis Frith in the 1850s–70s.

Waagen into English), German culture was the source of learning and understanding. France exercised an equally strong influence through the Musée Napoléon and the widespread interest in French culture and education, regularly described as superior to the British variety.

Along with the practical difficulties of establishing a national gallery in Britain, the theoretical context was equally fraught. The idea of displaying the art of the past – with Italian paintings standing for all foreign works – was viewed with suspicion, especially by artists, and seen as a dampener on the native school. Already in the 1740s David Hume,

an enthusiastic upholder of the social benefits of the arts and a champion of their growth in England, had argued that 'So many perfect models of *Italian* paintings brought into *Britain*, instead of exciting our artists, is the cause of their small progress in that noble art.'[11] Additionally, importing old foreign pictures would discourage patrons from buying new English ones: James Barry warned against the distracting nature of 'pictures of the old masters, separated, and in private hands', which might mislead the youthful artist because of the partiality their owners showed for them, and 'the excessive praise and admiration' lavished on their execution by sycophants,[12] while for the painter John Opie one cause 'of the discouragement of English art' was

> the vast and continual influx of old pictures into every part of the kingdom, more than nine-tenths of which, to the eye of true taste, offer nothing but a battered mediocrity, or worse bad originals, and bad copies of bad originals, smoked, varnished, and puffed into celebrity by interested dealers and ignorant connoisseurs, and sold for sums that would have astonished the artist under whose names they are fraudulently passed; to the utter starvation of all national attempts at excellence.[13]

The convention persisted that copying from paintings was a minor element of academic training, to be undertaken after the initial drawing from casts and drawings. The attempt to emulate the great artists of the past could, it was thought, have a depressing effect on the student. Hazlitt argued:

> [The] student who has models of every kind of excellence constantly before him is not only diverted from that particular walk of art in which, by patient exertion, he might have obtained ultimate success, but from having his imagination habitually raised to an over-strained standard of refinement, by the sight of the most exquisite examples in art, he becomes impatient and dissatisfied with his own attempts, determines to reach the same perfection all at once, or throws down his pencil in despair.[14]

At the centre of this debate was the question of whether the artist should be guided by the accumulated wisdom of the past, or should follow nature. Even the sculptor John Flaxman, while committed to the art of the past, was ambivalent about its educational value. Grateful that so much survived from antiquity, he yet felt that if more existed, this might 'rather overwhelm than assist the progress of modern genius'.[15] In many Victorian art museums these issues were neatly avoided, in that art of the past, and foreign art, were effectively excluded.

For those arguing in favour of the creation of art museums, instrumentalist considerations tended to be the most compelling arguments. The idea that art and the art gallery were valuable in their own right without any practical justification was only tentatively and occasionally proposed. Adapting the ideas of French theorists, Richardson had put forward arguments that were not intended, he said, for informed French audiences but that aimed to 'reform English attitudes to painting'.[16] Painting was to be seen as a 'Noble, Useful and Delightful Art',[17] a 'Pleasant, Innocent Amusement' ordained as 'an Ingredient in Humane Life, which the supreme Wisdom has judg'd necessary'.[18] Painting might be compared to music in its purely formal qualities: 'its beautiful Forms, Colours and Harmony, are to the Eye what Sounds, and the Harmony of that kind are to the Ear; and in both we are delighted in observing the Skill of the Artist in proportion to It, and our own Judgment to discover it'.[19] But while in his ninth discourse Reynolds reiterated the value of the visual arts as a means of expressing a 'general and intellectual beauty' able to 'raise the thoughts, and extend the views of the spectator', he felt bound in the academic tradition to associate this value with 'publick benefits', that is to say 'the means of bestowing on whole nations refinement of taste…disentangling the mind from appetite, and conducting the thoughts through successive stages of excellence'.[20] Although both writers expressed their faith in the value of art as an intellectual rather than sensual objective, its civic value remained a pre-occupation.

Romantic writers were more likely to endow art with sacred qualities. A painter and philosopher as well as art critic, Hazlitt was a passionate enthusiast for the art of the past. In a lyrical account of John Julius Angerstein's collection in Pall Mall, he invoked 'Oh! Art, lovely Art!'. There art could be seen in its 'plenitude' and 'power'; it was 'Time's treasurer', the only medium that could conquer time.[21] Paintings seen in the gravely sympathetic context of this gallery stood in contrast to the 'glitter and varnish', alluring but superficial, associated with Royal Academy exhibitions – this contrast being a *leitmotif* of contemporary discussion of the contrast between the museum's dignity and the exhibition's vulgarity. Hazlitt wrote in quasi-religious Germanic terms: the gallery was 'a sanctuary, a holy of holies, collected by taste, sacred to fame, enriched by the rarest products of genius'.[22] A gallery should display only art at its finest and arouse intense emotion, transporting the viewer to another level of experience, in contrast to the commercial atmosphere of the exhibition. Of

Angerstein's gallery, Hazlitt asserted:[23] 'This is not a bazaar, a raree-show of art, a Noah's ark of all the Schools, marching out in endless procession'.[24] The spectator is 'abstracted to another sphere; we breathe empyrean air…we live in time past, and seem identified with the permanent forms of things'.[25] In contrast to worldly pleasures, in this private space the visitor experiences 'the solitude, the silence, the speaking looks, the unfading forms within'. Art is seen as transcendent, 'the mind's true home. The contemplation of truth and beauty is the proper object for which we were created, which calls for the most intense desires of the soul, and of which it never tires.'[26]

The intrinsic virtue of art was differently interpreted by others. For Haydon, champion of history painting and believer in a distinct, romanticised, version of the academic tradition, public art should provide 'the illustration of a great moral principle, of the development of some sublime system, – heroic – poetical – or religious.'[27] He greeted the newly founded National Gallery with enthusiasm, seeing it as a training ground for artists: it was 'delightful at last to walk in to the Gallery just as you felt inclined without trouble or inconvenience'. The Gallery would promote a 'great and rapid advance to the Art of the Country from the facility of comparison this will afford the people.'[28] Haydon attacked the degeneracy of art in England, railing against artists' ignorance and incompetence, their getting 'money before they get knowledge'.[29] For these writers, the creation and contemplation of art represented a high ideal needing no material justification, but it was not an ideal that was often publicly stated.

ART AND THE NATION

The museum movement in Britain was inspired by recurring international competitiveness clouded by a strong sense of inferiority. The promotion of a national school addressed two persistent issues: innate British creative incapacity, and popular inability to appreciate the visual arts. However Britain might triumph in battle, or her poets and scientists excel, many felt that the country was doomed to artistic failure. This sense of inferiority was fuelled by foreign observers. In the eighteenth century such commentators as the Abbé Jean-Bernard Le Blanc, the artist Jean André Rouquet and Johann Joachim Winckelmann (who, unlike the others, never visited Britain) had postulated a theory of geographical determinism. It was impossible, they averred, for the visual arts to flourish in a country with so poor a climate – only in a country like Greece could the arts reach perfection. They pointed to the very small number of native-born English or Scottish artists, past or present, the deficiency being filled by immigrants. Their opinions exercised a devastating influence not only in their own time but in the nineteenth century, and the defiance with which the excellence of British art was often proclaimed by the Victorians was aroused by the lingering influence of such disparagement.

In the nineteenth century a partisan separation of attitudes developed. German commentators tended to be sympathetic towards England: the anglophile Waagen, eager to stress the relationship between the two countries, believed that it was in England that the fine arts might fully revive. French critics tended to maintain Rouquet's reservations. Louis Viardot, a conservative and staunchly Catholic writer, complained in 1843 that England, incapable of producing anything of quality herself 'under its sky of fog and smoke', threatened to suffocate the works of art amassed from the rest of the world.[30] The fine arts, including architecture and music, were not 'autochthonous' in England but were imported as objects of curiosity and fashion, 'to satisfy the caprices of idle wealth rather than the habits and needs of national taste, of popular feeling'.[31] For Francis Wey, a French critic visiting in the 1850s, the British paintings were the least impressive element of the National Gallery's collection: William Hogarth was 'the only incontestable glory of a non-existent school'.[32] He found the Vernon collection of British paintings recently left to the nation 'acutely offensive'. In mid-century the attitudes of foreign critics shifted, especially over the 1855 Paris Exhibition, where the British display was especially popular, not least because of its political associations and its newness: 'Britain seemed to present the last word in modernity and industry, commerce and political freedom'.[33] These paintings were seen to reveal the emergence of a new school across the Channel. The French must, Wey suggested, admit that their neighbours 'possess, not a school of painting, but a group of scholarly humourists trusting to their brushes to convey impressions too difficult to express in writing'.[34] Equally, the French art historian and critic Ernest Chesneau puzzled over English art: though the paintings were violent, '*criardé*' in tone, he was struck by their individuality. Almost alone among European countries, Britain possessed a national school, however hard it was to define.[35] British art remained a source of fascination for French critics and writers through much of the century, not least because it was Northern and therefore forward-looking and vigorous in contrast to the decadence of the Southern schools with which France had come to be associated.[36]

Pessimism about the native school extended beyond painting to the decorative arts in a way that was also to be highly significant for the development of museums. In 1755 Rouquet, well disposed after many years in England to that 'charming island', published *L'Etat des Arts, en Angleterre*.[37] Detaching himself from the fiercer criticisms of the Abbé Le Blanc, he analysed the fine and decorative arts. In each of the fields he discussed – textiles, silver and porcelain – the message was the same: English productions were remarkable for their high technical quality, but the design was unfailingly poor. The English could not bear to be criticised, and often ignored advice: even though a group of draughtsmen from Lyons had been established in a famous London manufacturer's and provided the best possible designs, 'A certain woman, who has neither skill nor fancy, has been for many years the principal source of the coloured designs employed in this manufacture'.[38] Fortunately at the Chelsea porcelain factory, 'a French artist of great abilities furnishes or directs the models'.[39] Equally, England had few silversmiths of any quality, the demand being slight.[40] For Rouquet, the artist was closely associated with craft – useful design – rather than with the liberal intellectual arts of the academy. He developed an issue that was to dominate the South Kensington Museum and the regional museums: the low standard of design in the decorative arts, and by extension the relationship of the fine to the applied arts, and the status of sculpture as an ideal or a useful art.

During the latter years of the eighteenth century and early period of the nineteenth, an extended effort was made to raise the status of the decorative arts by creating objects or sets of objects that would have a representational and avowedly artistic purpose, even at the risk of being relatively or wholly useless. In contrast to Josiah Wedgwood and Thomas Chippendale, manufacturers early in the nineteenth-century sought to create artefacts that sacrificed usefulness to artistic display and even ostentation. This tendency, in parallel to the campaign to raise the status of the fine arts, led to the production of such extravaganza as the Rockingham Dessert Service, a form of history painting in ceramic designed for William IV and displayed at the Rockingham factory's Piccadilly showroom in 1837 (Fig. 17).[41] Metalwork exhibited comparable vigour. The royal goldsmiths Rundell, Bridge and Rundell employed such figures as the sculptors William Theed, E.H. Baily and, above all, an internationally famous sculptor and draughtsman, Flaxman, as designers. The results included such pieces as Flaxman's *Shield of Achilles* of 1821, an imaginary recreation of the shield described in the *Iliad* (Fig. 18).[42] This extraordinary artefact, laden with historical and literary associations, could be seen as an equivalent to history painting, executed in the decorative arts and sculpture. With two of the four versions being acquired by the King and the Duke of York, the shield asserted the dignity of the applied arts and, like the Rockingham Dessert Service, succeeded as spectacle: a shield exhibited in the firm's showrooms in Ludgate Hill in 1823 attracted great crowds.[43] The ambivalent status of sculpture, seen variously as a fine art and as an applied art appropriate for the adornment of buildings, was to be a *leitmotif* of the nineteenth century.

ENGLISH IGNORANCE AND ASPIRATIONS

As early as 1719 Richardson was already commenting on English ignorance of the visual arts, not just among the general population but among supposedly educated people:

It is remarkable that in a Countrey as Ours, Rich, and abounding with Gentlemen of a Just, and Delicate Taste, in Musick, Poetry, and all kinds of Literature; Such fine Writers! Such Solid

17 Pieces from the Rockingham
Dessert Service, 1837 (Royal
Collection).

Reasoners! Such Able Statesmen! Gallant Soldiers! Excellent Divines, Lawyers, Physicians, Mathematicians, and Mechanicks! and yet so few, so very few Lovers, and *Connoisseurs* in painting![44]

He compared England to the situation 'not only in *Italy*, where they are all Lovers, and almost all *Connoisseurs*, but in *France, Holland,* and *Flanders*'.[45] A century later the theme remained current. Impressed though he was by Grosvenor House (one of a group of great London houses opened to polite visitors after their owners had been transported by the Musée Napoléon, which they would have visited during the Treaty of Amiens in 1802–3), Simond dwelt on the demeanour of the visitors:

It is amusing to sit in a corner, and observe, as they pass, the countenances of the visitors in places of this kind, staring round with a total absence of all pleasure and all feeling. Nine-tenths of them know and care absolutely nothing

about the pictures they look at, particularly the men. Why then do they come? Because it is fashionable, and because it is dear; you give gold at the door. The English appear to me to have more esteem than liking for the fine arts.'[46]

Haydon despaired of his countrymen's attitude to art, confined to an appreciation of the 'mechanical excellence' of Dutch painting and neglecting art's intellectual and spiritual powers:

It's a melancholy thing for those whose whole ambition is the advance of National taste – to see all the faculties of men, squeezed into an inside of a tasteless dutch Room, with a woman clouting a child – all the delight English men feel is in cocking their nose close to the Picture, and let its intellectual qualities be what they may, condemn or praise in proportion to its mechanical excellence…Wherever I dine, wherever I go, a string of technical phrases that are for ever on the tongue, without effort or reflection,

35

18 *The Shield of Achilles*, 1821. Created by Philip Rundell and designed by John Flaxman (who had studied Homer's description in depth and produced a plaster cast of the shield), this bravura silver-gilt evocation of the shield of the classical hero was supplied to George IV by Rundell, Bridge and Rundell and displayed at his coronation banquet. It was described by Rundells as 'a masterpiece of modern art'. Three other versions exist (Royal Collection).

are perpetually uttered – how that floor is imitated, what a colour that turnip is, how delightful is that cabbage, look at that herring – wonderful…[47]

These limitations could, however, be corrected through a national gallery. For one of the most successful art dealers, William Buchanan, writing in 1803, 'English taste' did not lie in 'Historical Compositions' or 'Subjects of Saints' – 'lively and pleasing Compositions are altogether the rage or the great and grand in Landscape principally'.[48] His experience of the display of the Orléans collection in London in the 1790s led him to advocate the estab-

lishment of a national gallery 'as tending to form and diffuse a more refined taste, or to improve the style of a national school of art, by reference to works of the first order'.[49] Equally, James Barry felt that 'without some proper public collection of ancient art, to refer to occasionally, both our pupils [at the Academy] and the public would be in the same bewildered situation so emphatically alluded to in the New Testament, of the people without guides'.[50]

This ignorance remained a constant plaint among gallery cicerones such as Hazlitt and Jameson in the 1820s and 1830s, Hazlitt complaining bitterly of the ignorance even of so-called experts: 'the opinion of those few persons whom nature intended for judges is drowned in the noisy decisions of shallow smatterers in taste'.[51] English Philistinism was attacked by George Agar Ellis, politician and advocate of the National Gallery. Shortly after its foundation, he wrote a (much-quoted) anonymous article in the *Quarterly Review*, applauding the event but attacking the bad taste of the English, notably in their love of portraiture. Agar Ellis expressed his contempt for the despicable taste of earlier generations, 'the kind of trash we see at Burghley, Corsham, and so many other houses', in contrast to the purity of the collections in Dresden, anticipating the reaction against sixteenth- and seventeenth-century Italian painting that was to gather strength in the 1840s.[52] He attributed the lack of understanding to the fact that 'the great body of the people, the middling classes, as well as very many of the higher orders', were unable because of their professional responsibilities to travel to Italy and see great works of art.[53] The solution lay in an effective national gallery.

A deep-rooted irony is evident in these discussions. During the eighteenth century, strict control was exercised over those who might visit princely galleries in, for example, Florence or Rome. In Britain, on the other hand, while fewer museums were open, admission was conceived on a more liberal basis. Although bureaucratic obstacles were put in the way of visits to the British Museum, in the end anyone with sufficient persistence was admitted without charge. As Pastor Moritz noted in 1782, reflecting current perceptions of cultural ownership in Britain: 'The company...was various, and some of all sorts; some, I believe, of the very lowest classes of the people, of both sexes, for as it is the property of the nation, every one has the same right (I use the term of the country) to see it, that another has.'[54] His reservations about the British practice of allowing access to all resemble those of his countrymen Zacharias Conrad von Uffenbach, appalled by the vulgarity of visitors to the Ashmolean Museum in 1710,[55] and Gustav Waagen, equally dismayed by the chaos and dirt of the early nineteenth-century National Gallery, where the hordes of visitors, admitted without hindrance, were damaging the pictures.[56] The convention of free admission to collections and libraries caused great anxiety to officials throughout the century, since it was believed that the British were particularly prone

to ill behaviour. Joseph Planta, the great reforming Principal Librarian of the British Museum, wrote to his trustees in 1814 that 'our popular Visitors...in the fervour of independence, pride themselves in shewing a disdain of order, & in doing essential mischief for which we have no means of obtaining immediate redress'.[57] Yet the principle of free admission was not abandoned.

In the face of recent suggestions that the nineteenth-century gallery operated as a supervised space in which the public was controlled physically and intellectually, the evidence suggests that on the contrary the museums (and libraries) that developed early in the nineteenth century offered an alternative approach to authority.[58] These were spaces where, in theory at least, people of all classes were offered the same experience, and permitted to see objects that in the past would have been the preserve of the few. At a time of wild disparities of educational provision, this was already a considerable, if sometimes grudging, concession. But not only that: the comments of Planta and many later officials suggest that the danger – and the promise – of these new cultural spaces were that rather than enabling they actually resisted supervision, and that 'popular Visitors' might show 'a disdain for order', since the rules governing access to sites of learning lent themselves to being flouted. The recurring expressions of alarm, by curators and librarians, that will be cited below suggest that popular audiences were not cowed, not intimidated, not controlled – and that (as this book aims to illustrate) these audiences were increasingly inspired by these galleries into curiosity and a desire to learn.

It was not only the general population and the nobility whose ignorance might be alleviated by the creation of a national gallery: artists too would benefit. The modest number of publicly accessible art collections in London and the near impossibility of foreign travel between 1793 and 1814 (except in 1802–3) underlay artists' reactions to the glories of the Louvre. Visiting Paris in the autumn of 1802, Joseph Farington encountered numerous fellow-artists whose experience of art had been transformed. John Hoppner 'said He had no idea before of the powers of the great Artists who executed those works',[59] while for Martin Archer Shee, portraitist and later President of the Royal Academy, 'The picture gallery [the Louvre] exceeded his utmost expectations. He had no idea of the perfection to which the Art had been carried'.[60] Farington himself was stunned by the museum, admitting that before seeing it, 'I could but ill judge what has been done in Art.'[61] He spent many days there, including a day 'studying the works of the earliest Flemish Masters from John Van Eyck to Brughel [sic]…having had no opportunity before of properly judging of the merits of the painters of that age'.[62] At a time when visiting Italy in any depth required several weeks of travel, and when the only other means of studying visual art was through the mediated and subjective medium of the print, a visit to a major art museum such as the Louvre was a revelation and inspiration. Britain, it was increasingly felt, should be able to offer the same opportunities.

HOPE FOR BRITISH ART

Self-doubt over British achievements in the visual arts to date was matched by a belief that the decline that was generally attributed to the Reformation could be reversed, and that permanent art collections, accessible to artists and to the public in general, could play a major role in educating and inspiring the public. One of the aspirations expressed by a succession of writers was that the English or the British school could become internationally prominent, and even supreme. Thus, celebrating the Royal Academy's new home at Somerset House, Reynolds expressed the hope that 'it will be no small addition to the glory which this nation has already acquired from having given birth to eminent men in every part of science, if it should be enabled to produce, in consequence of this institution, a School of English Artists'.[63] Acknowledging England's deficiencies, he stated that the nation's reputation would be assessed by neighbouring countries in terms of 'intellectual excellence' stimulated by trade and wealth. He warned that 'a people whose whole attention is absorbed in those means, and who forget the end, can aspire but little above the rank of a barbarous nation'.[64] The potential excellence of a native school of art became a favourite trope. Reynolds's fellow professor at the Academy, William Hunter, an enthusiastic patron, affirmed that with proper encouragement, the works of English artists

would rival those of ancient Greece and Rome.[65] National pride would be satisfied by the creation of a gallery fit for an emerging world power, and by the encouragement of the native school and a gallery dedicated to British painting.

A remarkable assertion of confidence in British art was made in the Louvre during the Treaty of Amiens, when Farington met two collectors, Abraham Hume and Charles Long. Faced by the modern French school, 'Of *Modern Art* they decided that the English School has the superiority.'[66] Contemporary French painting – partly for political reasons – was universally condemned by British artists and critics at this period, resulting in an almost total absence of French Neoclassical painting in British collections and initiating a debate over the rival merits of modern French and English painting that was to recur throughout the century.

The assertion of the superiority of the native school became a fundamental motif for nineteenth-century art galleries. Increasingly, the founders of new museums gave an honourable place to the modern British school even in collections concentrating on other works. As the recording of artistic achievement moved between the book and the museum, various collections took up the theme. Sir John Soane's Museum is filled with statements of the greatness of British culture, for which the Royal Academy (repeatedly represented in the museum) provided a metonym. Soane proclaimed the greatness of England's literature in his shrine to Shakespeare, and of its visual art in works by English painters, sculptors and architects, notably the school's putative founder, Hogarth. Sir Francis Bourgeois' bequest to Dulwich College included almost fifty British works among 370 pictures,[67] while the Angerstein collection contained works by Hogarth, Reynolds, Wilkie and West.[68] All this said, British art generally played a secondary role in these galleries and at the National Gallery. Only late in the nineteenth century, and notably in the new regional art galleries, did British art triumph.[69]

Some critics went so far as to suggest that the English might become leaders in the field. Richardson had already addressed this issue. Acknowledging the 'Uncouth Sound' of the 'very name…[of] the *English school of painting*',[70] he suggested, in view of the 'Greatness of Mind which has always been

Inherent in our Nation, and a Degree of Solid Sense not inferiour to any of our Neighbours', and the collections in England of drawings, antiquities and paintings, that 'if ever that Delightful, Useful, and Noble Art [of painting] does revive in the World, 'tis Probable twill be in *England*'.[71] Explicit here is the association between the nation's ownership of works of art and the possibility of national artistic success – an association seen as one of the strongest arguments for a national museum. Richardson's hopes for the revival of the arts were echoed by Hogarth and by Walpole in his *Anecdotes of Painting in England*:

At this epoch of common sense, one may reasonably expect to see the arts flourish to as proud a height as they attained at Athens, Rome, or Florence. Painting has hitherto made but faint Efforts in England....The Throne itself is now the altar of the graces, and whoever sacrifices to them becomingly, is sure that his offerings will be smiled upon by a Prince, who is at once the example and patron of accomplishments....When we abound with heroes, orators, and patrons, it will be hard if their images are not transmitted to posterity under gracefull representations.[72]

The visual arts were not only seen as intrinsically valuable: they had a public function. Walpole developed an idea that was to be much discussed: the value of a national school of painting and sculpture as a means of celebrating national victory and the nation's prominent citizens. Further, the arts were seen to offer a measure of the level of civilisation within a country, a point of view spelt out by Opie:

The progress of the arts in every country is the exact and exclusive measure of the progress of refinement;...we...find that the most enlightened, the most envied, and the most interesting periods in the history of mankind are precisely those in which the arts have been most esteemed, most cultivated, and have reached their highest point of elevation.[73]

For Haydon too, it was in the British Isles that the art of painting could be revived. He too believed there was no intrinsic defect in the English, and that the poverty of the arts should be ascribed to the artistic destruction of the Reformation; to the indifference of church and state; and to the low ambitions of 'the nobility and the opulent [who] are content with portraits of themselves and their beautiful families, till all feeling as to the public importance of painting is nearly extinct'.[74] All these factors could be obviated by proper public patronage.

THE ARTS IN SOCIETY

The perceived value of a public museum extended to the notion that it could improve society. The idea of art as a means of bringing together the social classes, and of taming the masses, became a commonplace early in the nineteenth century. A connection was often made between providing accessibility for the general population to the knowledge offered by museums (of all types), and ensuring their good behaviour. This crucial idea reflected the current German belief in the beneficial effects of *Bildung*, a word for which there is no precise equivalent in English, but which may be summarised as cultural and spiritual education. The concept of *Bildung* was to be essential to the development of the Victorian museum, not least because it was felt that within a museum, such training could be made available to everybody. Equally important was the prevailing idea that it was the duty of the privileged to educate and assist those seen as their economic, social and intellectual inferiors.

The notion of art as a humanising or taming force by which the angry masses could be softened has been regularly cited in the recent literature as evidence of the perception of museums as agents of social control.[75] Such an interpretation is certainly supported by, for example, the approving observation by the engraver Abraham Raimbach, visiting Paris in 1802, of 'the presence of the humbler classes and their decorous conduct in the numerous establishments open gratuitously to the public, and no one will deny the great and beneficial influence that must result from such facilities being so liberally and judiciously afforded'. He noted with 'some degree of mortification' that in Britain, dominated by class differences, 'the national establishments and the national monuments are so hedged in with what are called vested rights, that they are, in effect, as a sealed book to the great mass of the community'.[76] Notoriously, in the parliamentary debates of 1832, when London was in uproar over the Reform Bill, Sir Robert Peel suggested, as an argument in favour of the National Gallery, that 'In the present times of political excitement, the exacerbation of angry and unsocial feeling might be much softened by the effects which the fine arts had ever produced upon the minds of men'.[77]

This apparently manipulative statement needs to be put into context. It does of course reflect the privileged classes' terror of the mob, a terror that had been enflamed by the 1780 Gordon Riots – when for several days the mob took control of London – by the French Revolution and later upheavals in France, and by the civil dissension in Britain after the defeat of Napoleon. While it may appear that Peel was suggesting that art should act as an opium for the masses, the overriding theme proposed by this innovative Tory was that a national gallery could function as a place where all classes could be received at the same time, assisting 'the cementing of those bonds of union between the richer and the poorer orders of the State, which no man was more anxious to see joined in mutual intercourse and good understanding than he was.'[78] It was an argument deriving from German aesthetics during the political upheavals that followed the French Revolution. Friedrich Schiller, as James Sheehan has written, 'vividly expressed two convictions that came to be widely shared among German intellectuals late in the eighteenth century and early in the nineteenth: first, that modern society and culture...are fragmented and divided against themselves; second, that art can provide a new source of spiritual harmony and social cohesion'.[79] When Peel spoke of the taming effect of art and insisted that the selection of the new site for the gallery at Charing Cross was ideal because it lay at the very centre of the city and would become part of the lives of all sectors of the community, he was inspired not by ideals of repression but by optimism. Peel's hopes for the National Gallery seem particularly bold because he was speaking at a time when different social classes were segregated in almost all potential meeting places, including the theatre, the church and modes of transport. His views were not only current at a high level of society: when in 1835 a Parliamentary Select Committee asked an architect associated with the Norwich Society of Artists whether the institution of libraries, art schools and art galleries would 'have the

effect not only of improving manufactures, but the moral and social conditions of people', it received an affirmative answer.[80]

In fact, the siting of the National Gallery did not achieve this uniting effect. In 1850 a Select Committee met to consider 'the present Accommodation afforded by the National Gallery', and the possibility of moving the pictures to another site. There was no doubt about the Gallery's popularity: the report pointed out that whereas the Royal Gallery in Berlin received some 200 visitors daily, the average at the (smaller) National Gallery was over 3,000.[81] Eastlake, while not averse to the site on Trafalgar Square, remarked that the Gallery's popularity had a deterrent effect on more refined visitors. Discussing the issue of removing the paintings to a less accessible place, he said that 'many persons who are in the habit of visiting collections of pictures, especially ladies, avoid the National Gallery on account of the crowds that go there; and all that class of visitors would certainly be more numerous in the event of there being greater facilities for them to see the pictures'.[82] His views were reiterated a decade later, when a master printer giving evidence to a Select Committee remarked that printers enjoyed visiting museums 'as a better sort of relaxation' rather than for intellectual improvement, but that visiting the British Museum or the National Gallery on a public holiday was 'preposterous either as to comfort or instruction' on account of the crowds.[83]

In spite of these failures, the idea of promoting social harmony remained a constant argument in favour of municipal museums, exhibitions and libraries, even if it was sometimes rather nervously presented. While the National Gallery may not have succeeded as an agent of social change, the endeavour to diffuse a form of *Bildung* among the huge new urban population of Britain was to be a cornerstone of nineteenth-century cultural innovation.

This approach was based on a consciousness of what was perceived both as the ignorance and as the desire for knowledge on the part of large sectors of the population at a time when public education was disgracefully far behind parallel societies overseas. It was a programme with a quite different objective to Reynolds's or Haydon's: instruction in design for the working man. Numerous witnesses at Select Committees indicated 'that there exists among the enterprising and laborious classes of our country an earnest desire for information in the Arts'.[84] Addressing this problem was the prime objective of the 1835 Select Committee inquiry into 'the best means of extending a knowledge of the Arts, and of the Principles of Design among the People (especially the Manufacturing Population) of the Country'. The architect J.B. Papworth was typical in commenting that though 'there is innate talent enough in the country to supply all its wants in art', good taste was not generally prevalent in Britain, and the British were 'very far behind the French in…the manufacturing arts'. What the committee had in mind in its report was providing models to encourage the 'laborious' classes to draw, such as were already available in some mechanics' institutes. They remarked on how little artistic education had been encouraged in Britain, whereas in France the 'free, open and popular system of instruction…and the extreme accessibility of their museums, libraries and exhibitions, have greatly tended to the diffusion of a love of art, as well as of literature, among the poorer classes'.[85]

This idea of popular education recalls what is perhaps the most significant link between the theories of the eighteenth century and their application in the nineteenth: the notion of a double tier in society, divided by heredity (as many commentators would have it), by education, by social position. This notion had crucial implications for the arts and, as art came to be less a private and more a public sphere, for art museums.

As John Barrell has discussed, the civic humanist ideal of society enunciated by the third Earl of Shaftesbury early in the eighteenth century posited a fundamental and near-irreversible distinction between the 'liberal' man (educated and, at least in early versions, well-born), who was capable of exercising public virtues on behalf of the state, and the 'mechanic' or artisan, the person of ordinary attainments, only fitted to carry out manual activities to which he was unable to apply intellectual distinction or moral force.[86] The fact that the act of painting necessitated manual application was as anxiously debated in the eighteenth century as in classical times, writers regularly invoking Pliny the Elder's statement that painting was only carried out 'by people of free birth, and later by persons of station', and was forbidden to slaves. For the proponents of painting as a liberal art, it was important to stress that it was his intellectual and artistic qualities that distinguished the true artist.

Discussion of 'the common people' and of their fitness to appreciate art was a *leitmotif* in the discussion of art and by extension of museums. Reynolds enunciated a fundamental distinction in the creation, understanding and nature of art that was to run like a fault line through eighteenth- and nineteenth-century discussions. Since the society of men, Reynolds suggested, 'is divided into different ranks, and some are appointed to labour for the support of others, those whom their superiority sets free from labour, begin to look for intellectual entertainments'.[87] By implication, those who labour would be excluded from the creation – and to an extent from the proper appreciation – of great works of art. The true appreciation of art, in other words, could be attained only by the upper levels of society. Though our senses (opposed by Reynolds to reason) are necessary to support us 'in the lowest state of nature', they ought not to be needlessly gratified when we are in a state of plenty. '[It] is therefore necessary to the happiness of individuals, and still more necessary to the security of society, that the mind should be elevated to the idea of general beauty, and the contemplation of general truth'. By these means, the mind seeks 'something more excellent' and 'obtains its proper superiority over the common senses of life, by learning to feel itself capable of higher aims and nobler enjoyments'. While the practice of the visual arts necessarily 'is applied to somewhat a lower faculty of the mind, which approaches nearer to sensuality', sensual pleasure is purified by the exercise of sense and reason. Though his own art did not always fulfil his aspirations, Reynolds was constantly in pursuit of an ideal art dominated by reason, an art that could not be appreciated by all.

Reynolds was of course reiterating an old-established academic trope, and though the grip of academic art was to diminish in the nineteenth century, the idea of the difficulty for the uninitiated of understanding high art was to run through nineteenth-century discussions of art in a way directly at variance with the notion of the healing and socially redemptive effects of artistic appreciation. This book proposes that the idea of a double tier of galleries was peculiar to Britain and was to be fully, if not richly, developed there.

41

Education in design and in the production of objects of high visual quality was much more easily accepted than grandiose conceptions of the encouragement of history painting. After all, in parliamentary debates and Select Committees, one old-established note was insistently sounded: if art was to be supported by the state, it had to be economically useful. This might be achieved in various ways. In the 1824 debate over setting up the National Gallery, Agar Ellis cited its potential financial benefits in terms of tourism: like similar collections in Italy it might attract foreign visitors, coming specifically to view the pictures.[88] More insistent was the idea that a prime purpose of a national collection was to offer manufacturers, designers and workers ready access to art, so that their eye would be educated. As a result, the standards of design in manufactured goods produced in Britain would rise, making these goods more attractive to foreign buyers.[89]

As the nineteenth century advanced, the poor quality of design in Britain and the negative impact on trade that resulted were much discussed, though the ways in which this situation could be improved were not always elucidated. In 1832 Robert Peel, supporting in Parliament a new building for the National Gallery, stated that 'the interest of our manufactures was also involved in every encouragement being held out to the fine arts in this country'. While British manufacturers were superior to all foreign competitors in terms of machinery, 'in the pictorial designs, which were so important in recommending the productions of industry to the taste of the consumer, they were, unfortunately, not equally successful; and hence they had found themselves unequal to cope with their rivals'.[90] His forceful speech did not, however, make it clear how these objectives would be achieved, or how a study of Titian would assist manufacturers. The issue was aired again in the 1835 Select Committee, when the head of a firm importing manufactured goods commented on the stronger feeling for art that was being generated in the country, but declared that while, as the chairman, William Ewart, had suggested, education was needed to 'appreciate the beauties of the higher branches of art', this was not something that could be achieved by galleries and museums on their own.[91] A generation later, in Manchester and Liverpool, Glasgow and Nottingham, these arguments were to be rehearsed again.

For all the vigour with which these issues were pursued, no national policy for museums and the arts was enunciated during the first half of the century. The National Gallery's trustees, who might have served as leaders in the field, phlegmatically continued their business, having placed before them in 1848 the appointment of an assistant porter and stoker, and the loss of a visitor's umbrella entrusted to the 'servants of this establishment'.[92] They discussed picture conservation, the ventilation of the galleries, space shortage and the appearance of the rooms; they rejected the acquisition of Lawrence's drawings. What was lacking was any overall policy. In *The National Gallery: Its Formation and Management* (1853), the artist and arts administrator William Dyce attacked the 'miscellaneous and fortuitous assemblage of pictures, placed together without order or arrangement on any recognisable plan'.[93] He blamed the board of trustees, dominated by noblemen rather than savants, who were included only 'as a favour extended with a patronising hand, for which, of course, they are to be duly grateful'.[94] He criticised the fact that the Keeper of the Gallery was 'not a responsible officer, having definite duties…but a mere servant, acting under the orders of the Board'.[95] What was needed was a distinguished Keeper able to provide the trustees with 'the constant benefit of an experience and knowledge of art to which, either singly or as a body, they did not…lay claim, and which, at all events, public opinion did not ascribe to them'.[96] Above all, he railed at the lack of national policy:

> Our institutions, generally, and in particular those connected more or less with the arts, have grown up too much by accident, taking the shape of some ill-defined nucleus; or have been commenced with little more than a general conviction that such and such institutions were wanted, and ought to exist, in a country like Great Britain. What the institutions are to aim at becoming, – how they are to differ from others having similar objects, – what are to be their real nature and exact purposes, – how those purposes are to be fulfilled, – are inquiries which…have too frequently to be taken up when the progress of such institutions has not only been in wrong directions, but has grown so considerably as to throw serious obstacles in the way of their reconstruction.'[97]

Dyce's comments were not written in a vacuum. 1853 saw the publication of *The Organisation of the Permanent Civil Service* by Stafford Northcote and Charles Trevelyan, which attacked the Service's incompetence and preference for the well-born over the expert. Their comments led to the full-scale reform of the Civil Service, and the introduction of competitive examination for entry. In a direct parallel, Dyce's document led to the appointment of the 1853 Select Committee on the National Gallery. In the same years, the forerunner of the South Kensington Museum was set up, along with the Department of Science and Art. A new era of professionalism, in the visual arts as in the Civil Service, was on its way.

The themes outlined in this chapter constantly recur in the second half of the nineteenth century, when municipal and other galleries were being set up in great numbers. The negative views – the inherent incapacity of the British in the visual arts, including the decorative arts, the public's ignorance in this field and indeed the loutish stupidity of all levels of society when faced with works of art – were tempered by optimistic ideas, notably the belief in the potential triumph of the British school and the exciting results that would ensue. Any belief in the intrinsic value of art played a significantly less important part than the arguments for the moral force of art, its power to tame the unruly masses and introduce social cohesion, its ability to improve design and make British products more attractive to foreigners. And the notion of a double tier of art – and therefore of art galleries – would create a set of municipal art galleries in the same vein, intended to instruct working people in better carrying out their work, and to entertain the uneducated without requiring of them any special skills or knowledge. These ideas were to be realised in Henry Cole's vision for the South Kensington Museum and in the people's museums and galleries created all over the United Kingdom.

Northern Academy of Arts.

NEWCASTLE UPON TYNE.

3

STRUGGLING FOR
A VOICE

THE LEARNED SOCIETY AND ARTISTS' SOCIETY
IN THE PROVINCIAL CITY

Sociability was the key to the creation of many early museums. From the seventeenth century into the nineteenth and beyond, societies dedicated to the sciences and the arts developed throughout Europe and in the New World. They might be nationwide bodies, like the academies established by the French state or the Royal Academy of Arts in London, or local associations in regional towns. These societies had numerous objectives but they were all inspired by the Baconian empirical desire to study the natural world through observation and experiment: to collect and analyse antiquities, conduct experiments, engage in debates, correspond with scholars at home and overseas. To support these aims, the members of these quasi-colleges assembled libraries and archaeological remains, natural history specimens, exotic curiosities and technical apparatus for the conducting of experiments.

This was a remarkably cosmopolitan movement. Hundreds of societies were founded in the Western world, remarkably alike in their activities and their collections. Many have vanished, leaving perhaps a few archives, or nothing. But some survive, whether as archaeological societies (archaeology being a resilient discipline) or as the transformed modern versions of scientific bodies. In Görlitz, on the German-Polish borders in what was formerly Silesia, the *Oberlausitzische Gesellschaft der Wissenschaften* (the Philosophical Society of Upper Lusatia) was founded by a group of some twenty learned men in 1779 (Fig. 19). Its rich collections – cabinets of scientific machinery, graphics, geology, natural history, antiquities, topography, literature and of course a library – are preserved in the building acquired for them at an early stage, still testifying to the vigour of intellectual life in this provincial capital.[1] At Haarlem in the Netherlands the Teylers Museum, set up in 1784 to educate the public in the arts and sciences, remains a resplendent example of an eighteenth-century museum, complete with specimens of the natural world, scientific instruments and print room.[2] Nor was this only a

45

19 The library of the
*Oberlausitzische Gesellschaft der
Wissenschaften*, Görlitz. One of the
finest surviving learned societies, its
collections and library are
essentially intact.

European tradition. British influence extended to South Carolina, an especially rich colony earlier in the eighteenth century, where the Charleston Library Society, founded in 1748, displayed its British roots in the purchase of books, scientific instruments (inspired by the Royal Society's museum), prints by Boydell and a cast of the *Apollo Belvedere*. Ordered for the most part from London, these collections exhibited the members' desire to create in their prosperous but vulnerable community 'both an intellectual and social center…confident…of refining intellects and changing public culture'.[3]

For all the royal patronage extended in Britain and elsewhere, these societies were emphatically independent bodies, set up by men of learning, and financially dependent on private subscriptions. France was unusual in the encouragement provided,

or imposed, by the state. The first impetus for the French academies (as they were often known in France) emerged in the 1650s but the movement gained force in the 1680s with the foundation of the *Académie Française*.[4] The societies founded in such cities as Arles (1669) and Nîmes (1682) were controlled to a greater or lesser extent by 'the centralising universality of Parisian purism'.[5] They required letters patent and were informally supervised by the King's local representatives and by the upper clergy, since as forums that might permit free speech they posed a potential threat.

Gallic subservience to central authority was much remarked on in Britain. The British Institution announced on its foundation in 1805 its intention to compete with other countries that promoted 'the Arts of Painting, Sculpture, and Design, by great national establishments', threatening to 'wrest from

46

SOC·GEN·SPALDING·INSTITUTA·MDCCX·

us those advantages, which can only be retained by a pre-eminence in the Fine Arts'.[6] On a local level, in 1825 the Norwich and Norfolk Literary Institution stressed its healthily British character reliant on individual effort. In contrast to the Continent, where museums were 'instituted, solely by command of the respective governments…ours result from the disinterested and uncontrolled contributions of private individuals, and are established, not for the love of éclat, but from the genuine love of scientific improvement'.[7] Though the British tradition of independence was not as straightforward as its champions liked to think, and learned societies risked being seen as seditious, in many cases they engendered vigorous social and intellectual reform.

In Britain the learned society enjoyed two peaks: between 1660 (when the Royal Society was founded) and around 1720, and again between 1780 and the mid-nineteenth century. The Royal Society, with royal patronage but not public funding, assembled the keenest minds of the time. Of its many followers

only a few still exist, notably the Spalding Gentlemen's Society, established in that small Lincolnshire town in 1710. It showed its high ambitions in having Isaac Newton, George Vertue, Hans Sloane, Alexander Pope and Joseph Banks among its corresponding members (Fig. 20). Members of these societies yearned to explore the macrocosm of the universe (a number included observatories) while remaining loyal to the microcosm of their location through the study of local history. When they paid tribute to 'the arts', the term was used as in the title of the Royal Society of Arts, founded in 1754 to encourage all aspects of human creativity. In general the fine arts (in the modern sense) played a relatively minor role, other than for purposes of illustration and topography and as demonstrations of human ingenuity.

The period around 1800 witnessed an extraordinary development of semi-public bodies: antiquarian and archaeological societies, literary and philosophical societies, scientific institutions, athe-

47

naeums, lyceums, artists' societies, societies for the encouragement of the arts, subscription libraries, free libraries, academies for the training of artists, mechanics' institutes, musical societies and discussion groups.[8]

A new society in one town often stimulated others nearby, in a spirit of emulation that was to re-emerge later in the nineteenth century. Some societies were founded in rural county towns, such as Truro and Canterbury, but most developed in industrial and commercial centres.[9] Between 1800 and 1822 philosophical and literary societies or Royal Institutions were set up in Birmingham, Liverpool, Leeds, York and many other towns.[10] Smaller bodies were established on the Yorkshire coast in the 1820s, notably in Whitby, an old whaling centre, and Scarborough, a fashionable seaside resort. Both of their museums still exist, hauntingly reminiscent of their early days.

Members of literary and philosophical societies enjoyed at their best a spirit of civic humanism, intellectual curiosity and commercial self-interest that created an alternative to the scarcely existent culture offered by the state.[11] The societies of around 1800 differed from their earlier prototypes. Though both groups derived from the informal meetings of friends in a domestic setting, the later ones were more ambitious, materially and intellectually. Their premises regularly included lecture rooms and laboratories. Whereas earlier experiments and discussions had been directed at a core of initiates, the newer societies were more outward-looking, offering lectures and demonstrations. At the Newcastle Literary and Philosophical Society, public lectures were given from 1803, a much emulated innovation.[12] They might also be hubs of research: at the Rotunda Museum erected in 1829 at the expense of the Scarborough Philosophical Society, the displays were inspired by the pioneering investigations into fossils and geological strata of the geologist William Smith (Fig. 21).

These bodies played a crucial role in the development of museums in Britain. It was their collections of natural history, archaeology, geology and so forth that formed the basis of many of the municipal museums founded in the 1850s and later, while the concept of lecture programmes and research activities working in combination with collections was to be developed in the national and regional museums.

The learned society was not, however, without its awkward element. Predictably, societies reflected the character of their towns, which tended to be highly individual and were often marked by contentiousness between Tory and Radical, Anglican and Dissenter, employer and worker, even artist and merchant. This contentiousness might be played out in the activities of the learned society, which often relied on a narrow and partisan support base. As a focus for new ideas, learned societies could be seen as potentially dangerous, in Britain most dramatically during the French Revolution. In the 1791 'Priestley Riots' in Birmingham, Dissenting chapels and the houses of members of the Lunar Society and notably Joseph Priestley – associated with radical religious and political ideas – were destroyed by a drunken anti-revolutionary mob. The Church of England was a resolute enemy of any independence of thought, so that a society set up in Bradford lasted less than a week after being denounced from the pulpit the Sunday after its foundation.[13] As a result, excessive freedom of communication and dangerous topics tended to be avoided by these bodies. At Newcastle a Literary and Philosophical Society was founded in 1793, centred on the minister and congregation of a Unitarian chapel.[14] There caution prevailed from the beginning. In accordance with *Speculations on Attempting the Establishment of a Literary Society in Newcastle*, the founding paper written by the chapel's minister, the officers excluded from its business and its library any discussion of politics or religion.

In calmer times, and within the bounds of civil obedience, literary and philosophical societies functioned as hubs of intellectual life and social reform. In larger cities they responded to the lack of educational opportunities for non-Anglicans in England, which until the 1820s had only two universities: only Anglicans could take degrees at either until the 1850s. The societies' efflorescence in the 1820s and 1830s complemented the battle to create a non-Anglican university, consummated in the foundation in 1826 of University College London, the first secular seat of higher learning in England. For able and energetic men excluded from a university education or academic career for reasons of faith, the learned society provided an outlet not only for intellectual curiosity but also for implementing social improvement.

21 The Rotunda Museum at Scarborough. Internally, the museum illustrated the geology of the Yorkshire coast by means of fossils and rocks arranged in levels from the oldest to the most recent. It is an outstanding early survival of a learned society's museum. The wings were added later.

22 Manchester Mechanics' Institute, Cooper Street, Manchester. This was the first building of the Institute, founded in 1824 by manufacturers and scientists to offer technical training for working men. It was the site of the first mechanics' institute exhibition to be held in Britain, in 1837. The Institute moved to more imposing premises in Princess Street (still standing) in 1855.

Manchester illustrates the civic vigour of a private society in the absence of effective local government. The town rivalled its neighbour Liverpool as the primary industrial city of nineteenth-century England, expanding dramatically as a centre of the textile trade and as a customs port, one of the busiest in the country. Though depicted by its rivals as vulgarly ignorant and commercial, it enjoyed an active intellectual and political life and a long tradition of political independence, with continuing German, Italian and Irish immigration and a substantial Jewish community. Among its intellectual

leaders late in the eighteenth century were Nonconformists, Unitarians and Quakers. Excluded from public office or local politics until the 1820s, in a town unrepresented in Parliament until 1832, these businessmen, merchants, mill owners, engineers and doctors stood in direct opposition to the Tory Anglicans who through the workings of restrictive laws dominated local government.[15]

The Manchester Literary and Philosophical Society, 'one of the most vivid expressions of English provincial culture of these decades', provided a focus of activity from its foundation in 1781.[16] The Society was intended as 'a forum where the specialist and non specialist meet on common ground and where they can discuss problems of mutual interest'.[17] Members did not merely discuss such objectives, they implemented them. They were involved in the establishment of the first fever hospital in England; worked for the creation of a vocational college; helped to establish the Manchester Mechanics' Institute; and agitated for the improvement of social conditions (Fig. 22).[18] The Society's belief in political independence and human rights was reflected in the foundation in 1821 of the *Manchester Guardian*, champion of civil and religious liberty. And it was in Manchester that the hugely important Anti-Corn Law League was set up in 1839 to secure the abolition of the protective tariff on the import of corn, which kept up the price of bread for the benefit of landowners at the expense of the poor. The League became a symbol of opposition to greedy privilege.

In Manchester, as in other cities, a powerful impetus was given to social reform by a non-political body, the Unitarians. Unitarianism makes repeated appearances in the history of nineteenth-century reform in Britain. Developing late in the seventeenth century, it denied the divinity of Jesus Christ while acknowledging him as the supreme model of a human being. Rejecting predestination as well as fixed dogma, Unitarians believed in spiritual redemption through good works, and thence in the importance of improving this world rather than waiting for the blessings of the world to come: J.G. Robberds, minister at the large Cross Street Unitarian chapel in Manchester from 1811 to 1854, 'preached again and again about the Christian duty of *public* service: "Churches are not purely and perfectly churches of Christ, if they are merely associations of men for purposes, however praiseworthy, in relation to their own faith and worship – if they are not also intended to be diffusive sources of beneficial influence around them.'"[19] The Unitarians tended to attract, in addition to skilled working men, men of substance – merchants, manufacturers, medical men, lawyers, bankers – as well as intellectuals such as the young Samuel Taylor Coleridge, and were particularly strong in Northern towns such as Leeds and Manchester. A historian of their battle against slavery and the slave trade has described the British Unitarians as 'a small, highly educated, financially respectable, politically aggressive and articulate denomination that exerted an influence far beyond what their numbers, some 60,000 members in Great Britain and Ireland, would ordinarily command.'[20] They played a major part in public affairs, as MPs, mayors and aldermen and as members of city commissions, being regarded as radicals to a man, bent on reform in all walks of life, including prisons, temperance, education, and the rights of women.[21] Central was their belief in the importance of education for all. Their ideas inspired many of the figures who feature in these pages, from Joseph Priestley, William Roscoe and Elizabeth Gaskell to merchant patricians such as the Rathbones of Liverpool and the Kendricks of Birmingham. They played a major part in the creation of a liberal culture in Manchester in the nineteenth century, through their near-domination in the 1820s and 1830s of the new *Manchester Guardian* (its first editor was a Unitarian), the Manchester Literary and Philosophical Society and the Royal Manchester Institution, as well as Parliamentary representation after 1832.[22]

The Unitarian reformers were not angels, and no doubt their active role in public affairs brought advantages. But their belief in the perfectibility, or at least the potential for improvement, of the human condition, and in the duty of the privileged to assist their fellow human beings materially and by offering opportunities for self-improvement, offered a notable instance of the development of a liberal hegemony in the developing industrial cities, a hegemony that extended to mass education and to the creation of museums and galleries for the whole population. At the same time, they held an ambiguous role within society: their religious ideas were powerfully disliked and disapproved of by the Anglican Church, and it was a disapproval that

extended to individual Unitarians. They were hardly part of an oppressive upper class.

The Manchester Society's success was relatively rare. For all the fervour with which other societies were established, the 1840s and 1850s revealed the fragility of private groups dependent on financial and intellectual support from individuals. In Bristol, a shortage of funds was referred to in committee minutes as early as 1836,[23] while by the mid-1840s the annual reports of the Norwich Literary Institution were filled with pleas for more members and funds. The 1851 report complained that in running the museum the trustees had 'been obliged to practice an almost unseemly economy', and were hoping it might be taken into public ownership.[24] Many societies wobbled almost from the start and after a generation failed. Private endeavour without support from the public purse was no more secure in early Victorian Britain than it is today.

BRISTOL AND NORWICH

In this history the fine arts played an ambiguous part. The encouragement of painting and sculpture was not a prime aim of the societies, which tended to be tentative and inconsistent in this field. Often they followed the pattern of self-commemoration developed in old-established cities by acquiring civic portraits or images of their leading members, while encouraging the work of local artists, bought from their own exhibitions. In terms of collecting, donations were gratefully received: whatever was offered was taken, though it was seldom clear what would be done with these objects.

Two case studies – taken from Norwich and Bristol – illustrate the uncertain role of the fine arts within the learned society. Early in the nineteenth century, these old-established but economically static cities harboured the most creative schools of artists outside London, though that distinction was hardly acknowledged by their learned societies, founded respectively in 1824 and the 1790s. A comparison of the two bodies illustrates their contrasting approaches and the halting attempts to create a public forum for the arts.

The Norwich and Norfolk Literary Institution was dominated by a long-standing Nonconformist Radical tradition in a city whose intellectual life

23 *Norwich and Norfolk Literary Institution*, engraved by Robert Kitton in the 1830s. One of the most active learned societies, the Institution was originally in Exchange Street, Norwich, from 1833 to 1838, but changed premises several times. It was eventually absorbed by the Norwich Castle Museum.

THE NORFOLK & NORWICH MUSEUM.
Dedicated with permission to the Committee of the Museum
By their very obedient servants JOHN BROWN & ROBERT KITTON.

earned it the title of 'the Athens of England' – a title perhaps more used locally than elsewhere.[25] The *Prospectus of the Plan to Establish a Museum of Natural History, Antiquities, &. in Norwich*, announced that it would collect 'the…local natural productions of the district', for comparison with those held by the museums 'of greater or lesser Celebrity' in other towns.[26] Norfolk's Puritan traditions were reflected in the society's avowedly democratic nature: the subscription was 'designedly fixed' as low as possible with the aim of 'increasing the utility of the Museum, and of extending the circle of its supporters'.[27] This was an unusual statement for the time (Fig. 23).

In his chairman's speech of 1829, Dawson Turner, botanist, antiquary and patron of John Sell Cotman, enlarged upon these objectives. The museum would provide 'a receptacle for objects which would otherwise be neglected, dispersed, or lost, or…hidden in the obscurity of private houses'.[28] It would be 'the means of forming the minds of the young to pursuits the most worthy, by exciting their curiosity and teaching them the value and the pleasure of

mental cultivation'. Turner expressed a view that underpinned much discussion of scientific issues: the hope that the collection would help 'men of every age…[to] gain more exalted ideas of their Creator, and learn more and more to look through nature up to nature's God'. The belief that research and collections, especially in the field of natural history, could assert 'the power, the goodness, the mercy, and the infinite wisdom and justice of an Almighty Creator' was reiterated in 1861.[29]

In the Norwich Literary Institution, the visual arts played hardly any role. In contrast, in the old-established port of Bristol a relationship between scientific and artistic collections did evolve, if rather randomly. Boasting a city library founded as early as 1613, the city enjoyed a plethora of private museums, beginning with the fossils, minerals, plants, zoology and entomology assembled by the seventeenth century natural historian William Cole.[30] This tradition was encouraged by the exotic specimens brought home by sea captains, as well as the stimulus to geological and botanical research provided by local rock formations and flora. Societies flourished: the Library Society was founded in 1772, while the Philosophical and Literary Society was active from the early 1790s.[31] An 1820s guide listed twenty-six private museums, with holdings of natural history, fossils, incunabula, local history, antiquities and armour.[32] On the other hand, the city had a reputation for 'apathy in elegant and refined pursuits':[33] Passavant and Waagen could find only one art collection there.

Politically the city also differed from Norwich. Bristol tended towards conservatism and a close attachment to the Church of England (Fig. 24). The Dean of Bristol's words of encouragement to the new Bristol Philosophical Institution[34] asserted the ecclesiastical status quo:

Such societies, by becoming the repositories of important facts, collected from all quarters; and by the frequent communication of ideas which they produce between individuals engaged in kindred pursuits, furnish a powerful stimulus to the exertions of intellect and maintain habits of inquiry and perseverance.[35]

This Institution's investigations developed under the aegis of social elites interested in collaboration with the aristocracy. The lecture programmes

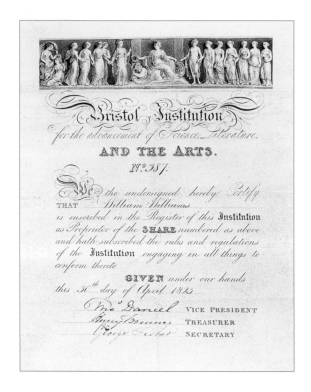

organised 'in a setting as deliberately patrician as possible' were non-utilitarian and conservative, stressing a creationist philosophy.[36] The aim was to bring together the natural sciences and the humanities, through the 'foundation of a Museum for objects of Natural History, including Zoology, Comparative Anatomy, Botany, Geology, &c', as well as 'exhibitions of Pictures, Statues, Casts, and other objects of the Fine Arts, and of Antiquities; also of Machines and Models in the useful Arts'.[37] This dual purpose was to lead to curious results (Fig. 25).

A city of such ancient wealth wanted its Institution to enshrine classical ideals, notably through architecture. In 1820 a prominent corner site was bought and the young C.R. Cockerell was appointed architect.[38] For the portico on the building's principal elevation he imitated Soane's use at the Bank of England of the circular Temple of Vesta from Tivoli, further displaying his erudition by employing the Corinthian order from the Temple of Bassae.[39] Since the Institution aimed to encourage local talent, the building was adorned with an allegorical frieze by the Bristol-born E.H. Baily, which depicts 'the Arts and Sciences and Literature...introduced by Apollo and Minerva to the City of Bristol; who,

seated on the Avon receives them under her maternal protection, and dispenses to them encouragement and rewards, whilst Plenty unveils herself to Peace, since under their happy influence, these expansions of the human intellect flourish and improve'.[40] Classical allegiances could not have been more clearly expressed. The interior, which included a laboratory in the basement, reading rooms and a lecture theatre on the ground floor, and a library and top-lit exhibition room upstairs, rapidly became a repository, if a chaotic one.[41]

The activities at the Institution anticipated the South Kensington Museum. The Philosophical Society, which shared the premises, organised many activities including lectures on chemistry, astronomy, architecture and the 'Arts of Design'.[42] Especially influential were the events considered appropriate for working men. An account based on contemporary sources describes the workers in terms of their childlike appreciation of demonstrations appropriate to their calling. In 1824 'an audience of working men' was excited 'by the exhibition of what was then a novelty – a series of working models of steam engines, and by...two lectures on their principles of construction, the climax of their delight being reached when he [the lecturer] showed them the operation of what is familiar enough now – the four-way valve'.[43]

Art did play a role in the Society's life, through artistic training, exhibitions and collecting. The Institution's wish to function as an academy was expressed by its acquisition of reproductions for the use of artists:[44] classical casts, like classical buildings, functioned in these societies as crucial didactic tools as well as symbols of learning and dignity.[45] It is not clear, however, that the educational role was fully realised. More prominent were the exhibitions, organised intermittently from 1824 onwards. But it was in its attempts at collecting and displaying art that the Bristol Institution most strongly revealed its *naïveté* in the visual arts. In 1828 it was announced that the Great Room was being fitted up in 'a style of elegance and utility, with a view to the reception of Works of Art, objects of Natural History, and other appendages of a Museum.'[46] An 1835 newspaper article lists a heterogeneous collection of scientific and artistic specimens.[47] The aquatic birds were shown in the Committee Room – presumably not with any symbolic significance – while the lobby,

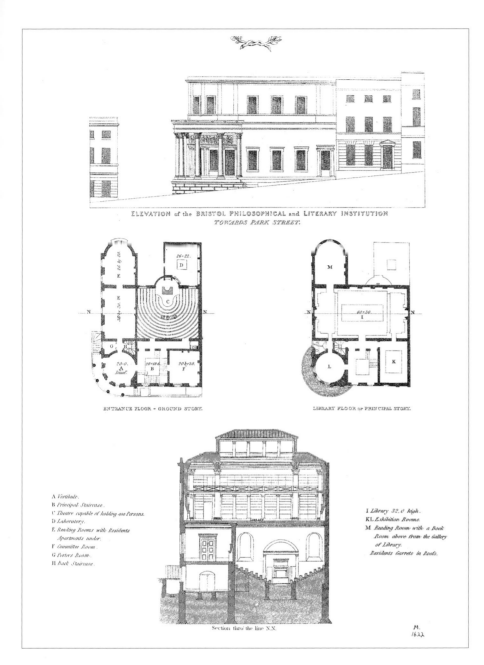

ELEVATION of the BRISTOL PHILOSOPHICAL and LITERARY INSTITUTION TOWARDS PARK STREET.

ENTRANCE FLOOR - GROUND STORY.

LIBRARY FLOOR or PRINCIPAL STORY.

A Vestibule.
B Principal Staircase.
C Theatre capable of holding 400 Persons.
D Laboratory.
E Reading Rooms with Residents Apartments under.
F Committee Room.
G Porters Room.
H Back Staircase.

I Library 32.0 high.
KL Exhibition Rooms.
M Reading Room with a Book Room above from the Gallery of Library.
Residents Garrets in Roofs.

Section thro' the line N.N.

Great Room. This contained casts from Aegina, as well as 'from the Apollo of the Vatican, the Venus di Medici, Dying Gladiator, Laocoon, etc., with several smaller figures'; a full-length portrait of General Sir John Moore (the hero of Corunna, but not a Bristolian) and 'the Temptation by Rippingille'. As at the Hunterian Museum, the works of art were supplemented, with no sense of taxonomical order, by shells and 'various reptiles, fish, and mollusca, in spirits'.

THE ARTISTS' SOCIETIES

Since the literary and philosophical societies offered such unsatisfactory hospitality to the fine arts, artists created another forum: the artists' exhibiting societies. These existed – it could hardly be said they flourished – from the 1810s onwards. It is suggested here that these associations were the ancestors of the municipal art galleries of the late Victorian age, more closely related to them, and more influential in shaping their character, than has been generally recognised.

It was in the field of temporary exhibitions that these societies most actively expressed contemporary attitudes to the display of the fine arts. As in many instances, it was a London model that shaped regional development: in this case, the British Institution, supplementing the long-standing influence of the Royal Academy. The Institution's history, rehearsed elsewhere, justifies a short summary because of its influence. Set up in 1805 and opening its first exhibition in 1806, the Institution was judged by Francis Haskell to have organised the first ever loan exhibitions drawn from existing collections rather than artists' studios.[48] It was a private undertaking, stimulated by the perception among artists and noble patrons that artists needed to be given 'a facility in selling their works', and that the Institution should 'form a school of painting for the rising generation, by furnishing exemplars by the old masters, from the collections of the nobility and gentry who formed and supported the plan'.[49] Patterns of patronage were extremely important: the Institution was supported by the royal family, leading collectors and philanthropists.[50] Significantly for later developments, no

25 A plan of the building of the Bristol Philosophical Society, designed in 1821 by C. R. Cockerell. It was bombed in the Second World War and only the façade survives.

hall and stairs held 'models, casts, bas reliefs, and busts, together with several mummies and mummy cases'. The octagonal room contained skeletons of the larger mammalia with coral, tattooed heads and implements from New Zealand, models and musical instruments, while ethnographical and archaeological materials, and minerals, were shown in other rooms. The gallery held some of the ornithological collections, along with 'over the door-way an enormous head of an elephant' and in the centre Baily's statue *Eve at the Fountain*. Most diverse was the

'professional Artist' (defined as an artist making a living by selling their work) might sit on a committee or vote as a Governor. The financial support system was meticulously organised, with grades of supporters listed in the catalogues, premises in Pall Mall, and two keepers. The Institution set about organising two types of exhibition: displays by living artists, and loan exhibitions. The contemporary displays were announced, quite overtly, as offering opportunities for artists to sell their work. Inclusion was restricted to artists resident in the United Kingdom, an important step towards the recognition of British art even at the cost of a mild xenophobia.

The Institution's declared ideals expressed a certain ambivalence. On the one hand, artists were urged, in a straightforward assertion of the academic tradition, to direct their attention to 'higher and nobler attainments, to paint the mind and passions of man, to depictive [sic] his sympathies and affections, and to illustrate the great events which have been recorded in the history of the world'.[51] '[P]ortraits…drawings in water colours, and architectural drawings' were regarded as 'inadmissible', a more rigid approach than the Royal Academy's.[52] On the other hand, the aims were also instrumentalist: the best reason to encourage artists was 'to improve and extend manufactures, by that degree of taste and elegance of design, which are to be exclusively derived from the cultivation of the Fine Arts; and thereby to increase the general prosperity and resources of the Empire'. The academic masterpieces were expected to contribute to a superior quality of national design 'in hardware, cotton, and porcelain'.[53]

The exhibitions organised by the Institution initiated the style of splendour on loan that was to prevail throughout the century and become a peculiarly British phenomenon. The Institution's events included monographic exhibitions dedicated to such deceased dignitaries as Joshua Reynolds, group shows in the same genre, and assemblies of Old Masters. They might be random or focused. In 1814 the summer exhibition featured four 'British' painters: Hogarth (characterised as the founder of the British school), Wilson, Gainsborough and Zoffany (actually a German). The catalogue discussed their place within the British school, and the astonishingly rich loans (opening with Gainsborough's por-

trait of the Prince Regent, and Zoffany's *The Tribuna of the Florentine Gallery*) were carefully arranged, Gainsborough and Wilson each commanding a room.[54] Although most of the exhibitions were a good deal less organised, the primary aim was always to provide models for artists. The general public was admitted only two days a week, on payment of a shilling. This dual identity – academy and public exhibition – was to be repeated at the National Gallery and regionally.

The formation of a permanent collection was investigated but never successfully sustained. It was announced that the Institution would compensate for the lack of a national gallery by 'endeavour[ing] to form a PUBLIC GALLERY of the works of British Artists, with a few select specimens of each of the great schools'.[55] In this spirit, the governors bought West's monumental *Our Saviour Healing the Sick in the Temple* for the enormous sum of 3,000 guineas, but the effort was not maintained.[56] Such well meaning but random patronage was also imitated by many artistic and learned associations.

The debt of the municipal art gallery to the artists' society cannot be over-emphasised. Haphazard, dependent on private initiative, vulnerable and parochial though these societies were, they developed a determination to represent their members that was finally rewarded from the 1860s onwards in the new public art galleries serving as exhibition spaces for local artists. In the Walker Art Gallery and many others, these societies at last found a home, even though it was a home from which they were to be dispossessed a century later.

The societies' initial objectives included the education of artists, collecting works of art and organising exhibitions. Their teaching role, at least in the early years, was much discussed, for example by William Carey, art critic and champion of British art. In 1810, after the opening in Liverpool of one of the earliest academies, Carey advocated the establishment of at least three or four similar institutions in England.[57] He cited France, where a network of academies had been set up, recognising that the artistic warmth shed by the *Académie Française* had not spread throughout the country.[58] Twenty years later, he had changed his mind: there was no call for provincial institutions to train more artists: there were enough artists in the provinces. What was needed was an outlet for their work, and

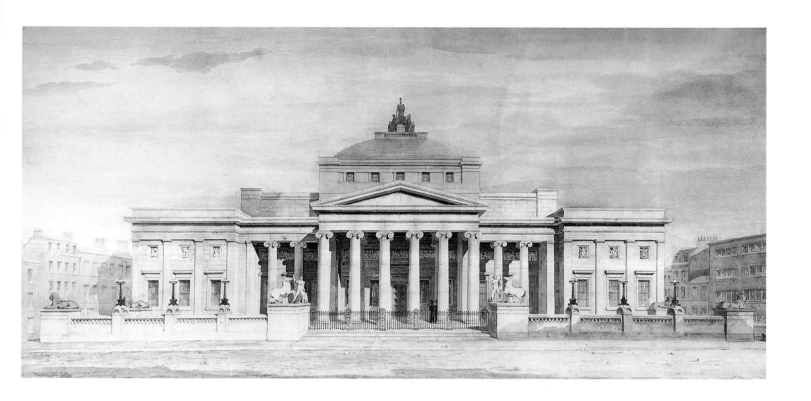

26 Exterior elevation of the Royal Manchester Institution, in a drawing from the office of its architect, Charles Barry, who won the competition to design it in 1824.

he saw '*annual exhibitions* of modern art, as a PRIMARY OBJECT TO THE NATION'.[59] They are necessary in London; and doubly so in provincial districts, since 'an exhibition is a powerful moral instrument', which 'holds forth the best opportunity of a sale for [artists'] work; and exalts the Arts, by kindling a noble spirit of emulation'.[60] It was true that such events were not universally well-received: Carey admitted that they had been attacked for being vulgarly commercial, like Vauxhall Gardens, or for resembling the private concerns of a joint stock company. In answer to reservations about the commercial taint, he cited the exhibitions' value in bringing 'the Arts into frequent communion with a portion of the public'. While Carey also acknowledged other objectives – the commemoration of those who had fallen for their nation, or the encouragement of a taste for 'the superior style of Art'[61] – the primary purpose of the societies, for him, was to bring 'modern Art' before 'the mass of the opulent classes…which remains [in its attitude to art] at a long distance behind, nearly on the same cold neutral ground, which our ancestors occupied a hundred years ago'.[62] The increase of patronage was 'the PRIMARY OBJECT and true end of all Institutions for the promotion of the Fine Arts, especially

of Provincial Institutions, whose support is scanty and uncertain'.[63]

Worth noting is the absence of any interest in the role that art could play in the instruction and entertainment of the population at large. Carey did not mention the potential role that artists' societies could play in making collections, and they were hardly very active in this role. As a result, few developed into municipal galleries, having generally acquired neither collections nor buildings. The Royal Manchester Institution, which formed the basis for the Manchester City Art Gallery in the 1880s, was a rare exception. Where the societies were important was in their fostering of a culture of annual exhibitions, and the promotion of art in a great range of towns.

Artists' societies proliferated but they developed a confused relationship, intellectually and politically, with scientific societies. This relationship is exemplified by the Royal Manchester Institution, where an artists' group intent on setting up a society to organise regular art exhibitions came into conflict with city worthies interested in a learned society, who eventually erected a building which combined both purposes and excluded artists from its organisation. The Manchester conflict, much

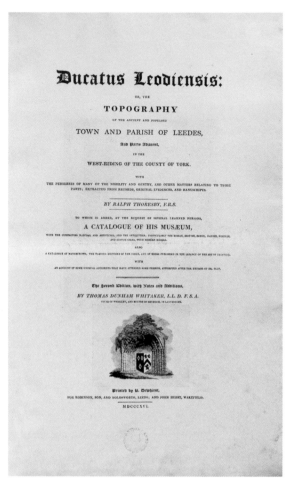

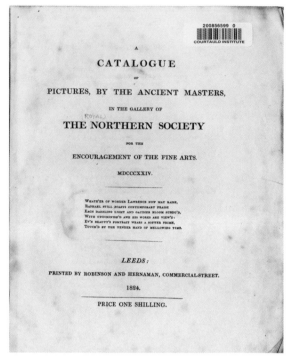

discussed elsewhere, exemplifies the urban power struggles of the period as well as the lack of confidence felt by men of business in artists as organisers (Fig. 26).[64]

Inevitably, the character and support patterns of these societies varied according to local civic identity and divergent relationships between town and country. Manchester, the paradigm of the new industrial centre, was inimical to the old social order, and as late as 1832 the Royal Manchester Institution could only muster four or five of the local gentry among its vice-presidents.[65] In Leeds, on the other hand, the Northern Society, one of the most successful artists' groups, was fostered by a proud and tightly knit community of bankers, wool merchants and manufacturers. It was a town with many old families, where *Ducatus Leodiensis*, the seventeenth-century record of the city by Ralph Thoresby, was reissued in 1816 with the family trees of the most prominent citizens brought up to date:

'The work…excluded all but the oldest Leeds families' (Fig. 27).[66] The early 1824 exhibition of the Northern Society included among its directors and members numerous men of this type, some of whom had moved and become country gentlemen while maintaining close links with the city (Fig. 28). They included such men as Benjamin Gott, merchant, pioneering manufacturer, collector and generous patron of contemporary artists (Fig. 29); William Beckett, head of the Leeds-based Becketts Bank; and John Sheepshanks, from an old Leeds family, who was to bequeath his British paintings to the nation; along with the local gentry, notably the Fawkeses of Farnley Hall, famous for Sir Walter's patronage of Turner. An organisation such as the Northern Society appealed to the civic pride of this well-established social elite, allied to the clubbable habits that survived in such cities. To Londoners, such an elite might be unexpectedly sophisticated. A Leeds historian has recorded the patronising attitude of visitors from the South: a metropolitan acquaintance of Beckett was astonished on being invited to his house at the quality of the dinner and the wine, the 'fine London people as guests', and the 'very fine London gentleman as (his) host'.[67] Such Southern condescension towards the North was to be a recurring feature of nineteenth-century

England, reflected in metropolitan attitudes to provincial museums (Fig. 30).

In Birmingham another pattern reflected the city's social mobility and concord.[68] There, the tensions found in Lancashire and Yorkshire between the old order and the new did not apply: 'Nor was the busy world of manufacture and commerce of itself anything new to the West Midlands...For many years...landed families like the Earls of Dartmouth at Patshull, near Wolverhampton, or the Viscounts Dudley, had been as interested in the industrial as they were in the agricultural profits of their estates.'[69] In this city of small family businesses set in the wealthy rural county of Warwickshire, the Society of Arts, established in 1821, was by 1832 basking in official approval. Headed by Lord Lyttelton, the future Queen Victoria and the Duchess of Kent, the list of supporters included three dukes (Wellington among them), nineteen marquesses and earls, assorted bishops, prominent collectors such as Robert Peel and George Agar Ellis, and numerous lords, baronets and Members of Parliament.[70] The list of donors and annual subscribers was as sophisticated as the British Institution's,

presaging the fund-raising techniques of a much later period.

ARTISTS' SOCIETIES AND EXHIBITIONS

It was above all artists' wish to provide a platform for their work that inspired artistic innovations in provincial towns, where artists came together to organise regular selling exhibitions. Such displays were arranged by the Norwich Society of Artists (which included John Crome and J. S. Cotman) in 1805, at Edinburgh from 1808, and at Leeds and Liverpool from 1809. By 1830 such events had been organised in some twenty English and Scottish towns, though the administrative side, dependent on private individuals, was frequently erratic and few societies were able to maintain annual displays.[71]

The British Institution shaped these societies through its primarily voluntary character, its selling exhibitions of contemporary work, loan exhibitions of historic and modern works, and the gestures towards permanent collections. What provincial societies could not emulate were the Institution's financial stability, and its handsome and well-located building. Financially the provincial groups were disastrously unstable, not least perhaps because they followed the Royal Academy in being governed by artists. Some exhibitions made money from sales and entrance fees, but sometimes, as in tight-fisted Norwich, the artists were regularly left to settle debts when the exhibition closed.[72]

The flavour of the displays mounted by these societies may be conveyed through the 1823 exhibition held by the Northern Society in the converted Music Hall in Leeds. Dedicated to modern artists, it offered 342 works, all (judging from the artists' names) paintings or watercolours.[73] Of the 126 artists, only seventeen were women. Two architects were represented, on the model of the Royal Academy, including the twenty-four-year-old Anthony Salvin at the outset of his successful career: representation at these exhibitions was a regular activity for ambitious youth. Locally based artists were balanced by those from further afield, particularly if the society had a good reputation, as at

11

No.		Painters.	Proprietors.
87	Landscape - - -	Ruysdael	*William Gott, Esq.*
88	St. Francis - - -	Quentin Matsys	*John Smyth, Esq.*
89	Inside of a church - -	Steinwyck	*William Smithson, Esq.*
90	Mrs. Anne Killigrew, the subject of Dryden's celebrated Ode, and one of King Charles's beauties	Sir Peter Lely	*A. A. Watts, Esq.*
91	Susannah and the elders -	Guercino	*Walter Fawkes, Esq.*
92	Cymon and Iphigenia - -	Rubens	*Miss Currer*
93	Sketch - - -	L. Caracci	*Walter Fawkes, Esq.*
94	Portrait of George Fox Lane, Lord Bingley - -	Sir Godfrey Kneller	*G. L. Fox, Esq. M. P.*
95	A Battle - - -		*G. L. Fox, Esq. M. P.*
96	Bacchanalians - -	Jordaens	
97	George III., the Earl of Harcourt, and a favourite yeoman of the guard - - -	B. West	*Archbishop of York.*
98	A Sketch - - -	Van Goyen	*Viscount Pollington.*
99	Landscape - - -	Hodges	*F. Vernon Wentworth, Esq.*
100	Portrait of the Duke of Cumberland	Sir J. Reynolds	*G. L. Fox, Esq. M. P.*
101	A Battle - - -		*G. L. Fox, Esq. M. P.*
102	Modern midnight conversation	Hogarth	*John Blayds, Esq.*
103	Bonfire - - -	Joseph Wright	*G. Wright, Esq.*
104	Game - - -	Rysbraeck	*R. Cracroft, Esq.*
105	Saint Catherine - -	Correggio	*B. Sadler, Esq.*
106	Landscape - - -	Gainsborough	*John Blayds, Esq.*
107	Landscape - -	N. Poussin	*Miss Currer.*
108	Landscape and animals -	Savery	*John Hardy, Esq.*
109	Study of flowers - -	Rachel Ruisch	*Walter Fawkes, Esq.*
110	His own portrait - -	Rubens	*F. Vernon Wentworth, Esq.*
111	Landscape - -	Salvator Rosa	*John Hardy, Esq.*

30 List of exhibits from the catalogue of the Northern Society exhibition, 1823.

where'.[74] Such events enjoyed a national reputation throughout the century (Fig. 31).

This was by no means a display of local artists. Apart from a smattering of amateurs, the exhibitors were established, British by birth or (occasionally) adoption. At Leeds in 1823 the northern artists included such relatively well-known names as the animal painter Charles Henry Schwanfelder and the landscape painter Joseph Rhodes, as well as Thomas Miles Richardson and H.P. Parker, leading figures in the Newcastle artistic world. They were rivalled by a constellation of Londoners, including Thomas Lawrence PRA (lending, not selling, as suited a man in his position), Alfred Chalon, Joshua Cristall, William Collins RA, Copley Fielding, C.R. Leslie, Richard Westall RA and the nineteen-year-old J.F. Lewis, as well as the youthful prodigy Edwin Landseer. Edinburgh was represented by Henry Raeburn, its most famous portraitist, and the landscape painter Alexander Nasmyth with three of his daughters.[75] The loans were strengthened by five Turner watercolours, mostly lent by the generous Walter Fawkes.

Such an exhibition fulfilled several functions. It operated as a proto-art museum in a city that – like every other British provincial city apart from Liverpool and Norwich – offered no permanent display of art. It celebrated British art. It also reflected contemporary taste. Of the 342 works displayed in 1823, 140 were landscapes (including seascapes and views of towns) or – in the antiquarian tradition – views of ancient buildings. There were substantial groups of portraits, regarded as a necessary if not altogether desirable element, genre scenes, and animal and still life pictures.[76] Numerous copies (often by anonymous ladies) were included, a genre excluded from more ambitious displays.[77] To the category of history paintings only eighteen works can be allocated: history painting exercised little market appeal.

The Leeds exhibitions varied in character and competence. As at the British Institution, private loans of works by living British artists or (more often) the great names of the past were customary. In 1824 the Northern Society showed 'the ancient masters' and in 1826 'ancient and modern masters', if possible heading the catalogue with a royal loan announced in capital letters. In 1824 the 214 exhibits, while they may have included optimistic attribu-

Leeds: works that had failed to sell in London could be presented again, and the inclusion of well-known names contributed to the event's financial viability. Of the identifiable artists showing at Leeds in 1823, fifty-three had addresses in London or the South of England, thirty-eight in the North of England (though only fourteen in Leeds), and twenty in Scotland, primarily Edinburgh. The figures underline the attractions of a prestigious venue such as the Northern Society in spite of the heavy 'expenses for the carriage of pictures, from London and else-

PICTURE GALLERY.

12

CURIOSITIES, &c.—SIDE A.

NO.	SUBJECT.	CONTRIBUTOR.
205	Two Wheel Lock Pistols	T. Fenteman
206	A piece of Wood perforated by the Ship Worm ; cut out of the centre of a ship's mast in Mount's Bay, Cornwall	J. P. Clapham.
207	Collection of British Insects	T. Blayds
208	Lichen Geographicus on stone from Skiddaw	S. Tarbotton
209	Four specimens of Jasper Ware, in different states of manufacture	— Mills
210	Ancient Copper Jug	H. Barton, Doncaster
211	Ancient Lock and Key, Buckle, and Punch Ladle	— Kerr
212	Brass Chafing Cup from Algiers	Mrs. Strother
213	Two Keys found near Conisbro' Castle	H. Barton
214	2 Links of an Iron Chain found in Lincoln Castle	Do.
215	Specimens of Stone Carving, A.D. 1150, 1240, and 1350	R. D. Chantrell
216	Specimens of Stucco from an Ancient Roman Bath discovered at York, whilst excavating the Railway	— Gawthorpe
217	Case of Foreign Insects	Wm. West

SIDE B.

NO.	SUBJECT.	CONTRIBUTOR.
218	Case of Crustaceæ	T. P. Teale
219	Two Cases of Foreign Butterflies	J. Bateson
220	Case—containing Specimen of Bead-work, supposed to be made by Mary Queen of Scots—Mr. Nunneley. Wax Model of the Triumph of Silenus, by Fiamingo—Wm. Hay. Dried Plant from Barbadoes—Wm. West. Inlaid Marble Table—G. K. Hirst. Mother of Pearl Box—S. J. Birchall. Piece of enamelled Porcelain—T. Fenteman. Forged Certificate, and Book of Subscriptions, taken from a begging Impostor—J. P. Clapham	
221	Books made of the different substances that have been employed in the Manufacture of Paper	W. West
222	Series of Skulls of Birds, Animals, &c.	Thos. Nunneley
223	Case of Articles of Tonguese Manufacture, &c.—such as Idols, (Teeth of the Whale and Stones), Axes, Clubs, Combs, Baskets, &c. with part of the New Testament in the Tonguese language.	John Jackson, Park-pl.
224	Case of Specimens of the Manufactures of the Natives of the North Coast of South America	W. Wildsmith

31 List of non-art objects from the catalogue of the Northern Society exhibition, 1820.

tions, came from distinguished local collections from the city and county, including Earl Fitzwilliam, Sheepshanks, Fawkes and Gott.[78] Most of the 'ancient' loans were Dutch and Flemish, with some Italian or older English paintings. The display in general reflected a style of collecting that was less Old Masterly, more British, than the taste seen in most great country houses, and closer to Victorian urban taste.

This style of event anticipated the major loan exhibitions of Victorian England in the generosity of private lenders and in the haphazard selection, eschewing thematic or chronological typology in favour of a more or less succulent artistic ragout. Only two principles of selection were evident: the traditional division according to size into gallery and cabinet works, and, at least in the modern displays, the concentration on British artists.

What is remarkable about these early displays is their wild eclecticism. At the Northern Society in 1820, a relatively small number of the works were for sale, the majority of the paintings shown in the Ante-Room and Picture Gallery being loaned Old Masters.[79] Paintings were supplemented by 'Natural History, Works of Art, Philosophical Apparatus, Curiosities &c', including cases of birds, anatomical preparations, a 'Group of Artificial Flowers, made from Feathers in a Convent in Madeira', minerals (many from the Leeds Philosophical Society), assorted models seen as miracles of craftsmanship, and objects including jasperware, an iron chain, foreign butterflies, and a model of a Swiss chalet. A didactic note was struck by industrial specimens such as flax (lent by a cotton mill) and scientific instruments (Fig. 32). Here art and science met in the tradition of showing advancing technology within a cabinet of natural and artificial curiosities. Although an attempt was made in this exhibition to impose a form of taxonomy on the museum specimens, they were generally shown in the same rooms as the works of art, and the typically laconic catalogue does not explain why such disparate objects should be shown together, or suggest that the natural history objects might provide artistic inspiration. No deeper significance was seen in the juxtaposition.

Such eclecticism reappeared more boldly in Leeds in 1839. 'THE EXHIBITION OF PAINTINGS, CURIOSITIES, MODELS, APPARATUS AND SPECIMENS OF NATURE AND ART', arranged on behalf of the

59

DIRECTORS.

THOMAS WALKER, Esq. *President.*
FRANCIS THOMAS BILLAM, Esq. *Secretary.*
JOHN BISCHOFF, Esq. *Treasurer.*

THE LORD VISCOUNT POLLINGTON, *Honorary.*
SIR JOHN BECKETT, Baronet.
WILLIAM BECKETT, Esq.
GEORGE BANKS, Esq.
THOMAS BENYON, Esq.
JOHN BLAYDS, JUN. Esq.
THOMAS BISCHOFF, Esq.
WALTER FAWKES, Esq. *Honorary.*
FRANCIS HAWKESWORTH FAWKES, Esq. *Honorary.*
BENJAMIN GOTT, Esq.
JOHN GOTT, Esq.
WILLIAM GOTT, Esq.
THOMAS GEORGE JAQUES, Esq.
THOMAS KINNEAR, Esq. *Honorary.*
DARCY LEVER, Esq.
WILLIAM LEE, Esq. *Honorary.*
JOHN MARSHALL, Esq.
JOHN ARTHINGTON PAYNE, M.D.
JOHN SHEEPSHANKS, Esq.
WILLIAM WALKER, Esq.
GEORGE WALKER, Esq.

Leeds Mechanics' Institute, included attractions such as George Hayter's portrait (lent by Buckingham Palace) of the newly crowned Queen, and other historical and modern paintings.[80] But it went further. Firstly, the exhibition included historical specimens thematically arranged to include a roomful of 'Fairfaxiana', material related to General Fairfax, the Parliamentary opponent of Charles I. Possibly thought suitable for an audience that might harbour radical sympathies, this kind of display anticipated the historical exhibitions of the 1860s and later. Secondly, it featured numerous practical appliances, with a Jacquard loom installed in the Lobby and a roomful of mechanical devices and models, no doubt aimed at the mechanic. An old-established technical display of this sort, already common in France and England in the eighteenth century, formed a strange alliance with the developing phenomenon of the art exhibition.[81]

These events early in the nineteenth century appear to have been fraught with problems, as over the arrangement of pictures (in the cantankerous tradition of the Royal Academy). The foreword of the 1832 Liverpool Academy exhibition explained that the pictures had been arranged by a sub-committee formed jointly of 'Members of the Society for the Encouragement of the Arts in Liverpool' and the artist Members of the Liverpool Academy: 'Fully aware of the difficulties that attend that part of their duty, and the utter impossibility of giving satisfaction to every Exhibitor, they feel, at the same time, a confidence that every possible justice has been done to the claims of merit.'[82] Statements of intent were limited to the occasional desire 'to support and to encourage the Arts in this Town and Neighbourhood', and the catalogues followed the British Institution formula, supplying only the title, artist and 'contributor' or owner of each work, with the occasional literary quotation.[83]

In addition, the exhibition rooms tended to be borrowed or converted spaces, eliciting many complaints.[84] Although Carey asserted that 'the primary duty' of 'the Nobility, Gentry, and the opulent classes, in any vicinity' wishing to 'step forward' in support of an artists' society, was 'to apply their funds to the erection of a public building' like the British Institution, this objective was rarely achieved.[85] Even the Royal Manchester Institution, sited in the wealthiest of towns, took over a decade to complete. At Bristol, as we have seen, art exhibitions and acquisitions were crammed into a building not primarily adapted for the purpose.[86]

Newcastle epitomised the problem of finances.[87] Carey exulted in 1829 over the recent erection of the Northern Academy of Arts designed by Newcastle's leading architect, John Dobson, for T.M. Richardson: 'the *Northern Academy* is a moral engine called into being by the highest authorities in the State, working for the honour and interest of Newcastle, for the public service, and for the advancement of the national prosperity and glory.'[88] His hyperbole was not justified. Richardson and his partner had over-extended themselves financially, received little support from the local gentry, and met fierce hostility from the Newcastle press. The Academy's exhibitions attracted too few works by artists from outside the city, and in 1834 it closed (Fig. 33).[89]

33 The Northern Academy of Fine Arts, Newcastle. The Academy was built by Richard Grainger, who with the architect John Dobson was responsible for the construction of Neoclassical Newcastle. It opened in 1828 but lasted only a few years before being converted to other artistic uses.

In the first half of the century Carey's assertion that 'a *public building* for *Annual Exhibitions*, ought to be the immediate object of any flourishing town or city' could not be answered by the efforts of private individuals, whether artists, local gentry or businessmen. What was realised in the 1860s and later, by the creation of the Walker Art Gallery and numerous public galleries like it, was the satisfaction – at least for a while – of the long-standing demand for a permanent exhibition space for con-temporary artists, supported not by private individuals but by public funds.

CONCLUSION

This chapter has dwelt at some length on these societies, in spite of their fragility, and on these exhibitions, ontologically and intellectually fleeting though they were. In their diversity and size they represented a novel phenomenon that was to shape provincial exhibitions and museums well into the twentieth century. In their shadow, many municipal art galleries were built primarily to house works for sale.

Though their supporters made various claims about their value to the larger community, in the end the prime objectives of these societies were for artists to sell and for the society to survive. Like the great majority of London exhibitions, they were subject to the rule of the marketplace. Just as many of the structures of the emergent national museums were intimately related to commerce, so were the institutions that served as the foundations of the municipal galleries. At the same time, the exhibitions associated with 'Modern Works of Art' represented the dissemination of a faith in the British school, a faith that was to sustain the Victorian art museum. From the union of commerce with civic and national pride, the Victorian art gallery was born.

PART TWO

CREATING THE ART MUSEUM IN VICTORIAN BRITAIN

4

PROMISING SOIL

THE CITIES OF THE INDUSTRIAL REVOLUTION
AND THE EARLIEST CIVIC ART GALLERIES

Looking back from the 1860s to the 1830s, George Eliot evoked the transition experienced on a coach journey from country to town:

> But as the day wore on the scene would change: the land would begin to be blackened with coal-pits, the rattle of handlooms to be heard in hamlets and villages…The breath of the manu-facturing town, which made a cloudy day and a red gloom by night on the horizon, diffused itself over all the surrounding country, filling the air with eager unrest…The busy scenes of the shuttle and the wheel, of the roaring furnace, of the shaft and the pulley, seemed to make but crowded nests in the midst of the large-spaced, slow-moving life of homesteads and far-away cottages and the oak-sheltered parks.[1]

Her description asserts the classic antagonism between country and town, with a new sharpened emphasis: the town no longer signified the challeng-ing civility of London but an indefinable and threat-ening urban monster, its breath powerful and disturbing (Fig. 34).

The industrial cities of Britain have suffered a bad press for two centuries, a reputation from which even now they are scarcely recovering. They have been regularly castigated for their physical ugliness and foul environmental conditions. The Lancashire poet Edwin Waugh in 1847 called Man-chester 'this great black city, full of rushing to and fro, and discordant tumults'.[2] Their own prominent citizens regularly criticised their appearance, with Whitworth Wallis, the long-term Keeper of Art at the Birmingham City Art Gallery, stating that one aim of a civic art gallery should be 'to excite a real discontent with the ugliness amidst which most of us unfortunately have to live'.[3] J.B. Priestley in his 1934 account of his travels around England wrote of the outskirts of Birmingham that 'it was beastly. It was so many miles of ugliness, squalor, and the wrong kind of vulgarity, the decayed anaemic kind', while 'Between Manchester and Bolton the ugliness is so complete that it is almost exhilarating. It challenges you to live there.'[4] Such cities were seen as slum-ridden and appallingly unhealthy by medical officers and observers of

OPPOSITE   Close No. 193, Glasgow, photographed by Thomas Annan in 1868 (detail of Fig. 36).

65

society, whether early sociologists or photographers, well into the twentieth century.[5]

It was an unhealthiness that extended beyond physical into moral and civil danger. They posed a risk to society. The first wholly industrial cities in the world, they elicited a routine hostility from the traditional orders of society – rurally based or least attached to a pastoral ideal – that persisted for many years: at an anecdotal level, the present writer recalls being assured as a child that these cities offered nothing of interest, and by citizens of Edinburgh (inspired by a more localised contempt) that Glasgow was not worth the detour. At the same time, they were always viewed with fascination. Friedrich Engels, who lived in Manchester from 1842 to 1844, could not restrain his admiration: 'Modern times can show few greater marvels than the recent history of South Lancashire', while Manchester was 'the masterpiece of the Industrial Revolution'.[6] To the French journalist Léon Faucher, writing in 1844, Manchester was 'an agglomeration the most extra-ordinary, the most interesting, and in some respects, the most monstrous, which the progress of society has presented'.[7] He found it 'the Utopia of Bentham', and felt it would be hard to devise a more practical or more hideous town (Fig. 35).[8]

The growth of old-established towns such as Leeds into huge new cities continued throughout the nineteenth century. In 1851 for the first time the national census showed that the population of Great Britain, almost doubled since 1801, was divided equally between town and country. Manchester had more than quadrupled its population. Most of the other major cities had tripled in size: Glasgow, enriched initially by its textile industry and the tobacco trade, and more recently by the iron and coal industries and by ship-building; Liverpool, which by mid-century had become the major British port and was soon to be compared with New York; Birmingham, the centre of the hardware trade; and Leeds, a leading textile town. Bradford, another textile town, had multiplied by a factor of eight. All these cities had become wealthy, at least for the benefit of the 15% or so of the population who could be described as middle class. In the last quarter of the century the growth accelerated.

One of the accusations made against these cities was that they were philistine and purely commercial. As we shall see, it was a charge that was frequently justified but which stimulated many assertions to the contrary. The history that informs this book results from the effort to sow the seeds of art in the

MANCHESTER ILLUSTRATED—BIRD'S-EYE VIEW OF THE CITY FROM THE NEW TOWN HALL TOWER

35 *Manchester Illustrated: Bird's-Eye View of the City from the New Town Hall Tower*, from the *Graphic*, 14 October 1876.

rough and seemingly barren soil of the industrial metropolis, within a national environment that, as we have seen, was plagued by meanness and unimaginative instrumentalism. Seeds did grow, but in this unpromising terrain their growth was unusual. These museums and galleries were the flowers of the Industrial Revolution (Fig. 36).

THE INDUSTRIAL CITY AS SYMBOL OF MALIGN POWER

For the traveller arriving in Manchester, the impression it made was physically and spiritually overwhelming. The French historian and social critic Alexis de Tocqueville, who visited England and Ireland in the 1830s, introduced into his discussion the dialectic of social conflict. He was appalled by the contrast between the 'palaces of industry' (Fig. 37) and the wretched habitations of the workers:

here is the slave, there the master…A sort of black smoke covers the city. The sun seen through

Close N.º 193 High Street,
1868.

it is a disc without rays. Under this half daylight 300,000 human beings are ceaselessly at work…Crowds are ever hurrying this way and that in the Manchester streets, but their footsteps are brisk, their looks preoccupied, and their appearance sombre and harsh….Here humanity attains its most complete development and its most brutish; here civilisation works its miracles, and civilised man is turned back almost into a savage.[9]

The savagery of the new urban class, dehumanised by their working conditions, was frequently reiterated. These creatures were seen to be savage because of the way they were obliged to live. In 1832 James Kay, pioneering physician and social reformer, depicted in the second and enlarged edition of *The Moral and Physical Condition of the Working Classes* the horrific living conditions in Manchester in a time of cholera. Throughout his description, physical illness is interwoven with what was seen as moral illness, and he suggests that the dangers posed to the established order are the responsibility of the privileged:

He whose duty it is, to follow the steps of this messenger of death, must descend to the abodes of poverty, must frequent the close alleys, the crowded courts, the overpeopled habitations of wretchedness, where pauperism and disease congregate round the source of social discontent and political disorder in the centre of our large towns, and behold with alarm, in the hot-bed of pestilence, ills that fester in secret, at the very heart of society.[10]

He described deformed and unhealthy people crowded into cellars filled with filth, who 'with an animal eagerness satisfy the cravings of their appetite', finding refuge only in alcohol and 'the grosser sins…which…enthral the idle and unwary'.[11] In such cities more than half the children died before completing their fifth year. Kay was concerned not only with the physical health of the poor but also with their character. He discussed the lack of religion or education: 'With rare exceptions, the adults of the vast population of 84,147 contained in Districts Nos. 1.2.3.4 [of Manchester], spend Sunday either in supine sloth, in sensuality, or in listless inactivity.'[12] This lack of social opportunities on a Sunday was hardly surprising, given that, in Faucher's words,

If the people of Manchester wish to go out upon a fine Sunday, where must they go? There are no public promenades, no avenues, no public gardens; and even no public common…Even the cemeteries and the Botanic Gardens, are closed upon the Sunday. What then remains but the brutal diversion of drunkenness?[13]

As Dickens put it, 'The day which his Maker intended as a blessing, man has converted into a curse.'[14]

Social and financial inequalities were a recurring theme. Gatherings where 'a gloomy spirit of discontent is engendered, and the public are not unfrequently alarmed, by the wild out-break of popular violence' were occasioned by the dissolution of the 'natural ties' between 'the higher and lower orders of the community'.[15] Just as cholera could not be kept within bounds but 'threatens, with a stealthy step, to invade the sanctity of the domestic circle; which may be unconsciously conveyed from those haunts of beggary where it is rife, into the most still and secluded retreat of refinement – whose entrance, wealth cannot absolutely bar, and luxury invites', so the discontent of the poor would lead to social disease.[16] In his plea for improved sanitation and medical care, Kay creates parallels between the physical and the moral failings of the poor, and between the linked threats of disease and revolution. He too stresses the division between classes, a division that was widely considered undesirable on grounds not so much of injustice as of the dangers of inadequate communication.

In this situation Engels, too, detected the breeding ground of revolution, denouncing the living conditions and the way that in 'those areas where the two social groups happen to come into contact with each other the middle classes sanctimoniously ignore the existence of their less fortunate neighbours', but to him the prospect of revolution was welcome. 'Everywhere one finds on the one hand the most barbarous indifference and selfish egotism and on the other the most distressing scenes of misery and poverty.'[17] The middle classes had no concept that 'the very ground beneath their feet is undermined and may give way at any moment'.[18]

Manchester and other cities that these writers discussed – Glasgow being reckoned as among the worst – became for contemporaries a canvas on which various images could be delineated. The idea of the two nations was endlessly reiterated, with the dark, oppressed but wealthy North opposed to the sunny pastoral beauty of the South, a geographical version of the familiar opposition of two female types. Under the influence of the threatening political situation – strikes, the Chartist movement of the 1840s and the Manchester Insurrection of 1842, in which eleven workers were killed – the industrial city under various soubriquets became a popular subject for novelists. They were no doubt further inspired by Thomas Carlyle's *Past and Present* of 1843, a passionate polemic on the evils of modern society and the sufferings of working people.

The novelists' approaches were widely different. In *Sybil or The Two Nations* (1845) the young Benjamin Disraeli presented a direct conflict between the two levels of society. At the climax, the (highly unconvincing) inhabitants of an industrial town storm the neighbouring castle of a (marginally less unconvincing) nobleman (Disraeli was perhaps recalling the mob's sack of Nottingham Castle in 1831 – a building that had exemplified feudal oppression and that was to have a very different future).[19] Unlike Engels, in his political subtext Disraeli was

advocating the union, at least in terms of mutual understanding, of the two sectors of society. Although *Shirley*, Charlotte Brontë's second novel (1849), is set around 1811, one of its principal themes is the Luddite hostility of Yorkshiremen to the replacement of individual handwork by the new mechanised mill: the Luddites are portrayed as a sinister force, operating violently and nefariously at night, and influenced by the equally misguided but comically vulgar forces of Nonconformism. In *Hard Times* (1854) Dickens satirised the inhuman good will of manufacturers and reformers in the Utilitarian town of 'Coketown', where people are perverted into cruelty by the setting in which they are forced to live, in contrast to the natural if chaotic kindness of a troupe of actors. George Eliot's *Felix Holt*, published in 1866 but set around 1832, evoked the violent hostilities between political groupings, giving a relatively sympathetic account of the Radical cause, and set the morally and financially decaying gentry in opposition to the forceful Nonconformists of the industrial city. Only Elizabeth Gaskell, who lived in Manchester, painted in *North and South* (1855) a convincing picture of life in a great industrial city, with the North-South conflict personified (and gently eroticised) in the leading male and female characters. At a time when the genre of the novel exercised a powerful pressure on the public consciousness, these writers aimed to raise their readers' awareness of social injustice. In their novels the industrial city, crudely though it is generally depicted, becomes a character in itself. But however strong the writers' sympathies, these fictitious Manchesters are dominated, except in Gaskell's pages, by a sense of alterity: their inhabitants are definitely 'other' in manners, attitudes and religious affiliations, while the cities are hectically lurid and vulgar.

A more positive attitude, celebrating technical or industrial marvels, was taken by local writers of guidebooks. For *Fraser's Guide to Liverpool*, published in the 1850s, the 'wonderful line of docks is the great boast of Liverpool. These inventions for commercial convenience originated with this town, and have been imitated all over the world'. (Fig. 38)[20] In the same spirit the guide claimed that the city's churches were unparalleled for architectural excellence anywhere in England.[21] A similar approach was taken by Benjamin Love, the author of a guidebook to Manchester, which encouraged

38 *The Custom House, Liverpool, Looking South*, painted by John Atkinson Grimshaw in the 1880s. Oil on canvas, 58.7 × 87.6 cm. Grimshaw's atmospheric paintings of cities and ancient houses made him widely popular (National Museums Liverpool).

appreciation of the city in all its guises. While admitting that 'Manchester may be termed a soil on which the plant of business thrives the best' and offered few obvious attractions, he expatiated on the appeal of the mills:

> If the reader of this be a stranger, we recommend him to take a walk among the Mills of Manchester: and although his notions of smoke and darkened waters, may not be the most agreeable, still, these will soon vanish, and feelings of wonder take their place…A visit to one of the largest mills, if an introduction can be procured, is a gratifying treat.[22]

This statement by a member of the Literary and Philosophical Society of Manchester, as he proclaimed himself on the title page, conveys the growing sense of pride felt by thoughtful citizens.

An affectionate picture of Manchester emerges from the pages of a young journalist. In October 1849, after one of several cholera epidemics, Angus Bethune Reach travelled to Manchester on behalf of the *Morning Chronicle*. His brief was to partici-

pate in a survey of the 'moral, intellectual, material, and physical condition of the industrial poor throughout England' while the great proto-sociologist Henry Mayhew conducted equivalent enquiries in London.[23] Reach joined a throng of observers – social reformers, political agitators, the earliest sociologists, medical officers of health, journalists – in studying the living conditions of the poor in the new industrial centres and particularly the 'Queen of the cotton cities', as he called Manchester. Acute, unprejudiced, a sparkling writer, Reach was interested in individuals as well as social conditions, and invested the inhabitants of 1840s Manchester with individuality and even cheerfulness.[24] At one level he was overcome, like others, by the drama of the place. The approaching traveller was struck 'by the dull leaden-coloured sky, tainted by thousands of ever-smoking chimneys, which broods over the distance' (Fig. 39).[25]

You shoot by town after town…they are all little Manchesters. Huge, shapeless, unsightly mills, with their countless rows of windows, their towering shafts, their jets of waste steam continually

MANCHESTER, FROM THE ENTRANCE TO THE LONDON AND NORTH-WESTERN RAILWAY.

39   A view of Manchester around 1870.

puffing in panting gushes from the brown, grimy wall. Between these vast establishments, a network of mean but regular streets, unpicturesque and unadorned – just the sort of private houses you would expect in the vicinity of such public edifices and...scattered amongst all this, great irregular muddy spaces of waste ground, studded with black pools and swarming with dirty children.[26]

Though Reach wrote at length about the filthy lodging houses and the danger of cholera (he reckoned conditions to be less bad than in parts of Glasgow or London), he also noted improvements in working people's way of life, notably as a result of the recent Ten Hours Act, which limited work times for women and children.

A revealing comparison may be made between Reach's reactions in 1849 and Faucher's in 1844. Faucher, like other observers from France, where industrial cities had hardly developed, was astonished by the city's inhabitants. He found the businessmen severely practical, the male workers silent but highly intelligent. 'The Lancashire operative is, indisputably, the best workman on the face of the earth; the best spinner, and the best mechanic...But this untiring, this excessive and unceasing energy, carried beyond certain limits, tends to enervate and

undermine his frame.'[27] One result of the new way of life of an anonymous proletariat, divorced from the middle and upper classes, was laxity of sexual morals, a phenomenon that few English writers referred to so straightforwardly. Faucher was shocked by the behaviour of the 'Manchester girls' (it was of course the women he condemned):

The factory girls are strangers to modesty. Their language is gross, and often obscene; and when they do not marry early, they form illicit connexions, which degrade them still more than premature marriage. It is a common occurrence to meet in the intervals of labour, in the back streets, couples of males and females, which the caprice of the moment has brought together.[28]

His comments were echoed by a surgeon writing in 1836 on the social results of a population newly thrown together in an uncontrolled environment and viewed by their employers merely as mechanical accessories:

The bringing together numbers of the young of both sexes in factories, has been a prolific source of moral delinquency...The stimulus of a heated atmosphere, the contact of opposite sexes, the

72

example of license upon the animal passions – all have conspired to produce a very early development of sexual appetencies…[29]

The atmosphere of 'considerable sexual laxity' represented the triumph of economic sense over morals.[30]

Reach's analysis presents Mancunians in a more considered and sympathetic light. He expressed considerable sympathy for the city's inhabitants, describing the conviviality of the streets in the evening – 'the people all appear to be on the best terms with each other, and laugh and gossip from window to window, and door to door'; and the boys in the Lyceum Factory Schools, 'tolerably ragged, to be sure – and some of them shoeless – but full of life, fun and devilry'; and the 'factory girls, somewhat stunted and pale, but smart and active looking, with dingy dresses and dark shawls, speckled with flakes of cotton-wool wreathed round their heads' (Fig. 40); and the cotton-spinners, often 'hard-headed, studious, thoughtful men, who pass brooding, meditating lives' and yearn for knowledge.[31] He

might have dwelt longer on the role of women in these communities: according to a later commentator, looking back on his youth in the 1840s, in the worst cases, 'It was the woman who was mainly the salvation of an otherwise deplorable situation.'[32] Reach characterises the mill workers as dirty, with faces that are 'cadaverous and overspread by a sort of unpleasant greasy pallor', and neither as well grown nor as healthy as they should be.[33] But in contrast to most other witnesses, he conveys their liveliness, their thirst for self-improvement, and early indications of general prosperity and self-esteem: 'The people are uniformly well shod and their general appearance is that of unostentatious comfort.'[34] They were hampered by their ignorance and lack of education: 'the ignorance of these young English savages is dense and deplorable', while the adults who did read consumed such 'literary garbage…utterly beneath criticism' as the illustrated novels (with such titles as *Angelina* and *Gretna Green*) published in penny weeklies.[35] It was not intelligence that was wanting but the chance to develop it (Fig. 41).

First Process
The Opener

Last Process
The Loom

Dinner time

This was the population to which, a generation later, the new civic museums and art galleries would be opening their doors. Though the memories (and the continuing presence) of illness and slums may have haunted these museums, they were also animated by the vigour, the sense of curiosity and the desire for self-improvement described by this acute observer.

THE HOPELESSNESS OF LOCAL GOVERNMENT

To their problems, the new cities were for some years incapable of delivering solutions. They suffered – and 'suffering' is the apposite word – from the English habit of unambitious pragmatism that led them to preserve and minimally adapt old institutions rather than embark on wholesale reform. By the early nineteenth century there were some 25,000 instruments of government in England and Wales, a situation felt by many to be the natural order. Over two hundred towns were corporate – that is to say, they had been granted charters and were governed by corporations, or councils – but the allocation of charters depended on ancient demography and was unrelated to modern needs. These corporations were largely self-appointing, resistant to change, and notoriously corrupt, often dominated by Tory Anglicans who considered that their responsibilities ended in the administration of charities and the maintenance of property. Whereas Liverpool and Leeds did have corporations, up to the 1830s Manchester, Birmingham and Sheffield were governed like villages, with county Justices of the Peace administering the law, and parish authorities and medieval manorial courts dealing with other issues. These bodies were incapable of reform or innovation.

In 1835 the Municipal Corporations Act abolished the old corporations in favour of elected bodies, allowing non-corporate towns to apply for corporate status. Birmingham, Manchester, Sheffield and Bradford all applied successfully. In almost every instance when a town became corporate, the old Tory administration was swept away in favour of a Liberal or Radical council. But reform was spread over many years. While the personnel in local government changed and for the first time a town's voters could elect their own council (if on a severely limited suffrage), the new councils' powers were ill defined. Civic improvements, pressingly needed in health and education and many other fields, were only slowly introduced. The tenets of the Manchester school of economics, which held that the state should intervene as little as possible in economic matters, exerted a wide influence, as did many people's reluctance to contribute to the well-being of their poorer fellow-citizens. The battle to keep down public expenditure remaining a dominating force. In Birmingham, reformers of the 1840s and 1850s were impeded by two successive leaders of the ratepayers' associations, who prevented even the implementation of effective measures for public health. In these circumstances it could not be expected that art galleries would immediately flourish.

The difficulty of taking an art collection into public ownership is illustrated by the McLellan collection in Glasgow, where the idea of a city owning works of art met with resistance to, or at least incomprehension of, public support for the arts. When Gustav Waagen visited in the early 1850s, he noted that in a city where 'The taste for collecting has at present but little obtained among the rich merchants and manufacturers...a carriage-builder, Mr Alexander [sic] McLellan, forms an honourable exception.'[36] This exemplary collection, extending well beyond the Dutch seventeenth-century landscapes and modern British works favoured by newly rich business people, had a didactic purpose, to represent all the national schools then recognised as important (Figs 42–44).[37] The collection, and the building that McLellan had erected to house it, were acquired by the city in 1856 against much opposition: according to James Paton, who later served as Curator and then Superintendant of Glasgow Museums, 'In this way the Town Council...became somewhat reluctant patrons of art, and the owners of an art gallery rather against their will.'[38] Glasgow did, however, pay the astonishing sum of over £44,000 for the paintings, an amount that would have been illegal in England, where the Acts allowing public expenditure on museums and libraries did not permit such purchases. This was one of the most important acquisitions of a collection ever made by a gallery in Britain, particularly remarkable for having taken place at such an early date, when the

42 *The Annunciation* by Sandro Botticelli and Studio, 1490–5. Tempera on panel, 49.5 × 61.9 cm. One of the works from the collection of Archibald McLellan acquired by the city of Glasgow in 1856, it is an example of his forward-looking taste (Glasgow Museums).

43 *Christ and the Woman taken in Adultery* by Titian, *c.* 1510. Oil on canvas, 139.3 × 181.7 cm. This painting from the McLellan collection was in the past frequently attributed to Giorgione. It was cut down at the right at some stage. Part of the missing section, a fragmentary head of a man, was acquired by Glasgow in 1971 (Glasgow Museums).

44 *Cottages and Fishermen by a River* by Jan van Goyen, 1631. Oil on panel, 29.2 × 45.7 cm. Like many nineteenth century and earlier collectors, McLellan was fond of Dutch landscape painting, and this fine example is less unusual in an early nineteenth century collection than many of his pictures (Glasgow Museums).

concert of the municipal art gallery had scarcely been developed, but it set no precedent for a long while.[39]

Once the purchase had been made, the City Council's difficulties in coping with an art collection became apparent. Having sold several works, the Council came to regard the galleries 'as rent producers' and let the halls for 'public lectures, balls,

concerts, bazaars, and other similar entertainments'. 'These applications of a gallery of art', Paton severely remarked, 'were manifestly inconsistent with its proper use of a public institution; but the whole matter was looked upon, in the early days, merely as a matter of investment'.[40] After a financially unsuccessful attempt in 1867 to mount an exhibition of portraits, the collection 'fell into the most regrettable and detrimental condition of public neglect', with the pictures regarded 'as a hindrance to the free use of the halls for miscellaneous purposes'.[41] The concept of what could be done with such a collection, or of how its ownership might reflect favourably on the character of the city, had not reached even such a vigorous and forward-looking city as Glasgow.

THE VALUE OF THE ARTS

The public value of museums, as well as of libraries, was much discussed at Westminster. The findings of the 1835–6 Parliamentary Select Committee, for example, anticipated some crucial themes in the development of Victorian museums. The Committee's aim was 'to inquire into the best means of extending a knowledge of the Arts, and of the Principles of Design among the People (especially the Manufacturing Population) of the Country'. It debated the poor quality of British commercial design and the consequent difficulty of exporting products, and concluded that British decorative artists must be taught to understand the principles of fine design. The 1836 report agreed that the Fine Arts had received too little attention in Britain.

Accessibility was a recurring theme in the report. Free access to museums and libraries would lead, as in France, 'to the diffusion of a love of art, as well as of literature'.[42] Principles of design should be introduced into 'any permanent system of national education', and the committee regretted the lack of any 'general instruction even in the history of art at our universities and public schools'.[43] The idea that the universities ought to play a larger role in art education was reiterated throughout the century. The report remained cautious over the role of Government in art education, believing that Government 'should aim at the development and extension of art; but it should neither control its action, nor

Museum & School of Art Warrington, Lancashire

force its cultivation'.[44] The fear of foreign competition and superiority remained a *leitmotif*. The report supported the formation of

open PUBLIC GALLERIES or MUSEUMS OF ART in the various towns willing to undertake a... share in the foundation, and...maintenance, of such establishments. In nothing have foreign countries possessed a greater advantage over Great Britain than in their numerous public galleries devoted to the Arts, and open gratuitously to the people...[since] the poor are necessarily excluded....Everything which exhibits in combination the efforts of the artist and the workman, should be sought for in the formation of such institutions...[45]

The writers embraced both leading principles. Visitors to these new museums would imbibe 'the pure principles of art' and at the same time learn technical skills. In many ways – free admission, the use of reproductions, the didactic nature of galleries – the report anticipated the standard Victorian conception of an art museum.

As a result of such reports, a Bill allowing municipal authorities to set up museums and libraries with funds from ratepayers was introduced into Parliament in 1845 by that stalwart of cultural education, William Ewart, and passed into law under Peel's administration.[46] For the 'instruction and amusement' of the people, towns with populations of over 10,000 were permitted to devote a rate of a halfpenny in the pound to the establishment of museums and to buy specimens that would be vested

permanently in the corporations. It was known as the 'Beetle Act', being primarily directed at scientific museums. Permission to make an admission charge (of not more than one penny) was initially granted, though the further 1850 Act for Enabling Town Councils to Establish Public Libraries and Museums, which extended the powers of local councils, stipulated free admission.

These ambitious pronouncements from Westminster and Kensington took some time to be realised in the provinces. By the late 1850s only six towns had established libraries or museums, often by taking over ailing Literary and Philosophical Societies. As in the old learned societies, art played a minor and equivocal part, and often none. The first municipal museum (combined with a library) was set up in 1848 in Warrington, a town known for its long-standing radical tradition (Fig. 45).[47] The basis of the collection was natural history, fine art playing no part until the addition of an extension dedicated to painting and sculpture in 1877. Warrington was followed by Ipswich, where the town took over the existing learned society's museum, and by Norwich, where a library service opened in 1857, with an art gallery following some ten years later.[48] Significantly, both Ipswich and Norwich are sited in the famously free-thinking Nonconformist region of East Anglia (Figs 46, 47). In the early 1860s further delays were caused by the American Civil War, which created the 'Cotton Famine' in Manchester. In general, twenty years elapsed between the passing of these acts and any substantial action.

EXPANSION OF THE PUBLIC REALM

In many cases it was a courageous individual who managed to appeal to the latent enthusiasms of their fellow-citizens and to shift opinion. One of the most revealing early episodes in the civic expansion of Birmingham was the campaign for the purchase of Aston Hall. This was the city that Alexis de Tocqueville had described in 1835 as having 'no analogy with other English provincial towns... One only sees busy people and faces brown with smoke. One hears nothing but the sound of hammers and the whistle of steam escaping from boilers. One might be down a mine in the New World.

46 Ipswich Museum's first building. The museum opened in 1847, with a brief to educate working people in natural history and other subjects, in the absence of any initiative by the old universities to provide scientific or technological training. Originally run by a private society, it soon became financially unviable and in 1853 was one of the first learned society museums to be taken over by a town under the Public Libraries Act of 1850. It has had a distinguished history under several notable curators. This building, by Christopher Fleury (which survives, in another use), was replaced by a new museum in 1881.

47 Ipswich Museum's main hall.

Everything is black, dirty and obscure, although every instant it is winning silver and gold.'[49] The Jacobean Aston Hall and its park on the outskirts of the city were threatened with demolition and development. Prominent in the preservation campaign was 'the towering figure of John Walsh'.[50] Walsh, a member of the Town Council and a manufacturer of soda water, isinglass and gelatine, cigars and glass, was typical of the energetic businessmen who regarded the improvement of their city as their

duty, as well no doubt as a means of shining up their own reputations. He was eager to achieve the best results: 'he used to chafe at the thought that double the area of the present park might have been purchased, for less money than was paid for the portion now held.'[51]

In 1856 and 1857 Walsh organised two 'colossal fetes', ostensibly to support the Queen's Hospital but also to advertise Aston's importance (Fig. 48).[52] These events were conducted in the spirit of the Great Exhibition at its most rambunctious. Business in the city was temporarily suspended:

> Scores more barrels of ale and porter came slowly into the park…crates upon crates of tumblers, earthenware mugs, and plates arrived. Soda water, lemonade, and ginger beer were provided in countless grosses, and in fact everything for the comfort and convenience of visitors…was provided in the most lavish profusion.…As noon approached, train after train deposited at the Aston station hundreds and thousands of gaily attired Black Country people [transported by] omnibuses, wagons, cabs, carts, and every other imaginable vehicle.[53]

50,000 people attended the first fête, 90,000 the second, all paying an entrance fee to benefit the hospital. Apart from 'the merriment in the gardens', the Old English games, the dancing, fireworks, swings, Punch and Judy shows and the piggy balloon, the Old Hall was 'thrown open, and hundreds of people strolled through its quaint rooms and noble galleries'. The day finished with fireworks, which culminated in the words, 'in glowing fire…SAVE ASTON HALL'.[54]

This enthusiastic description conveys the character of a people's festival in support of a good cause: the huge mixed crowds, the reliance on a medley of traditions, the new-found accessibility in terms of transport and cost to a broad sector of the population, and above all the vigour of private initiative working increasingly in co-operation with the rising movement to create municipal institutions. The Aston Hall celebrations also represent an early example of the involvement of a large sector of the population in the preservation of parkland and a historic house. It was not only Walsh who worked to save the hall: in an innovative move a committee of working men was set up to aid the cause, and

shares and donations were accumulated.[55] Inspired no doubt by the Great Exhibition, this was a new type of virtuous communal event, reflecting a growing sense of civic and regional identity before the development of regulated sport.

THE PARK MOVEMENT

The creation at Aston of a public open space was characteristic of the movement to develop public parks, which offers revealing parallels to the foundation of museums. The link between museums and gardens dated back at least to the foundation of botanical gardens at the universities of Pisa in 1544 and Padua in 1545, each with curators and a developed taxonomical system. These academically based gardens were reflected in Britain in the establishment both of university botanical gardens (as at Oxford) and of recreational public gardens and parks. The first of these was the park opened in Exeter in 1612, where private and municipal initiative combined in the earliest civic provision of a public amenity.[56] It was followed in the eighteenth century by public walks in towns such as Tunbridge Wells, Shrewsbury, Bath and York – walks that tended to cater for the affluent classes as places to promenade, rather than for the whole population.[57] In 1833 a Select Committee investigated public walks, aiming to find out what parks were available and to recommend future action.[58] Reflecting contemporary thinking about museums, the Committee concluded that parks were essential for public well-being and the easing of class tension: contact between the social classes in parks would promote friendly communication.

From the 1840s onwards the growing inaccessibility to town dwellers of the countryside and fresh air gave a further impetus to the movement. The authors of the 1845 *Second Report on the State of Large Towns and Populous Districts*, published after successive cholera epidemics, emphasised the beneficial effect of open spaces on public health.[59] The realisation of this programme began in Manchester, with the opening of Queen's Park and Philips Park, and of Peel Park in neighbouring Salford, all in 1846. The even more ambitious Birkenhead Park, designed on picturesque principles around a lake and studded with pavilions, was laid out from 1843 to 1847 at public expense to the designs of Joseph Paxton (Fig. 49). These pioneers were followed by many others, so that by the end of the century any self-respecting

topia, within the city and yet outside it, an escape from the regular demands of domesticity, work and social pressures.

THE GROWTH OF CIVIC PRIDE

The heroic city in this narrative was Birmingham, notable above all other British cities for its civic improvements. A writer at the end of the century discussing 'The Art Treasures of America' characterised it as having been in the 1830s 'in every respect more parochial, more unrelievedly dismal, more devoid of any mental atmosphere save that of commercialism and a sad religiosity, than is Pittsburg [sic] or any other as dismal or more dismal American manufacturing centre'.[63] In spite of this dreariness, he concluded, the city did give birth to Edward Burne-Jones. The process of civic improvement began in 1839 with the appointment of a coroner, followed in the next decade by the creation of institutions paid for by the Town Council, individuals or public subscription: a lunatic asylum, a hospital, a medical college and the first public park. In the 1850s the new amenities included the Birmingham and Midlands Institute (a training college for teachers), public baths and a second public park, as well as Aston Hall. The process accelerated in the following decade. Birmingham – to John Bright, as 'liberal as the sea was salt'[64] – was to gain from 1870 one of the most active and enlightened of City Councils under the reforming Liberal administration of Joseph Chamberlain.

It was the belief of Liberal Nonconformists in society's duty to provide for the needs of all its citizens that stimulated many innovations, not least the foundation of cultural and learned institutions for all. In the context of this 'civic gospel' Birmingham became a national leader, so that in 1887 the *Magazine of Art* could describe it as 'perhaps the most artistic town in England'.[65] The reforming political mood was personified by such men as George Dawson, from 1848 until his death in 1876 a charismatic preacher at the Unitarian Church of the Saviour, which had been built by his admirers, and Henry William Crosskey, Unitarian minister and preacher at the Church of the Messiah from 1869 until 1893. Both men were associated with a range of advanced views, including extension of the suffrage

49 The official opening of Birkenhead Park, from the *Illustrated London News*, 10 April 1847. 10,000 people attended the opening of the first park in Britain to be provided at public expense. It was laid out on a grand scale by Joseph Paxton in 1843–7 on marshy land, irrigated to provide lakes and mounds. It contains numerous pavilions and the elegant housing around it helped to defray the costs. F.L. Olmsted visited the park in 1850 and it influenced his designs for Central Park, New York.

town had at least one public park, just as it had at least one museum. In several cases, museum and park were brought together, the museum occupying a central position in the open space in the way that a house would dominate a private garden (Figs 50, 51). The Queen's Park Museum in Manchester,[60] which opened in 1864, and the library and natural history museum in Peel Park (1870), were early examples of a union that continued into the twentieth century.[61]

These parks offered many advantages. They were innovatory in breaking down social divisions, at least in principle. The historian of Aston Hall proudly stressed the social heterogeneity of the crowds at the 1850s fêtes:

> All classes were represented…Here you might see a group of well-dressed folks from Edgbaston, next some pale-faced miners from the Black Country, and then the nut-brown faces of some agricultural people. All seemed intent upon fun and pleasure…[62]

The parks also offered the chance to enjoy visual spectacle in the form of floral displays and romantic landscapes, to take healthy exercise, increasingly with the provision of games pitches, and to enjoy musical entertainments from the bandstand. Just as museums and galleries would provide for the people's intellectual and social well-being, parks would ensure their physical health. Both offered a hetero-

80

50 The Mappin Art Gallery and Weston Park, photographed in about 1950. Created in the grounds of Weston Hall, a private house bought by Sheffield Corporation, this was the city's first municipal park. Designed by the celebrated (Sheffield and London) gardener Robert Marnock, it contains entrance gates designed by Godfrey Sykes, another son of Sheffield, best known for his work at the South Kensington Museum.

51 A fountain in the gardens of Weston Park.

and (in Crosskey's case) universal free education, female suffrage and state old age pensions, but they had many other interests. Dawson's church became a centre of social and political reform: seventeen of the church members became town councillors and six mayors of Birmingham during the period after the late 1860s, when a movement for reform was purging the old council in favour of more able and active members.[66] In spite of this influence, it should be stressed that both men stood outside the mainstream not only of the established Church but also of most Nonconformist churches and aroused much animosity. These men were indeed radicals and it

was in this radicalism that the improvements they advocated had their roots.

These allies worked to make the city a pleasant and more civilised place to live, Dawson helping to secure Aston Park as well as leading the public libraries movement. According to his biographer,

It is beyond all question that he so educated and influenced his personal friends and occasional hearers, that they went forth to work; and he really gave the first impulse to that public life, high municipal spirit, political energy, and literary and artistic progress which have so distinguished Birmingham during the past thirty years. His constant pressure and personal influence infinitely improved the quality of the Town Council, which, when he came, was in but indifferent repute…No one man ever had so large and so evident an influence in a great town. He came when, after the Reform Bill, the town was resting from its labours. He evoked a new spirit, and aroused a new life, and became an important power.[67]

They also believed in the need to make cities more civilised places to live in. For Crosskey, the key lay not only in efficient government but also in 'making the town cleaner, sweeter, and brighter;…providing gardens and parks and music;…erecting baths and free libraries and free libraries, an art gallery and a museum'.[68] As Crosskey wrote in a personal memorandum, the Liberal Association's aims included sanitary reform, slum clearance, the purchase of gas and water services to provide high standards and additional income, 'The provision of Public Parks and Recreation Grounds', as well as:

The more extended provision of such civilising agencies as
    The Free Libraries,
    The School of Art,
    The Art Gallery,
and making them more useful and more acceptable to the people at large.[69]

This enthusiasm for literature and the arts, as well as for appealing to a wide public, was to be fulfilled by their ally Joseph Chamberlain, a notably active mayor of Birmingham in the mid-1870s who remained closely involved with city politics during his subsequent Westminster career. As champions

52 Leeds Town Hall. Built to the designs of the Hull architect Cuthbert Brodrick between 1853 and 1858, it symbolised the city's dignity, even though funds were found only with great difficulty. One of the most splendid of all Victorian city halls, it housed municipal offices, courtrooms and the richly decorated Victoria Hall, intended for concerts and major events.

of the city wrote in the 1930s, at a time when Victorian civic grandeur was still intact, a Brummie Rip van Winkle reawakening to the city would enquire 'was there anything that this "corporation" did not do or provide, any human activity that it did not control'?[70]

Like the city republics of Continental Europe, the Victorian cities were anxious to proclaim their pros-

'Glasgow has attained the high position which she now holds among the great municipalities of the world'.[73] Its account of the city's history and present government – the police, health provision, tramways, libraries, the navigation of the Clyde, the art galleries and museums and many other subjects – resounds with civic pride. Public service is emphasised: the city's administration conduces 'to the health, happiness, and prosperity of the citizens'.[74] Bell's text also reflects Scottish discomfort over the relationship with the British Empire, asserting Scottish excellence and independence. He opines that in most of 'the important modifications of social legislation the towns and cities have been pioneers', in contrast to the 'timid hesitation and doubt' shown by the Imperial Parliament.[75]

> The power for good or evil of a Corporation such as Glasgow, dealing with the daily life and wants and interpreting the aspirations of three quarters of a million people, is almost inconceivably great. The city has a revenue of £2 million yearly, and employs more than 10,000 'officials and servants'.[76]

Such figures were equal to those of a small country. Though Glasgow was exceptional in size and wealth, it is in the context of such optimistic pride and impatience with national or imperial Government that the overall development of provincial museums and galleries should be seen. The belief that one of the most effective ways of expressing local success was through a civic museum parallels the more or less contemporary development of museums in Boston, Chicago and Pittsburgh.

SETTING UP THE NEW GALLERIES

As we have seen, the process of setting up new art galleries was a slow one. In the early stages, some interest was shown in acquiring historic buildings, especially if they enjoyed royal or noble associations: the Royal Pavilion at Brighton in 1851, Chillington Manor in Maidstone in 1858. Brighton Corporation's decision to acquire the Royal Pavilion, abandoned by Queen Victoria in favour of the more private Osborne House, was an early example of municipal initiative in the cultural field,

53 A postcard of Manchester Town Hall, built to an Early English Gothic design by Alfred Waterhouse from 1868 to 1877. Romantic in its skyline, it was also well planned and technically innovative. It cost the enormous sum of around £1 million.

perity. Though the visual analogies are not immediately evident, Birmingham was compared to Florence, Siena or Venice; Manchester to Florence; Liverpool to Florence or Bruges (and New York). According to Crosskey's biographer, 'Sometimes an adventurous orator would excite his audience by dwelling on the glories of Florence and of the other cities of Italy in the middle ages, and suggest that Birmingham, too, might become the home of a noble literature and art'.[71] Rejoicing in a considerable degree of political independence, the cities celebrated their grandeur in physical terms. In many cases an ostentatious town hall, sited in the principal square and constituting the earliest civic building, proclaimed the excellence of the city's government: Birmingham Town Hall of 1833, and the Council House of 1873; Leeds Town Hall, from 1853 (Fig. 52); Manchester Town Hall, from 1868 (Fig. 53). The sites and architecture of these buildings recall the independent city states of earlier centuries. A further assertion of civic dignity was provided by the plate and mayoral chains that in the second half of the century were presented to many town halls, notably to celebrate royal jubilees and other great occasions.[72]

The sense of purpose of these councils are conveyed in such books as *Glasgow: Its Municipal Organization and Administration*, published in 1896. This imposing volume was written by Sir James Bell, the influential Lord Provost of Glasgow, and James Paton, Superintendent of the Glasgow Museums, and local historian. It illustrates how

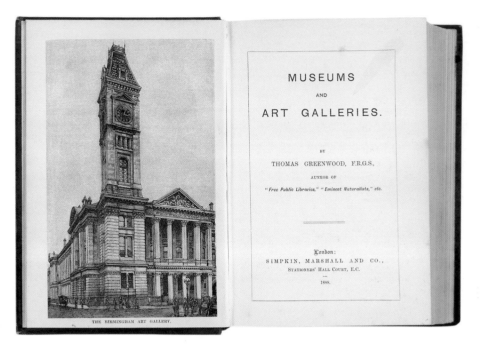

54 *Museums and Art Galleries* by Thomas Greenwood (1888). A campaigner for public institutions who had already written on free public libraries, Greenwood argued that museums and galleries had 'ceased to be luxuries, and should be considered as absolutely necessary for the welfare of every Municipality throughout the country. Gaols and workhouses are provided as a matter of course, and why should not Museums and Free Libraries be looked upon as of equal importance?'

achieved through the efforts of an enlightened town clerk.[77]

It was not until the late 1860s that museums with some bias towards the visual arts and history were created, in Birmingham and Exeter. In the 1870s municipal museums and galleries were set up in large cities such as Liverpool and Birmingham and in smaller towns, while in the 1880s the emphasis on the establishment of museums and art galleries in the North became apparent in Scottish towns such as Aberdeen and Inverness, in the rich towns of Lancashire, such as Manchester and Oldham, and a little later in Yorkshire, notably Sheffield and Leeds (see Appendix).

The new museums followed the learned societies in being hybrid institutions containing both scientific specimens and works of art, though it was scientific collections that led the way until the last years of the century. Among the 211 provincial museums listed in the 1887 *Report of the British Association for the Advancement of Science on the Provincial Museums of the United Kingdom*, only thirty-two included 'Art' or 'Industrial Art' in their collecting policy. A mere dozen institutions were described as 'art galleries only'. Much more strongly represented was geology, an extremely popular subject, as well as botany, zoology and archaeology.[78] Even this small

total seemed excessive to another observer: in 1888 Thomas Greenwood's *Museums and Art Galleries* (Fig. 54), which offered an overall survey of the British field, found in the whole of the British Isles (including Ireland) fewer than 200 museums. As he remarked, 'many which are included in this estimate should really not be in the list, for, although they have been established with worthy aims, they hardly deserve the name'.[79] In the 1890s the foundation of new museums continued, with an increasing emphasis on art galleries – an emphasis that may have been inspired by the well-publicised high attendance figures at Liverpool, Birmingham and Manchester art galleries.[80] At least fifteen major galleries were set up all over the country: not only in the industrial North but also in naval centres and in old-established towns such as York and Norwich.

To a modern eye it may at first appear that these galleries possessed a degree of uniformity, that they all owned collections of modern art, primarily British, and were housed in Victorian galleries of eclectic but traditional design. Actually, what is striking about these galleries is their variety. Founded in some cases by private individuals, sometimes by civic enterprise, they were created with varying agenda, not all surviving to this day. Four main types recur: the galleries based on a private collection and paid for privately, including the 'collection museums' (discussed in Chapter Seven) and such municipal collections as Bury; the ones that concentrated on building up a permanent collection, such as Manchester City Art Gallery and Kelvingrove Art Gallery, Glasgow; the galleries erected with the prime purpose of accommodating temporary exhibitions by contemporary artists, such as the Walker Art Gallery; and those that concentrated on large-scale loan exhibitions, such as Birmingham. These categories are not mutually exclusive – Kelvingrove engaged heavily in temporary loan exhibitions – but they illustrate the variety of solutions to setting up a new institution with limited funding.[81]

PUBLIC PARSIMONY

In many cases, these new museums and galleries came into existence through private contributions. Day-to-day funding became the responsibility of

55 The junior staff at Cartwright
Hall, Bradford, in about 1904.

£1,000 on running costs, with many finding only a few hundred pounds, at a time when the annual cost of running the National Galleries of Scotland and Ireland was estimated at £10,000 each.[84] The number of staff too was usually very low. The Walker Art Gallery was unusual in employing a relatively large staff: in 1911 two curators and an assistant, a typist, a foreman and six uniformed attendants, three housemaids and two cloakroom boys. Manchester City Art Gallery survived on a mere two professional staff members (Fig. 55).[85]

In an attack that recalls A.W. Pugin's 1836 depiction of the modern British city in *Contrasts* in which he savagely caricatured the punitive meanness of the day, Greenwood wrote,

> The only adjuncts to a Municipality which are…looked upon as absolutely indispensable beyond street improvements, drainage, lighting, and waterworks, are a gaol and a workhouse, with their concomitants of police, magistrates, and a share in a lunatic asylum and the national hangman. We are most lavish in our expenditure under these heads, but when we come to the expenditure for education…we resort to rigid retrenchment. If a few millions are required for an impossible and useless railway in a desert, or for powder and shot to blow away into space…up go the thumbs of a large section of our legislators, and the money is forthwith voted. But let the object be a few extra thousands for the British Museum, the endowment of research…or Free Libraries, down go the thumbs, and strangulation forthwith proceeds. A new torpedo is considered of greater value than a hundred Museums…[86]

It was in these peculiar circumstances that municipal libraries, galleries and museums struggled into existence. It is remarkable that they achieved so much.

the councils, which exercised extreme caution. Greenwood substantiated his polemic on British meanness towards the arts by furnishing details from the museums of their 'aggregate annual expenses'.[82] Though many authorities refused to co-operate, the results supported his strictures. Birmingham was easily the most lavish corporation, spending in the years around 1888 an annual £3,500 on its Museum and Art Gallery, and a further £1,000 on Aston Hall. Greenwood agreed with the city's 'proud boast that it possesses the finest Art Gallery out of London', setting an example to the country.[83] Birmingham's contribution was almost three times that of the next most generous city, Nottingham, which spent £1,220. In total only five museums (four rate-supported, one private), other than the national museums, spent more than

5

THE UNIVERSAL
EXHIBITION

Municipal art galleries and museums were shaped by the dizzying phenomenon of the universal exhibition. Within twelve years, Europe and the United States witnessed the Great Exhibition of 1851; the Exhibition of Art-Industry in Dublin and the Exhibition of the Industry of All Nations in New York, both in 1853; the *Exposition Universelle des produits de l'Agriculture, de l'Industrie et des Beaux-Arts de Paris*, shown in the purpose-built *Palais de l'Industrie* in 1855; and the International Exhibition of the Industrial Arts and Manufactures, and the Fine Arts, of All Nations, held in a vast new building in South Kensington in 1862. Though the catalogues of the British exhibitions repeatedly mention the earliest industrial display, held in 1798 in Paris and followed by a number of similar manifestations, they make it clear that in their view the Great Exhibition, held in the Crystal Palace in Hyde Park in 1851, was the culmination of these earlier events. It was a culmination that transformed the genre.[1] Its huge success, with over six million visits, created a new phenomenon, the visual spectacle aimed at a mass audience (Fig. 56). The phenomenon became increasingly large-scale and aggressive during the second half of the century: as Paul Greenhalgh has written, 'Between 1855 and 1914 an event involving more than twenty nations was held somewhere in the world on an average of every two years', with Paris playing a particularly prominent and competitive part.[2]

For the development of museums and art galleries in Britain, the exhibition movement played a crucial role – more so, it is suggested, than anywhere else in the world other than the United States. In London, the South Kensington Museum's emergent collections were based on purchases from the Great Exhibition and later displays. In the provinces, the Manchester Art Treasures Exhibition of 1857, housed in an enormous temporary iron-and-glass basilica, applied the language and buildings of the trade fair to a quite different event, an art-historical display that proclaimed the greatness of British collections and the potential achievements of provincial cultural life. It was on the foundations of such exhibitions – entrepreneurial, commercial, entertaining, accessible – that many provincial galleries were built.

THE GREAT EXHIBITION OF 1851

The ambitious objectives of these exhibitions have not been well received in the recent historio-

MANCHESTER in 1851.

56 'Manchester in 1851', from
George Cruikshank and Henry
Mayhew, *World's Show 1851, or The
Adventures of Mr and Mrs Sandboys
and Family* (1851). This account of
a country family's adventures
includes a satirical depiction of
the city denuded of people, since
'all the world' had gone to see
the Crystal Palace.

graphy. The Great Exhibition in particular has been classed as a dubious, even malevolent, force, an early promoter of the self-evidently expensive object that is intrinsically useless, and as an agent of conspicuous display and mass consumption to ensnare a newly prosperous public (Figs. 57, 58). This point of view was dramatically posited by Walter Benjamin: 'World exhibitions are places of pilgrimage to the commodity fetish'.[3] His analysis encouraged a flow of comparable assessments in the 1980s and 1990s. In *Ephemeral Vistas* (1988) Greenhalgh argued for an intimate connection between the world exhibition and the presentation and exploitation of Empire. For Thomas Richards in *The Commodity Culture of Victorian England: Advertising and Spectacle, 1851–1914* (1990), the Great Exhibition served as 'a monument to consumption…where manufactured objects were autonomous icons ordered into taxonomies, set on pedestals, and flooded with light'.[4] Its ultimate purpose was a 'middle-class end: the continuing extension and ultimate consolidation of the capitalist system in England'.[5] Jeffrey Auerbach's *The Great Exhibition of 1851: A Nation on Display* attacked its artificial spectacle and crude commercialism.[6] More recently, however, historians have viewed the Great Exhibition in less censorious terms. For Celina Fox, 'it can also be seen as the last triumphal representation of the arts of industry, the

grand finale of the old unified world of knowledge'.[7] John Davis, commenting on the enormous volume of relevant material, saw it as a subject lending itself to subjective and selective interpretation. Aiming to 'present an account of the Great Exhibition that is free of the generalisation, partisanship and moral censure of past writing, and that incorporates and summarises the findings of more recent works', he explored the organisers' attitudes to social polarisation, notably the exclusion of the working classes from any active role.[8] He studied the conflicts embodied by the Great Exhibition between the forces of industrial progress and the conservatism of an anti-industrial old order, and between the ethos of Free Trade (intrinsic to the event) and the forces of protectionism. For Lara Kriegel, the event was notable for its 'explicit glorification of skilled labor', with its catalogues embracing 'the broad liberal values of hard work, free trade, imperial expansion, and democratic consumption' where 'design became the stuff of enchantment, edification, and entertainment'.[9]

Negative interpretations of the Great Exhibition would have astonished most of the visiting millions. Its innovatory quality was celebrated in the massive literature produced at the time and in memorial publications recording 'a display never equaled [*sic*] in the world's history'.[10] For Prince Albert, more given to idealistic public statements than most of his British-born contemporaries, the event enshrined lofty purposes. It offered 'a true test and a living picture of the point of development at which the whole of mankind has arrived in the great task, and a new starting-point from which all nations will be able to direct their further exertions'. Man must use his God-given reason to 'discover the laws by which the Almighty governs his creation, and, by making these laws his standard of action, to conquer nature to this use, himself a divine instrument'.[11] Such sentiments were to be echoed in the proclamations made in opening speeches and in the semi-sacred texts that adorned this and later exhibition halls. According to this agenda, the Crystal Palace offered an amphitheatre in which happy crowds could contemplate humanity's economic, social and cultural progress, while themselves offering a spectacle for officialdom's approving gaze.

It was the grandeur of the concept, the bringing together of many nations, the celebration of pro-

57 The British Department at the Great Exhibition, 1851, a view towards the transept.

58 The Foreign Department at the Great Exhibition, 1851, a view towards the transept.

paintings intended for Royal Academy exhibitions were seen as garish and over-blown, so many of the Great Exhibition exhibits applied sculptural qualities to supposedly practical appliances, which as a result lost any practical application. The 'most exquisite TEA AND COFFEE SERVICE, manufactured by M. Durand, of Paris', was created in the form of a fully sculpted Renaissance fountain, while a 'Group, in bronze and or-morlu [sic], of the Queen and the Prince Consort, modeled by Mr. John Bell, the distinguished sculptor' was acclaimed as 'in all respects, a good example of English Casting', making it an object notable for both artistic and technical virtuosity.[12] The traditional hierarchy of the arts, and artistic decorum, were flouted in the displays: as early in the nineteenth century, the creators of industrial or domestic objects strove to refer to classical art or landscape and still life traditions. The relationship between the arts was given a further fluidity by the display of figurative sculpture in close relationship to quite other artefacts: M. Engelhard's 'very lovely statue of LURLINE, the dangerously beautiful resident of Lurley-berg, who woos the boatmen to destruction' stood close to a table and sideboard from Gillow's, an ecclesiastical candelabrum from Birmingham and knives from Messrs. Mappin of Sheffield.[13] Pieces regarded as of particularly high quality were sited in the Fine Art Court, which was dedicated not to paintings (which were not shown in 1851) but to objects that displayed what Henry Cole defined as the application of beautiful design to mechanically produced pieces (see chapter 9). Inclusion in the Fine Art Court constituted 'a very marked testimony to the merit of a really beautiful work'.[14] This Court was distinguished by its dignity and quietness in comparison to the clamour and heat in the rest of the building, filled with machinery in action. This close but ambiguous relationship between the fine and the decorative arts was to remain a theme in many later exhibitions.

THE 1857 EXHIBITION

The lofty intentions of 1851 reappeared in the Manchester Art Treasures Exhibition of 1857, but in a wholly different form. The event was seen by a writer in the *Art Treasures Examiner* as 'the most

gress and modernity, that captivated champions of the Great Exhibition. The physical essence of the displays had a less glorious quality. The insistence of Henry Cole, the prime manager of the exhibition (Fig. 59), on the importance of 'taste' and the need for the applied arts led to an attempt in many of the pieces designed for these displays to create a strong artistic effect, often with curious results: much as

58 *Henry Cole* by A.J. Melhuish. Cole's achievements at the Great Exhibition and the South Kensington Museum, and his belief in setting up a chain of regional art galleries supplied with loans from South Kensington, made him probably the most influential individual in Victorian England for the creation of regional galleries.

60 Sir George Scharf, photographed by Nadar on 21 August 1867.

beautiful and attractive feature' in the entire history of Manchester: 'Now she steps forward in her aggregate character to emulate the glorious example of Florence of old, under her prince-merchants the De Medici, to display to the world the richest collection of works of fine art the resource of the country affords.'[15] It was an astonishing event, organised within a year by a group of Manchester businessmen anxious to achieve recognition for their city and to prove that Manchester – habitually sneered at as a city of boors,[16] and described by Faucher as a city where 'industry…knows nothing but itself…literature and the arts are a dead letter'[17] – was capable of cultural enterprise on the grand scale. The 16,000 objects aimed to represent the entire canon of Western art, including the fine and industrial arts, and were accompanied by an ambitious if hastily assembled scholarly apparatus. Scholars such as George Scharf (Fig. 60), shortly to become Director of the National Portrait Gallery (founded four years before), and Gustav Waagen helped select the loans. This was a new manifestation in British and indeed international terms: a didactic universal survey of what was considered the art of the world. A crucial message was that, as a matter of principle and as a triumphant assertion of Waagen's researches, all the exhibits came from British collections, sometimes institutional but largely private: if Britain did not yet excel in the creation of art, it was supreme in its art holdings (Figs 61–63).

Shown in three vast halls with numerous subsidiary rooms, the 1857 exhibition included over 2,300 paintings. The representation of Western art was shaped by the sophisticated eclecticism of Waagen, although, as Elizabeth Pergam has suggested, his connoisseurial approach may have appeared old-fashioned to newer scholars interested in the detailed analysis of individual works.[18] The paintings featured such (then) little-known artists as El Greco and Grünewald, with a strong representation of early German and Flemish paintings. The display of the Spanish school moved well beyond the previous restriction of British taste to Murillo and Velázquez. Contemporary prejudices were ignored, to embrace such currently unpopular artists as Nicolas Poussin and the Bolognese. The exhibition's principles were reflected in the chronological arrangement of the historic works on either side of a long hall, with Italian and Spanish paintings facing Northern

61 Plans of the Manchester Art Treasures exhibition from the one-shilling *Catalogue of the Art Treasures of the United Kingdom: Collected at Manchester in 1857* (1857), published by Bradbury and Evans. Note the symmetrical plan, with 'Ornamental Art' balanced by the British Portrait Galleries and then by ancient and modern pictures; the provision of refreshment rooms, with a free-standing kitchen; and the essential provision of a railway station immediately next to the main entrance.

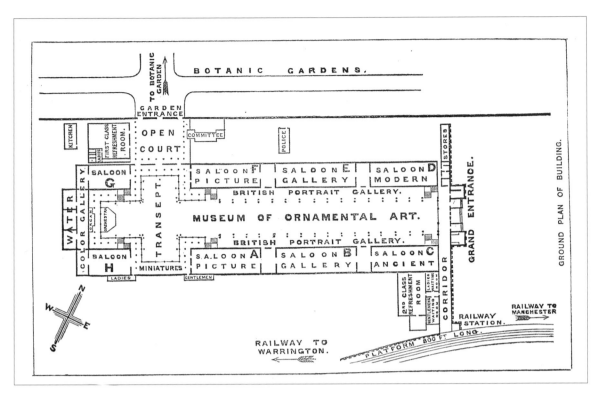

62 A view of the central hall, the Manchester Art Treasures Exhibition, 1857.

63 Setting up the Manchester Art Treasures Exhibition, 1857. The complex task of mounting this enormous display was accomplished with remarkable speed.

ones. This interest in the parallel development of various schools contrasted with the approach taken at the National Gallery, where Western art's history was traced primarily through Italy. One of the exhibition's strengths was that it allowed scholars to contrast schools and artists that had never been brought together in such strength: for the first time direct comparisons could be made between Florentine and Sienese paintings, allowing a re-evaluation of their respective character and importance.[19]

Manchester also aimed to be encyclopaedic in its representation of different media, although for example African art was (as the period dictated) excluded, while India and China were represented only through the decorative arts. The official catalogue set works of art in their social and intellectual context, as in the discussion of ivories: 'there is no other branch of Art which can to an equal degree afford us a knowledge of the different styles of successive epochs, of the guiding spirit, dominant ideas, customs, and manners of past ages, from the com-

mencement of the Christian era down to the seventeenth century'.[20] Close to a thousand watercolours represented a genre regarded as 'indisputably an English invention, and hitherto…only…practised as a School in England'.[21] The display of over 2,000 prints, divided by medium, was a further innovation. Though a display of the masterpieces of printmaking had been held at the Bibliothèque Royale in Paris in 1819, it had been almost entirely restricted to works by French artists, and the Manchester print exhibition appears to have been the first of its kind.[22] The national boundaries applied in Paris were no longer considered valid in the newly international context.

Such a display provided an ideal arena for asserting the merits of a national school. The exhibition included a major representation of British art, both historical and modern, artists having been invited to nominate examples of their own work. The selection in the British Portraits and Miniatures section, drawn primarily from historic collections, was intended to complement the new National Portrait

64   *Handbook to the Fine Art Collections in the International Exhibition of 1862* by Francis Turner Palgrave. Employed in the education department of the Civil Service, Palgrave was also active as an art critic and became famous for his poetry anthology, *The Golden Treasury*. He was friendly with the Pre-Raphaelites, and this handbook, incisive and sometimes crusty in tone, was attacked for excessive partiality towards them.

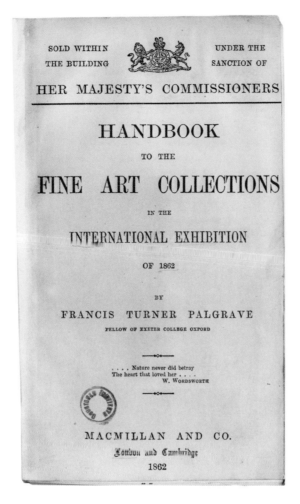

SOLD WITHIN
THE BUILDING

UNDER THE
SANCTION OF

HER MAJESTY'S COMMISSIONERS

HANDBOOK

TO THE

FINE ART COLLECTIONS

IN THE

INTERNATIONAL EXHIBITION

OF 1862

BY

FRANCIS TURNER PALGRAVE

FELLOW OF EXETER COLLEGE OXFORD

.... Nature never did betray
The heart that loved her ....
W. WORDSWORTH

MACMILLAN AND CO.
London and Cambridge
1862

64   *Handbook to the Fine Art Collections in the International Exhibition of 1862* by Francis Turner Palgrave. Employed in the education department of the Civil Service, Palgrave was also active as an art critic and became famous for his poetry anthology, *The Golden Treasury*. He was friendly with the Pre-Raphaelites, and this handbook, incisive and sometimes crusty in tone, was attacked for excessive partiality towards them.

Gallery by illustrating 'in an effective and instructive manner English life in bygone times' – an early exploration of social history.[23] One continuance of the 1851 ethos was the importance of what was described as ornamental (meaning 'decorative' or 'applied') art: the central aisle of the exhibition hall contained a Museum of Ornamental Art, explaining the historical development of each type of object as well as manufacturing techniques. Education for the worker and the manufacturer remained a dominant consideration.

With its pictures displayed in several tiers on the lofty walls of the exhibition halls, organised in educational categories but to the modern eye extraordinarily prodigal and exuberant, the Manchester Art Treasures Exhibition initiated an interest in the large-scale survey of the history of art that was to persist for many years. Its organisers imposed order and reason on the chaos of the artists' society.

THE 1862 INTERNATIONAL EXHIBITION

Just over a decade after 1851, the exhibition movement in Britain showed signs of a loss, not of energy but of idealistic freshness. The 1862 International Exhibition, held in London, was not the happiest of events, and the discussions around it convey a developing sense of strain, notably after the death in December 1861 of Prince Albert, who had been closely involved. The display was of course hailed by official publications as a triumph. The joint authors of *The Illustrated Record of the International Exhibition* considered that it marked 'an immense step in human progress' compared to 1851, with a much larger number of exhibits. They celebrated the inclusion of paintings, drawings and engravings, which meant that 'for the first time in this country, the painting and sculpture of all Europe' were on display, allowing interesting comparisons to be made with the art of Britain.[24] The emphasis was on contemporary work, which was for sale in a special art pavilion (Fig. 64).

While the official text on the walls proclaimed 'Gloria in excelsis deo, et in terra pax', and cited William Cowper in declaring the interdependence of nations – 'Each climate needs what other climes produce' – the actuality was less positive.[25] As in the art world of the early part of the century, the frontier between idealism and commerce tended to be indistinct. For some critics the commercial element was excessive. They were unhappy with exhibits such as the tobacco pipes from Austria, which sold 'by the bushel',[26] and with the two weeks of a frankly commercial sale offered after the exhibition's official closure. An aura of dishonesty and inefficiency surrounded the event, with many of the French works of art arriving late. For some critics, the commission for the building, granted to the engineer Francis Fowke without a proper competition, had resulted in 'a building, the ugliness and absurd unsuitability of which have disgraced the architectural knowledge and taste of England in the eyes of the whole world'.[27] This attack on a competent man responsible for such major buildings as the Albert Hall and the Royal Museum in Edinburgh illustrates the rancour that had entered the public debate (Fig. 65).

Numerous exhibitions followed during the nineteenth century and well into the twentieth. Paris

65   Edmund Walker, *Interior of the Eastern Dome, The International Exhibition, London*, 1862. Watercolour. Held in a building on the site of the present Natural History Museum and Science Museum, the exhibition attracted over six million visitors (Victoria and Albert Museum).

and London were in perpetual competition, Paris often leading in terms of innovation through such events as the 1867 Exposition Universelle (visited by over nine million people) and the Exposition Universelle of 1893. In the United States the great world exhibitions marked milestones in the declaration of civic identity and national pride, notably the Centennial Exposition held at Philadelphia in 1876 (Fig. 66) and the World's Columbian Exhibition at Chicago in 1893, a vast affair that helped to shape the city centre. In Britain the large-scale exhibition became a regular feature of civic cultural life, sometimes in cultural terms, as in universal survey exhibitions, but more often in the events blending spect-

acle, profit and entertainment that were organised all over the country and found perhaps their most vigorous manifestation in the world exhibitions held in Glasgow (see Chapter Eight).

THE IMPACT OF THE EXHIBITIONS

The history of such exhibitions is key to an understanding of the late Victorian art museum. These enormous events were frequently undiscriminating in their choice of objects; they combined the desire to instruct and amuse with a commercial impetus

THE CENTENNIAL—BALLOON VIEW OF THE GROUNDS.

that challenged the accepted distinction between an 'exhibition' and a 'bazaar' – defined as a sale intended 'to raise funds for particular objects'[28] – and they were aimed at and attracted vast publics. The officials obsessively chronicled daily attendance figures, ticket sales, weather conditions and exhibitors' prizes; they provided for the body as well as the mind, with graded refreshment rooms and (profitable) lavatories; and they were suffused, at least on an official level, with optimism and energy. Most of these characteristics were transmitted to the public art gallery, not least because several of the new museums occupied the physical infrastructure created for an exhibition. Additionally, the organisation of temporary displays often served as a weapon to persuade city fathers to found a permanent gallery. The novel character of these events was underlined by their iron and glass buildings, which abandoned the classical and aristocratic language associated with the traditional art museum in favour of the forms of the industrial age, the railway station and the market hall. Cautiously but steadily, Victorian art museums were to follow this pattern.

As Alison Adburgham has shown, the 1862 exhibition exerted a major influence on the development of high-class retailing, in the inclusion of diverse objects under one roof and in the type of object on sale. Whiteley's, opened in 1863 as one of the earliest department stores in London, was described in the language of the great exhibitions as 'an immense symposium of the arts and industries of the nation and of the world',[29] while it was from the 1862 event that A.L. Liberty, later to be the founder of the fashionable shop Liberty's, gained his first understanding of Japanese art.[30] In the same spirit, the borders between art and commerce were blurred in the developing regional museums and galleries, especially in their early days. One aspect of this blurring was the concept of the commercial museum. At Liverpool, the Library and Museum Committee discussed in 1853 the 'great demand for the establishment of a Commercial Museum, where specimens of the various products which make up the commerce of this emporium of the world, might be always at hand to be consulted, and form the basis of a high class commercial education'.[31] It was suggested that a gallery of sculpture and painting 'might

95

easily be added, at little or no expense'. Though unrealised, the proposal indicates the close association for city councillors between art and trade. The notion persisted: when the Manchester Whitworth Institute was being set up in the late 1880s, a 'Museum of Commerce and Manufacture' was initially identified as one of its objectives.[32] Britain never possessed a major institution on the lines of the enormous and for some years highly successful commercial museum in Philadelphia,[33] but a version of the trade museum survived in such relatively modest twentieth-century enterprises as the Clark's Shoe Museum in Street, Somerset, an example of an old-established family business celebrating its heritage.

FRIENDSHIP BETWEEN CLASSES AND BETWEEN NATIONS

The most important objective reiterated in the discourse around these exhibitions was the creation of friendship, between social classes and between nations, aims that were sometimes conflated. Richard Cobden, 'Apostle of Free Trade' and champion of the people, declared in a speech in Birmingham that through the 1851 Exhibition, 'We shall…break down the barriers that have separated the people of different nations, and witness one universal republic'.[34] In his view, 'The Exhibition would make all the classes better known to each other…and would prove how wrongly those estimated them who set these workers down as a rude ferocious mob'.[35] In Cobden's perception, the mob, a source of terror to previous generations, would become a benevolent and self-supporting community. In similar terms, the writer of the *Routledge's Guide* asserted the fraternising influence of business and trade. The exhibition would 'teach the politicians, merchants, manufacturers, and labourers of different nations, that the whole commercial world constitutes one vast community in which the true interests, advancement, and well-being of the people are as mutual and as much bound up together as those of the people of any one nation'.[36] Social and international conflict would give way to universal co-operation in striving for human perfection.

These aspirations were practically based, since the development of the international railway system meant that for the first time a display could bring together not only objects but also people from around the world: 'From Turkey, Tunis, Greece, Algeria, and Egypt, from the East Indies, even China, from South Africa, and from our colonies in the Australasian region, visitors will flock to the exhibition.'[37] Trade and commercial links would create international friendship. In uniting the nations and throwing 'aside the cold garb of nationality and exclusiveness', the Great Exhibition promised 'a long peaceful future': 'Other triumphs have been won, other victories celebrated, but none greater or more glorious than this'.[38]

In actuality, this concept of a great exhibition as a metonym of the world – somewhat on the lines of Disneyworld or Las Vegas today – was realised in unexpected ways. Already in 1851 it was gently parodied by Mayhew. His story of the Sandboys family, humorously conflating the British provinces with the most distant parts of the world, describes how

> The GREAT EXHIBITION was about to attract sight-seers of all the world – the sight-seers, who make up nine-tenths of the human family. The African had mounted his ostrich…The Yakut-sian SHILLIBEER had already started the first reindeer omnibus to Novogorod. Penny cargoes were steaming down Old Nile…[The] whole of the British Provinces likewise were preparing extensively to enjoy themselves.[39]

While many nations were indeed represented in the 1851 and 1862 exhibitions, whether in their own right or as colonies, the juxtaposition of so many forms of national self-presentation actually created an atmosphere of aggressive competition. In such a setting the host nation always commanded the largest area. In the British exhibitions France paid for a place of honour, since by mid-century the two countries were close allies, and the dominating role of France was to remain an element of art exhibitions throughout the Victorian age. In 1851 France occupied a quarter of the space available for foreign exhibits. It was also seen (in the continuance of the eighteenth-century tradition) as superior to Britain in the quality of its design, though a decade later Britain was felt to have made notable improvements.[40] France was acknowledged as the leader among foreign nations in the 1862 exhibition, culturally ahead of Britain, having 'always had the start

M. Taschereau le rétrospectif venant exposer une découverte
de son invention.

67 *L'exposition de Londres, croquée par Cham.* This satirical interpretation of the 1862 London International Exhibition included illustrations of large-scale displays of armaments.

when the American Civil War had just begun and Garibaldi was leading an insurrection against the Papal States. In fact, they became a forum for attacks on unpopular foreign governments. *The Record of the International 1862 Exhibition* castigated the Austrian Empire as 'a despotic power',[43] while 'Rome' (meaning the Papal States) was characterised as 'the most backward and Cimmerian of all European governments'.[44] *L'exposition de Londres, croquée par Cham*, published in Paris in 1862 and illustrating a fictitious French visitor's experiences (Fig. 67), also subverted the ideal of peace by referring more than once to the armaments firm of William Armstrong, whose wares were prominently displayed. Armstrong had gained a reputation for the innovative field gun that he devised and supplied to the British Government during the Crimean War but his firm was controversial in the 1860s, its supply of arms to both sides during the American Civil War rather stretching the concept of international friendship.

THE PRINCE AND THE COTTON-SPINNER

Even if international accord had to be abandoned as a realisable objective, the relationship between classes, and the encouragement of workers' activities, remained constant preoccupations. One of the most important themes was the role of the working man (and occasionally woman). In one of the serious passages interwoven by Henry Mayhew into *1851*, the exhibition was hailed as a triumphant recognition of working people's contribution to modern society:

The Great Exhibition of the Industry of all Countries is the first public national expression ever made in this country, as to the dignity and artistic quality of labour…It is only within the last ten years, perhaps, that we have got to acknowledge the artistic and intellectual quality of many forms of manual labour, speaking of certain classes of operatives no longer as handicraftsmen…but styling them artisans, or the artists of our manufactures. It is because we have been so slow to perceive and express this "great fact" – the artistic character of artisanship – that so much intellectual power has

of us in time and tide of civilization and its train of arts'.[41] Not only did French works dominate the foreign art displays, but France again purchased a larger area than any other foreign country. In 1862 the French sections in two buildings stretched over almost 120,000 square feet, close to half the area allocated to foreign powers, and much in excess of any other nation – Russia's barely reached 10,000.[42] Britain and her colonies, by contrast, extended over some 700,000 square feet. Subsequent exhibitions in Paris and London continued this form of contest, the French and the British constantly competing to offer the most successful event and the highest quality of design.

In 1862 the numerous commentaries on the exhibition referred to universal peace, ironically at a time

been lost to society, and there has been so much more toil and suffering in the world than there has been any necessity for.[45]

Mayhew develops a theme that would have been inconceivable to earlier generations, a theme that does not follow the accepted division between the dignity of intellectual artistic creativity and the lower value of labour. Particularly significant is his association of manual labour with artistic creativity.

It was a theme close to the heart of Henry Cole. Quoting an entry from the *Encyclopaedia Britannica* that distinguished in timeworn fashion between 'useful or mechanic, fine or liberal' arts,[46] Cole deplored the distinction recently made between 'Fine Art', meaning painting, sculpture, and architecture, and the applied or useful arts, characterised as 'Industrial Art', a term covering any useful object produced by mechanical means. The term 'Fine Art' meant 'beauty applied to mechanical production', or, in his own phrase, 'Art Manufactures', as opposed to 'the Polite Arts' of painting and sculpture. This definition of Fine Art had to be followed if the useful arts were to reach the high standards of craftsmanship and design that were usually lacking in Britain. The newly made distinction between the polite and the applied arts was destructive in that the effectiveness of mechanical reproduction removed the expectation of creative energy from architectural adornment and the useful arts, giving the polite arts a higher status on account of their supposed originality. Here, Cole was subverting the traditional hierarchy of the arts and the long-standing division between the liberal and the mechanical. By extension, the people who produced the applied arts, and particularly the craftsmen, deserved a new consideration.[47]

In analysing the Great Exhibition's lineage, a contrast was regularly made between 'the entirely aristocratic nature' of earlier displays and the current adaptation of manufacture 'to the wants of the *masses*.'[48] Industrial art provided for all classes. In addition, the ability of such exhibitions to eliminate social divisions was a constant official theme.

Have not the Prince and the cotton-spinner, the peer and the merchant, the Celt and the Saxon, the Greek and the Frank, the Hebrew and the Russ, sat down, for the first time in the history of the world, at one table with one common object in view – the advancement of the mass?[49]

blithely enquired *The Illustrated Exhibitor* in 1851, addressing geographical and class union and introducing as an objective the improvement of working conditions. In general, the exhibition discourse dwells on two elements of the relationship between the classes: the dignity of the workers and the obligations of the upper orders. Both ideas could be realised through the benevolent medium of art.

THE WORKING CLASSES

An interesting development in the literature around these exhibitions, and highly relevant to the municipal museum and gallery, is the changing definition of the term 'working classes'. The phrase, emerging early in the nineteenth century, predicated a collective identity for workers seen not as a riotous mob but as people gainfully employed. They came to be viewed as a positive force, economically and even culturally.

This approach took some time to develop. In 1851, as we have seen, one of the proclaimed purposes of the exhibition was to bring together the classes through cultural osmosis. In fact the organising Royal Commission excluded the working classes from active participation: during the planning process it suppressed the Central Working Classes Committee (a body which in fact hardly contained anyone who could be identified as working class) to the annoyance of such prominent members as Dickens and Thackeray.[50] Working people were consigned to the role of spectators (Fig. 68). With experience, particularly of the commercial benefits of attracting a huge popular public, these attitudes shifted. The minutely prepared business plan for the 1857 exhibition stated that while the sale of season tickets was important it was the popular audience taking advantage of the reduced admission price who would make the greatest financial impact: 'It is…to the shillings we must look mainly for success; and if one million and a half…visited the Dublin collection…we may fairly hope that a much larger number would visit the Manchester Exhibition of 1857.'[51] Care was taken to lower the admission charge

68 'The First shilling Day', from George Cruikshank and Henry Meyhew, *World's Show 1851, or The Adventures of Mr and Mrs Sandboys and Family* (1851). Cheap admission days to the Great Exhibition began about three weeks after the opening. Though Mayhew commented on the disappointingly low attendance, the days were regarded as symbolic of friendship between social classes, and commentators remarked on the visitors' good behaviour. The crowds, eager on arrival, leave in a state of exhaustion.

on some days to allow all but the very poorest to visit. In 1857 it was reduced on Saturday afternoons (which were becoming increasingly free for workers) as low as sixpence, while in the reverse direction a specially high fee of 2s 6d for the first ten days (and on Thursdays) allowed the wealthy their customary privileged viewing (Fig. 69).

While the *Manchester Guardian* published a series of 'critical notices' in its columns, reprinted as handbooks for an educated audience, a new type of

69 *Visitors to the Manchester Art Treasures Exhibition Looking at Nelly O'Brien* drawn on a page of the catalogue by Richard Doyle. One of the most famous and fantastical Victorian illustrators, Doyle worked with Dickens and Thackeray and illustrated his own fairy stories (Victoria and Albert Museum).

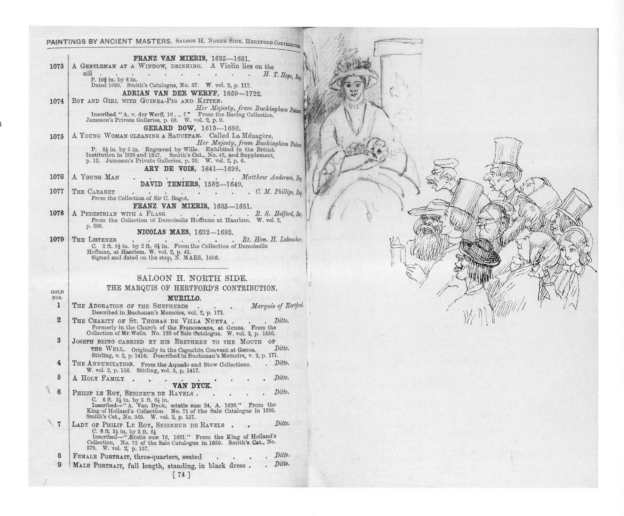

exhibition literature was also on sale. *What to See, and Where to See It!*, priced at a penny, offered 'An Operative's Guide' to the exhibition: it was 'dedicated to the Working Classes of Lancashire and Yorkshire' and given an official imprimatur by being sold at the exhibition bookstall. The booklet's assumption was that workers would be interested and pleased by seeing fine examples of craftsmanship in their own fields: in cognitive terms the operative needed to be kept at the level appropriate to his working life, while being imaginatively engaged in the spectacle. 'The carpenter, the joiner, the cabinet maker, and the carver will be specially interested in the examination of the works of ancient and modern execution' and by the 'beautiful Bed, by Charles of Warrington' while 'the smith, the founder, and the worker in the precious metals' would find it 'profitable and amusing to notice how the ancient workers managed to overcome the difficulties of converting to the purpose, and adorning the most

stubborn metals'.[52] The language expressed the close links between pleasure and instruction: by studying older methods of production workers would improve their skills but they would also be 'amused' – that is to say, engaged and interested. Only in the field of textiles was it suggested that such reactions might be elicited from all levels of society, and even then this shared response was limited to women: 'This department will afford pleasure…to the female sex in general, rich and poor, who exercise the needle for pleasure and profit.'[53] Though the tone evokes a lecturer addressing the operatives, the importance of this guide lies in its identification of working people as a discrete and valuable audience. The tone anticipates the information offered by municipal museums and galleries a few years later, as well as their displays directed at an attentive, sober and acquiescent working-class public.

This newly positive definition of working people reflected the recognition among a group of influen-

100

INTERIOR VIEW OF THE EXHIBITION—EAST END.

70   Interior view of the North London Working Classes Industrial Exhibition 1864, from Wilson 1864.

71   *Illustrated Memorial of the North London Working Classes Industrial Exhibition 1864* by James French Wilson (1864).

ILLUSTRATED
MEMORIAL
OF THE
NORTH LONDON
WORKING CLASSES
Industrial
EXHIBITION
1864

categorised during the mid-century. The old idea of labour as a punishment or as an evil and unpleasant necessity necessary for the well-being of society and the individual, lost ground in mid-century under the influence of such sages as Carlyle and Ruskin. In the execution of 'expressive work', men were able to fulfil themselves through work: as Barringer notes, 'Ruskin asserts that expressive work, properly conceived, is the process by which the ungendered human being, what he calls a "working creature," is "made a man." Work is the process through which identity, human wholeness, is formed.'[54] Various meanings came to be associated with this concept, notably the idea of salvation through work advocated by Carlyle in *Past and Present*. In this discourse hard physical labour, previously regarded as the lowliest of occupations, gained at least in theory a newly honourable status.

These ideas were expressed in the endlessly fertile and flexible theatre of the temporary exhibition by such events as the North London Working Classes Industrial Exhibition of 1864, an event in the long tradition of Mechanics' Institutes displays and recently described as 'the efflorescence of working men's exhibitions' (Fig. 70).[55] It was held in the Agricultural Hall in the then strongly working-class area of Liverpool Road, Islington. This display enjoyed the support of prominent public figures, including two past or future Liberal Prime Ministers, in Earl (Lord John) Russell and W. E. Gladstone, as well as that great campaigner for the rights of the deprived, the seventh Earl of Shaftesbury.[56] All three made speeches at various ceremonies. The exhibition was elevated by being presented as a successor to 1851 and 1862 but in a new guise: since 'In those undertakings the Working Classes were chiefly represented by their employers, who devoted their capital to the production of the best specimens of skilled workmanship, and received the honours awarded', it was now time for 'a fair representation of the Working Classes'.[57] Labour was increasingly viewed as a strength and a virtue. With a realisation of the 'perennial nobleness and even sacredness in Work', workers were to be dignified for their ability to be creative in a setting that abandoned the old barriers between liberal and mechanical arts (Fig. 71).[58]

The displays consisted exclusively of paintings, drawings, models and craft objects made by working

tial writers, notably Thomas Carlyle, of the dignity of labour, an expression that was repeatedly used. As Tim Barringer has discussed with reference to paintings, including Ford Madox Brown's *Work* (created between 1852 and 1865), labour was variously

people for their own enjoyment. Although the patrons included clergymen and other worthies, the event asserted what would today be called the social empowerment of the workers, with the organising committee including a tailor, watchmaker, gas-meter maker, house decorator and schoolmaster, but no grandees. The enterprise confirmed, for Russell, the impression that 'the working classes of London are…the highest working classes in the world, [making this great community] the head of the civilised world in all those works which betoken civilisation and progress'.[59] His thesis that the working people of London – and by extension, Britain – should be rated among the justifications for national pride and constituted an element in the 'civilization and progress' of the capital was a novel idea in the light of the concurrent doubt about the possible bad behaviour of such people in privileged places. Russell was not alone in his views. Attended by enormous crowds – almost 100,000 in the second week – the exhibition attracted widespread favourable reviews, in *The Times*, *Daily News* and *Morning Star*.[60] Though these articles tended, in the manner of the time, to cast the working classes in the role of others, with *The Times* referring to the unfortunate tendency of the working classes during leisure hours to engage in 'idleness of the lowest sensual enjoyment',[61] the ode for the opening ceremony conveys a more positive attitude:

> All honour to the working man,
> Who worketh "with his might,"
> In patience and in honesty,
> At what he knows is right;
> Whose life, though pass'd in poverty,
> Will bear the light of day,
> Nor fears his works should follow him,
> Die when or where he may.[62]

Staged a very few years before the municipal art museum movement gathered strength, this exhibition represented an acceptance of art (at least, home-made art) as an instrument of virtuous pleasure and self-expression among all social classes. As *The Times* remarked, 'it is not easy to overrate its influence upon the career of a workman brought within its sphere'.[63]

Continuing for some years, such workers' exhibitions were seen as valuable in various ways. The *Art Journal* in 1880 acclaimed 'Workmen's Industrial Exhibitions' for encouraging 'industrial, artistic, and even scientific pursuits' by those for whom 'their daily occupation affords no scope' – not only for their own good but as a means of maintaining 'ingenuity, skill, and effort' for the benefit of the country, faced as it was with formidable international competition.[64]

SHARING THEIR CHOICEST TREASURES

Within the discourse around the 1857 exhibition, the propertied classes were regarded as bound to contribute to social harmony by extending their possessions to as broad an audience as possible. The *Report of the Executive Committee for 1857* stated that when the event was conceived by J.C. Deane, organiser of the 1853 Dublin exhibition, he wrote to Thomas Fairbairn of Manchester, 'urging…that the Art wealth of England would supply examples of equal interest and an aggregate of greater value than any other country in the world, and that application for the loan of these treasures for an object of public utility would be met with promptness and liberality by their owners'.[65] Accordingly, the display presented the wealth of the (largely private) art collections in Britain that had recently been published by Waagen, whose books were seen as a prime motive for the exhibition. Foreign loans were by and large excluded, no doubt for practical reasons but also because the event was intended to emphasise the capacity of native collections to illustrate the entire narrative of world art.

The idea of the sharing of treasures was enunciated by the Prince Consort in his speech at the opening:

> We behold a feast which the rich, and they who have, set before those to whom fortune has denied the higher luxuries of life – bringing forth from the innermost recesses of their private dwellings, and intrusting to your care, their choicest and most cherished treasures, in order to gratify the nation at large…[66]

By and large these hopes were realised. The exhibition organisers were indefatigable in their researches: the Duke of Portland had 'given Mr. Cunningham the fullest liberty at Welbeck [Abbey], and the vast historical collections of the huge house have been rummaged – not the reception rooms, or bedrooms, or corridors only, but the attics, and still-rooms, and grooms' and coachmen's lodgings over stables'.[67] For the *Art Journal* the exhibition demonstrated the 'matchless wealth which…might one day make up the sum of the national treasure'.[68] This was the time when British private collections were arguably at their richest, amplified by specialist collections of early German and Italian paintings or of drawings.[69] Ownership was held to bring obligations, and non-lenders were identified in such publications as the *National Review*, *Jerrold's Guide to the Exhibition* and the *Manchester Guardian*. The *Guardian* also pointed out in its discussion of the British Portrait Gallery that 'Cashiobury, Hatfield, and Petworth – three of the houses which contain the most valuable treasures of historical art in England – contribute nothing'.[70] For the owner of an important collection a refusal to participate in this patriotic exercise was seen as a dereliction of duty – a further stage in the concept of private collections becoming part of a national heritage.

THE EXHIBITIONS AS A FORCE FOR EDUCATION

The Manchester exhibition was viewed in advanced circles as a means of educating all sectors of the community: aesthetically, socially and morally. The morally beneficial effect of art had been a theme of exhibition literature since at least 1851, when a commentary had declared that 'within the crystal walls of the palace…forms of beauty yet undreamed of rise before the student's eyes in rich and glorious profusion, each telling its own tale of wisdom, and learning, and power, and might, and greatness, in words of great and unmistakable meaning'.[71] In 1856 Prince Albert expressed the educational purpose of the Manchester exhibition in a letter to Lord Ellesmere, President of the General Council of the Exhibition:

> That national usefulness [of the exhibition] might, however, be found in the educational direction which may be given to the whole scheme. No country invests a larger amount of capital in works of Arts of all kinds than England; and in none

almost is so little done for Art-education! If the collection you propose to form were made to illustrate the history of Art in a chronological and systematic arrangement, it would speak powerfully to the public mind, and enable, in a practical way, the most uneducated eye to gather the lessons which ages of thought and scientific research have attempted to abstract; and would present to the world for the first time a gallery such as no other country could produce…[72]

He enunciates a cardinal principle, the hope that 1857 would serve as a grand demonstration of art history suitable for 'the most uneducated eye' rather than just the connoisseur's.

In all these exhibitions, the visual displays were supplemented by printed material so voluminous as to create a dual but united discourse, exhibition and literature functioning as a pedagogic unity. The literature was addressed to various levels of reader: the educated, the middling, the simple. Thus the 1857 *Official Catalogue* was supported by *A Walk through the Art-Treasures Exhibition at Manchester, Under the Guidance of Dr Waagen*, which offered brief summaries of important works of art, largely drawn from Waagen's previous publications. This was intended 'not for the small number of connoisseurs, but for the larger proportion of lovers of art who seek both pleasure and instruction within the walls of this Exhibition'.[73] Explanatory catalogues on individual subjects were also produced at short notice, such as the *Handbook to the Museum of Ornamental Art* by J.B. Waring, the artist who acted as superintendent of the works of ornamental art and sculpture.

In addition to their role in softening social and national divisions, exhibitions came to assume a pedagogic function not only in the field of industrial art but also in relation to 'the fine arts', at a time when the didactic art-historical exhibition of the twentieth century did not exist. They were seen by contemporaries as shaping the reputation of individual artists and of whole schools, especially contemporary British art. In 1874 Samuel Redgrave outlined the events that had contributed to the rising popularity of the native school: the 1862 London and the 1867 Paris International Exhibitions with their strong representation of British painting, the Special Exhibition of Portrait Miniatures (which he had organised) in 1865, and the three exhibitions of 'National Portraits' put on at South Kensington between 1866 and 1868, which covered the history of England from the late Middle Ages to the present.[74] Ernest Chesneau, one of the most enthusiastic (if sometimes guarded) upholders of English art, also stressed the importance of international exhibitions, singling out the 1855 Paris Exhibition for opening the eyes of the French public to the British school: it offered 'a revelation of a style and a school, of the existence of which they had hitherto had no idea'.[75]

The interest shown in British art in the Manchester exhibition was extended in 1862. Francis Turner Palgrave's *Handbook to the Fine Art Collections in the International Exhibition of 1862* set out the explanations parallel to the displays, providing an assiduous reader with a history of art that was reasonably comprehensive, though by no means universally enthusiastic. Palgrave gave particular attention to the British paintings dominating the 'Modern Masters' department, which out of almost seven hundred works showed only some fifty by foreign artists (Dutch, German and French, notably Ary Scheffer). Homage was paid to Reynolds, as father of the English school, along with Hogarth, Gainsborough and Wilson, Turner, Landseer and Wilkie. The wide range included many recent young artists, some forgotten today. This was the first time that an organised historical overview of the British school had been created, and it anticipated the first major book on the subject, Richard and Samuel Redgrave's *A Century of Painters of the English School* of 1866.[76]

In terms of academic organisation, many of the protagonists of 1851 reappeared. Waring's intellectually ambitious and richly illustrated *Art Treasures of the United Kingdom from the Art Treasures Exhibition* contained essays by authorities including the designer Owen Jones, who had directed the interior decoration and planning of the Great Exhibition; the architect Matthew Digby Wyatt, secretary to the executive committee of the 1851 exhibition, on *The Industrial Arts of the Nineteenth Century*; A.W. Franks, a rising young curator at the British Museum; J.C. Robinson from the South Kensington Museum, established on its new site in that year; and George Scharf, the exhibition's art secretary. This publication, like the exhibition itself, gathered together many members of the influential new cadre

of art administrators around the South Kensington Museum. Through the Wallis family at Birmingham and Nottingham, and through Henry Cole, this group was to make a major contribution to the creation of municipal art galleries, reinforcing links between the provinces and South Kensington that were to be much stronger than their links with other national museums.

VISITORS TO THE 1857 EXHIBITION

However much thought was given to these publications, the educational success of 1857 – and of other displays – seems to have been limited, depending, contrary to the Prince Consort's hopes, on the intellectual attainments of each visitor. The better educated appear to have found the material on offer gruelling but ultimately inspiring. The ardent young Henry Gibbs, recalling his youth in later life as a Manchester cotton manufacturer, made regular four-hour visits to what he saw as 'the glory of Manchester', an exhibition that contained 'the cream of art, collected from the highest sources'.[77] Determined to miss nothing, he found himself repeatedly drawn to Turner. For the public in general, he recorded, two landscapes by John Linnell and *The Death of Chatterton* by Henry Wallis were the big draws, though 'the mothers had a difficulty in removing their children' from a Snyders still life (Fig. 72).[78] He gave no time to 'the forests of statuary, of which there appeared to be no end', or the applied arts.[79]

What emerges from his account is the painstaking desire for improvement of a largely self-educated man, along with a patriotic passion for the British school and a preference for painting above all other media. His comments are corroborated by a man of higher social standing, who had travelled some distance to attend. A copy of the one-shilling *Catalogue of the Art Treasures of the United Kingdom Collected at Manchester in 1857* (a thick little volume) survives that belonged to John Peck of the village of Wisbech St Mary in Cambridgeshire.[80] Peck was a wealthy farmer, road surveyor and churchwarden, and a regular visitor with his family to the theatre and to exhibitions.[81] During his three-day visit in August, he thoroughly annotated his catalogue, not with

72 *Figures with Fruit and Game* by Frans Snyders, *c*.1635. Oil on canvas, 125.8 × 122 cm. This was one of the most popular paintings in the Manchester Art Treasures Exhibition. It belonged to the Earl of Aylesford, and was sold from that collection through Thomas Agnew and Sons in 1888 – a characteristic example of the aristocracy disposing of works of art in the late nineteenth century (Kenwood House, The Iveagh Bequest).

73 Nathaniel Hawthorne photographed by James Wallace Black, *c*. 1860–4.

personal comments but with remarks on the genesis of the exhibition and on individual pictures largely taken from Waagen's commentaries. Peck's painstaking transcriptions testify to the authority wielded by these publications, as well as the seriousness of such a visitor.

An even greater determination fully to experience the exhibition was recorded by Nathaniel Hawthorne (Fig. 73), already a successful novelist and coming to the end of his service as American consul in Liverpool. Hawthorne arrived in Manchester in July 1857 at the beginning of a stay of almost a month, primarily to study the exhibition. 'I mean to go again and again', he wrote after his first visit, 'many times more, and will take each day some one department, and so endeavour to get some real use and improvement out of what I see.'[82] His initial enthusiasm was soon countered by the *Angst* that must have affected many: 'I was unquiet, from a hopelessness of being

able to enjoy it fully'.[83] But he persisted. The Dutch masters pleased him most, at first, among the Old Masters, his comments ('Such life-like representations of cabbages, onions, brass kettles, and kitchen crockery') echoing the enthusiasm for technical virtuosity that Haydon had mocked.[84] Gradually he found himself appreciating other historic paintings, rating Murillo 'about the noblest and purest painter that ever lived'.[85] Such assiduous application was not possible for most visitors.

Several visitors expressed doubt about the success of the educational objectives. Interpretation (in the modern sense) was not addressed outside the traditional medium of the printed publication: a proposal that exhibits should be comprehensively labelled was rejected on the mean-spirited grounds that labelling would reduce catalogue sales.[86] Hawthorne, for one, realised that his enthusiasm was not universally shared. Characteristically for the time, he studied the reactions of other visitors, concluding that for many people the exhibition was unbearable, partly because it was unexplained other than through catalogues aimed at the highly literate. Though he was touched by the eagerness of the 'shilling visitors' to learn, in the end 'the Exhibition, I think, does not reach the lower classes at all; in fact, it could not reach them, nor their betters either, without a good deal of study to help it out'.[87] He commented after a later visit, 'The exhibition must be quite thrown away on the mass of spectators'.[88] Charles Dickens wrote in similar terms, remarking in his discussion of the exhibition in *Household Words* that

> The working man has not come forward eagerly, neither with his shilling, nor with that glow of enthusiasm for the thing of beauty, which, it was promised him, would be a joy for ever. Even when he has been admitted gratis, the attractions of Knott-Mill Fair and Belle Vue Gardens have beaten the Art Treasures hollow.[89]

Ever energetic in his views and sympathetic to the cause of popular education, Dickens regretted that

> The plain fact is, that a collection of pictures of various "schools" excites no interest, and affords but little pleasure to the uninstructed eye. The ancient way of imitating nature at different epochs, or the manner of copying her in various countries, is, to the factory-worker or the farm-labourer, simply unintelligible. The only school he has the wit to recognise, is the school of Nature; and that era or that nation in which she is imitated with the greatest truth and fervour presents the only school which his unlearned taste can appreciate.[90]

He was no more impressed by the behaviour of the middle classes – 'the majority of the well-dressed crowd gossiped and grouped round the music, promenaded and looked at and admired each other – did everything, in short, except examine the pictures'.[91] His comments can be taken to epitomise the views of many of the philanthropically inclined regarding 'art for the people', that Old Master paintings held no interest for the working man or woman (Figs 74, 75).

The disparity between the organisers' ambitions and the inability of visitors to cope with these unmediated visual feasts was developed in other commentaries that suggest a growing interest in popular education related to the artistic or scientific display. For the engineer Robert Mallet analysing the 1862 exhibition,

> To one observant of human faces, nothing was more clear than the expression of vacant bewilderment of the vast majority of those who wandered about the Exhibition, like sheep without a shepherd, dazed and confounded by innumerable objects, all exciting curiosity, but of the nature, origin, use, or even names of most of which, they knew nothing. To thousands thus the Exhibition has been a dazzling but meaningless phantasmagoria. This want hand-books, however, cannot supply. We had ourselves, on more than one occasion, abundant proofs of the eagerness with which men, and women too, some with rough visages and hard hands, listened to explanations given with lucid brevity and distinctness, in reply to some inquiry for information, by one…[who] is…inscribed high upon the pedestal of scientific discovery.[92]

Such stupefaction must have been general. Although Victorian illustrations show spectators reading or listening to official texts, the comments of Hawthorne and Mallet reflect a growing recognition that such texts were inappropriate for less educated people. In short, the didactic intentions of this, and other, exhibitions – the intentions that had raised them to the highest level – had failed. From such perceptions of failure developed the educational programmes of the municipal art gallery (Fig. 76).

The doubts expressed by these perceptive viewers were reflected in official figures and, to a lesser extent, official reports. The many thousands of 'shilling' visitors who had been hoped for did not attend, or at least not voluntarily (many were brought by their employers). While impressive, the total attendance of 1,336,715 missed the early target, and though the reports resonate with triumphalism, they also convey an undercurrent of disappointment.[93]

A FORUM FOR INNOVATION

The world exhibitions, with their great open spaces and their championing of modernity, provided a fertile field for technical innovation. Numerous

74 *Two Rooms of Visitors to the Manchester Art Treasures Exhibition* by Charlotte Ellis. This drawing and Figs 69, 75 and 76 are taken from a copy of the *Catalogue of the Art Treasures of the United Kingdom, Collected at Manchester in 1857* that belonged to Maude Stanley, a notable activist on behalf of women's rights who initiated a series of clubs for working girls and would have been interested in, and amused by, the reaction of the audience to the Manchester exhibition. It is interleaved with blank pages to which drawings of paintings in the exhibition as well as satirical sketches by Ellis, Richard Doyle and Stanley herself were fixed (Victoria and Albert Museum).

75 *Outraged Lady at the Manchester Art Treasures Exhibition* by Richard Doyle (Victoria and Albert Museum).

DRAWINGS IN WATER-COLOURS.

MISS FANNY CORBAUX.

690	THE STRANGER	Thomas Kibble, Esq.

F. O. FINCH.

691	COMPOSITION PASTORAL	Thomas Griffiths, Esq.
692	PLEASURE GROUNDS—MOONLIGHT	George Hanbury, Esq.
693	LANDSCAPE AND CATTLE EVENING	Lord Hadde
693a	COMPOSITION PASTORAL	Miss Griffiths.

HARTMAN.

694	LE BENITIER	Carl Haag, Esq.

NUIJOU.

695	THE PORCH	J. H. Hawkins, Esq.

EDWARD H. CORBOULD.

696	SCENE FROM THE PROPHÈTE	Her Majesty the Queen.

PRITCHETT.

698	MARKET PLACE	John Pender, Esq.
699	VIEW IN VENICE	J. F. Bateman, Esq.
700	VIEW IN VENICE	T. Schunck, Esq.

I. R. HERBERT, R.A.

701	FALIERO AND FOSCARI	G. P. Kenworthy, Esq.
702	ABDUCTION OF THE BRIDES OF VENICE	H. W. Capes, Esq.
703	THE TWO FOSCARI	Ditto.
704	THE OUTCAST	Charles Pemberton, Esq.

D. MACLISE, R.A.

705	SPIRIT OF CHIVALRY	Ditto.
706	MARRIAGE OF STRONGBOW WITH EVA	W. Turner, Esq.
707	THE DISENCHANTMENT OF BOTTOM	T. Birchall, Esq.

BROCKEDON.

707a	COMO	Messrs. Brockedon.
707b	CIVITA CASTELLANA	Ditto.
707c	AMALFI	Ditto.
707d	BASSANO	Ditto.
707e	ASSISI	Ditto.
707f	TERRACINA	Ditto.

CHARLES LANDSEER, R.A.

709	AN OLD BARONIAL HALL	R. Freeland, Esq.

J. B. PYNE.

710	LAGO MAGGIORE	Miss Ashton.
711	LAGO MAGGIORE	John Pender, Esq.
712	THE DRACHENFELS	John Barratt, Esq.
713	THE LOWER END OF THE CAMPAGNA	Messrs. Agnew.
714	HEIDELBERG ON THE NECKAR	Ditto.
715	CASTLE OF ISCHIA	R. Freeland, Esq.
715a	VENICE	Charles Pemberton, Esq.

GEORGE BOWLES.

716	PART OF CRUMLIN VIADUCT	R. W. Kenneard, Esq.
717	THE AVENUE, SOUTHAMPTON	H. J. Prentice, Esq.

[198]

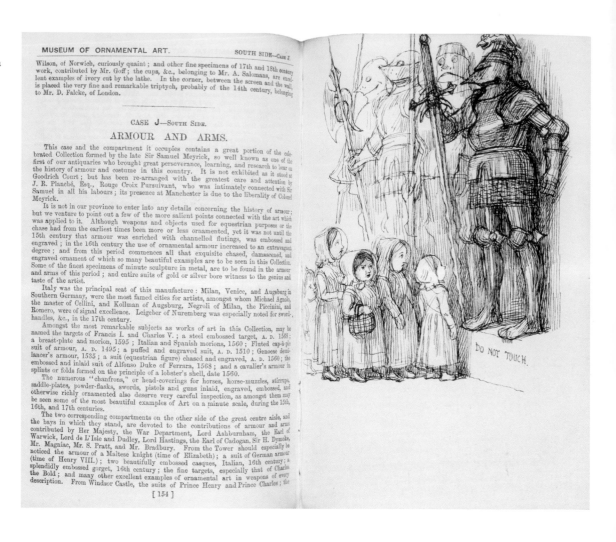

photographs from various countries were displayed at the Great Exhibition: 'It was the moment at which the new medium achieved critical mass'.[94] Both in 1857 and 1862, the expansive and exploratory nature of a temporary exhibition encouraged innovation and the recognition of new technology. At Manchester in 1857 a section was devoted to photography, in which the celebrated photographer P.H. Delamotte was invited 'to undertake the collection and arranging of Specimens of the Photographic Art, and to adopt such measures as he might consider desirable to secure an attractive collection'.[95] The emphasis on the visual attractiveness of 'Photographic Art' was significant at a time when its status as an art form was controversial. As the first Director of the new South Kensington Museum, Henry Cole embraced photography both as a means of recording the collections and as an artistic medium, setting up a department of photography

and acquiring works by pioneering and artistically ambitious photographers such as Julia Margaret Cameron, as well as documentary images.

This approach was taken further in 1862, when almost a thousand prints were shown, accompanied by a dedicated catalogue filled with the advertisements considered an appropriate accompaniment to photography. The catalogue commented that at the time of the Great Exhibition photography had been insufficiently advanced to be put in a class of its own, whereas now it deserved its own section.[96]

This reflection of the importance of technical innovation was characteristic of the exhibition material, since these exhibitions offered the best means of announcing and advertising technical progress in every sphere. A notable feature of 1862 was the hall dedicated to electric telegraphy: 'Telegraphy, which in 1851 was still in its infancy, has progressed so rapidly throughout the world, that the

WRITING ROOM

TELEGRAPH OFFICE.

SMOKING ROOM

POST OFFICE

POLICE

POST OFFICE

POLICE OFFICE

77   The Telegraphy Hall at the 1862 International Exhibition, from the *Illustrated London News*, 16 August 1862.

more cautiously as pageants of the past. In the museums that followed them, a similar appetite for technical novelty was also apparent.

THE PLEASURES OF THE SENSES

Once the universal exhibition encompassed the fine arts, it exploded the restraints that confined the traditional art museum: art could be presented in conjunction not only with objects never seen within the portals of the National Gallery but also with activities that would have seemed equally incongruous there. For a start, the ear as well as the eye was addressed, whether through musical recitals or through loud, intrusive noises from machinery.

The gratification of physical pleasure was a further innovation, notably the provision of food and drink. Its attractions were conveyed in a sensually charged description from a *Manchester Guardian* handbook in 1857. The visitor who has viewed the whole exhibition 'will indeed have earned that sustenation of his inner man which Mr. Donald has catered for so vastly, by anticipation, and oh! how he will enjoy that marbled sirloin of Aberdeen beef – those plump thighs of Dorking chickens – and a cool and sparkling bottle of Moet, topped up with a becoming share of a magnum of that '40 port now piled in fabulous numbers of dozens under the floor of Mr. Donald's strong room'.[98] The association of gustatory with artistic pleasures had existed for many years in the festive setting of the theatre and the opera house, while sporting events, notably racing, have been associated with such pleasures for centuries: food and wine were sold in ancient Rome at the Circus Maximus and the Colosseum, but never in modern art galleries.[99] At a large-scale temporary exhibition, the epitome of Free Trade, such licence was permissible. The idea that refreshments should be available to all visitors at all times was of course fuelled by commercial considerations and a wish to retain visitors longer, but also by a new sense of an exhibition as an event not limited to beholding. If people could pay to enter, they could pay to eat and drink (Fig. 78).

For all the earnestness of their declared purposes, these exhibitions introduced the idea of a huge public forum in which physical or mental activity

whole globe may be said to be encircled by its wires; and the new inventions and contrivances for the more rapid transmission of intelligence by this means, form one of the most interesting courts in the Exhibition.'[97] Such excitement over exploring, and announcing, technological advances was characteristic of the thirst for new ways of improving the human condition that pervaded the exhibitions (Fig. 77). They served as theatres for innovation, and

could hardly be controlled. They made possible the broadening of the Victorian museum into an arena of entertainment. The novel idea of physical satisfaction in a place dedicated to the arts was given permanent form in the famous refreshment rooms at South Kensington, the first museum in the world with a purpose-built restaurant pavilion.[100] Shortly afterwards, this approach extended to provincial galleries. At Liverpool's Autumn Exhibitions a fully equipped refreshment bar was installed among the pictures (Fig. 79), while from its opening Nottingham Castle Museum offered refreshments, including beer, in what was described in the licensing register as 'Nottingham Castle. Ale House'.[101] These

innovations signify a new attitude to the role of the gallery within society, as a place that satisfied the demands of leisure.

Catering represented only one of the pleasures for body and mind on offer. Ovid in *The Art of Love* recommended a horse race at the Circus Maximus as a suitable place to make amatory advances. A comparable erotic interest emerged in the Great Exhibition. Much energy was expended in discussing the potentially disturbing nature of some of the sculptures, with a group of bishops refusing to take part in the opening ceremony if some erotic sculptures were not covered up, a request met by the introduction of temporary fig-leaves.[102] In the same

80 *View of the Great Exhibition showing Hiram Powers' The Greek Slave* by John Absolon, 1851. Lithograph. Executed in 1844, the statue aroused such controversy that it was exhibited with a protective canopy for use when necessary. Powers successfully interpreted it, however, as a moving depiction of an enslaved Christian, awaiting her fate 'with intense anxiety, tempered indeed by the support of her reliance upon the goodness of God'. The work became a symbol of enslaved virtue for American abolitionists (Bridgeman Art Library).

spirit, a curtain was introduced to be drawn when necessary around the naked figure of the *Greek Slave* by Hiram Powers, disturbing because it showed a supposedly living woman rather than a mythological figure (Fig. 80).[103] In the 1853 Exhibition of Art-Industry in Dublin this discourse was taken further. The Exhibition was of course a decorous event, which for the first time juxtaposed paintings with industrial art (Fig. 81). Through a judicious selection of the foreign schools (and countries) most in favour in Britain, the Fine Arts Court offered a contrast between 'the productions of British Artists, and on the other [wall] of those of the artists of Germany, Belgium and France'.[104] *The Illustrated Catalogue*, issued in connection with the *Art Journal*, sounded

another note (Fig. 82). Amid the serious and impeccably loyalist explanations of the exhibits, the publisher inserted at intervals full-size prints of statues which were 'judiciously scattered' through the exhibition. Without exception, these showed near-naked and relatively revealing full lengths of women – an interesting choice of subject in a Catholic country at a time when nudity, however artistic, was a delicate phenomenon.

MUSIC AND ART

The remit of the universal exhibition also included an element of synaesthesia in the status given to

112

music. In 1851 choral singing and orchestral playing enjoyed an important role in the ceremonies, and this role became even more significant in 1857. From the earliest stages of planning, music was envisaged: it was 'deemed expedient, to enhance the general attraction of the Exhibition, that there should be a daily performance of music in the building'.[105] Its role in a public context and as an accompaniment to outdoor recreation belonged to a long tradition, from the music played in Vauxhall Gardens early in the eighteenth century to the bandstands erected in Victorian parks.[106] The development of concert halls and museums runs in parallel, in each case in com-

petition with a popular counter-culture represented by the music hall and the print shop.

Like learned societies, musical performances late in the eighteenth century were fostered by private bodies such as the Manchester society that from the 1770s onwards organised an annual programme of twelve 'Gentlemen's Concerts'. As with learned societies, it cost a substantial sum to join (four guineas), with 'ladies and strangers' attending by invitation.[107] This was a society made up of bourgeois Mancunians, including the city's numerous German-born inhabitants and favouring German music.

82 Catalogue of the Exhibition of Art-Industry, Dublin, 1853. This event was notable as the first world exhibition to include paintings, a precedent that was widely followed.

tion, the commission was awarded to Hallé, who 'undertook to form a permanent Orchestra for daily performances, and choral performances at the Inauguration of the Exhibition, and on other occasions'.[109] His exhibition orchestra was the first wholly professional orchestra to be established in a British city, and was much admired. For Henry Gibbs, the concerts were 'instructing and delighting thousands upon thousands of thirsty musical souls', and he wondered 'how can any of these men [the players] be so human as to die?'[110] At the exhibition's close, Hallé, determined that the orchestra should survive, personally funded an annual series of concerts aimed at a wide audience (Figs 84, 85).[111] Under such leadership, by the 1880s it was accepted that 'musical cultivation is the safest and surest Method of popular culture'. This approach was to spread far beyond Manchester and was followed in many other towns (fig. 83).[112]

Such events operated in direct opposition to popular entertainment on the other side of the social division: music halls and entertainments in public houses. Faucher found in the gin-shop 'a species of palace' where music, dancing and exhibitions had been added to the attractions, 'in Liverpool, so [in Manchester], the swelling of the organ, and the sounds of the violin and the piano, resound in their large saloons'.[113] Here as elsewhere much of the alarm aroused by popular culture derived from the observer's preconceptions: Faucher's translator into English, an anonymous member of the Manchester Athenaeum, commented more positively that these musical events were signs of 'increasing temperance, and improved habits amongst them [the workers]'.[114] Reach characteristically took an optimistic approach to the Apollo in the London Road, Manchester. There he found a long narrow room, packed with 'a dense swarm of people', almost all decently dressed and including several family parties: 'just as I entered, nearly two hundred voices, male and female, were entreating Susanna not to cry for the minstrel who was "going to Alabama with his banjo on his knee."'[115]

In parallel to art galleries, large-scale concerts became increasingly popular. The Leeds Philharmonic Society, established in 1870, was one of several large choral societies, often associated with Nonconformism.[116] At the Crystal Palace, reopened in Sydenham in 1854, concerts – including massed

Like municipal museums absorbing the collections of learned societies, Victorian musicians transformed the existing semi-private provision for the genteel into a public resource, supposedly superior to vulgar popular entertainments. The Gentlemen's Concerts orchestra formed the basis for the famous Hallé Orchestra, created by the German-born Karl/ Charles Hallé, who had been appointed Director of the Gentlemen's Concerts in 1853.[108] When tenders were received to provide music at the 1857 exhibi-

83 The chorus of the Sheffield Musical Union outside the Mappin Art Gallery, Weston Park.

84 *Sir Charles Hallé* by C.A. Duval, 1851.

choirs of 2,500 and more – dominated London's musical life, a situation that lasted to the end of the century.[117] These concerts, which included triumphant Handel festivals, were on a huge scale: the opening ceremony of the reconstructed palace included a concert featuring singers from many provincial choirs, which were considered superior to London ones (Fig. 86). Following this example music and the visual arts came to be closely linked in some of the larger new museums, with an organ often a central element of the principal hall.[118] The hall at the first Glasgow Art Gallery, with its organ played every Sunday afternoon, was an excessively successful example of the conjunction of the two art forms, the concerts proving so popular that the crowds became a danger and the recitals were terminated.[119] The new Kelvingrove Art Gallery was furnished with an even larger, even finer, organ (Fig. 87). In the case of both music and the visual arts, mass popular participation in the arts was regarded, for the first time in Britain, as possible and desirable.

While this wish to extend an enjoyment of music to a general audience was analogous to the work of museums, the level of sophistication and experiment of the music programmes was considerably higher

than the level of art collecting. Like August Manus at the Crystal Palace, who in pursuit of 'the establishment of a classical repertory' introduced his audiences to such unfamiliar works as Schubert's and Schumann's orchestral music, Brahms and Smetana, Hallé regularly played Mozart, Beethoven, Weber, Mendelssohn, Berlioz, Verdi, Wagner, Dvorák, composers who were half-forgotten or new and unfamiliar in Britain.[120] Progressive in his tastes and aware of his audience's weaknesses (he remarked in his diary in 1855 that 'public taste in England is still rather backward'), Hallé was determined that their taste could be improved, much like the German-inspired organisers of the Manchester Art Treasures Exhibition.[121]

A disparity emerges between the provision for music and for art in late Victorian cities. With one or two exceptions, the curators and committees of Victorian art galleries, as we shall see, would not attempt to introduce their audiences to unfamiliar or difficult works. Rather, they were buying paintings

and watercolours from popular exhibitions, often works that had achieved local success and were executed by artists with local associations. This disparity leads one to question the reasons for the popular nature of the art collections assembled in late Victorian art museums. Were they motivated by a desire to appeal to popular taste, or by a feeling that (on the evidence of 1857) high art would not attract working-class audiences? Or were these popular works forced on galleries by a shortage of funds and the near-impossibility of obtaining Old Master paintings and work by the most expensive contemporary artists?[122] In such places as Glasgow and Liverpool where more generous funding and patronage were available, a style of collecting somewhat analogous to Hallé's programmes was indeed developed in conjunction with repeated statements about the need for popular culture. The overall evidence suggests that it was financial problems, a desire to encourage local artists, and timidity over the acquisition of high art, that limited the collections.

87   The Great Hall at Kelvingrove,
Glasgow, in 1902, showing the
mighty organ acquired for the
exhibition that originally occupied
the building, as well as the major
display of sculpture at the opening.

CONCLUSION

Although 1857 may have succeeded as an assertion of the feasibility of exhibiting major works of art in the provinces, it did not succeed in inspiring municipal authorities with a conviction that they could create permanent collections on historical principles, not least because none of them could afford to. In typological terms, its influence was limited to a number of (generally more modest) exhibitions, and a few museum displays, aiming to tell the whole story of art.

The style of the universal exhibition, its breaking with convention, its attitude to the visual arts, was to shape in the South Kensington Museum and the regional art galleries that followed it a museum of a wholly new type – as it were, the exhibition-museum. Whereas the great majority of art museums in Continental Europe (though not necessarily in the United States) saw their collections as their first priority and the organisation of temporary exhibitions as a later and subsidiary activity, temporary displays with a determined purpose were the moving force at South Kensington and its offspring. Exhibitions are of their nature temporary and chameleon-like, and it is on account of this lineage that provincial art galleries in Britain became such changeable sites of activity, volatile, responsive but also vulnerable. So they remain, to their peril, to this day.

TANGYE COLLECTION.

WEDGWOOD GALLERY, ART GALLERY, BIRMINGHAM, FROM N.W.

6

FOR INSTRUCTION AND RECREATION

The creation of new art museums in late Victorian Britain was an erratic process shaped by competing bodies, the wishes of donors, and an uncertain notion of the museums' purpose. Many of the ideas surrounding them derived from earlier generations, notably the belief in their value in taming the rougher elements of society and in elevating standards of design. Equally, the idea of the validity of art on two levels, liberal and mechanic, was, as we have seen, forcibly expressed in the emergence of a double tier of art galleries.

The nascent art museums could hardly rely on any body of literature: as Thomas Greenwood remarked in 1888, 'The subject upon which this book treats is almost without a literature'.[1] In 1904 the solicitor and historian David Murray also commented on the shortage of relevant texts in *Museums, their History and their Use*, one of the first attempts to study the intellectual and institutional history of the museum in Europe.[2] Though both men were primarily writing about scientific museums, their comments also applied to art galleries.

Scientific museums did receive more attention. The periodical *Nature*, founded in 1869 as 'A Weekly Illustrated Journal of Science' and aimed at a popular but also an expert audience, regularly dis-

cussed museums. They were already assuming the reputation for shabby neglect that haunted them for many years. Thus, in 1877 the distinguished geologist W. Boyd Dawkins, Professor at Owens College, Manchester, and curator of the Manchester (University) Museum, writing on *The Need of Museum Reform*, ridiculed collections found 'in the holes and corners of Free Libraries and Museums' and cited an (actual) glass case containing a fragment of human skull and a piece of oatcake labelled 'Fragment of human skull very much like a piece of oatcake'.[3] Reflecting the confusion to be found in the collections of learned societies, he lamented that in many museums art was not separated from natural history or ethnology. Dawkins expressed a passionate belief in the importance of scientific museums, both learned and popular, and their contribution to the health and prosperity of society.[4] For Dawkins, the role of the provincial museum was primarily to offer popular instruction: he too believed in a double tier of museums, with the provincial museum at the popular level.

The increasing professionalisation of curatorship around 1900 – a field in which Britain was advanced in the scientific field but much less so in the visual arts – led to a growing corpus of literature. The

Museums Journal, first published in 1901 by the recently formed Museums Association, addressed both particular and general issues under its first editor, the lively and articulate Elijah Howarth, Curator of Public Museums in Sheffield from 1876 to 1928. These reflections paralleled the work of Sir William Flower, a distinguished zoologist who spent most of his career in museums and served as Director of the Natural History Museum from 1884 to 1898. His *Essays on Museums* (1898), distilling a lifetime's experience, stressed the crucial importance of the well-trained curator.

These limitations did not reflect any shortage of literature on the fine arts, especially after 1850. In theory, writing on art was hampered by the exclusion of art history as an academic discipline from any English university until the foundation of the Courtauld Institute of Art in London in 1932, although at Edinburgh University the Watson Gordon Chair of Fine Art, the first of its kind in Britain, was set up in 1880. Nevertheless, a number of important and innovative writers on the history of art were active in Britain in the second half of the century, and their work was enriched by translations. In addition to Eastlake, Jameson, Robinson and Ruskin, many others contributed to this discourse. The provision of a general history of art, especially if directed at a particular school and aimed at the enlightenment of the educated public, was a recurring objective. For Italian art such a text was provided firstly by Luigi Lanzi's *The History of Painting in Italy*, translated into English by Thomas Roscoe in 1828, and then by F.T. Kugler's *Handbuch der Geschichte der Malerei* of 1837. This was translated into English and edited by Charles Eastlake and his wife, Elizabeth Rigby, the Eastlakes' involvement underlining their association with German intellectual circles as well as the idea that the role of the Keeper or Director of the National Gallery should extend into scholarly publication. Kugler's work was succeeded by the three mighty volumes of J.A. Crowe and G.B. Cavalcaselle's *A New History of Painting in Italy* of 1864, 'Drawn up from fresh materials after recent researches in the archives of Italy, and from personal inspection of the works of art scattered throughout Europe'.[5] Numerous monographs were published in the second half of the century, including works on Leonardo da Vinci and Michelangelo, Claude Lorrain, Poussin and Holbein, while the 'discovery' of Spain was prompted by Richard Ford's *A Handbook for Travellers in Spain* (1845) and Sir William Stirling Maxwell's *Annals of the Artists of Spain* (1848). Improving standards of book production meant that books on art developed into powerful means of communication, so that whereas Roscoe's Lanzi was unillustrated and even in the 1840s only a scanty provision of engravings or etchings was generally available, by the 1850s an art book might well be supplied with a substantial and visually revealing corpus of illustrations, assisted by the rapid development of photography.[6] In addition, museums, and notably the South Kensington Museum, published an extensive expert literature.

This literary output was strongly international. The texts by British writers were enriched by the speedy translation into English of key texts, notably from the German: not only Kugler, Passavant and Waagen, but works by later writers, including Karl Woermann, whose *History of Painting* was edited in English by Sidney Colvin in 1880; the controversial connoisseur Giovanni Morelli; and such experts on classical sculpture as Adolf Michaelis, whose *Ancient Marbles in Great Britain* of 1882 applied scholarly investigative recording and analysis to classical sculpture. In the light of Steven Conn's comments in *Museums and American Intellectual Life* (1998), discussed above (see p. 4) on the transference of intellectual power in the scientific field from the museum to the academy late in the nineteenth century, it is worth remarking that in Britain almost none of these writers was working within the university system. Many were employed in museums, notably Eastlake, Colvin, and a formidable array of scholars at the British Museum. At least until early in the twentieth century museums played a leading role in the enunciation of art-historical ideas, a role that extended to the development of the museum catalogue. This creative activity was, however, largely restricted to national and university museums: municipal gallery curators seldom had the time or experience to extend beyond catalogues of their collections, at least until the end of the nineteenth century. How far this corpus of literature reached the museum curators and the public for regional art museums can at this stage hardly be defined, although scholarly curators such as Whitworth Wallis would certainly have been aware of it.

The stirring works of John Ruskin were of course widely known, as well as the introductory essays in exhibition catalogues, notably the catalogues of the Manchester Art Treasures Exhibition by such luminaries as Gustav Waagen and William Michael Rossetti. Museum publications were seen as having a didactic function, whether in the catalogues of the National Gallery or in such luxurious books as Emile Molinier's *The Wallace Collection* of 1903: as Lady Dilke wrote in her introduction, 'he who now visits Hertford House with the text of M. Molinier before him, may, if he will, recognise the teaching value of this, in its way, unrivalled collection, and see also, under his direction those fine shades of difference which are visible only to the trained and experienced eye.'[7] There is, however, a disjunction between writing at this level and the material contained in the cheap catalogues available in provincial art galleries. The two nations structure applied to publications just as it did to collections.

GALLERIES TO SOOTHE THE WILD

One of the themes that emerges most prominently from Victorian discussions of libraries, museums and galleries is their value as agents of social reconciliation, a theme already encountered in this book. The workers of the North were endowed with a character that was dark, yet open to redemption. Visiting Manchester in 1871, Hippolyte Taine expatiated on the people's noble savagery:

> The brute in man is very strong in this country… The spark of mind is choked by the dark, heavy vapours of instinct, and does not flash forth, spontaneous, lively, a thing of air and light, as among the Southern peoples…When this is accomplished the flame is very powerful; but nowhere is the task of civilizing the people so urgent and so necessary as it is here.[8]

'Civilizing the people' was one of the prime objectives of municipal libraries and museums. This objective was given additional force by the growing realisation in official circles that leisure and leisure pursuits, which for many years had acted as demarcators of social privilege, were becoming available to all. In 1869 Matthew Arnold wrote of 'that vast portion…of the working class which, raw and half-developed, has long lain half-hidden amidst its poverty and squalor, and is now issuing from its hiding-place to assert an Englishman's heaven-born privilege of doing as he likes, and is beginning to perplex us by marching where it likes, meeting where it likes, bawling what it likes, breaking what it likes'.[9] As Peter Bailey has noted, the growing availability of leisure and the consequent demand for more entertainments caused irritation and alarm in certain circles.[10] The Church of England discussed the problem at length, in the 1860s deciding to tolerate billiards and dancing but not the theatre or racing. In the following decades much resentment was expressed at the amount of leisure time enjoyed by working people, and their rowdy way of spending it.

Some observers were more positive. The writer and social commentator T. H. S. Escott remarked in the 1870s on the 'eager, actively enquiring, socially omniscient citizen of the world, ever on the outlook for new excitements, habitually demanding social pleasure in fresh forms'.[11] The need to provide more opportunities for working people to enjoy themselves was widely acknowledged at a time when *per capita* annual income in Britain was the highest in the world. The average annual income stood in 1860 at £32 6s in Britain compared to £21 1s in France and £13 3s in Germany,[12] and in the last third of the century working people's wages rose by between a third and a half.[13] Given that towns offered few recreations, notably on Sundays, it was felt that libraries and museums would deter working people from the public house and the music hall; they would reduce crime; they would offer a glimpse of a better life. Whitworth Wallis reflected in 1911 on the successful opening of Birmingham City Art Gallery, in which libraries and museums were linked:

> It is of some interest to note that the first attempt to form an Art Gallery was under the fostering care of the Free Library, and, all things considered, a provincial museum can hardly be started under better auspices. The intimate connection of Free Libraries and Museums in their aims, and the functions they perform in the education and culture of the people, must be apparent to all who take the trouble to consider these institutions

from the standpoint of a general principle in relation to the elevation of the masses. In one case, that of the Free Library, the mind in its wider aspects is appealed to; in the other, that of the Museum, the eye is the organ through which the perception of beauty and proportion is conveyed to the mind.[14]

Early official reports of the civic libraries in Liverpool indicate how educational taming was officially viewed. A year after the public library opened in 1852, it had proved its popularity: more than 111,000 books had been borrowed, each loaned book (in the librarian's opinion) having been read by some thirteen people. In spite of 'a slight degree of disorder and irregularity...apparent in early days', the atmosphere in the reading room had become stable, so that users now 'cheerfully and cordially co-operate with the officers...In the most crowded state the utmost order and silence are preserved. No instance of willful defacement or injury to any book has occurred.' (Fig. 88)[15] The justification for this public provision was clear: even if a quarter of readers did prefer to read 'works of amusement' (meaning novels), the Library and Museum Committee was convinced 'that the love of reading in any form must tend to counteract the propensity to low and degrading pursuits'.[16] The authorities noted two years later 'a greater degree of appreciation in the public mind, of the benefits resulting from the ready and free access to the treasures of literature, science and natural history'.[17] By 1856 the 'good conduct of the visitors ceases to be a novelty'.[18] Official statements of the wide popularity of libraries and museums, and of visitors' good behaviour, recur repeatedly.

By the 1870s it was accepted that museums and exhibitions, especially if opened on the Sabbath or in the evening, provided a particularly attractive diversion. In *Glasgow: Its Municipal Organization and Administration,* published in 1896, James Bell and James Paton emphasised the provision for instructive entertainment in their city. Temporary exhibitions offered working-class people for the first time the opportunity to enter gratis a socialised space that had no dubious connotations, where they would be exposed to valuable and instructive objects and learn to behave with civility and politeness. Greenwood enunciated the ideal of the humanising museum:

I have watched minutely the faces of visitors at many an Art Gallery and Museum, especially in the evening, and the faces of the working-class visitors have provided a study in physiognomy so gratifying that I never now enter a Museum without giving some attention to [them]...How the eyes light up at some picture, where the "one touch of nature makes the whole world kin," and I have more than once seen a wife with a pale careworn face cling more closely to the arm of her husband as some picture of child life was being looked at, or something else suggestive to them, perhaps, of little fingers lying cold in mother earth. Let any opponent of these institutions open to conviction go some weekday evening or Sunday to the Birmingham Museum and study for himself the faces of those who come to see perhaps for the twentieth time the pictures and other art objects, and he will be convinced.[19]

Here is a statement of benevolent authority, presented in various aspects: the constant gaze exerted by the middle-class official, the well-conducted sentiment-bathed appreciation of visitors who are scarcely accorded a voice (or to whom words are attributed), the perception of art as a means of offering a sympathetic commentary on contemporary life and deprivation, and the confidence (misplaced, as it turned out) that such visits would be endlessly repeated.

POPULARITY OF GALLERIES

The new museums and galleries were extraordinarily popular, with the larger institutions attracting – at least until the end of the century – hundreds of thousands of annual visitors (Fig. 89). Over a million people visited Birmingham City Art Gallery in 1888, two years after the new building opened. This was more than the whole population of the city, and the annual figures remained at well over half a million until 1900. Early in the twentieth century numbers began to decline but remained relatively strong until 1914: 800,000 visitors were recorded in Bradford in 1907, two years after it had opened, with regular attendances of 4,000 on Sundays and almost 2,000 on weekdays, at a time when the city's population was 280,000.[20] In 1910, when the National Gallery

88 This illustration from *Cassell's Magazine* in 1882 shows a free public library on a Saturday evening, filled with working men (some straight from work) virtuously reading newspapers and books. No women appear to be present. In their generous opening hours and welcoming approach to the public, the free public libraries anticipated the development of civic museums and galleries by some years.

SATURDAY NIGHT IN A FREE LIBRARY.

89 *Bank Holiday at the Bethnal Green Museum,* from Thomas Greenwood's *Museums and Art Galleries* (1888). Greenwood was not overly impressed by the Bethnal Green Museum (opened in 1872), commenting that the 'building is a painfully plain structure' as though 'designed with a feeling that anything would do for the East End', and enquiring 'Why should the privileged West Enders possess the cream of the national building and the best be kept for them?' He also deplored the lack of a general guidebook, as well as the 'elaborate display of the diet for convicts'. The sign in the background refers to the exhibition of Lord Bute's paintings shown here in 1883.

in London attracted 738,000 visitors and the Victoria and Albert Museum just under a million, Birmingham City Art Gallery welcomed (as in the previous five years) between 700,000 and 800,000 people, while Glasgow's figures were 650,000 and Bradford's 600,000. Given the respective populations, the provincial museums were proportionately much more heavily visited than their national equivalents.[21]

Already in the 1840s the growing ease of railway travel opened up unfamiliar cities – as well as rural attractions such as country houses – to new audiences who could not afford to take holidays abroad but were curious to see new places. Enabling such travel was seen as part of the educational brief of an active Mechanics' Institute. Sir Benjamin Heywood, a pious Manchester banker and one of the founders of the Manchester Mechanics' Institute, proposed that the Institution should organise 'occasional excursions of pleasure, on any holiday',

and suggested a three-day jaunt from Manchester to Liverpool on the railway line opened in 1830.[22] Such travel was seized on with enthusiasm by a new style of organisation, the agency typified by Thomas Cook (Fig. 90). In 1841 Cook, then a publisher active in the temperance movement, began to arrange railway journeys between cities for members of temperance groups and Sunday schools. He saw the railways as 'a medium for bringing about reform in the social condition of the working class', a characteristic statement of the social value of new technology.[23] These improving journeys soon proved financially beneficial, as visiting other towns or rural locations for pleasure became popular. Such new visitors were welcomed, if with some trepidation, to new museums. In 1854 the Earl of Derby's natural history museum, which belonged to the Borough of Liverpool, attracted well over a hundred thousand visitors, of whom 'a considerable proportion… have consisted of excursionists, chiefly from

90 Poster advertising a Cook's Tours railway excursion, 1850. Initiated in 1841 for temperance groups, Thomas Cook's travel company expanded with the large number of travellers visiting the Great Exhibition. Cook collaborated with the railway companies, at first to provide excursions in Britain, and later to organise foreign travel. This kind of mass travel contributed to the high visitor numbers to the early museums and galleries.

Five Days' Trip to the West of England

T. COOK, Excursion Agent, Leicester, has received authority from the Directors to announce a

CHARMING EXCURSION

TO

CHELTENHAM, GLOUCESTER,

BRISTOL,

EXETER & PLYMOUTH.

TUESDAY, JUNE 18, 1850,

SPECIAL TRAINS

Will run from NOTTINGHAM and LEICESTER and thence to BURTON, where they will be united and attached to a Train from Macclesfield, and proceed, *via* Birmingham, to Bristol.

TIME OF STARTING AND FARES THERE AND BACK.

PLACES and TIME of STARTING.	To Cheltenham or Gloucester. 1st.	2nd.	3rd.	To BRISTOL. 1st.	2nd.	3rd.
Nottingham, 8-40 a.m.; Leicester, 8-30; Ashby, 9-20.	12s. 6d.	9s.	7s.	18s.	12s. 6d.	9s. 6d.
Derby, 9-30; Burton, 10; Tamworth, 10-30	11s. 6d.	8s. 6d.	6s. 6d.	17s.	12s.	9s.

A SPECIAL-TRAIN WILL LEAVE BRISTOL FOR EXETER & PLYMOUTH,

On WEDNESDAY MORNING, JUNE 19th, at 7 a.m.

FARES from BRISTOL to EXETER & BACK :—First Class, 12s. Second Class, 8s. Third Class, 7s.

FROM EXETER to PLYMOUTH & BACK :—First Class, 7s. Second Class, 5s. 6d. (No Third.)

Passengers may return from Plymouth to Exeter, or Exeter to Bristol, by the ordinary Trains (Express and Mails excepted) on payment of an extra Shilling to each company, at any time previous to the hour fixed for the return of the Special Train, which will leave Plymouth at 3-30 p.m., and Exeter at 6 on Friday, June 21.

The Train will return from Bristol on Saturday June 22, at 9 a.m.: from Gloucester at 10-30: and from Cheltenham at 10-45. Passengers may return on Friday, June 21, on payment of 1s. extra, by the Trains leaving Bristol at 11 a.m. Gloucester at 12-35, p.m. Cheltenham at 12-55, and Birmingham at 3-30.

TICKETS are issued at the Stations and any additional particulars may be had on application by letter, with stamp for reply, to the Manager of the Trip,—T. COOK, 28, Granby-street, Leicester.

T. COOK will be in attendance at GIRAUD'S Victoria Temperance Hotel, Corner of Bath-street, Bristol, on Tuesday Evening, after the arrival of the Special Train, for the purpose of issuing Tickets for Exeter and Plymouth.

N.B.—By the arrangements of this Trip, Tourists will be introduced to districts full of natural, artistical, commercial and historical interest and importance. The bare mention of the names of the deeply interesting Cities of CHELTENHAM, GLOUCESTER, BRISTOL, BATH, EXETER, &c., call up a thousand pleasing associations which cannot be set forth in a handbill. Visitors to Cheltenham will have the privilege of attending the Great HORTICULTURAL EXHIBITION, which takes place on the 20th instant. From Bristol, River and Sea Trips may be made to CHEPSTOW, TENBY, and other places of note on the Western Coast. Excursions may also be made to various places in SOUTH WALES, such as MONMOUTH, TINTERN ABBEY, &c. &c. The Plymouth tourist will be conveyed over the most astonishing Railway in the world, running along the Coast, over Craggs, Promontories, &c. extending into the sea. The Docks, Arsenal, Fortifications, &c. of PLYMOUTH and DEVON-PORT, will be viewed with intense interest; and should the tourist desire to reach the "Land's End" in Cornwall, he may accomplish that object, and return in time to avail himself of an arrangement of the Manager of the Trip, in the month of July, for an Excursion to "John o' Groat's House," at the extreme northern point of Scotland! Such are the glorious facilities afforded by Railways and Steamboats. Let the people appreciate and rejoice in them!

T. COOK, PRINTER, 28, GRANBY-STREET, LEICESTER.

the manufacturing districts, the conduct of whom has been orderly and respectable'.[24] Two years later it was remarked of the previous year's visitors that 'the great majority have been excursionists – many from Birmingham, Leeds, Nottingham, Preston, and other distant towns'.[25] *The Report of the Executive Committee of the 1857 Exhibition* stressed that the railways had always been seen as 'absolutely imperative…as the chief source of success'.[26]

These museums satisfied a demand for instructive entertainment from a newly mobile and relatively prosperous urban population, a demand stimulated by the Great Exhibition. Far from being socially controlled members of an oppressed proletariat, the people who participated in these excursions were evidently avid for entertainment and liberated from the constraints of home and factory by their relative prosperity and the democratisation of transport.

A SET OF JUSTIFICATIONS

The new galleries and museums had a good deal to say about themselves, in the speeches made at the opening of new buildings, in committee papers and annual reports, newspapers, personal memoirs and occasional formal documents. Varying objectives were posited. At one extreme, an aesthetic purpose, tinged with utilitarianism, was enunciated by the Prince Consort at the 1851 opening of the National Gallery of Scotland. This is an articulate statement of the intrinsic value of art, its sacredness, and its role as a signifier of civilisation – the attitudes understandably reflecting German theory of the time. The new gallery, said the Prince, was to be 'a temple…to the Fine Arts – the Fine Arts which have so important an influence upon the development of the mind and feeling of a people…it is on the fragments of the works of art come down to us from bygone nations, that we are wont to form our estimate of the state of their civilisation, manners, customs, and religion'. He hoped that the 'daily increasing attention bestowed upon [the culture of the Fine Arts] in this country…will not only tend to refine and elevate the national taste, but will also lead to the production of works', which will serve as 'memorials of our age [and] will give to after generations an adequate idea of our advanced state of civi-

lisation'.[27] This idea of the museum as a memorial of the present age was relatively rare but the National Gallery of Scotland was not a typical institution, any more than the Prince's views were typical.

Many statements of purpose expressed less idealistic arguments. Repeatedly, it was stated that the gallery would redound to the fame of a city: laying the foundation stone of a new building at Bury (Fig. 91), the Mayor commented that the generous donation of the collection of Thomas Wrigley had 'raised the status of Bury among the municipalities of the kingdom'.[28] Cities were constantly looking at their rivals and determining to out-do them. The *Annual Report of the Walker Art Gallery* in 1896 commented:

> The Gallery had already a high reputation, but it is most desirable that efforts should be made to render it as complete as possible, in order that its prestige may be in no way eclipsed or diminished by the patriotism and munificence of the wealthy in other cities.'[29]

In a similar spirit, a museum might be set up with the more commercial aim of attracting tourists. Sir Merton Russell-Cotes, eponymous founder of the Bournemouth art gallery which opened in 1919, expressed not only his hatred of Darwin, (Thomas) Huxley and Post-Impressionism but also his wish to promote the town by inducing 'the patronage of visitors to a health resort, because of there being at that time no attraction whatsoever in Bournemouth'.[30]

DEMOCRATIC OWNERSHIP

Art galleries were repeatedly presented as democratic institutions, referring both to their legal ownership by the state or the city, and to their ownership by the people. It was not a new notion: already in 1838 *The National Gallery of Pictures by the Great Masters*, published commercially, had expatiated on the shared ownership of pictures, books and parks:

> [if we] divest ourselves of the worldly ideas of personal and exclusive property…in the instance of the NATIONAL GALLERY, we have even no occasion for this abstraction: it *is* our own. Every Englishman has a positive and physical, as well

91 Bury Art Gallery, erected to the designs of the Manchester firm of Woodhouse and Willoughby in 1899–1901, a time when the town was keen to assert its increasing wealth. Its style was described as 'the English Renaissance style of the eighteenth century, freely treated'. A great deal of trouble was taken to create richly harmonious interiors.

as an intellectual, property in it; and we feel honour and pride in *thus* identifying ourselves with our country, and in combining our own happiness with its prosperity.[31]

One of Greenwood's principal themes was the need to transfer collections still in the hands of learned societies into public ownership. Analysing the ineffectiveness of private museums, he quoted the museum in the historic little town of Welshpool on the borders of England and Wales to illustrate 'that for which this book pleads, namely, general Museums becoming in the fullest sense the property of the citizens'.[32] A sense of shared ownership, replacing outmoded privilege, was trumpeted by Bell and Paton in 1896 at a time when Socialism was spreading among intellectuals and workers. Art, proclaimed Paton, had previously been collected by churches, emperors and kings: 'Now that it is the turn of the municipalities to exercise democratic rule and authority over the people, they, in turn, have become

collectors; but their modest museums, as become strictly democratic times, are for the instruction and the gratification of the people at large.'[33] In cooler, more curatorial, terms, Whitworth Wallis wrote in 1911 that in twenty-five years of Birmingham City Art Gallery 'not a single object has ever been damaged', due to the fact that 'people know the place is their own'.[34] The idea of the museum as the possession of the 'people at large' was one of the most important tenets of the Victorian municipal gallery. Equally, this sense of ownership was localised: most galleries were viewed as existing primarily for the benefit of the local population.

A vision of the educational mission of a large museum service was developed by Paton: 'All in all the Glasgow Gallery is one of which the citizens have just reason to be proud, it has to be taken into account in reckoning the art wealth of the race; it is a treasure-house for the serious student; it affords invaluable material for tracing the history of schools; and to the people generally it is an undying source of that gentle enjoyment which imperceptibly elevates and refines.'[35] His statement was typically generous in its inclusion of the 'serious student', the schoolchild and the general population among the targeted audience, but more ambitious than many Victorian or twenty-first-century museums in including the expert.

Amid all these objectives, it is worth considering what is lacking. The intrinsic significance of a work of art was rarely discussed, nor were galleries often envisaged as institutions for systematic study, unlike scientific museums or university art galleries. The idea of showing any canon of Western art was seldom enunciated. Only at Birmingham – supreme among Victorian provincial museums – did the earliest collecting policy aspire to 'a thoroughly representative character as regards the historic development of Art, both pictorial and ornamental'.[36]

JOHN RUSKIN

One of the most active champions and analysts of the art museum was John Ruskin. His innumerable pronouncements on the subject, many of them offered as evidence to Parliamentary Select Committees, constitute an important, if eccentric, museological corpus.[37] Ruskin's ideas rested on his belief in what he called 'Typical Beauty', the reflection of the hand of God in the forms of natural, animal or human beings. Art's purpose was to express the universal truths potentially visible in the physical world. The artist must possess high moral qualities and must belong to a moral society, since the quality of art was inextricably associated with the society engendering it. The purpose of an art museum was to offer examples of Typical Beauty in natural phenomena (plants, minerals) and in works created by humanity: buildings, paintings, manuscripts, or depictions of such man-made, if originally natural, creations as cultivated landscape. In Ruskin's museums, diligent students, through extended application and under supervision, would come to understand Typical Beauty and be enabled to apply this knowledge to their own creative activity, however humble the field. They would gain the power to contend against the spiritual and physical degradation of an industrialised and materialistic society. This attitude towards the improvability of

the general population was phrased in paternalistic terms, insisting on the acquisition of knowledge before access was permitted.

An essential element in Ruskin's thinking was his insistence on the role of art in a corrupted society: the whole population, and notably the working man, must be involved in the process of social, moral and artistic improvement. He believed that the National Gallery should be a structure very unlike the actual building: 'a stately place – a true Palace of Art, pure in the style of it indeed, and as far as thought can reach, removed from grossness or excess of ornament … especially precious in material and exquisite in workmanship'.[38] Such an institution, showing the finest 'high art' of the past, was for the initiated. Necessary education in the development of painting, sculpture and architecture would be provided by a network of local museums throughout the country in suburbs, smaller towns and villages. These would teach the true principles of Beauty through reproductions of masterpieces (primarily of the Italian Renaissance) and modest examples of contemporary work, which the student would comprehend by extended verbal instruction and copying. At the Walkley Museum, set up outside Sheffield by Ruskin's Guild of St. George in 1878, and in its larger successor at Meersbrook Park, which opened in 1890, the plaster casts, drawings by Ruskin and his pupils, copies of Italian Renaissance paintings and views of Italian (notably Venetian) buildings, coins, gems and minerals, were arranged according to Ruskin's principles (Fig. 92). The perfect order of the arrangement was intended to inspire.

These people's museums had additional purposes: to educate the population in appreciating historic buildings and the countryside; to give an understanding of the buildings and scenery of unattainable foreign countries; and to depict Britain's glorious history. They were to be accessible, physically and intellectually, with labelling and accompanying literature to educate the worker in visual principles and qualify him or her to study the great works kept in shrines of art. Ruskin did not believe that fine art museums should be open to all. The most elevated types of museum (such as the National Gallery) should not be accessible to the uneducated working man or woman, and steps should be taken to ensure that the 'palatial' rooms that were suitable for the display of high art should not admit 'the

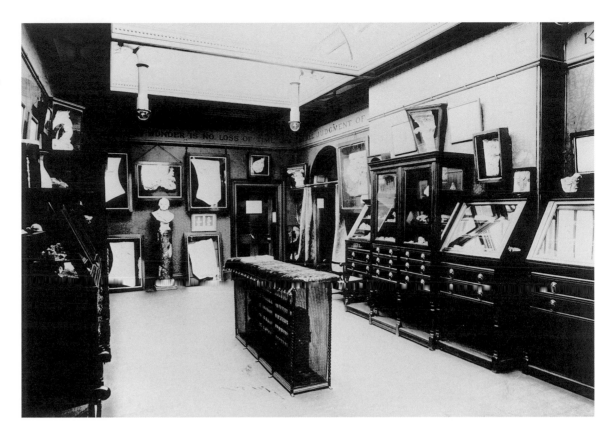

utterly squalid and ill-bred portion of the people'.[39] Ruskin's advocacy of the worker's museum was not inspired by a desire to exclude the less socially privileged from 'high art' museums, but by his belief in the over-ruling importance of art. He exerted an enormous influence on the development of municipal museums and galleries, particularly through his influence on prominent, as well as less well-known, individuals. And in some cases, such as the Victoria Jubilee Museum at Cawthorne in Yorkshire, opened in 1889 at the instigation of the local rector and supported by the artist Roddam Spencer Stanhope, the squire's brother and a friend of Ruskin, he inspired the whole museum (Figs 93, 94).[40]

THE SCIENCE AND ART DEPARTMENT AND THE SOUTH LONDON MUSEUM

Probably the most important creative force for the Victorian art museum was a child of the Great Exhibition, the Science and Art Department. Set up initially as the Department of Practical Art and attached to the Board of Trade, with Henry Cole as its first Superintendent, it was innovatory as a public body promoting education in science and the 'practical arts', that is to say, design. The Department gained a wide brief, supervising, in addition to the South Kensington Museum, the Royal Dublin Society, the School of Mines, the Geological Museum in Jermyn Street and the Government Schools of Design. As Cole put it, 'these institutions had in view the promotion of scientific artistic knowledge of an industrial tendency, at the expense of the State'.[41]

At Somerset House, the first Government School of Design was set up in 1837 under the direction of William Dyce, who advocated training in 'Ornamental Art' as opposed to the 'High Art' of the Royal Academy. Life drawing and drawing from casts, as well as the study of classical history and mythology – staples of academic training – were excluded from the syllabus. Instruction was limited to the basic principles of design in order to cultivate a standard of work suitable for practical commercial production.[42] Dyce intended that in place of classical casts, his school would display for educational

purposes ornamental art, which would be primarily English. From 1852 onwards the Department created a network of Government Schools of Design, which imitated the teaching style of Somerset House. The purpose of these schools was, in Cole's official explanation, 'to provide for the architect, the upholsterer, the weaver, the printer, the potter, and all manufacturers, artizans better educated to originate and execute their respective wares, and to invest them with greater symmetry of form, with increased harmony of colour, and with greater fitness of decoration; to render manufacturers not less useful by ornamenting them, but more beautiful, and therefore more useful.'[43] This system of art education was highly technical, depending on the minute copying of prescribed specimens.[44] Casts of architectural fragments played an important role, since the stimulation of fine architectural design, as well as good construction, was a leading aim, as was the encouragement of sculpture, architecture's sister. Painting was theoretically irrelevant, except fresco painting applied to the decoration of buildings.

These Government Schools were seen as purely practical institutions for the working man and woman. Already by 1854 schools had been set up in 'Aberdeen, Bristol, Burslem, Carnarvon, Chester, Dudley, Durham, Hereford, Llanelly, Merthyr-Tydvil, Newcastle-under-Lyme, Penzance, Swansea, Warrington, Waterford, Wolverhampton'.[45] This apparently strange selection of middle-sized and small towns reflects what was seen as the importance of locating such schools in developing centres of industry rather than in large cities. The principles enunciated in these schools were to shape the first phase of collecting in the regional galleries.

The character of the early South Kensington Museum also anticipates the provincial galleries. In its early days it combined its art and science collections in a spirit of broad generalisation – indeed, it could scarcely be described as an art museum. As defined in 1858, the museum had a multivalent and overtly didactic character that is hardly comprehensible today. True to its descent from a temporary exhibition and its governance by the Department of Science as well as of Art, it contained nine departments: the Sheepshanks collection of British paintings; modern sculpture; 'Ornamental Art'; architectural casts; a 'Circulating Art Library'; models illustrating methods of building; models

'used in Education' (Fig. 95); 'Materials illustrating the uses of Animal Materials'; and 'Models of potential inventions'.[46] The *Guide to the South Kensington Museum* of 1865 suggests a didactic bazaar, full of individual assemblages of stuff. The visitor who had negotiated the Museum of Building Materials filled with interesting patents and processes, and who had not been too much startled by a poultry house built for the Queen next to a model of the Church of the Holy Sepulchre, would proceed to the Educational Museum, where the displays were aimed at 'those engaged in teaching' and illustrated school buildings and equipment. The Gallery of Naval Models was followed by the Food Museum, with its alarmingly realistic models, including wax ones, 'In order to make people acquainted with the appearance of diseased meat, and meat unfit for human food'.[47] Only then did one reach the Art Library, the South Court with its 'Rare and choice

examples of Art Workmanship', the casts and architectural specimens (Fig. 96), and the ten Picture Galleries, which had been established in South Kensington because the pictures could not be accommodated in Trafalgar Square.

This attempt to create a museum that would instruct builders, teachers and craftsmen in bettering their work and their lives constituted a radical departure from any museum of the past. It also shaped one of the prevailing characteristics of the provincial museums: the presentation of practical and moral homilies. Not all observers admired the results. Ruskin, who was often critical of South Kensington, described the museum as 'a Cretan labyrinth of military ironmongery, advertisements of spring blinds, model fish-farming, and plaster bathing nymphs with a year's smut on all the noses of them'.[48] In more general terms, however, Ruskin was not as different from the South Kensington

96 The architectural and cast
gallery at the South Kensington
Museum in the 1860s.

circle as he pretended. Both considered the combination of improvement and enjoyment to be the ideal goals for a museum, and both agitated for an extension of the role of the state.

In terms of art, the museum's initial brief was to collect, in place of valuable originals, specimens of design and craftsmanship such as easily available originals or casts, electrotypes or photographs. In the long term, this programme lost force at South Kensington, not least because of the diminishing reputation of reproductions, but in the short term it dominated the museum's activities. On the other hand, the concept of a collection of reproductions did not suit some of those involved in the museum's early development, notably J.C. Robinson (Fig. 97), its Curator and Art Referee.[49] Comparable to Eastlake in his pioneering connoisseurship and his European travels, Robinson concentrated on assembling original works of art, notably Italian Renais-

sance sculpture and maiolica. His approach was innovative internationally: museums that collected such objects as maiolica did not exist elsewhere in Europe or North America, and collecting Italian and Northern Renaissance sculpture was almost unknown in British or European public institutions (other than Berlin and Paris) until the 1870s. At least in theory, Robinson had to work within the South Kensington remit. The acquisition of maiolica, Limoges enamel, mediaeval metalwork, could all be justified as examples of craftsmanship serving an educational purpose. On the other hand, his view that only important and finely decorative objects should be acquired subverted Cole's goal of establishing a collection of facsimiles. As Robinson made clear at an early point in the development of the Museum of Ornamental Art, 'Libraries, Museums, Galleries, even shops and workshops, – these too are schools, it is felt that the eye should be trained to

134

but at their most fruitful periods it was Robinson's example, not Cole's, that they followed.

THE TREASURY OF SCIENCE AND ART

Through the South Kensington Museum, the Department was seen as 'the central storehouse or treasury of Science and Art for the use of the whole kingdom'.[52] In the dry words of an early *Annual Report*, 'The action of the Department being chiefly to stimulate and encourage the efforts made by localities for obtaining instruction in Science and Art, its operations are directed to the creation of such means as will sustain…active local co-operation in the promotion of the general objects entrusted to it.'[53] What this pronouncement entailed was a major programme of proselytisation across the country, in which the Department (with its limited budget) would collaborate with local individuals and bodies. It would provide reproductions of works of art for schools, extend elementary and higher instruction in practical art, train teachers for the provinces, and make 'as publicly useful as possible the central schools, museums and libraries of the Department'.[54] From South Kensington, artistic specimens would be distributed as loans or as modest purchases to schools of art, as well as to the promised museums that had been on the national agenda since the 1830s. It was Cole's hope that reproductions of great works of art could be systematically gathered from the major art capitals of Europe 'by means of electricity and photography' and distributed 'as prizes to local museums and schools, and thus…lay the foundations for the establishment of local museums of Art, wherever the people themselves may make the necessary arrangements for housing and preserving them'.[55]

In 1855 a modest loan system of art objects for provincial art schools came into operation at South Kensington, offering works on paper – 'Engravings of the English School' and so forth – and oil paintings.[56] In 1867 Robinson reported that in the past year exhibitions of etchings and coloured 'photograms' (i.e. photographs) 'mounted in suitable glazed frames', had been shown all over the country, arousing great interest.[57] The display of historical reproductions and the loan of material from London

seize and appreciate'.[50] In this educational spirit (and betraying his contempt for contemporary art), he saw the museum of ornamental art in Hegelian terms as leading 'the art student, by clear and definite steps, to the upward level of his own time, rendering him familiar with every link of the chain of gradual development, enabling him to profit by the true inventions and progress of the contemporary mind, and at the same time to detect and avoid the spurious affectations of originality, the empty revivals and false adaptations, which are so rife in modern Art'.[51] Robinson's interest in Italian Renaissance sculpture, in particular, stimulated a focus on the works of major artists in the style of the traditional fine art museum. His objectives were found to be incompatible with Cole's and he was dismissed in 1867, but in the long run his approach formed the museum's collecting policies.

Robinson's work at South Kensington was reflected in many other art museums. Provincial galleries started, in many cases, as collections of facsimiles, and ironically Robinson was one of those who late in the century still considered this their proper role, along with the assembly of works of local interest. Curators found themselves struggling, as Robinson had, to acquire original works of art,

museums would play a crucial role in the development of the provincial museum. This centralist approach constituted a remarkable episode in the history of the visual arts in a country where state intervention had traditionally been seen as an alien concept.

In its attitude to the public, the Department was particularly influential. Cole repeatedly emphasised the importance of opening up the South Kensington Museum to the broadest possible audience. He believed passionately in its duty to provide physically and intellectually accessible entertainment and instruction for all. Nationwide, not only better housing and education were needed, but also cultural attractions, parks, music, sports grounds, available as far as possible without charge. The authorities should 'open all museums of Science and Art after the hours of Divine service; let the working man get his refreshment there in company with his wife and children, rather than leave him to booze away from them in the Public-house'.[58] As the Department's 1858 *Annual Report* declared, it had 'been the aim to make the mode of admission as acceptable as possible to all classes of visitors' by opening the South Kensington Museum free of charge to everyone except unaccompanied children, three days a week.[59] That same year the experiment was tried 'of opening a public museum in the evening to ascertain practically what hours are most convenient to the working classes'.[60] The Department insisted that 'It would appear to be less for the rich that the State should provide public galleries of paintings and objects of art and science, than for those classes who would be absolutely destitute of the enjoyment of them unless they were provided by the State.'[61] The experiment of extended opening hours at South Kensington, made possible by the innovative introduction of gas lighting, was justified by the huge evening crowds that were satisfyingly identifiable as working class, especially on Mondays, a day workers traditionally took as holiday. Even though the evening opening times were shorter, the number of evening visits exceeded daytime ones. Cole published comparisons between the visitor figures at South Kensington and at the National Gallery that indicated (at least by his reckoning) that the older museum had lost the advantage.

The accessibility of South Kensington was enhanced by free lectures with special places reserved for working men, and by simply worded guidebooks written by Cole under the name of Felix Summerly. Much importance was attached to labelling: it was reported in 1865 that 16,138 labels had been put up in the past year, offering information on the material and uniqueness of each object, the artist's or maker's name, its price, in certain cases its provenance, and its country of origin.[62] The museum made a point of organising appealing temporary displays: the Prince and Princess of Wales's wedding presents, shown during seventeen days in 1864, attracted almost a quarter of a million visitors, making it the museum's most popular exhibition of the century.[63]

These experiments were widely followed in provincial museums, notably the principle of extended opening hours. By the end of the century many of the larger museums were open not only on Sundays but also well into the evening. According to a survey made in 1911, many municipal museums, including Glasgow, Leeds, Manchester and Nottingham, followed South Kensington in staying open from ten in the morning until nine at night, several days a week.[64] In a revealing contrast, at the National Gallery and the British Museum, in spite of numerous petitions and much discussion, no artificial lighting was introduced on the grounds of fire risk and damage to works of art from gas, a situation that did not change until the twentieth century.[65]

THE CASE OF BIRMINGHAM

One major example illustrates how the South Kensington Museum shaped the new galleries. The old-established town of Birmingham was famous for the independence of its economic units, made up of many small businesses specialising in engineering and metal goods. A mid-century commentator remarked that although there was 'no town in the United Kingdom whose prosperity [was] so fully dependent on the intelligence and skill of its artizans as Birmingham', the development of adult educational institutions was less advanced there than elsewhere.[66] As we have seen, the Liberals, in power in Birmingham from the early 1870s, sought to transform the city, and supported the creation of a civic museum and gallery.[67] As Robinson wrote, it was to the Liberal Party that 'is unquestionably

98 The Round Room,
Birmingham City Art Gallery.
This hall has always served as one
of the Gallery's most important
rooms for displaying works of art.
Its 1885–6 catalogue listed around
a hundred paintings here, all
British, which included the
Nettlefold bequest of works by
David Cox.

mainly due the fostering of the art movement of the second half of this century in England'.[68]

Following abortive attempts by private initiative, the first Birmingham Corporation Art Gallery opened in 1867. The catalogue produced three years later lists a characteristically inchoate assembly of works.[69] One or two paintings attributed to such masters as Elsheimer and Ribera were outnumbered by images of local worthies and works by Birmingham artists. The initial lack of an acquisitions budget made the Gallery dependent on gifts and loans, whether from individuals or from such bodies as the Birmingham School of Art and Design. These holdings were supplemented by reproductions, notably Arundel Society prints depicting the development of Italian art from the earliest days, and 'Electro Deposited Copies of Objects of Art Manufacture'.

From the beginning it was found that visitors came to see special exhibitions rather than the improving but hardly exciting permanent collection.

In the early years, annual visits of around 200,000 were recorded, with the *Annual Report* for 1874 noting that a gratifyingly large number of visitors were artisans.[70] The exhibitions organised for these visitors and for students at the School of Art tended to be technical, such as the 1874 display of a 'Collection Illustrative of the History and Practice of Etching', lent and organised by a private owner, or the Tangye Collection of Old Wedgwood, shown in 1885, with a catalogue containing a long chapter on Josiah Wedgwood's career and technique. Underlying many of these exhibitions, as well as the material related to the permanent holdings, was the message that the determined viewer could attain equal success. This message, contemporaneously being propounded by the popular polemicist Samuel Smiles to a receptive public, was a recurring theme in the discourse around the provincial gallery.

A high proportion of the loans at Birmingham came directly from South Kensington on a short- or

long-term basis, as its first major loan experiment. In an innovatory move in 1855, the Department lent to an industrial art exhibition at the Birmingham Government School of Design a selection of 'Works of Industrial Art…adapted, as far as possible, to the industrial wants of the town and district'. These loans were intended to supplement the standard course of instruction laid down by Cole and his colleagues.[71] This initial emphasis on didactic displays of industrial art remained a vital element in the museum's development: when in 1881 an acquisitions fund was set up, it was chiefly for 'objects of Industrial Art'.

By 1885 Birmingham Art Gallery had acquired permanent premises in the centre of the city through the generosity of a private patron. Its six rooms epitomised the dialectic between industrial art and fine art that marked the emergence of some Victorian galleries. On arrival, visitors found themselves in a circular hall hung with a hundred or so paintings, almost all of the modern British school (Fig. 98). This room was separated from the other picture gallery by a suite of three rooms dedicated to the

institution's declared purpose of instruction in design. The Italian Gallery, the next room on the route, contained a *mélange*, with statuary and paintings treated as subsidiary to the decorative arts (Fig. 99). Metalwork naturally played an important role in a city of metal production, and the catalogue, emphasising materials, included extended observations on 'Decorative Iron Work'.[72] Etruscan vases, maiolica, wooden furniture, stone doorways and balconies, ceramics and 'Della Robbia Ware', and enamels were also on view, some in the wooden and glass show cases patented by the South Kensington Museum. Borrowing heavily, the Industrial Hall contained in rows of cases on two levels assorted bronzes, enamels and ivories, many from the Far East, together with jewellery, textiles, arms and electrotypes representing European and Asian work from the fifteenth century to the eighteenth. The Wedgwood Gallery exhibited the collection of the Tangye brothers, whose offer to establish a purchase fund for works of art, along with the loan of their Wedgwood collection, had stimulated the erection of the building (Fig. 100). The Great Gallery – a

100 The Wedgwood Gallery, Birmingham City Art Gallery. From 1885 this Gallery showed 'The Tangye Collection of Old Wedgwood', lent by Richard Tangye of Tangye Brothers, a successful Birmingham engineering firm and major benefactors to the city's museum and art gallery.

descendant of the Great Rooms of the early nineteenth century – reverted to paintings. Here indeed was a museum of the fine and of the decorative arts, cohabiting, though in a relationship that was to become increasingly strained.

CONCLUSION

To modern eyes there is something naïve and almost hobbledehoy about these early art galleries. Given that many of them opened with no collections, they often had the character of *Kunsthallen*, spaces intended for temporary exhibitions, rather than permanent collections. In these spaces, at least in the early years, they housed a whole range of activities, always energetic, often chaotic.

They had, on the other hand, a very particular character. A century and more later, the rules surrounding museum collections have become so strict over such matters as deaccessioning, conservation, the hieratic character of the museum space, that it is difficult to imagine the entrepreneurial nature of these early museums, with their wide-ranging temporary exhibitions substituting for permanent collections, their avoidance of constricting social propriety, and above all their huge popularity. The prominent buildings, simple guidebooks and programmes of instruction aimed at the working man and his family made them the reverse of intimidating. They could accommodate gargantuan exhibitions on a scale that would dumbfound modern curators and publics. In so far as they accumulated collections, these were often planned with the aim of pleasing an unsophisticated public.

At a time when the provision of public education remained partial and inefficient, municipal art galleries functioned both as educational spaces and as places of entertainment. Non-purist though they may have been, their achievements were far from negligible. The idea of the art museum as a source of education, with displays and didactic material aimed at an audience that was neither well educated nor socially privileged, was to shape their development. In contrast to earlier museum types, they were not intended primarily for the privileged classes or for artists; to a great extent they were museums and galleries for the workers.

7

ART ON SHOW

The years before 1870 witnessed the construction in Britain of important museums in the capital cities and the old universities but few elsewhere; the history since 1914, at least until recent years, has been surprisingly meagre; it was between 1870 and 1914 that the majority of public art galleries were built in Britain. With some exceptions, this narrative is not impressive. It is marked by an obsession with economising and a fear of the grand gesture that the museum often demands, as well as by a lack of confidence in the position of a museum within the city or society. Looking back at the period from early in the twenty-first century, when the art museum has become one of the most publicly discussed and celebrated building types, it is surprising to realise how, at least until around 1900, many art galleries in what was one of the richest and most powerful countries in the world were erected on a modest scale, often through piecemeal development, and that the architectural language in which they were couched was variable and uncertain. As Carla Yanni has discussed, the same applied in other disciplines: 'architects could not devise any one distinctive building type for natural history museums', resulting in buildings that ranged from Italian Renaissance to Ruskinian Gothic to Germanic Romanesque.[1] For most clients, 'the practical arrangement of rooms' and not the choice of style was the prime concern.[2] Although issues around museum design were much discussed, the aesthetic results were often disappointing.

The history was complicated by two conflicting factors. The prevailing belief in the virtues of economy in public finances was counterbalanced by a sense that national (or local) glory should be expressed through imposing structures.[3] It was a dilemma that had been discussed (in relation to such public buildings as temples) by Vitruvius, by Renaissance theorists, and again in the eighteenth century. As Joseph Baretti explained in *A Guide Through the Royal Academy* (1781), Sir William Chambers' Somerset House – intended to accommodate cultural institutions, including the Royal Academy, as well as government offices – was originally to be plain, but since prominent figures such as Edmund Burke felt that such a structure should be 'at once an object of national splendor [*sic*] as well as convenience', plans were set in train to make the building a chastely magnificent celebration of the public realm.[4] A similar ambivalence attached to the long debate over the rebuilding or extension of William Wilkins' National Gallery. In one episode, the 1847–8 Select Committee considering accommodation for works of art, following the donation of the Vernon collection, concluded that the existing Gallery was too small and 'wanting in the dignity and elevation due both to its purpose and its site', and that a new building designed by 'the most eminent talent of the nation' was required. The desirability of a central location in London was a recurring theme: in this instance it was felt that the existing site should be retained, since it enjoyed a commanding location close to 'the chief thoroughfares, and centres of business'. But the site was also valued because it offered scope for economy, since, given the closeness of the surrounding buildings, only one ornamental front would be needed.[5] Dignity and the patronage of local talent were sought, but on the cheap. No such reservations dogged the triumphantly palatial history of museum building in France, or the adaptation of the temple to urbanistic and scientific needs in the German states (other than in Protestant Prussia, where strict economy was imposed on Schinkel at the Altes Museum).

In the early part of the century the physical appearance of most museums in Britain hardly recalled either temple or palace. The dirt, disorderly picture hang and shortage of space in the National Gallery were repeatedly castigated. Francis Wey in the 1850s felt that 'public buildings are in general very inferior in arrangement, the Englishman being far better at understanding private than public comfort'. The National Gallery shocked him: 'The structure is meagre, out of proportion, badly lit, skimpy and surmounted by a diminutive dome, as though some waggish jockey had stuck his cap on it. It ought to be entirely rebuilt.'[6] It seemed strange to him that in a country 'where cleanliness is a tradition, the only badly kept and neglected buildings are those devoted to art…The National Gallery, if for its disgraceful flooring only, could not bear comparison with a racehorse's quarters.'[7]

Foreign museums presented an ideal for British lovers of art. Just as Italian *palazzi* and archaeological museums had inspired private owners in the eighteenth century, the Louvre became an ideal in the early nineteenth. It was, however, German museology and museums that exerted most influence in Britain, at least in aspiration, such architectural specialists in museums as Leo von Klenze being regularly consulted. The evidence of the 1836 Parliamentary Select Committee on extending a knowledge of the arts included Klenze's description of his own Alte Pinakothek and Glyptothek in Munich, with substantial comments by Gustav Waagen, while in 1855 the *Art Journal* devoted an extended review to the new picture gallery in Dresden, praising the exterior of the building and its iconography, 'the perfect simplicity and total absence of elaborate ornament which is alone suitable to the purposes of a picture gallery', the wall colouring and decoration.[8] German expertise extended to technical issues, so that when the new Ashmolean Galleries were being planned, opinions on lighting the galleries were solicited from Waagen, the painter Schnorr von Carolsfeld, and other authorities in Germany.[9]

One of the difficulties was that the ideas of such a writer as Waagen were too ambitious for a British audience. In 1853 he discussed the creation of particular rooms for particular works, addressing one of the most pressing display problems that faces any art museum, the removal of a work from its original context:

A Museum is simply a means of rescuing works of Art from otherwise certain destruction, or of exhibiting to general view those which would otherwise be seen by few, if any persons, who feel a want for such enjoyments. It is, therefore, the duty of those entrusted with the arrangement of Museums, to lessen as much as possible the contrast which must necessarily exist between works of Art in their original site, and in their position in a museum. But, to realise in some degree the impression produced by a temple, a church, a palace, or a cabinet, for which these works were originally intended, and where a certain general harmony reigned, such works alone (and in moderate number) ought to be collected in a room, which belong to the same period and school.[10]

He also suggested that the problem of the alien environment of a museum should be assuaged by the subtle juxtaposition of works of comparable scale and character, creating an intellectual synthesis. While such an approach – along with the division of rooms into larger galleries or cabinets – was sometimes discussed in Britain, it required too much space and planning to be followed there with any regularity, at least until late in the century.

❖

CONFIDENCE IN THE DESIGN OF THE GALLERY SPACE

A remarkable feature of the discourse around the character of museums and exhibition spaces in the brave new world of the 1850s was the confidence expressed by architects and patrons in the straight-forwardness of the process. The design of the Crystal Palace and other recent exhibition halls had seemingly resolved problems that in actuality tease architects and patrons to this day. In 1853 two architect brothers, J.W. and Wyatt Papworth, writers on architectural history and practice, published *Museums, Libraries, and Picture Galleries, Public and Private; Their Establishment, Formation, Arrangement, and Architectural Construction.*[11] The book, no doubt prepared with an eye to commissions, is remarkable for its strong opinions. Referring to such authorities as Eastlake, Waagen and Klenze, the Papworths offered recommendations for the dimensions of galleries, the hanging of paintings, lighting, the use of screens and many other elements, writing as though such issues had been resolved for good.

Similar self-assurance was expressed by Thomas Fairbairn, promoter of the Manchester Art Treasures Exhibition, whose letter to a local paper on the need for an art gallery in Manchester was reported by the *Art Journal* in 1860. Making the 'bold proposition to the wealthy classes of the great manufacturing districts' that they should combine to create an art gallery and museum in their city, years before such galleries had become the norm, he wrote as though the arrangements for the 1857 exhibition had left no questions unanswered. The new building was to 'attain a national importance from its extent and largeness of design', and to enjoy a central and convenient location. Fairbairn had no doubt about practicalities, briskly remarking that 'We now possess the experience of what well lighted and properly decorated picture and sculpture galleries should be, and there need therefore be no waste of money in experimental investigations and frequent failure'. In some ways his recommendations anticipated the municipal galleries of a generation later: large saloons for pictures, corridors for original sculptures and plaster casts, and (particularly relevant for later developments) 'one extensive hall [devoted] to the portraits of Lancashire worthies and local benefactors; – a Hall of Fame, where aspiring youth might muse upon the features of the mighty dead'.[12] Architectural style and creating a building attractive to audiences were scarcely touched on. An efficient container was enough.

Museum architecture was not always very ambitious in artistic terms. Addressing Victorian museums in general, John Summerson (admittedly writing in 1955, at a time when Victorian architecture was generally despised) considered that 'not more than one or two [were] built by an architect of distinction'.[13] It is hard to question his assessment, although it should be borne in mind that relatively few major buildings in the great new cities were designed by nationally known architects. Unlike the first half of the century, when such figures as John Soane, John Nash, Charles Barry senior, William Wilkins, Robert Smirke, George Basevi and C.R. Cockerell all worked on museum design, during the most active age of museum building from 1870 to 1914 few British architects of more than local reputation – with the exception of Alfred Waterhouse, Gilbert Scott, the partnership of Deane and Woodward and arguably James Pennethorne and Sir John Simpson of Simpson and Allen, with J.J. Burnet at the very end of the period – applied themselves to the genre.[14] The majority of provincial museums, galleries and libraries, even when built on a considerable scale, were designed by such competent local architects as T.C. Hine of Nottingham. In pursuit of economy, they seldom engaged in flights of fancy. On the other hand they often reached a high level of quality and were well-equipped to address the needs of contemporary art display and conservation.

CONTAINER OR SHOWPIECE?

An issue that perennially affected both national and regional museums was the conflict between the functionalist approach of regarding a museum structure as a container, and the temptation to treat it as a major work of architecture.[15] The conflict is no less strong today, and is often won by the champions of architecture for its own sake.[16] A closely related issue was the degree of elaboration appropriate in the exterior and interior of an art gallery, an issue that reflected varying concepts of the museum and its place in society: whether it was to be seen primarily as a statement of national, local or personal grandeur, an architectural masterpiece, a people's palace or a box.

The idea that spaces for showing works of art should defer to their contents was long established. Baretti had outlined such an approach in discussing the Great Room at Somerset House, one of the first public purpose-built spaces in Britain for displaying works of art (Fig. 101): 'As the Pictures of the Exhibition were to be the great ornament of the place, very few decorations are introduced on any part of the Room, that the attention of the Beholders might not be called off from the main object.'[17]

Early in the nineteenth century, the French theorist J.-N.-L. Durand – well-known to such scholarly architects as Soane – commented that a museum resembled a library in being 'on the one hand, a public treasury enshrining that most precious of deposits, the knowledge of humanity, and on the other…a temple consecrated to study…[where] the greatest security and the greatest calm may prevail'. He did not mention magnificence and display. Museums were 'built to conserve and to impart a precious treasure, and they must therefore be composed in the same spirit as libraries'.[18] Nineteenth-century writers repeatedly stated that the architect's duty was to provide the essential facilities for showing art to advantage, within an interior as simple as was consistent with dignity. Charles Eastlake agreed with Lord Morpeth, the Chairman of the 1847–8 Select Committee, that 'the interior of the National Gallery should be tolerably free from much decoration', even though 'the present bare and frigid effect' was inappropriate.[19] In 1853 Waagen published a series of articles in the *Art Journal* on the planned rehousing of the National Gallery in South Kensington.[20] Rather surprisingly, in view of the general disdain for the building, he singled out the National Gallery as an instance of the extravagance of museum spaces in contemporary England, even though most commentators viewed it quite differently:

> Although I am far from asserting that there are not architects in England, who in the execution of a building keep its chief object steadily in view, treating everything as subordinate to this, yet experience shows that there are also archi-

tects who regard a building for the exhibition of works of Art merely as offering an opportunity to indulge every kind of caprice – such as the erection of magnificent halls, in which works of Art are introduced only as a decoration, sacrificing the principal object, of presenting an exhibition of Art under circumstances the most favourable for affording enjoyment and instruction.'[21]

For a new building, he recommended simple external design without columns or sculpture since 'Beauty of proportion, grandeur of form, and outline in the single parts, are quite sufficient to give the appearance required'.[22] The idea of restraint extended to the interior, in that 'the entrance-hall and staircase should not occupy such a disproportionate waste of room as in the present National Gallery', while the 'decoration of the rooms must be simple, and its effect always subordinate to the pictures'.

This point of view was fairly general, notably in the circles around the South Kensington Museum. Discussions about the proposed new building for the National Gallery of Scotland reflected similar reservations. The *Art Journal* reported in 1850 that the architect 'considered a picture gallery ought to be constructed, so that the pictures may be seen to the best advantage, instead of having it stand as a monument of architectural display', and expressed the hope that similar principles would apply at the proposed new National Gallery in London.[23] Richard Redgrave, equally, lamented the frequent sacrifice of good lighting to the vanity of architects: 'even within everything must be sacrificed to classical examples, to Vitruvian proportions, to lofty vaultings, to cornices and covings, which leave the pictures to the accident of being seen well or ill…The shrine is elegant, but the pictures are entombed…In a gallery for art, the art is the one thing to which all should be subservient.'[24] In 1880, when the erection of new art galleries and museums in provincial towns was routine, the issue was revived by J.C. Robinson: 'Of late years provincial towns have developed a great propensity for the erection of showy architectural structures, and museums and galleries of art, in particular, seem to be regarded by ambitious promoters of public works, and by architects, as of all institutions the most fit and proper to be gorgeously housed.'[25] Too often the elevations determined the planning, since they started with a

false premise: 'Rigidity and completeness of plan are necessary in such structures in order that the exterior elevation, which is usually more considered than the interior arrangements, may shape itself in the desired lines.'[26] There was no need for museums to be pretentious buildings:

> As a matter of fact, plain substantial brick-built galleries, with little interior decoration, and that little of the most subdued and sober kind, are what is required. They should be long and spacious galleries, not suites of separate rooms, and so placed as to admit of ready extension and alteration in response to the demands of ever-growing collections.[27]

Equally, they should be solidly constructed, not 'Flimsy glass and iron structures' like some of the museums that followed the 'Brompton Boilers' at South Kensington (the first building of the South Kensington Museum, and much ridiculed).

A museum could be a purely functional unadorned space if it was accepted that it need not express permanence or dignity, or make any effort to attract visitors. Robinson's approach reflects the South Kensington creed of employing a military engineer rather than an architect. Not many buildings were erected in this spirit, but the Queen's Park Museum in Manchester, a functional brick structure set in a suburban park and opened in 1884, may serve as an example. It is a rare instance of a Victorian museum that no longer serves its original purpose: closed to the public, it acts as a store (Fig. 102).

This concept of a museum was by no means universally accepted later in the nineteenth century, any more than it had been in early generations: as museums became increasingly important building types around 1800, such visionary designers as Etienne-Louis Boullée had advocated the creation of huge, grand spaces in which the individual object would be sacrificed to the effect of the whole.[28] In Britain, the advocates of ornament tended to focus on interior fittings and decoration. In 1851 the *Art Journal* commented (no doubt with reference to the National Gallery) on 'the dreary homes which England provides for her treasures of Art', with

The Museum, Queen's Park, Manchester

pictures crowded 'together in shabby rooms of a monotonous dingy tint, with dirty floors, and miserable furniture and fittings, everything offending the eye of taste, depressing the spirits, and annoying the senses'. The article suggested that paintings and sculpture could be shown together with fine materials on the walls, and asked in relation to Palazzo Pitti or the galleries designed by Klenze, 'Do the marbled columns, the frescoed ceilings, the gilded cornices, the silk hangings, the superb furniture, the parquet flooring, – make the pictures less interesting, less effective, less important? Is not the contrary the case?'[29]

This point of view was developed by Ruskin, who was saluted by Thomas Greenwood for his 'marked and beneficial' influence on museums and his 'predominant desire, that there should be a beautiful England, filled with people living beautiful lives, in unison with the beautiful objects by which they may be surrounded'.[30] Avowed enemy of the commercial-seeming, undecorated, pragmatic Crystal Palace, both at Hyde Park and in its second guise as 'the big Norwood glass bazaar', Ruskin stressed the need for museums to create a sense of order and of visual and intellectual beauty.[31]

His views (not only on art galleries, it may be noted) are epitomised in letters quoted in the *Art Journal* in 1880:

The first function of a Museum – (for a little while I shall speak of Art and Natural History as alike cared for in an ideal one) – is to give example of perfect order and perfect elegance, in the true sense of that test word, to the disorderly and rude populace. Everything in its own place, everything looking its best because it is there, nothing crowded, nothing unnecessary, nothing puzzling. Therefore, after a room has been once arranged, there must be no change in it.[32]

He developed the idea of 'elegance' as addressing 'chiefly architecture and fittings. These should not only be perfect in stateliness, durability and comfort, but beautiful to the utmost point, consistent with due subordination to the objects displayed.'[33]

The degree of splendour suitable for a gallery, and technical issues such as lighting and wall colours, were debated at length, critics variously attacking galleries for disorder or excessive fineness, and ridiculing the public for their lack of discrimination. In the view of Harry Quilter,

146

The reason for our indifference to the bad arrangement of our picture galleries, is that we do not care for our pictures…Pictures or statues are nothing to us, except appropriate objects, to fill spaces on our walls and dark corners in our drawing-room, and, were we able, we should degrade all the best art of England, to the decoration of a sofa or the pattern of a plate.[34]

The dichotomy was nicely expressed in an article in the *Art Journal* in 1876. Commenting on the ambitious new set of rooms designed by E.M. Barry at the National Gallery, the critic wrote that both the dinginess of the old rooms and the splendour of the new ones could 'detract from that repose in which the eye should be enabled to rejoice in the works of the immortal masters'.[35] Only in the late 1880s could critics accept that for the first time in its history the recent additions to the National Gallery had made it 'one of the best in Europe, and for the first time worthy of the splendid collection of pictures'.[36]

Comparable debates were vigorously pursued in the regions. At the Walker Art Gallery the display of works of art, particularly in the temporary exhibitions that dominated its early history, was a constant theme. When it inaugurated new rooms in 1884, the *Art Journal* approvingly commented:

On entering the first room the eye is gratified by a fountain. Looking along the vistas formed by the successive rooms, and getting glimpses of statuary, gilding, and draperies, the visitor feels that his surroundings are the results of liberal expenditure, judiciously employed, and methodical arrangement guided by judgment and good taste.[37]

What the Walker offered was a luxurious environment and a sense of significant (but controlled) expenditure, with the assurance that these material benefits had been governed by both aesthetic and moral considerations (Figs 103, 104). Comparable accounts of Walker Art Gallery exhibitions continued in later years, the *Annual Report* remarking in 1895 that 'a great improvement was effected in the arrangement of the Exhibition, the rooms being handsomely draped with cloth and plush hangings, which gave a richness and completeness to the Exhibition which was highly appreciated by visitors'.[38] Although the gallery was open to all who could pay the modest admission charge, it presented a bourgeois and even aesthetic character some way from the ideal of the popular gallery but in accordance with the prevailing taste for the elaborate decoration of public and private interiors – though towards the end of the century this approach was superseded by a more austere aesthetic. Equally at Kelvingrove, where the admission of the whole population had always been a watchword, a 'sumptuous style of decoration' was considered appropriate when the new building opened in 1901.[39] This approach parallels the idea posited at Toynbee Hall, the middle-class educational 'colony' in Whitechapel, that the spectacle of beautifully furnished interiors would inspire impoverished spectators to create more dignified interiors in their own dwellings.

The emphasis on the importance of an elegant setting for displays extended (as Ruskin suggested it should) to the science museum, with an American authority commenting that 'The value of a specimen as an instructive or educational implement…depends very much on the perfection of its display'.[40] Leicester Museum in the 1880s was noted for the 'pictorial treatment of the mammals and birds in the general collection' and for the 'artistically modelled rock work' on which the specimens were shown,[41] while at Liverpool Museum much thought was given to evocative and realistic natural history displays aimed at a popular audience.[42] Equally, when W.H. Flower wanted in 1896 to alter the displays in the Mammals and Birds section in the Natural History Museum he consulted Leighton before altering the 'stands of pale polished sycamore' to 'dull wood stained to dark brown'.[43]

THE CLASSICAL TRADITION

In the first half of the nineteenth century, classicism – in a wide variety of forms – was the almost exclusive architectural language of the museum in Britain, whether in national, university or local museums, literary and philosophical societies, or artists' societies. Appropriate to a place of learning, classicism expressed continuity and stability. It was established as the regular language for the art museum in such innovative structures as the Hunterian Museum in Glasgow, the Royal Manchester

Boots l° Pub.

Institution (Fig. 105), and the Yorkshire Museum in York, completed in 1830.[44] Classicism was seen as universally valid, so that at York the classical building was inserted into a new botanic garden, on a site filled with relics of the city's medieval past, to create an interesting dialogue. Classicism extended to scientific institutions, such as the circular Rotunda Museum at Scarborough (Fig. 106), and in museum terms reached its apogee in the British Museum and the National Gallery of Scotland.

Sometimes transmuted into Italianate forms, the language of classicism remained in regular use to the end of the century in such structures as the Hancock Museum of Natural History in Newcastle (1884), the Mappin Art Gallery in Sheffield (1887), and the monumental Harris Art Gallery and Museum in

Preston (1893; Fig. 107).[45] Classicism was not seen as necessarily traditionalist: the Mappin was described as having been designed in 'a modern adaptation of the Greek Ionic style'[46] and was praised for its novel conception, its system of alcoved recesses, and its lighting.[47] The amazement expressed by the modernists Nikolaus Pevsner and John Summerson at the late use of classicism – Summerson called the Harris 'an almost incredible anachronism'– is irrelevant in the face of a solution that was lastingly appropriate in its associations and flexible in its provision of internal spaces.[48]

This adherence to classicism in the museum was not an isolated pattern. As Irina Steffenson-Bruce has discussed, in the United States the imitation of the South Kensington Museum that characterised

148

1. Exterior of the Building.—2. The Opening Ceremony.—3. Lord Derby Unveiling the First Picture.—4. View in One of the Galleries.

OPENING OF THE NEW WALKER ART GALLERY AT LIVERPOOL

105 A nineteenth-century view
of the entrance hall of the Royal
Manchester Institution, later
Manchester City Art Gallery.

106 The Rotunda Museum at
Scarborough. Completed in 1829,
the museum's design was inspired
by William Smith, 'father of
English geology'. It was built at
the expense of the Scarborough
Philosophical Society.

107   The Harris Art Gallery and Museum, Preston. Built in 1882–93, it was paid for from a munificent bequest to the town by
E. R. Harris, a local lawyer and businessman. Designed by Alderman James Hibbert of Preston in a severely flamboyant Greek
Revival style reminiscent of the work of Karl Friedrich Schinkel, the building cost almost £80,000. It towers over the Market
Square, which contained the town hall and other civic buildings, emphasising the museum's importance within the city. The
building contains the library in noble classical rooms on the ground floor, with the museum upstairs. Extensive research into
other museums and libraries in England and overseas was carried out as the building was being planned.

PERSPECTIVE VIEW · AMGUEDDFA GENEDLAETHOL CYMRU · FROM THE SOUTH WEST

the early major museums was supplanted by the internationally dominant vogue for Beaux-Arts classicism, following the success of the 1891–3 Art Institute of Chicago building, with its pure elevations and symmetrical planning.[49] Steffenson-Bruce's suggestion that in the United States the re-recreation of pure Greek architecture in museum buildings was associated with democratic, Progressive Party and even Socialist ideals is not reflected in Britain, though in such buildings as the austere and windowless Mappin or the National Museum of Wales in Cardiff (1905–27; Fig. 108), Beaux-Arts Classicism served as a dignified civic style appropriate to most public purposes.[50]

ALTERNATIVES TO CLASSICISM

In the culturally excitable context of Victorian Britain, however, classicism in museum architecture co-existed with a range of other styles. The first divergence involved Romanesque or Gothic architecture. In mid-century the received classical language was challenged by a newly functional and didactic Italianate architecture, didactic because it demonstrated the visual power and durability of certain favoured materials which were recom-

108 The National Museum of Wales, Cardiff. Pen and wash, 48.5 × 95 cm. The museum was founded in 1905 but as a result of the First World War the building, by Smith and Brewer, did not open to the public until 1922. It was completed in 1927.

109 The Oxford University Museum of Natural History (1855–60).

110 The Royal Albert Memorial Museum, Exeter. Postcard. Designed by John Hayward, an Exeter architect with an extensive West Country practice. The building was completed in 1869. (The building proceeded in several stages, as funding allowed). Originally intended to house a multiplicity of functions, it was the ancestor of the city's university and art college.

Exeter Museum.

JWS 1009

mended for use in other buildings. It was a style devised by a succession of military engineers at South Kensington from the 1850s onwards and defied the classical hegemony expressed by the National Gallery and the British Museum.[51] The use of terracotta was widely imitated, especially in early American museums, where it became a symbol of adherence to South Kensington.

It was in the field of the natural sciences that the boldest non- or even anti-classical experiments were made. A precedent was created by the buildings of Deane and Woodward, first at Trinity College Dublin and then at the University Museum in Oxford (Fig. 109). Erected between 1855 and 1860 in a version of Venetian Gothic strongly influenced by Ruskin, the Oxford museum housed the university's natural history and geological collections as well as laboratories and professorial rooms, and in its wake versions of medieval styles were accepted as appropriate for natural history museums. Leading examples were designed by Alfred Waterhouse, notably the Natural History Museum in London (1881), built in a version of German Romanesque and described by Summerson as 'by far the largest and most impressive building, apart from the British Museum, to be built for museum purposes in Britain',

and the Manchester Museum, part of the ambitious structure of Manchester University erected in the 1880s.[52] Ruskinian Gothic, and Gothic architecture in general, were less widely applied in art galleries, perhaps surprisingly in view of his links with many of their founders.[53] In Britain, museums in the Gothic manner, as at Dundee (completed 1869;) and Exeter (1870; Fig. 110), tend to date from the early days of the municipal museum and were aimed at scientific collections as much as at art. At Exeter the architect, John Hayward, intended 'to reproduce some of the picturesque character of the old city, without copying any of the old forms of its architecture'. In what might be seen as a concession to Ruskin, the windows were inspired by Italian forms and the ornaments 'have more of that free and bold treatment which is to be found on the Continent rather than in old examples in this country'.[54] Given the general waning of enthusiasm for Gothic revival architecture in Britain after 1870, it is a late and relatively rare Gothic gallery.

As provincial museum and gallery buildings became increasingly varied architecturally, the choice of style tended to depend on the whims of patrons and committees rather than on a canon of taste. Style appears to have been a matter of personal

111 Wolverhampton Art Gallery, which opened in 1884 as part of the Fine Arts and Industrial Exhibition for Wolverhampton and South Staffordshire. Postcard. Designed by the Birmingham architect Julius Chatwin, the building is adorned with a frieze illustrating the arts and crafts, and science.

Art Gallery, Wolverhampton. 43/12

inclination. If a chronological development can be detected (other than the shift away from Gothic), it is a movement towards buildings of increasing size and pretension.

In an age of rampant eclecticism, few stylistic conventions applied to the design of museums other than entrance by an imposing hall and the erection of two storeys, with picture galleries on the upper floor and sculpture or scientific specimens beneath. A new museum or gallery building might be 'a classic structure, the lower part being of the Doric, and the upper story of the Ionic order', with 'panels sculptured in bold relief' depicting all the arts, as at Wolverhampton Art Gallery and Museum (completed in 1884; Fig. 111).[55] Its style could be Gothic; or 'the English renaissance of the eighteenth century, freely treated' as at Bury Art Gallery (1901);[56] or Italianate or 'modern Renaissance' in the New (Feeney) Art Galleries (1912) at Birmingham City Art Gallery – the term 'Renaissance' was freely and optimistically applied. It might adopt a Second Empire style, as at the Bowes Museum (begun 1869, completed 1892); or a daring combination of Roman classicism with French mansard roofs, as at Sunderland Art Gallery and Museum (1877–9; Fig. 112); 'composite Italian classic-baroque', as at the Atkin-

son Art Gallery, Southport (1878);[57] or Eclectic Jacobean (a rare style for a museum) for the Sedgwick Museum in Cambridge (1904). Alternatively it might be clothed, as at the Kelvingrove Art Gallery and Museum (1902; Fig. 113), in a celebratory manner described as 'a kind of Spanish Renaissance'.[58] Alongside these boldly affirmative structures ran a trickle of nondescript buildings erected in no particular style, such as Leeds City Art Gallery, of which up to 2009 the *Buildings of England* could only bring itself to say that it provided 'an addition to the Municipal Buildings of 1887–8'.[59] It may be suggested that the uncertainty of the architectural language reflected the multi-faceted definition of the museum's purpose. As Simon Bradley notes, this extreme variety also reflected the taste of individual cities, with Newcastle retaining a tradition of civic classicism from the great Neoclassical days of John Dobson into the twentieth century, and Manchester showing a propensity for Gothic.[60]

PRACTICAL ISSUES

At the unacknowledged heart of the discourse over the design of the art gallery, as of the science

112 Sunderland Museum and Winter Garden. Postcard. One of the earliest municipal art galleries, it opened in 1879 in a city that had become wealthy through ship-building. The building backs onto a park and includes an impressive Winter Garden. Many art galleries and museums were commemorated in colour postcards such as this, evidence of their central place in the popular consciousness.

museum, was the issue of iron construction, already used by Smirke throughout the British Museum but concealed from view, and still controversial late in the century. While the Crystal Palace may not have been accepted as architecture, it had incontestably provided the most admired and successful exhibition space to date, permitting display on an unparalleled scale. It 'involved machinery in almost every possible aspect of the construction process – the creation of the pillars, the glass, the famous Paxton gutters, the wrought-iron arches, the patented trolleys that transported the glaziers along the roof'.[61] The building inspired in Britain and all over the Western world comparable temporary or semi-permanent structures, though none that shared Paxton's courage in making his building transparent.

As Pevsner and Andrew Saint have discussed, construction in iron and glass was associated with temporary needs and immediate convenience, as at an industrial mill. It could therefore be exposed internally for a temporary exhibition building, even though the façades were usually, as in London in 1862, given architectural elevations. Iron and glass construction, more or less unconcealed, was also considered appropriate for places for the entertain-

ment of the urban population – notably in such prominent adornments of Glasgow as the spectacular Kibble Palace, re-erected in the city's Botanic Garden in 1873 and used as a conservatory and as a gallery for the display of (frequently sensuous) sculpture. In such a building art was on show, but it was primarily contemporary art intended to appeal to a broad audience. Saint suggests that the need in exhibition spaces for rapid construction and up-to-date technology meant that 'in the mid-Victorian building world a permanent, symbolic museum architecture was incompatible with efficiency'.[62] On the whole, the symbolic language won, at least superficially, since '[c]onventionally, the values of architecture had been set upon permanence, and thus upon monuments'.[63] For a museum that embodied eternal values, as opposed to the temporary pleasures of the exhibition, the ephemeral would not do. This belief meant that although iron and glass construction was central to museum buildings late in the nineteenth century from the Brompton Boilers at South Kensington and Oxford University Museum to York City Art Gallery and Kelvingrove, the construction had to be, as far as possible, clothed – as in a railway station – by the addition of a piece of 'true architecture'. Thus, the

155

113 Kelvingrove Art Gallery and Museum, 1902. Glasgow's Superintendent of Museums travelled extensively in order to research the best solution for the city's new museum. The result, designed by a London firm, Simpson and Allen, received a mixed press but has always succeeded as a museum for all.

most innovative elements of the nineteenth-century museum and exhibition buildings – not only the means of construction, but the vast spaces that they were able to provide – had to be concealed.

The interest in new technology that characterised the great exhibitions extended to their children, the new museums and galleries. Heating and ventilation were extensively discussed by builders and curators, along with the introduction of gas (and later electric) lighting into display spaces. In 1851 the *Art Journal* devoted an extended article to 'lighting picture and sculpture galleries', criticising the inadequacies of many British galleries and pointing out

that such problems had generally been resolved in France and Germany (with the Munich Glyptothek receiving the usual plaudits as a model of good lighting).[64] At Nottingham the official 1878 *Statement of the Objects of this Institution*, issued on its opening, emphasised the attention that had been given to heating and lighting in planning the building,[65] while at Bury the modern technical provision included 'ventilation and heating by the *plenum* system', an early form of air circulation.[66] The availability of electricity produced a rapid reaction. At Glasgow it was reported in 1894 that 'The installation of lighting…has proved an unqualified success',

156

114 The interior of Victoria Gallery, Dundee. To celebrate Queen Victoria's Golden Jubilee, a group of civic leaders and businessmen commissioned the Victoria Galleries, which were added to the existing Albert Institute. The extension opened in 1889, offering picture galleries on the first floor and museum rooms downstairs. It was funded by the generosity of John Keiller, manufacturer of marmalade and jam, together with an energetic money-raising campaign that included a four-day 'Indiapolis Bazaar'.

being both 'more efficient' and much cheaper than gas lighting,[67] while three years later at the Walker it was judged that the new electric lighting enhanced the paintings' appearance.[68] At the Victoria Galleries in Dundee, the introduction of natural lighting benefitted from the industrial expertise of one of its patrons, James Guthrie Orchar, a manufacturer of machinery for the textile industry. Seeking to obtain the best light, he constructed in his engineering works a full-size model of the proposed interior in order to test 'the unique curved walls (which angle the higher pictures down towards the viewer) and the double-skinned glass roof (which diffuses the daylight)'. After some adjustments these features were incorporated, along with the innovative use of electric light, as early as 1889 (Fig. 114).[69]

THE DISPLAY OF ART

Although metropolitan critics of provincial museums often commented on their disorder, it is clear that considerable efforts were made to provide sympathetic settings and to arrange the works of art com-

prehensibly. Nottingham Castle Museum's 1878 *Statement* stressed that 'The colouring of the galleries has been the subject of special consideration, and acknowledged masters of colour have been consulted thereon'. It explained the principles, advanced for the time, on which the pictures had been arranged (Fig. 115) in opposition to the densely crammed hangs applied at the Royal Academy:

> The immense wall space at the disposal of the Council will enable them to give an ample margin to every picture; and it is the intention of the Castle Museum Committee to act upon the principles which have been found so successful in some modern Galleries, namely, so to isolate every picture and work of art as to bring out its inherent beauties, and give it room to produce its full and natural effect.[70]

By the 1890s, with the increasing professionalisation of museum curatorship and the impact of aesthetic displays at such places as the ultra-fashionable Grosvenor Gallery, the subject was being regularly aired. In an address to the Museums Association in 1893, Flower extended his remarks beyond the realm

of science to the 'too great crowding' of works in art galleries, their poor visibility, the incongruities of display and the unsuitability of many of the settings:[71] 'Correct classification, good labelling, isolation of each object from its neighbours, the provision of a suitable background, and above all of a position in which it can be readily and distinctly seen, are absolute requisites in art museums as well as in those of natural history.'[72]

The argument was taken further by Walter Armstrong, Director of the National Gallery of Ireland. In 1913 he read a 'forceful paper' on 'The Necessity for Aesthetic Harmony between Museums and Galleries and their Contents', urging that 'the walls, cases, frames, backgrounds and fittings in art museums should be more in harmony with the nature of their contents'.[73] Armstrong, a distinguished director who had battled with the poor state of the Gallery since his appointment some twenty years earlier, reflected his time: it was not just Flower's desiderata – the need for order and visibility – that were being enunciated, but a sense that a

gallery should offer a wholly sympathetic setting for the works of art.

In spite of these rousing comments, standards of display and arrangement in provincial museums were often attacked. In 1906 a contributor of three articles on 'English Provincial Museums' in the *Burlington Magazine* remarked that while the standards of classification and arrangement of the collections had 'witnessed an enormous advance',[74] the 'degree of order' remained unsatisfying: 'Things good and bad are labelled and displayed side by side with an impartiality that can scarcely fail to mislead the designer who comes to the gallery in search of models or suggestions.'[75] Visitors (presumably the writer had uneducated ones in mind) risked being corrupted by experiencing poor works shown without discrimination, in that the inferior quality of pictures at the Bowes Museum (a curious choice, to modern eyes) could in a more populous place than Barnard Castle 'hardly fail to have a disastrous effect upon those who visited it with the view of increasing their taste and knowledge'. Hardly one in ten of provincial museums could offer the visitor a logical and orderly understanding of their collections or effect the education of the eye so evidently missing at the Bowes. The *Burlington* wrote in a similar vein: praising Birmingham City Art Gallery for its 'consistent good judgement' in acquisitions, it contrasted its 'definite character' with Manchester and Liverpool, where 'the masterpiece hangs surrounded by its artistic enemies – by pictures which are a denial of its earnestness'.[76]

Some regional galleries did give increasing attention to providing attractive and comfortable spaces, particularly when new buildings were created. At the newly established Bury Art Gallery, the former Director described the new building in 1907 as 'admitted to be architecturally imposing, well designed, judiciously arranged, and in appearance and character well worthy of its dedication'. His eulogy of the interiors reveal the care taken in their installation, with the pictures hung in a single line, a double lighting system and 'cream-coloured curtains' for the watercolours, with polished oak parquet floors (see Fig. 91).[77]

The choice of wall colourings was controversial. By 1900, in a reaction against the dark colours of the Victorian gallery, it was common for curators to employ subtly modulated tones and even white under the influence of proponents of the Aesthetic Movement, as expressed in the *Studio*. This approach was not greeted with universal approval, the *Museums Journal* lamenting in 1913 that 'At present, with very few exceptions, the walls and ceilings of our museums are…an indescribable drab colour, if they are not painted white.' White might be a suitable colour for a bathroom, but 'Dark and strongly coloured objects in a museum look doubly dark against white walls.'[78] Certainly it was not the colour of choice at the newly extended Birmingham City Art Gallery in 1912. A press account ecstatically described 'the splendid interior', rhapsodising that

> Indeed, one cannot realise that this airy, elegant salon is merely the portal to the galleries. Beautifully moulded columns of white, owing something to Tuscan design for their style, carry an arched roof ornately fashioned, and divide each wall of the vestibule into three bays. The floor reflects the general colour scheme with its mosaic pavement of marble of delicate green and white. In the bays

are the richly coloured and beautifully designed tapestries, in whose production Sir Edward Burne-Jones and William Morris collaborated.[79]

Here was an Aesthetic interior executed in the boldest manner.

The Museums Association, through the *Museums Journal*, was a strong voice in favour of restrained decorative schemes and pale colours, often citing foreign instances and notably those associated with the German museum reform movement. It published an extended article by the Curator of the Industrial Art Museum in Christiania in Denmark, who on the basis of two European tours asserted the overriding excellence of unobtrusive colours. His paper, read at the Museums Association conference in 1904, appears to have met with approval, Mr Lowe of Plymouth commenting that 'there was a very simple way to ascertain whether or not the rooms and backgrounds were of a right colour. When a visitor had completed his round of the museum, let him be asked what was the colour of the walls. If he did not know, then one might be sure they were the right colour.'[80] This point of view came to be widely accepted. When the Tate Gallery opened its extension in 1910, the *Museums Journal* lamented the rich decorative scheme selected for the Turner rooms, citing 'a pathetic lament…from a colleague':

> Ye gods! Walls covered with crimson silk tapestry; a dado and floor border of green marble with appalling variegations; and a parquetry floor! Such is Tate's terrible treatment of Turner. Turner the colourist, who has here no colour. It is taken out of him by the background!…Woe is me, for we are back in early Victorian days, and the voice of the Museums Association has been as that of one who cries in the wilderness. Go ye, my brethren, and profit by this magnificent example of how *not* to do it.[81]

The hanging of paintings was another recurring theme in the art press. From its first publication in 1893 onwards, the *Studio* attacked the bad hangs at the Royal Academy in contrast to the arrangements at the New Gallery, which allowed pictures to breathe. It discussed J.M. Whistler's attitude to displaying art, and publicised the exhibitions of the Vienna Sezession and exhibitions in Turin and

Mannheim. By the opening of the new century, Eastlake's desire to arrange pictures in a single row at eye level was increasingly being realised: as his nephew Charles Lock Eastlake wrote in 1887, the paintings at the National Gallery were now thinly hung, and that 'no one is likely to complain of this who remembers the immense superiority in effect which every picture gains by comparative isolation on the walls'.[82] At Birmingham City Art Gallery, photographs taken late in the century show the (dark) walls draped with swagged fabric at around half the height of the room, presumably to minimise the height and avoid the earlier style of paintings hung from floor to ceiling (Fig. 116).

By the 1910s the idea of creating a harmonious environment for works of art was widely accepted, with the Wallace Collection, opened to the public in 1900, generally regarded as a model. This approach was particularly evident in collector museums, which realised the founder's intention to create a small perfect universe away from the daily world. For Lord Leverhulme, the construction of an ideal community for his workers extended beyond housing

and community halls. As his apologist wrote, Leverhulme extended his concern with his own visual surroundings to his 'villagers':

> He felt ill at ease in a mean, commonplace, or ugly environment, and to this feeling may be largely ascribed his creation of Port Sunlight. What advantages he enjoyed he was always desirous of sharing with his employees, and his keen perception of beauty inspired him with the wish to render their everyday surroundings as beautiful as possible.

Throughout Port Sunlight, 'there exists no jarring or incongruous note'.[83] In the spirit of Ruskin, the new community was to be dominated by the beauty and art enshrined in the Lady Lever Art Gallery, which would house his lovingly acquired personal collection while commemorating his wife. Its location within the village was a rare example of an art gallery at the centre of a planned layout (Fig. 117). The Gallery's character was strongly defined: it was not to be 'a morgue of art objects – the unfortunate

160

fate of so many provincial galleries…He wished, and rightly, that it should form an integral part of the everyday life of the community, a place which should be a second and more splendid home for them.'[84]

INTERNAL PLANNING

It is hard to generalise about the internal planning of Victorian and Edwardian art museums, since the proud individuality of the towns and the scattered nature of patronage made for a wide variety of approaches. The planning of museums has been subjected to critical scrutiny by followers of Foucault, with the museum categorised as a space dedicated to supervision where visitors could be controlled intellectually and physically through long sightlines and viewpoints from on high.[85] In an extended analysis of this approach, Kate Hill has concluded pragmatically that 'the prevailing idea of Victorian museums as disciplinary institutions which produced self-policing, improving citizens…has to be modified', not least on account of the limited resources of these museums, which would scarcely permit supervision at this level. As she concludes, 'Victorian museums were not disciplinary spaces, they were

relatively unplanned, underdetermined spaces which responded to local conditions.'[86] This analysis is convincing, and it is suggested here that Victorian museums of the popular type were notable for their variety and adaptability, for the unconstrained enjoyment that, like parks, they were able to offer to audiences that previously had been deprived of such pleasures. It is significant that these museums were always free in the nineteenth century (as they largely remain today).

Sophie Forgan has identified four major circulation systems for scientific museums in nineteenth-century Britain: 'the domestic, articulated by a staircase'; a circuit of rooms, leading the visitor back to the starting point; rooms that can be entered in a series from a linking corridor, as in Continental picture galleries; and 'the 'dispersed' system, 'where from a central hall one could choose a number of points from which to start a perambulation'.[87] To an extent, these types are reflected in Victorian art galleries. The domestic approach hardly applied to art museums except in the case of collector museums housed in domestic interiors, such as the Russell-Cotes Museum in Bournemouth. Equally, the plan based on rooms accessible from a linking corridor was not regularly used, though such an arrangement exists (on two levels) at Kelvingrove. On the other hand, the circuit of rooms set around a central hall (or two halls) or staircase was a classic type, going back to Durand's plans for an ideal museum and frequently applied by the designers of Beaux-Arts museums. It was executed in such early buildings as the Royal Manchester Institution and remained a regular choice in the new century, as in the Aberdeen Art Gallery (1905) and the Feeney Art Galleries at Birmingham. The straightforward plan made it well suited to inclusion within classical elevations, but even in such an externally bombastic building as Glasgow Art Gallery and Museum the essential symmetry of the plan resembles Beaux-Arts prototypes.

In some respects, art gallery design diverges from the pattern posited by Forgan. The top-lit picture gallery, a type derived from seventeenth- and eighteenth-century prototypes, and sometimes the culmination of a series of rooms, provided a module for internal planning.[88] The enfilade of galleries derived from the Baroque palace was used by Soane at Dulwich and reappeared as two parallel enfilades at

118 A plan of Kelvingrove Art Gallery and Museum. In keeping with the original purpose of the building as an exhibition hall, much thought was given to creating impressive large spaces suitable for housing major events and objects, an effective circulation system and the demarcation of separate zones for the very various collections.

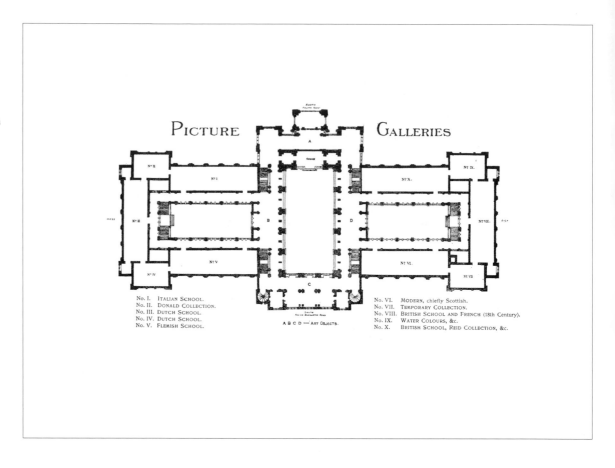

PICTURE GALLERIES

No. I. ITALIAN SCHOOL.
No. II. DONALD COLLECTION.
No. III. DUTCH SCHOOL.
No. IV. DUTCH SCHOOL.
No. V. FLEMISH SCHOOL.

No. VI. MODERN, chiefly Scottish.
No. VII. TEMPORARY COLLECTION.
No. VIII. BRITISH SCHOOL AND FRENCH (18th Century).
No. IX. WATER COLOURS, &c.
No. X. BRITISH SCHOOL, REID COLLECTION, &c.

A B C D — ART OBJECTS.

the Mappin Art Gallery. More usual, however, was a form of accretive planning, the addition of rooms or suites of rooms as and when necessary, an approach pioneered (if the word is appropriate for such a piecemeal process) at the National Gallery. This approach can be identified in many municipal galleries, which offered serviceable sets of rooms as advocated by Robinson. Even in such a relatively ambitious building as Birmingham, the circular hall at the top of the stairs – a modified grand statement – leads either to the Industrial Hall or to the picture galleries, with no sense of an overall plan. Equally, the Walker Art Gallery grew section by section from modest internal beginnings into a structure suited to the grandeur of its façade and its collection. While an enfilade or a great hall might express confidence and pride, modular development reflected practical limitations.

The creation of a central hall allowing a variety of routes around a building was realised at a number of galleries, including Kelvingrove and the Glynn Vivian Gallery in Swansea (1911). Erected in the Baroque style, the Glynn Vivian has a large central hall surrounded at first floor level by an open balcony. James Paton had outlined the advantages of this approach in his prospectus for Kelvingrove. The design (Fig. 118) would be clear and practical: 'A simple, well-ordered plan, so that visitors may always know where they are, and where they have been, with ready access to all stages and departments, to enable them to return with ease to any department they may wish to revisit, are the essential and meritorious features of internal design.'[89] He mentions the influence of the 'Dresden Gallery', underlining the rarity of such an ideal plan in Britain. The rooms for natural history, arms and armour and so forth were arranged on the ground floor around the hall, with the art galleries on the upper storey, while a liminal space between hall and exhibition spaces was created by the arcades processing around the central space at both levels.

In both these buildings, the location of the hall expresses more than an interest in circulation. These plans provided the kind of socialised experience offered by a major exhibition building where the hall functioned like an indoor city square, suitable for

162

congregating and promenading. Since a museum was 'of the people and for the people, for rich and poor, high and low…it becomes a duty to render such an institution cheerful, bright, and gay, and to attract the people into it by every honourable device', in Paton's words. The central space would be a suitable place to listen to music, with an additional function: 'Such a hall, adorned with shrubs and flowering plants, would form a suitable centre for the accommodation and refreshment of a vast number on the occasion of any public festival or rejoicing.'[90] More strongly than in any other civic art museum, the Great Hall at Kelvingrove (Fig. 119) epitomises the museum and art gallery as a palace for the people. Far from Robinson's dour practicality, this attitude

reflects the joyous, festive quality, the almost carnival atmosphere, of some late Victorian museums, especially those that were closely linked to exhibitions. Equally, there can have been nothing dour about the evening parties and the conversaziones held over many years at many galleries, some but by no means all for the social elite (Fig. 120).

With its elaborate sculptural programme, marble floors, splendid Art Nouveau light fixtures and rich internal decoration, Kelvingrove offered – and still offers – a welcome to all comers. In such an interior, the organ recitals, played on an instrument built in 1901 and acquired for the exhibition, presented in the tradition of Hallé's concerts at the Manchester Art Treasures Exhibition a virtuous alternative to

163

THE FINE ART INSTITUTION : THE PICTURE GALLERY—OLD MASTERS

YORK ILLUSTRATED

120 York City Art Gallery, a wood engraving from *York Illustrated* (1879). This lively representation of the Yorkshire Fine Art and Industrial Exhibition of 1879 conveys the social aspect of Victorian galleries and exhibitions.

the raucous and improper entertainment of such venues as Glasgow's Britannia Music Hall, famous for the improprieties of the performers and the rowdiness of the audience. In addition to all the other achievements of the Gallery (notably the success of its great mid-twentieth-century director T.J. Honeyman in making it integral to Glaswegian life), one reason why the people of Glasgow feel an intense pride in their art collections must be this extraordinary building.[91]

The new building cost the enormous sum of around £250,000, which was found with some difficulty.[92] Not to the taste of purists, it was given a

cautious welcome in the art press. The *Art Journal* wrote that 'As without, so within, a sumptuous style of decoration has been adopted, and the galleries are of many sizes, and suited for classification of art exhibits…in its broad features the building must be pronounced a satisfactory piece of architecture, though architects may criticise many of the details'.[93]

THE EDWARDIAN CLIMAX

With a quite different patronage background to Kelvingrove, Cartwright Hall in Bradford expresses

Edwardian confidence in museum and patron at a time when grandiose public buildings in the style subsequently dubbed Imperial Baroque were being erected all over the country. It represents the apogee of gallery building around 1900: redolent of wealth, edging towards a definition of the municipal museum as a statement of financial security, celebratory in the provision of public spaces while addressing complex technical issues. Like Glasgow, Cartwright Hall originally functioned as the centrepiece of a 'world exhibition', and the ability of these festive events to liberate patrons and public from the mundane world is reflected in its expensive *panache*.

A complex history existed behind the philanthropy of Samuel Cunliffe-Lister, later Lord Masham. The building was named after Edmund Cartwright, whose invention of a wool-combing machine leading to mechanisation had formed the basis for Bradford's wealth. Cunliffe-Lister was one of the leaders in developing such mechanisation but it was a leadership he had been obliged to dispute lengthily and in public with a former business partner.[94] Having sold his family house and its

grounds to the city, he offered £40,000 for the erection of a public art gallery. This prominent gesture of patronage to the city that had given him his wealth was expressed in the entrance façade, bearing the arms of Bradford and of Masham.

Cartwright Hall was no ordinary gallery. It had numerous purposes, summarised in the President's speech to the Bradford Conference of the Museums Association in 1902 when he discussed the advantages of a central art gallery and museum in 'large commercial cities'…As an example of beautiful architecture, it would stimulate buildings of equal quality in the city; it would be a centre of industrial art, and 'help the people to see the possibilities of the future through the examples of the past, and thereby be an incentive for future prosperity'; and the contents would 'give to the community happiness and pleasure through seeing the beautiful creations of man' (Fig. 121).[95] Additionally – an objective not stated in the Presidential Address – the lavish interiors were designed for civic processions and banquets, necessitating halls, imposing staircases and large kitchens, with a south entrance treated as the main façade of the building since it

165

122 Oldham Museum, Art Gallery and Library. Opened in 1883, the building cost £26,748, heavily over estimate. The architect was the Oldham-based Thomas Mitchell, who had an extensive practice in the North-West. He worked here in a Gothic style intended to combine 'simplicity of outline with dignity of character and economy of construction'.

was originally intended to be reserved for guests at civic functions.[96] Here the Baroque Revival style was executed on a scale and with a degree of internal splendour that distinguished it from all but its most ambitious peers. The fittings proclaimed the excellence of the patron, the gallery walls being covered in silk tapestry made by his company, Lister and Co.[97] The building was acclaimed, the *Museums Journal* calling the building 'one of the finest of its kind in Europe' and remarking that 'The richly ornamented courts opening into one another, and built with the creamy stone from Giffnock Quarries, are in themselves objects for admiration.' Lighting, as always in a gallery, was important, and the hall, lit by 'ten massive electroliers...has a beautiful effect'.[98] Naturally, the heating and ventilation systems were fully up-to-date.

ART GALLERIES AND OTHER FUNCTIONS

In terms of buildings, art galleries often co-existed with other types of collection and function. The continuing link between the arts and the sciences dominated the British Museum, which housed the natural history specimens until the creation of the Natural History Museum in the 1880s, while the South Kensington Museum included the Department of Science and Art's scientific collections into the twentieth century.[99] In regional cities, the relationship between science and the arts was usually expressed by their accommodation on different floors of one building: typically at Brighton Museum and Art Gallery (1902), where the new art gallery was sited upstairs, with the natural history and archaeological collections downstairs, and the town library next door.[100] The same pattern was to be found at Oldham in a building that opened in 1883 and housed art gallery, museum and library, with a lecture hall added a few years later (Fig. 122), and applied in many other towns.[101] Rivalries might emerge, as a speaker at the Bradford 1902 conference celebrating Cartwright Hall intimated when suggesting 'that too much allowance had been left for rooms to be devoted to art in proportion to the space allotted to the scientific collections'.[102]

In many instances a gallery found itself sharing a roof with other building types. Providing housing for the director or curator was an old-established practice, initiated in Britain at the original Ashmolean Museum with its Keeper's Lodging, and developed on a grand scale at the British Museum and South Kensington. The practice was followed in some regional museums: the 1878 floor plan of Nottingham Castle indicates a modest self-contained two-storey 'Director's Residence' next to his office.[103] Following the British Museum, again, the museum often shared premises with the public library, which frequently occupied the more prominent space.[104] Equally, the museum or gallery might co-exist with an art school, as at Exeter, where art school, library and museum were intermixed: in this case the multi-purpose building resembled a prototype such as William Hunter's house-museum in Great Windmill Street, London, which combined a school of anatomy, a library, a museum, a picture gallery and a residence.[105] The modern role of the museum as a place of entertainment was anticipated at Cartwright Hall, while at Birmingham the City Art Gallery was accommodated (for reasons of economy) above the ground floor Gas Hall, headquarters of the city's innovative and remunerative gas service. All these instances illustrate the municipal gallery's equivocal identity. The multiple functions of a municipal museum are well illustrated by the Museum, Art Gallery and Library in Oldham (Figs 123–126).

❖

THE POSITION OF THE MUSEUM WITHIN THE CITY AND THE PASTORAL ALTERNATIVE

This ambivalence extended to the geographical position of the gallery within the city. Greenwood opened his 1888 survey of museums by describing their obscure location in many towns:

> Should the inquirer...be persistent in his determination to find the local Museum, he will perhaps, in the smaller towns, eventually drop upon it only to find it situated in some narrow and unfrequented street, or some out-of-the-way yard where the chief ornament is a pump...[and indoors] immediately he casts eyes on the cases he finds dust and disorder reigning supreme.[106]

Although the idea of an association between the museum and the public square as a site of national commemoration and celebration was sometimes addressed in nineteenth-century Britain, the civic supremacy of the museum that can be seen in Munich, Berlin and Dresden, or later in Chicago and Boston, was seldom achieved.[107] The British Museum's principal façade has always faced a row of unexceptional town houses. By contrast, for Trafalgar Square in front of the National Gallery Charles Barry had envisaged 'an opportunity...of giving scope and encouragement to sculptural art of a high class, and of giving that distinctive and artistic character to the square, which is so much needed in the public areas and squares of London, to excite amongst all classes that respect and admiration for art, so essentially necessary to the formation of a pure and well-grounded national taste'.[108] In fact, the square did not develop as an external display space: until recently it was cut off from the gallery by a busy road and contained a modest and incomplete sculptural programme.[109]

The tradition of understatement in the placing of galleries tended to apply in regional cities. They were not alone in this among public buildings. Although universities, schools and hospitals were frequently handsomely constructed or rebuilt, notably the Board Schools in London, they were seldom incorporated into any overall urban concept. Equally, buildings associated with the armed services tended to be kept well away from the centre: as Saint has put it, 'a phobia about flagrant military

presence in English cities persisted'.[110] Only town halls tended to enjoy a fine central site. In some cities the art museum was treated as part of the streetscape, as at the Royal Manchester Institute, or the Fitzwilliam Museum (Fig. 127). But in many cases the site was less distinguished, whether the central but under-exploited setting of Leeds City Art Gallery or, in the noble Neoclassical city of Newcastle, the location of the Laing Art Gallery in Higham Place, an alleyway inconsequentially related to the city centre and originally facing a row of mean commercial premises, which even at the time was not regarded as a suitable location.[111] The same lack of ambition applied in such burgeoning towns as Oldham, Rochdale or Bury, where insignificant sites accommodated relatively imposing museum and gallery buildings.

Sometimes the art museum was given a more prominent setting. In a few cases it served as an annexe to the town hall, a juxtaposition that – as Bruno Foucart suggests with reference to French civic museums – placed the galleries at the centre of local power.[112] Thus in Birmingham the Gallery is sited on Chamberlain Square, an important public space to the rear of the Council House, though secondary to the main square (Fig. 128). Only in a few instances was the museum or gallery given a central situation, to triumphant effect. In Liverpool the Walker Art Gallery enjoys a striking site as part of a ceremonial group of structures dedicated to justice, the arts and learning (Fig. 129), while at Preston the extraordinary bulk of the Harris Art Gallery and Museum dominates the Market Square and is juxtaposed with the leading civic buildings.

MUSEUMS AND PARKS

Late in the nineteenth century North America saw the emergence of the concept of the City Beautiful.[113] In Philadelphia and Chicago the great Beaux-Arts museums were given visually conspicuous settings approached by avenues linking them to the city centres, in a manner inspired by Washington and ultimately Versailles. Such grand schemes almost never applied in British cities, since even in Edinburgh the ruling principle of planning was Picturesque rather than Baroque. Cardiff offers a rare exception: the set of public buildings around Cathays Park, erected from around 1900 onwards and including the majestic Beaux-Arts National Museum of Wales (1905–27), constitutes what has been called 'the finest civic centre in the British Isles'.[114] But in general the avoidance of assertive public statements and the neo-pastoral tendencies of urban planning were so firmly established in Britain that they stimulated an alternative approach.

During the later years of the century the creation of a sylvan setting for a museum became increasingly popular. This principle was not without precedent. Since the seventeenth century the botanical garden had been the sister of the museum, and in the Victorian city the relationship revived, in a new guise. The proponents in the 1850s of moving the National Gallery to semi-rural Kensington believed that the Gallery and its visitors would benefit from the clean air and the surrounding gardens, which would complement the works of art. William Ewart summarised this approach when he asked an 1853 Select Committee on the National Gallery, expecting an affirmative answer, whether 'it is desirable to prepare the minds of visitors to the gallery by the distribution in the surrounding grounds of statues, fountains, and other decorations of an artistic character?'[115] Various themes emerge in these discussions: firstly, the creation of a suburban Arcadia where works of art and other collections would shine more beautifully; secondly, the health, physical and moral, of the population; and, thirdly, the contribution a gallery's collection and building could make to a city's beauty.

Given that one of the most common complaints made about provincial cities was their ugliness, made up of mean buildings, poor atmospheric conditions, and a divorce from natural surroundings, the art museum had an important role. In Manchester, still in the 1880s considered a long way behind other major towns 'in the question of art galleries', the new City Art Gallery was felt by a councillor to be 'doing a great deal to take away what was called the "unloveliness of Manchester"'.[116] Museums should be beautiful and, if possible, beautifully sited. At Sheffield, the Mappin Art Gallery and the city museum were located

127 The Fitzwilliam Museum, Cambridge. The museum was founded in 1816. The Founder's Building (1837–45) was designed by George Basevi and completed by C.R. Cockerell, architect of the Ashmolean Museum. It opened in 1848.

in a park on the (then) outskirts of the city. As Greenwood wrote, 'The possession of such a building and its contents by the people of Sheffield must exercise profound influence on both the commercial and the moral future of the town. It cannot fail to be humanising and elevating on all who resort to the Gallery'.[117] By the end of the century it was generally expected that a new museum would enhance its city: at the opening of Cartwright Hall the President of the Museums Association expressed his wish 'to impress upon my own citizens how much it is their duty to encourage the erection of all buildings in such a manner that they will make the city attractive'.[118]

A generation later a similar approach was taken in Glasgow. Councillor Robert Crawford emphasised (in the speech cited above) that

To get at the people we must attract them. They must get pleasure or they will not come…a first essential is to attract. How is this attraction to be obtained? In many different ways. Among these I place first the site – attractive surroundings, fresh air, trees, grass, flowers, and birds; water if you can. Let your building and its contents be a diamond set in pearls, Art and Nature intertwined. I am quite fixed in my belief that the hard definiteness of a rigid building in a stony street, with the exhausting tread of ten thousand daily

170

INDEX TO KEY-BLOCK

BIRDS-EYE VIEW OF BIRMINGHAM IN 1886

554 31.

128 Chamberlain Square, Birmingham. The Museum and Art Gallery stands along one side of this imposing square, which contained the old Town Hall of the 1830s, and Mason College (the ancestor of the University of Birmingham). The difficulties over raising money from the rates required the museum to be located on the first floor, over the premises of the profitable gas board, which was also run by the city. Locally the building was considered 'second only to the galleries in which the national collections are exhibited'.

feet, is fatal to a permanent Art Gallery in a place like Glasgow. I am, therefore, of opinion, that the people's parks are the proper situations for the people's galleries.[119]

Whereas the 'Renaissance' City Chambers of the 1880s, resoundingly expressive of civic pride, stand foursquare on George Square at the heart of the Victorian city, Kelvingrove inhabits a sylvan second world. The art gallery opened in 1902 at the centre of a landscaped park, where the picturesque terrain, with its river and valley and hills, sets the visitor in an enchanted landscape that excludes the ordinary

life of the city. For a romantically inclined enthusiast for Glasgow, this was

the most beautiful public pleasure ground in the kingdom. With the noble façade of the University towering on one height, and the terraced mansions which were once the homes of the city's merchant princes on another, while the Art Galleries, with their clustered gables and turrets, rise on the haugh below, and the brimming flood of the Kelvin winds beautifully between its bosky banks, the park combines many of the finest features of nature and of art.[120]

171

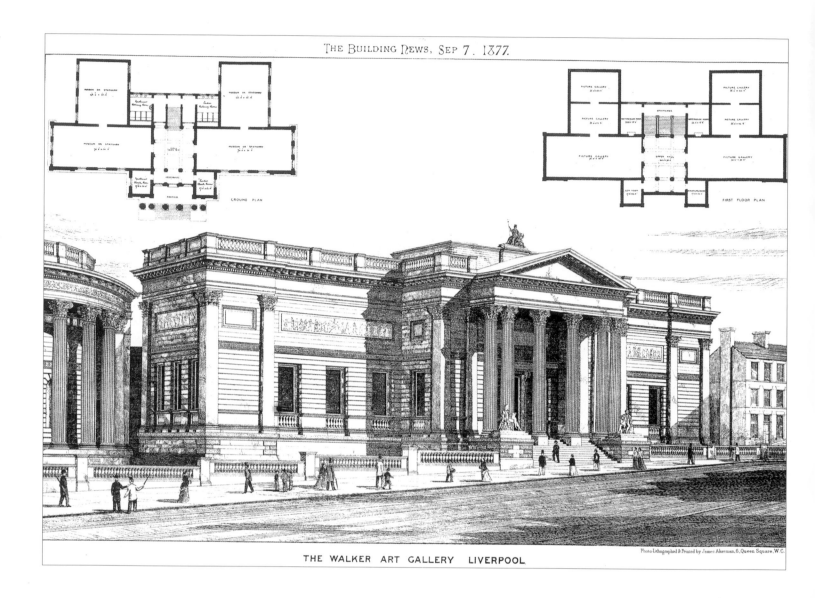

THE WALKER ART GALLERY LIVERPOOL

129 The Walker Art Gallery, Liverpool, a façade and plan from *The Building News*, 7 September 1877. Built in 1847–77, the Gallery was designed by the Liverpool architects Sherlock and Vale. It is flanked by statues of Raphael and Michelangelo. The original building has been extended on numerous occasions.

Here and in other museum-parks, the ensemble was intended to offer the visitor pleasure for the whole day: walking on the lawns, listening to music from the bandstands, studying plants and aviaries. It provided a vision of natural and artificial beauty combined (Fig. 130). In such a setting even the poorest citizens could imagine themselves in the 'ideal city' that Canon Barnett of the Whitechapel Art Gallery envisaged[121] or that George Dawson and Henry Crosskey dreamt of for Birmingham, achieving via beneficent Liberalism 'the enjoyment by the great mass of people of the blessing of a beautiful and civilised life'.[122]

CONCLUSION

Between the late 1860s and the 1920s Britain gained museum and gallery buildings in almost all its major towns. Following the complacency of the 1850s over gallery design, the subject came to be energetically studied. During these years the buildings gained in ambition and practicality, with their hard-headed patrons wishing them to function as efficiently as contemporary technology allowed. This provision of practical facilities represents one of their most important contributions to the development of museum architecture, and explains why in almost all

130 The park at Kelvingrove with the new university building in the background. Postcard. The old university, founded in 1451, and originally in the High Street, reopened in 1870 in new Gothic buildings by George Gilbert Scott. The choice of an English architect for this prestigious commission was much attacked in Scotland.

KELVINGROVE PARK & UNIVERSITY GLASGOW

cases these museums and galleries retain their original function, testimony to the high quality of the original execution. Although the proportions and architectural character of a Victorian gallery may not always be ideal for the art of today, this set of buildings constitutes, for the regions, probably the most important legacy of the late Victorian museum movement.

RRYING THE MAILS   PENINSULAR & ORIENTAL. S.N.C°.   TO   INDIA .

8

THE TEMPORARY
EXHIBITION

NEST OR CUCKOO?

In the context of the traditional museum, the temporary exhibition is an anomaly. Museums, like temples, aspire to the eternal: they are predicated on the notion of preserving the relics of the past and the present, and on the belief that material culture is worthy of preservation and study. Like temples, they create a realm of their own, in which the objects on display possess an aura removed from the outside world and freed of base associations. That at least is one of their underlying theses, however complex and loaded their links with wealth and power may actually be.[1]

Exhibitions, by contrast, are intrinsically ephemeral. They were born in the marketplace, at a time when the art market as it is now known did not exist. Although eighteenth-century exhibitions of contemporary art at the Paris Salon, or at the Royal Academy of Arts in London, theoretically eschewed any dealings with money, cash was in fact central to their activities: one of their prime objectives was to provide artists with the opportunity to reach a new buying public, since no mechanism for this purpose existed other than the (habitual) transformation of the studio into a commercial space. In the nineteenth century – when the temporary exhibition, in a sense that would be recognised today, came to maturity – its role as a marketplace, albeit frequently a concealed one, was maintained. Exhibitions, in their various guises, were usually seen as potentially profitable financially. Dealers regularly charged for admission to temporary exhibitions,[2] and at the humble level of the Mechanics' Institutes or in the more elevated municipal art gallery and Royal Academy, the temporary display was expected both to turn a profit and to remain artistically inspiring (Fig. 131). In France, additionally, the exhibition organised at national level was loaded with political significance.[3] What is more, the exhibition depended, as it does today, on a broad but not unlimited public, entitled by a modest payment to enter the realm reserved for the contemplation of art. This approach was in striking contrast to the scientific museum, predicated on the basis of the informed accumulation of objects, where no exhibit was ever for sale.

Even in its most scholarly modern form, the temporary exhibition – surrounded by the paraphernalia of sponsorship, the resonance of the stellar loan, competitive visitor figures, sensational publicity – still operates as a spectacle. Through the accumulation and arrangement of its constituting objects, most exhibitions today also function as narratives: that is to say the objects on display are chosen as individual elements in a coherent discourse, each object – at least in principle – making an individual contribution to the whole. Although the creation of a narrative was sometimes attempted in the nineteenth century, the idea of paring down the content to only the most illuminating works was unfamiliar even to the organisers of such an intellectually ambitious event as the Manchester Art Treasures Exhibition of 1857.

In spite of its closeness to the marketplace, part of the exhibition's aim is to persuade the viewer that it is an authoritative event, in which the status – the 'genuineness' – of the objects, and of the narrative they embody, can be trusted. Such an ambition applies both when the exhibition is held within an institution such as a museum that is dedicated to conveying knowledge and understanding, and more dubiously when it is presented in a commercial

forum. Many museum exhibitions have asserted their distance from commercial pressures by refusing, for example, to include objects from the art market, which might be given spurious credibility by their inclusion. The relationship between didacticism and the quest for pure knowledge on the one hand, and on the other commercial imperatives (however subtly these may be promoted), forms a constant sub-current in this narrative.

Traditionally, temporary exhibitions were not a feature of the high art museum. Like their peers in France or Germany, the National Gallery and the British Museum traditionally did not mount temporary exhibitions of any size: at the National Gallery, not until the late 1970s. Such events were not considered part of their territory, unless a modest display addressed a recent purchase or a conservation issue (such as the 'Exhibition of Cleaned Pictures' held at the National Gallery in 1947).[4] In contrast, a pragmatic approach was taken at the South Kensington Museum, derived as it was from the Great Exhibition and predicated on the idea of a vast public consuming inexhaustible quantities of visual and factual materials. This museum – entrepreneurial, unacademic at least in its early days, and receptive to the discourse of commerce – always regarded temporary exhibitions as an essential part of its business. This, too, was the approach taken in the Victorian regional museums. While they used the language associated with sites of knowledge and trust, they often depended on the temporary exhibition for creation and survival.

In Victorian Britain, as in many European countries and in the United States, huge numbers of temporary exhibitions were organised in museums and art galleries, purpose-built halls and commercial galleries. Highly influential and particularly well recorded were the Winter Exhibitions at the Royal Academy, which succeeded the British Institution exhibitions in 1867. Initiated by Frederic Leighton, these displays included hundreds of works,[5] They were organised on modest budgets and regularly made a profit: the 1870 Winter Exhibition (the first) cost £1,300 1s 5d and took £3,124 6s 6d in admissions and catalogues, and this pattern was repeated.[6] In the same year, a press view was instituted, possibly for the first time in Britain, an acknowledgement of the increasing importance of the press and the Academy's growing professionalism. In place of the years of negotiation required for the loan of major works in the twenty-first century, schedules were rapid: a standard letter requesting the loan of paintings for an exhibition opening at Burlington House at the beginning of January 1870 was sent out only the preceding November. Apparently these caused no agitation to potential lenders; as late as 14 December a letter was written on behalf of Lord Spencer, agreeing to lend 'the four pictures [by Rubens] in Ball Room at Spencer House' for the following month.[7] Given this administrative ease and the cheapness of arrangements, as well as the surviving riches of private collections, the frequency and size of exhibitions both at the Academy and at regional galleries were not surprising. It was emphasised that the events were organised 'solely in the interest of Art'[8] – that is to say, with no commercial incentive – even though, as it turned out, the display of works from private collections did often contribute to their eventual exodus to the United States.

The first Winter Exhibition was on a relatively small scale, with only 152 pictures, many of them drawn from such famous (and still partly or wholly surviving) sources as the Westminster, Bute, Sutherland and royal collections.[9] Although some of the loans were of extreme splendour, no curatorial supervision applied: in the first room two views of Llangollen were juxtaposed with a portrait of the Prince of the Asturias, *St Jerome* by Savoldo, and Holbein's *Lord de la Warr*, while the second gallery contained works by Ostade, Rembrandt, John Crome, Zurbarán, Giulio Romano, Van Dyck and Wilkie. As at the British Institution, living or recent British artists were given special attention. In this first display the two chosen artists – C. R. Leslie and Clarkson Stanfield – were well represented, with no apparent sense of bathos. Both artists were recently deceased, an advantage in terms of eligibility for selection.[10]

Succeeding Academy exhibitions followed a similar pattern. Henry James memorably commented on their impact on 'the log smitten wanderer [who passed] out of the January darkness of Piccadilly into the radiant presence of Titian and Rubens.'[11] Although as early as 1877 James was suggesting that 'there is an end to everything, even to the picture-list of English castles and Mayfair mansions' these events lasted until the First World War.[12] Their influence was widely felt in the provinces, where major loans from private (and occasionally public) collections formed an essential feature of late Victorian gallery programmes.

'SOMETHING ALMOST MADDENING'

For some observers, notably professional visitors, the volume of exhibitions was overwhelming. Harry Quilter wrote in 1892,

> There is something almost maddening in the apparently unending range of the galleries, as well as in the gigantic size and interminable number of the pictures which they contain, in view of the attempt to grasp within the compass of an ordinary visit…the merit and meaning of so many works of art. Many folks, I fancy, leave the exhibition, wishing for the moment that there was no such thing as a picture or a statue in the world…[13]

Though Quilter was writing primarily about exhibitions held in London, at the Royal Academy, the Grosvenor and the New Galleries and numerous other commercial or semi-commercial premises, his remarks could almost equally have applied to the regions. The major manifestations in provincial cities included thousands of objects assembled in a spirit of comprehensive instruction, testifying to an almost gross ambition to entertain, instruct and sell. Only early in the twentieth century did a more selective approach emerge.

Victorian provincial galleries offered a wide range of exhibition types, some familiar today, some obsolete or diminished. The oldest type of display was the (usually) annual artists' selling exhibitions, descended from the Royal Academy's Summer Exhibitions, which formed the mainstay of many of the new public art galleries in their early years. Shows of industrial art included the loan exhibitions distributed by the Circulation Department of the South Kensington Museum and frequently directed at the display of technical processes. In many cases, world exhibitions included a fine art section, often a significant display in its own right. Another early type, frequently commercial in aspiration, was the show devoted to a single artist's work: this type had a mixed history, only being transformed relatively late in the century into the non-selling retrospective.

The period's mania for large educational exhibitions was apparent in other manifestations. Displays of works of art from private collections were variously configured: whether as a random selection of works (as at the Royal Academy), as a group of loans loosely arranged round a general theme, or as an entire private collection displayed on its own. The good nature of private owners made possible the grand survey, as at Manchester in 1857 and at Leeds in 1868. A closely related type was the historical (as opposed to art historical) exhibition, often a display of portraits supported by manuscripts and relics.

Late in the century other genres developed. Photographic exhibitions became increasingly usual, either as elements of a larger event (as at the Manchester Art Treasures Exhibition) or as independent shows. Often dedicated to an individual photographer, these were frequently an extension of the display of local artists: for example, in 1889 the first exhibition of photographs by members of the Leeds Photographic Society was organised at Leeds City Art Gallery, and became an annual event. Only one style of exhibition that was to become prominent in the twentieth century was hardly to be found in Victorian Britain, at least until the 1890s: the thematic or monographic show, based on scholarly research and including international loans.

PROVINCIAL ART GALLERIES AS EXHIBITION VENUES

To a considerable extent provincial museums, large and small, were the children of the temporary exhibition. In provincial towns early in the nineteenth century, the exhibitions organised by artists' societies had represented the earliest structured events in the visual arts. Erected with this purpose, late Victorian galleries often derived their collections from the sale of exhibited works. Many galleries were born on the foundations of temporary exhibitions that were intended to provide the capital necessary to construct permanent buildings. York City Art Gallery (Fig. 132), opened in 1892, and Kelvingrove Art Gallery, opened in 1902, were both accommodated in exhibition halls conceived for long-term use. At York, the Gallery occupied a building originally intended for the Yorkshire Fine Art and Industrial Exhibition of 1879, and bought by the City Council for its art gallery after years of miscellaneous use, while at Glasgow two large-scale exhibitions paid for the building and the foundation of the museum. The new buildings established in former exhibition halls sometimes retained vestiges of the razzmatazz of the popular events they originally housed (albeit, at Glasgow, a rather solid Scottish razzmatazz).

The staple annual showpiece of the artists' society was central to many of the new galleries. When the new civic art gallery opened in Leeds in 1888, it was expected that exhibitions, particularly the annual displays by the artists' societies, would play a crucial role in the programme as well as providing funding for purchases and maintenance. As the official catalogue put it, 'The future of the Gallery will depend very much on the success of these special Exhibitions'.[14] Often a new art gallery was regarded, especially by artists, primarily as an exhibition venue. These events made a heavy demand on space: at Leeds, as in many other galleries, during the artists' show little or nothing else could be displayed. In addition, as the source from which purchases were made, they shaped the emerging collections, often in a self-perpetuatingly conservative way.

FINE ART EXHIBITION BUILDING, YORK.

132 York City Art Gallery. From 1892, the Gallery was housed in the 'Italian Renaissance' building originally erected for the Yorkshire Fine Art and Industrial Exhibition of 1879.

133 The catalogue for the Autumn Exhibition at the Walker Art Gallery, 1908.

The Walker's Autumn Exhibition of 1888, to take one example, represented the fusion of temple and marketplace. Presented with the trappings of civic dignity and philanthropic didacticism, it of course functioned as a selling enterprise, with prices listed beside each picture.[15] Under the patronage of the Lord Mayor of Liverpool and the City Council, and with the Town Clerk as Honorary Secretary, it was directed by an acting Committee that included several Consulting Artists. Among them were the recent President of the Liverpool Academy of Art and a Corresponding Artist in London, charged with maintaining links with the London artists who, it was hoped, would send in their work. The 'Notice to Exhibitors' declared that the City's Library Museum and Education Committee considered it desirable 'in the interest of Art' (a phrase echoing the Royal Academy's) to hold regular displays of paintings, which would open as soon as was practicable after the closure of the Royal Academy's summer show. The annual reports indicate that the exhibitions were also regarded as educational, allowing Liverpudlians to see works that would otherwise be unavailable.

The scale of these events was a matter of competitive pride: as the 1885 *Report* commented, the new Walker extension opened 'with an exhibition of works of art on a scale hitherto unequalled in the Provinces' (Fig. 133).[16] The Walker exhibitions were swelled by the considerable number of societies that were invited to participate. Each was accorded its own room, rather on the principle of the modern trade fair: this arrangement became possible when an extension to the building allowed the 'exhibition proper' to be hung in the new rooms, with the Royal Society of Painters in Water Colours, the Grosvenor Gallery and so forth shown in the old ones (Fig. 134).

The exhibitions were surrounded by an apparatus of related activities celebrating not only the Gallery and its Autumn Exhibition but more broadly, the city; in Liverpool, as in other cities, such activities formed a focus for the city's social life, often aimed at the upper-middle classes, though not at them alone. In 1884 the Medical Association laid on a conversazione at the Walker, attended by 4,000 people.[17] The following year the Mayor 'held a Reception for the Working Classes, when 10,000 artizans and their wives and daughters were present

134 Title page of the Autumn
Exhibition catalogue, Walker Art
Gallery, 1884.

Corporation of Liverpool.
1884.

FOURTEENTH AUTUMN
Exhibition of Pictures
In Oil and Water-Colours,
And INAUGURATION of the
Extension of the Walker
Art Gallery.

to inspect the Autumn Exhibition and the Library and Museum'.[18] In 1888 the National Association for the Advancement of Art held its first congress in Liverpool, an event involving a glittering array of notables under the presidency of Leighton, with sections on such advanced subjects (for the period) as 'Art History and Museums'.[19] No less impressive as a recognition of the Gallery's importance was the list of 'Distinguished Visitors' included in the Curator's history of the first decade, a list that featured (not surprisingly, in view of Liverpool's importance as a port) assorted princes and ministers of foreign countries, as well as such notables as Ruskin, Gladstone, and Sir Coutts and Lady Lindsay of the Grosvenor Gallery.[20]

Many galleries made a point of maintaining close links with the Royal Academy and with prominent artists in the capital. Proud though they were of their local identity and attachments, adherence to metropolitan and academic ideals remained a constant. One aim was to persuade London artists, especially Academicians, to continue the long-established tradition of sending work to provincial exhibitions: in 1895 the *Annual Report* reported with satisfaction that three councillors and the curator, 'who formed the deputation to visit the London Studios in the early Spring, met everywhere a cordial reception'.[21] In 1883 the Mayor of Oldham, where a new museum had just been set up, reported that he and a town councillor had travelled to London and met the Town Clerk of the City of London, the Chief Librarian of the British Museum, the Director of the South Kensington Museum and other influential persons, and had solicited loans for their forthcoming exhibition.[22] The custom remained alive into the twentieth century: representatives of the Harris Museum and Art Gallery made an official visit to Burlington House almost annually up to 1971.

These displays could be justified in budgetary terms only if they cost the City Council nothing, or made a profit. At Liverpool the public paid to enter and buy catalogues, and visitor figures were minutely recorded and analysed. These were formidable – well over 400,000 every year until 1896. The catalogue – unlike the more discreet publications issued at Burlington House – was overtly aimed at facilitating sales, giving prices but providing no editorial information other than the occasional quotation submitted by the artist (as at the Royal Academy). The 1888 exhibition presented some 430 oils, 450 watercolours (reflecting the growing importance of this medium in the art market), a mere seventeen sculptures, and a few works in other media, to the considerable total of 930 works. The greatest number of oils and watercolours were genre pictures, narrative scenes and landscapes, with local

views especially prominent. Only a few images showed subjects drawn from the Bible or from literature, though illustrations of episodes from Scott and Dickens did feature. Portraits were rare, though homage was paid to the recent donor to the city's museums, Joseph Mayer. Most of the artists were from Liverpool, and on this occasion the number of works by what might be described as 'national' artists was modest: only fourteen pictures were sent by Royal Academicians or Associates, including Leighton.

The early success of these temporary exhibitions did not last. As permanent collections became established, the annual exhibitions often led to problems, especially when they had to displace the expanding permanent holdings. The relationship between artists' societies and curators tended to be difficult. As early as 1877 the *Annual Report* of the Glasgow Museums complained that for the sake of temporary exhibitions, 'the Corporation pictures have yearly been removed from the walls and stored for several months, whereby the pictures have been endangered, frames and mountings injured, and the Corporation Collection detrimentally depreciated in the public estimation'.[23] Such events required 'careful consideration'. These complaints continued for many years, not least because the artists' exhibitions increasingly lost popularity. At Nottingham, the Curator, dissatisfied with the standard of work, stopped the annual exhibition from 1904 to 1907. The annual reports of Leeds City Art Gallery, beginning in 1892, record rapidly falling attendances at the (fee-charging) artists' exhibitions, from over 50,000 in 1892 to 21,000 four years later. The Curator ascribed this drop to a corresponding rise in free visits to the rest of the building.[24] By 1911 the appeal of the Leeds exhibitions had so declined that it was decided to end admission charges, 'on account of the increase in size and importance of the Permanent Collection which is opened free to the public; the abandonment of Musical Recitals at the Special Exhibitions; and the existence of other varied attractions in the City'.[25] By 1914 they retained little validity – at much the same time that the Summer Exhibition at the Royal Academy was waning in critical if not popular esteem – though they often lingered on for years. The Walker abandoned its Autumn Exhibition only after 1938 (Fig. 135).[26]

135 The Hanging Committee
of the Liverpool Autumn
Exhibition and the gallery staff,
1893. They are posing for a *tableau
vivant* inspired by an unidentified
work of art. Councillor Rathbone
is fifth from the left. The sole
woman is Henrietta Rae, the first
woman artist to be represented in
the collection and the first female
member of the Hanging
Committee.

INDUSTRIAL ART EXHIBITIONS

Temporary exhibitions featuring industrial art (in its broadest sense) were of course central to the museums' programmes (Fig. 136). At Glasgow, before the erection of the present buildings at Kelvingrove, a series of ambitious displays of decorative arts offered demonstrations of handicraft, often flavoured with what would have been perceived as a strong element of exoticism. This programme brought its own problems, not least the increasing indifference of the public to anything that was seen to be less than exciting. In 1879 Glaswegians were regaled with a display of the 'Collection of Indian Presents' made to the Prince of Wales during his Indian tour three years earlier. The catalogue commented that these demonstrated the 'finest examples of the highest and most elaborate handicrafts', stressing that European manufacturers should be stimulated by these artefacts from far-away lands.[27] In this scheme, non-Western applied art was emphatically regarded as worthy of a place within the canon of industrial art, even though it did not

as yet feature in the high art category (something not achieved until the twentieth century). An ambitious 'Oriental Art Loan Exhibition' was organised two years later, comprising 'principally the Decorative Arts of Japan and Persia'.[28] As the *Annual Report* pointed out with characteristically competitive complacency, the selection of objects 'for exhaustiveness, beauty and commercial as well as artistic value, has never been equalled in any provincial town in this country'.[29] The Oriental exhibition, it concluded, had been 'fruitful of much good'.

In spite of these recurring statements of optimism, there appears to have been a growing dilemma over the nature of industrial exhibitions, and over the public to whom they were addressed. As time passed, a wider public than the aspiring artisan had to be satisfied. Thus, in 1882 an exhibition of Italian art was organised in Glasgow. Including assorted paintings, early Italian prints belonging to the Duke of Buccleuch, medals, metalwork, and six cases of miscellaneous pieces from South Kensington, with an emphasis on objects appropriate for study and copying, it seems to have been aimed at a general

136 The Glasgow International Exhibition, Kelvingrove, 1888. A case advertising Nobel's Explosives dominates the display.

audience.[30] Even that fierce critic J.C. Robinson commented that the Italian exhibition had induced a 'marked change of the public tone in regard to the Galleries and their contents' among the citizens of Glasgow, who had discovered that they possessed an institution 'entitled to rank with famous galleries'.[31] In spite of these efforts, by the 1880s the art exhibitions, concentrating in succeeding years on the industrial arts of Persia, India, Japan, Italy and France, were attracting only modest audiences: 38,000 for the Italian, 30,000 for the Persian. They had become relatively specialised events aimed at a particular audience: 'It is to art students, designers, and to persons connected with art industries generally, that such Exhibitions are specially valuable', the Curator defensively argued.[32] It may have been the decline in visitor figures that encouraged the organ-

isers of the 'French Art Loan Exhibition' that followed to spice up the display with historical delights in the manner of the Romantic Interior. One section was dedicated to 'Historical Relics and Miscellaneous', including Napoleon I's table and 'Mary Stuart's Hand-bell…one of the objects of personal use, doubtless, which garnished the chamber of the captive Queen'.[33] But however charming such relics may have been, the style of exhibition with which they were associated was giving way to more ambitious events.

STYLES OF EXHIBITION

In the context of modern thinking about cultural institutions, these exhibitions triumphantly realised

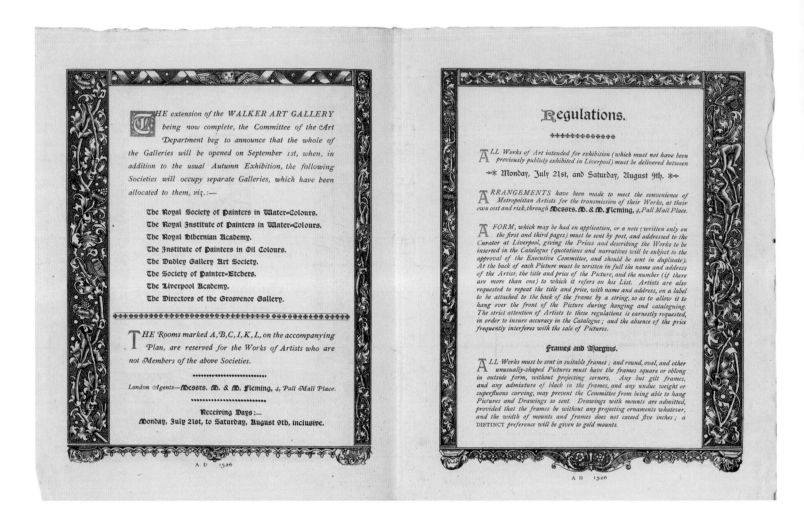

137 Regulations for the Walker Art Gallery's Autumn Exhibition of 1884. The regulations show how the display included several ancillary exhibitions organised by individual societies – emphasising the event's resemblance to a sale in a department store.

the goals of community involvement and social inclusion. Although in the early days of almost all municipal galleries, the artists' exhibition was seen as the principal annual event and the justification of the whole enterprise, such places as the Walker did not go 'dark' during the rest of the year. On the opening of its extension in 1884 it was resolved that a variety of societies – the Royal Society of Painters in Water-Colours, the Liverpool Academy and several others – would be allocated space (Fig. 137).[34] A curious array of exhibitions was accommodated in a building that functioned for several years primarily as a *Kunsthalle*: they included such events as the 1892 Liverpool Naval Exhibition, filled with nine rooms of ship models, displays of navigation and telegraph cables, and paintings of the sea (Fig. 138).[35]

It was not only the Royal Academy that benefitted from the generosity of private owners. Individual

lenders to London exhibitions also lent to provincial galleries. In 1884 Glasgow enjoyed the loan of some 200 paintings belonging to the Marquess of Bute, accompanied by a catalogue written by the esteemed scholar John Paul Richter. These works had previously formed one of the most ambitious displays organised at the Bethnal Green Museum. The transfer of the exhibition to Glasgow suggests the existence of a circuit of regional venues, and well-established links between the provinces and London's limited number of non-commercial venues.

Exhibitions played a role as advocates of civic expansion and the excellence and utility of the visual arts. In some circumstances displays were organised in temporary premises, to promote the foundation of an art museum when none existed. Leeds, for example, was slow to set up a municipal art gallery. A series of special events, mostly exhibitions, was organised by local and national well-wishers, culmi-

184

138 The Naval Exhibition at the Walker Art Gallery, 1893, photographed by Bedford Lemere.

tions, including Italian paintings from the fourteenth century, around eighty from the fifteenth century and similar groupings up to the eighteenth, as well as drawings, miniatures and prints. In its ordered chronological hang, the Leeds exhibition was considerably more sophisticated than the Burlington House Winter Exhibitions that followed close upon it. It also included works from the private collection of Lord Dudley (shown as a group, like the Marquess of Hertford's pictures in Manchester in 1857), almost 500 oil paintings by British artists, close to 400 watercolours, and the Museum of Ornamental Art, containing over 3,000 objects from 'the earliest period to the present century'. Particular attention was given to 'MODERN FOREIGN ARTISTS', the catalogue claiming that 'This is the first time that a really important series of works showing the state of pictorial art in Europe has been formed in this country, except in the metropolis'.[37] Additional elements included 'A Portrait Gallery of Yorkshire Worthies' (such local portrait galleries being a regular feature of such events); and 'An India Museum', also a fairly regular attraction.[38]

Ironically, in neither Manchester nor Leeds did a major 'universal art' exhibition lead with any rapidity to the foundation of a civic art gallery; in spite of much lobbying, Manchester did not gain its gallery until 1882–3.[39] The Leeds National Exhibition did at least stimulate the foundation of the Yorkshire Fine Art Society, 'formed for the promotion of a taste for the Fine Arts among the inhabitants of this district, and as a means of giving encouragement to Artists'.[40] The programme of exhibitions was maintained, with the support of Yorkshire collectors: in 1884 the display included early German and Italian paintings and seventeenth-century French and Dutch works, though with British pictures of the eighteenth and nineteenth centuries predominating. The hope was again expressed by the Society in 1886 that the popularity of these events 'would lead to the establishment of a permanent gallery, and to periodical Exhibitions'.[41] Although in this parsimonious city this did not actually happen until 1892, an exhibition was clearly an effective campaigning tool.

Temporary exhibitions could be useful in other ways. Several new museum buildings were launched at a moment when they possessed no collections

nating in the 'National Exhibition of Works of Art' of 1868.[36] This major event was installed in temporary premises, the newly completed but not yet functioning Leeds Infirmary, which provided generous circulation spaces and large wards/galleries suitable for a large-scale display (Fig. 139). Typically for the period, the exhibition's General Council included the established national leaders in promoting artistic enterprises, mostly with South Kensington affiliations. Among them were the President of the Royal Academy; Sir Thomas Fairbairn of the Manchester Art Treasures Exhibition; Owen Jones, designer of the interiors of the Crystal Palace; Richard Redgrave; and Ruskin. In many respects the 1868 Leeds exhibition resembled 1857 in Manchester. Though on a smaller scale, it numbered thousands of works, and its mode of operation, with numerous departments each curated by an individual expert, followed the Manchester pattern (Fig. 140).

The revealingly named 'National Exhibition' aimed to illustrate the whole development of Western art as conceived at the time, supplemented by a strong representation of contemporary art. The display featured over 400 paintings in both the Northern and the Southern Old Master sec-

139   Plan of the galleries at the
National Exhibition, Leeds, 1868.

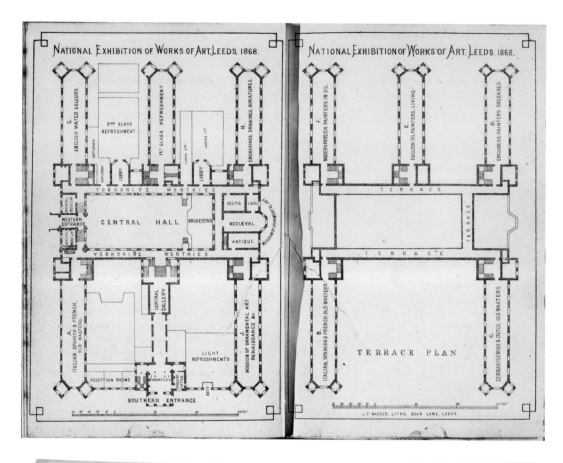

140   'Plan of Leeds' from the
official catalogue of the Yorkshire
Exhibition of Arts and
Manufactures, Leeds 1875. The
map illustrates the uninhibited
attitude to raising money through
advertising to be found in some
exhibition catalogues.

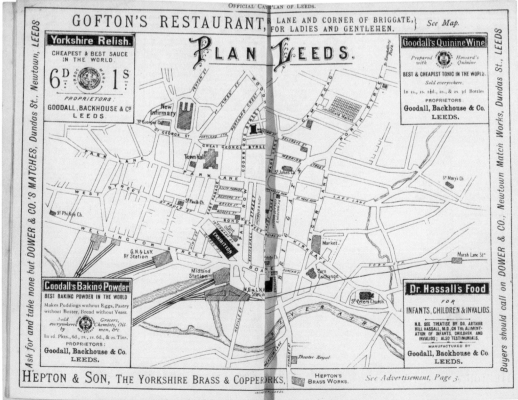

and relied on loans to fill their walls. When Nottingham Castle Museum opened in 1878 the ambitious loan exhibition, drawn from national and local collections, was a huge success, attracting almost 700,000 visitors and encouraging the city to form a permanent collection. A more popular style was adopted at Oldham, a town close to Manchester and deriving its prosperity from textile spinning and weaving. It was a town 'of wealth and opulence',[42] as the Mayor remarked in a speech on the presentation of what was officially described as 'a very handsome painting by a celebrated local Artist, Mr Charles Potter, entitled "A Winter's Tale" (value 120 guineas)'. The Art Gallery was inaugurated in 1883 with a display in the style of the Mechanics' Institutes rather than the Manchester Art Treasures Exhibition (Fig. 141).[43] The Fine Art and Industrial Exhibition, under the patronage of members of the aristocracy and that aristocrat of art dealers, William Agnew, contained objects from private collections, mostly in Oldham, supplemented by tankards and modelled figures lent by W. E. Gladstone, students' work from the Polytechnic Institute in London, and numerous loans from South Kensington. Any visitor exhausted by the power looms, shuttles and mixing machines lent by local firms and displayed on the ground floor would be relieved on ascending the stairs (ornamented, for no particular reason, with prints after Landseer) to find themselves in a display that anticipated the varied experiential delights later developed in Disneyland. At Oldham the influence of the country house park was also apparent, the display featuring a 'Grotto and Hermitage, built of Tufa stone, showing a stalactite dripping cavern', which led to 'a primeval forest, with natural ferns and ivy, afterwards arriving at the Hermitage'.[44]

The general survey exhibition has pretty much disappeared in the twenty-first century for reasons including the strengthening of public collections, the huge expense of transporting and insuring works of art, and the cheapness of publishing high-quality images, whether printed or digital, compared to the cost in the nineteenth century even of black and white photographs. The recent questioning and redefining of the artistic canon may also make this style of display less easy to accommodate. In general it has to be said that the direct influence of Manchester Art Treasures Exhibition was limited.

HISTORICAL EXHIBITIONS

The Victorian rage for history inspired a small but revealing group of historical exhibitions, events that constantly negotiated the tension between portraits as documents and portraiture as an art central to the British tradition. These events took several different forms. Already in 1820 the British Institution was displaying 'Portraits, representing Distinguished persons in the History and Literature of the United Kingdom'.[45] At this early stage the organisers were motivated by a desire to 'interest, rather than instruct', to illustrate the appearance of distinguished persons, and to 'extend to a wider circle' a love for the arts.[46] This enthusiasm for portraiture gathered force and seriousness throughout the century. An antiquarian exhibition of portraits copied from famous originals in local collections and illustrating a publication called *Lodge's Gallery of Historical Portraits* was on view at the Society of Arts in Leeds in 1832. In the 1857 exhibition the large historical section, based primarily on portraits, initiated an ambitious approach that was maintained in the three Exhibitions of National Portraits held at South Kensington from 1866 to 1868, and in historical displays in Glasgow. They illustrated the power of images that were as much political as academic in defining local identity and pride.

A succession of huge exhibitions emphasised the wealth, the technical accomplishments and the cultural fecundity of Glasgow, a city that considered itself the 'Second City of Empire' and was anxious to assert its superiority to its immediate neighbour, Edinburgh, and its industrial competitor Manchester. The 1888 exhibition, sited in Kelvingrove Park, trumpeted Glasgow's industry, its heavy machinery, its shipbuilding. The relative lack of foreign exhibits was compensated for by a strong imperial element, including a picturesque Indian Street alongside displays about Canada, at a time when the Canadian Government was anxious to recruit immigrants from Scotland. In the Fine Art section some 2,700 exhibits were shown in ten galleries: they included many British, and especially Scottish, painters, and helped to establish the up-and-coming Glasgow Boys (Fig. 142).[47]

The success of this event encouraged several others. The 1901 exhibition, which also occupied Kelvingrove Park and launched the new Glasgow

141 Poster for the Oldham Fine Art and Industrial Exhibition, 1883. The exhibition that opened the Gallery brought together loans from many sources and disciplines, announced in a striking poster reminiscent of publicity for a theatre or music hall.

OLDHAM
FINE ART & INDUSTRIAL
EXHIBITION

TO BE HELD IN CONNECTION WITH THE OPENING OF THE

FREE REFERENCE LIBRARY,
ART · GALLERY · & · MUSEUM,
ON WEDNESDAY, THE 1ST DAY OF AUGUST, 1883,
AT 2 P.M.

→ PATRONS: →

His Grace the DUKE OF DEVONSHIRE, K.G.
  "   DUKE OF SUTHERLAND, K.G.
  "   DUKE OF WESTMINSTER, K.G.
The Right Hon. the EARL OF DERBY.
  "   "   EARL OF WILTON.
  "   "   MARQUIS of HARTINGTON, M.P.
  "   Sir STAFFORD NORTHCOTE, Bart. M.P.
  A. J. MUNDELLA, M.P.
Sir PHILIP CUNLIFFE-OWEN, K.C.M.G, C.B, C.S.I.
W. FARRAR ECKROYD, Esq., M.P.
J. G. McMINNIES, Esq. M.P.
ROBERT N. PHILLIPS, Esq. M.P.
EDWARD WHITLEY, Esq., M.P.

J. T. HIBBERT, Esq., M.P.
The Hon. E. L. STANLEY, M.P.
WILLIAM AGNEW, Esq. M.P.
ROBERT LEAKE Esq. M.P.
The Hon. ALGERNON EGERTON, M.P.
JACOB BRIGHT, Esq., M.P.
BENJAMIN ARMITAGE, Esq. M.P.
ARTHUR ARNOLD, Esq., M.P.
JOHN P. THOMASSON, Esq., M.P.
PETER RYLANDS, Esq. M.P.
THOMAS KNOWLES, Esq. M.P.
GEORGE J. HOWARD, Esq., M.P.
W. E. M. TOMLINSON, Esq., M.P.

WILLIAM SUMMERS, ESQ., M.P.

Sir J. LUBBOCK, Bart.
F.R.S., D.C.L., M.P. FOR THE UNIVERSITY OF LONDON,

⚜ WILL ⁂ OPEN ⚜
THE NEW BUILDING & EXHIBITION.

THE EXHIBITION WILL COMPRISE

PAINTINGS ❖ STATUARY,
CARVINGS IN WOOD AND IVORY,
AND OTHER WORKS AND OBJECTS OF ART; COTTON, WOOLLEN, AND OTHER

MACHINERY IN MOTION,
ELECTRICAL APPLIANCES,
MODELS OF SHIPS, DESIGNS, SCIENTIFIC APPARATUS,
AND VARIOUS OTHER OBJECTS OF INTEREST.

Machinery and Appliances illustrative of the development of the Cotton and other Textile Industries will be a Special Feature of the Exhibition.

The Works and Objects of Art include contributions by the Prime-Minister, His Grace the Duke of Devonshire, K.G., His Grace the Duke of Westminster, K.G., the Earl of Derby, the Science and Art Department at South Kensington, the National Gallery Trustees, the President and Council of the Royal Academy, the Royal School of Art Needlework, the Corporation of the City of London, the Drapers' Company, the Ironmongers' Company, and many others.

PRICES OF ADMISSION: **On the Opening Day 5/-;** after that day,
ONE SHILLING. CHILDREN under 15 HALF PRICE.
SEASON ... ... issued on and after the Opening Day, will be 21s. Applications for Tickets to be made to
Mr. JOHN WEST, the Cashier of the Exhibition. *CATALOGUES 6d. EACH.*

ARRANGEMENTS HAVE BEEN MADE WITH THE

MANCHESTER, SHEFFIELD & LINCOLNSHIRE RAILWAY CO.
For First, Second, and Third Class Tickets
To be issued to Oldham (Glodwick Road or Clegg Street Stations) every Week-day at a
SINGLE FARE & A QUARTER
FOR THE DOUBLE JOURNEY,
From Stations on their Line within a radius of 20 Miles
THE MINIMUM FARES WILL BE:
FIRST CLASS 1/6, SECOND CLASS 1/2, THIRD CLASS 10d.
For particulars of Trains and Times see Bills issued by the Company.
JOHN WEST, SECRETARY.

THOS. DORNAN, PRINTER, STATIONER, AND ACCOUNT BOOK MAKER, UNION STREET, OLDHAM.

142 *State Visit of Her Majesty Queen Victoria to the Glasgow International Exhibition* by John Lavery, 1890. Oil on canvas, 256.5 × 406.4 cm (Glasgow Museums).

Museum and Art Gallery, was attended over six months by a staggering 11.5 million visitors (Fig. 143).[48] By this time the political climate in the city had changed, a change that was reflected in the displays. In Glasgow, a rich city eager to establish its cultural credentials as well as its claims to political independence, the historical tradition was notably strong. The city was particularly partial to portrait exhibitions with a Scottish and especially Glaswegian emphasis: a display on 'Prominent Glasgow Citizens and Scots', was organised in 1868, long before the existence of a public art gallery.

The next generation saw two major historical exhibitions. The 'Old Glasgow Exhibition' of 1894 featured portraits of prominent citizens, accompanied by a mass of supporting material, including stone carvings, plans of the city, pedigrees of the leading families and such everyday but evocative relics as tickets for banquets, soup handles and snuff boxes.[49] This approach reached its apogee in the enormous 'Scottish Exhibition of National History, Art and Industry', also held at Kelvingrove in 1911 (Fig. 144). The exhibition campus was announced by a gateway in an extravagantly historicist style, with portcullis and battlements, and intended to

induce a sense of appropriate excitement (Fig. 145). According to the keenly Scottish writer George Eyre-Todd, secretary of the historical section, the exhibition 'with its beautiful white buildings, like so many palaces of Aladdin…was thronged every day and all day throughout the summer with happy pleasure-seekers'.[50] They could enjoy 'the gay amusement section…with its scenic railway and other attractions' and the vast Industrial Hall, but 'the beautiful Palace of History was the solid attraction which brought visitors in streams from all parts of Scotland, and from many countries overseas'. This Palace took the form of an invented building temporarily added to Kelvingrove Mansion, with architectural references made to Falkland Palace and Holyroodhouse in its round towers and battlements. Alluring as it may been outside, internally the displays illustrated the remorseless comprehensiveness considered appropriate for these events, given additional *gravitas* in this case by the organisers' aim to use the profits to fund a chair of Scottish History at Glasgow University.

Drawing on private lenders in the spirit of Manchester in 1857 but also, more heavily than was usually the case, on public bodies such as the Scottish

143 A panorama print of the 1901 Glasgow International Exhibition. This huge event at Kelvingrove featured the new art gallery and museum, which served as 'the Palace of Art'. The highly eclectic buildings included numerous pavilions erected by foreign countries.

144 The Palace of History, at the Scottish Exhibition of National History, Art and Industry in Glasgow, 1911. Postcard.

OPPOSITE 145 Catalogue of the Palace of History in the 1911 Scottish Exhibition of National History, Art and Industry in Glasgow. The illustration shows the interior of the palace, which contained panoramic historical displays.

universities, the College of Physicians and the Corporation of Glasgow, the exhibition included portraits by the hundred (accompanied by biographies in the catalogue); pewter (domestic, tavern and ecclesiastical); silver and jewellery; Stewart miniatures; brooches and knee and shoe buckles; personal relics, such as Charles I's watch and the coat and helmet of the romantic Scottish Jacobite James Graham of Claverhouse (displayed close to his portrait, in the National Portrait Gallery tradition); the memorabilia of such writers as Burns, Scott and Stevenson; naval and military relics; 219 Scottish coins, 133 medals and 619 seals; armies of weapons; and books, from Bibles and early mediaeval literature onwards.[51] The second section of the exhibition concentrated on more quotidian considerations, such as mining, agricultural implements, umbrellas and shoes, but also found space for a prehistoric gallery, heraldry and stained glass.[52] Sections explored Scotland's links with France and Sweden,

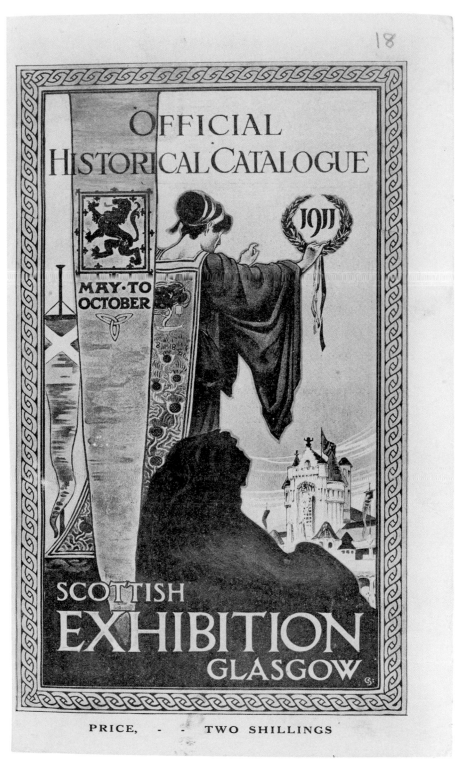

Here was an exhibition that was altogether uncommercial and wholly didactic, at least in appearance. According to Eyre-Todd, 'The feature which appealed especially to me was the suggestion that the proposed exhibition should be Scottish Historical in character. If successful it could hardly fail to quicken interest in a neglected but most important field. Besides, Glasgow had had no exhibition on the grand scale since 1901, and no enterprise was more certain to bring visitors, and consequently business, to the city and to Scotland at large.'[53] This was a canny mixture of motives. At one level the exhibition aimed to provide popular education in history at a time when universal education was still haphazard. It strove to proclaim the wealth and longevity of Scottish culture in the context of the campaign for political independence. But it was also seen as a shrewd business venture, appropriate to the city's commercial needs at a time when its fortunes were beginning a slow decline.

These various events illustrate the ways in which the temporary exhibition, particularly when organised on a large scale, could act as theatre. In such a setting it became possible to express, however clumsily and obliquely, the deeply felt desires of a community, in a manner impossible in the more circumscribed art gallery or museum.

A NEW APPROACH TO THE EXHIBITION: THE SINGLE ARTIST SHOW

The large-scale exhibition sometimes came under contemporary attack. Writing in 1888 the philosopher Frederic Harrison commented on their pointlessness and triviality, asking whether 'the custom of holding *Exhibitions* of paintings really tends to the advancement of art?'[54] Pointing out that 'in no great epoch of art were Exhibitions ever imagined', he enquired:

Can we conceive of Pheidias and Lysippus, Zeuxis and Apelles carting their works into a gallery, as the month of April came round, and all the young aesthetes in town, in new chiton and chlamys, noisily criticising the folds of 'Nike's' drapery, the curves of Ilissus' ribs, the soft limbs of 'Aphrodite,' and the proud glances of 'Athene'?

but not England: after all, the exhibition secretary was President of the Scottish Patriotic Association, and packed an early meeting to discuss the event with supportive Association members.

Fancy Giotto, Angelico, Bellini, and Giorgione, closely crammed into long galleries, numbered 3785 and so forth, and catalogued with little snippings from Dante, Petrarch, and Boccaccio! …Was the 'Sposalizio' sky'd by the Hanging Committee; was the 'Madonna di San Sisto' jammed between a 'Storm at Sea' and a 'Portrait of a Gentleman'?…an Annual Exhibition is almost the only spot conceivable where no picture ever can be in its place, where the local environment of every picture is turned upside down, where every note in the gamut of art is sounded in discord.

He went on to attack the jokey triviality of much contemporary art, fostered by the 'nineteenth-century mania for Exhibitions', which persuaded the viewer that 'drollery, riddles, anecdotes, novelettes, sentimentalities on canvas, [which] are so horribly irritating', were worth acquiring, regardless of the fact that 'to have them eternally dinned into us is maddening'.[55]

Harrison's objections to the discordant and inappropriate displays, the arbitrary selection by hanging committees, the general diminution of art, were written at a time when the huge miscellaneous exhibition was still a commonplace. A more selective approach both to the display of art and to large-scale exhibitions was, however, developing. The cult of the artist, and in particular the campaign to establish the reputation of British artists, encouraged the increasing popularity of the single-artist (or even single-picture) show. In particular, the last years of the century witnessed what might be defined as an emerging art-historical exhibition, which aimed neither at a universal survey nor at the grand-scale presentation of contemporary works of art, but at the analysis of an individual or a cohesive group.

The display of a single artist's work had emerged late in the eighteenth century, when a number of painters such as Thomas Gainsborough had organised independent showings of their work in opposition to what they saw as the unsympathetic setting of the Royal Academy, a practice continued by Turner from 1804. This approach was extended early in the nineteenth century to the monographic displays of the *oeuvre* of deceased artists at the British Institution. Opening in 1813 with an exhibition of

paintings by Joshua Reynolds, these were probably the first of their kind in Britain or elsewhere. At the same time, rentable spaces, notably the Egyptian Hall in Piccadilly, were taken by artists to display a group of their own works, or even just one piece: among the most famous single-picture exhibitions was Géricault's *Raft of the Medusa*, shown there in 1820.

During the nineteenth century the single-artist exhibition remained a regular, if not always esteemed, element of the art world. In 1843, for example, George Hayter organised a major exhibition of his work at the Egyptian Hall (Fig. 146), and a substantial show of works by William Etty was held at the Royal Society of Arts in London in 1849: arranged very shortly before the artist's death, it offered a retrospective view of his achievements since 1820. This event was a tribute to a senior artist with a high reputation, at the end of his career. Very much in contrast was the exhibiting career of J. M. Whistler, who organised a notable succession of carefully staged displays of his own work, beginning in 1874 at the Flemish Gallery, a commercial space off Pall Mall that Whistler leased and entirely reinstalled for the occasion. In general, however, a single-artist exhibition organised by the artist himself (it was seldom a woman) was motivated by an interest in self-promotion and sales. Income could be gained from exhibition admission, reproductive prints and ultimately the sale of the work, but it was a form of self-promotion not generally considered respectable. Richard Altick has pointed out the repugnance felt for the one-man show: 'To many traditionalists, inside as well as outside the Academy, there was something flagrantly unprofessional about putting on, and advertising, a pay-as-you-enter exhibition devoted to one's own works.'[56] This ambiguity and suspicion also applied if the exhibition was organised commercially by an art dealer. In this vein W. Archer Shee in 1883 caricatured the promotion of a painting by 'some well-known if not strikingly eminent artist': he characterised the painting as heavily puffed, if possible approved by royalty, exhibited in 'a *public* 'private view'…probably sent on a provincial tour, and…duly heralded in every important town throughout the country, the walls being placarded with the announcement that Mr. So-and-So's "great picture" is to be seen at the principal art shop "*for one week only*" for a small admission fee'.[57]

146 A poster for an exhibition of works by Sir George Hayter, held at the Egyptian Hall, Piccadilly, in 1843. Hayter had a lively career, partly in Italy, partly in London, and was much favoured by the young Queen Victoria, who knighted him in 1842. This ambitious single-artist exhibition brought together many of the composite portraits for which he was famous. Bringing him revenue from the sale of tickets, it allowed him to show his depiction of the first post-Reform Bill House of Commons, a painting he had recently completed but for which he did not find a buyer until 1854.

EXHIBITION
OF
SIR GEORGE HAYTER'S
GREAT HISTORICAL PICTURES,
EGYPTIAN HALL, PICCADILLY.

THE GREAT PICTURE OF

THE HOUSE OF COMMONS,
Painted on One Hundred and Seventy Feet of Canvass,
WITH FAITHFUL PORTRAITS OF ALL THE MEMBERS,
Who sat expressly for this Work.

THE HOUSE OF LORDS,
DURING THE CELEBRATED TRIAL OF THE
LATE QUEEN CAROLINE.

THE MUCH ADMIRED PICTURE OF THE

TRIAL OF WILLIAM, LORD RUSSELL,
IN 1683.

THE PORTRAIT OF HER MOST GRACIOUS MAJESTY

QUEEN VICTORIA,
IN THE IMPERIAL DALMATIC ROBES,
Removed, by Her Majesty's permission, from the Corridor in Windsor Castle,
expressly for this Exhibition.

AND VARIOUS OTHER WORKS, COMPRISING UPWARDS OF

EIGHT HUNDRED PORTRAITS,
Of Eminent Characters, all painted by the same Artist.

Open from Nine o'Clock till dusk, at the Egyptian Hall, Piccadilly.
Admission, 1s. Descriptive Catalogues, with Eleven Plates of Reference, 1s.

COOK AND CO., PRINTERS, 76, FLEET STREET, LONDON.

The organiser would make a profit from both admission charges and the sale of prints after the advertised painting. These satirical comments exemplify the continuing ambiguity of the one-man show or work, and the tendency of critics to regard it as self-promoting and vulgarly commercial.

There are few records in provincial museums or in London of displays of living or recently deceased artists, at least until the 1890s. Harry Quilter observed of the exhibition of the hugely admired G. F. Watts at the Grosvenor Gallery in 1882, 'It is, as far as I am aware, the first time that anything like a complete collection of an artist's pictures have been exhibited in his lifetime, and with his assistance and approval.'[58] The shows at Birmingham in 1885 dedicated to Burne-Jones and to Watts innovatively reflected the Gallery's far-sighted approach. The experiment was followed the next year by the display of paintings by a Birmingham artist, Walter Langley, while a fellow-citizen, Frederick Henshaw, received the same honour in 1887. He was eighty years old at the time, a not insignificant fact, since advanced age was apparently seen (*pace* Lady Bracknell) as a guarantee of respectability: when Liverpool organised a Holman Hunt exhibition in 1907, he was seventy and an established national treasure. Both of the Birmingham artists are largely forgotten but their works were evidently found appealing, Henshaw attracting 180,000 visitors. In spite of these successes, after 1887 displays of works by living artists were temporarily discontinued.

Generally, living artists were expected to demonstrate a sense of communal duty by contributing to group exhibitions. Once dead, then acceptable, was apparently the rule – a supposition supported by an 1897 show at Leeds unalluringly entitled 'Four Recently Deceased Local Artists' (including the ever-popular Atkinson Grimshaw), in which the works were all borrowed from existing collections that seemed unlikely to be put on the market, removing the event even further from the marketplace. A valedictory event was also in order at the 1913 Birmingham exhibition dedicated to the lately deceased Alphonse Legros.

❖

THE SCHOLARLY EXHIBITION

The conservatism of City Councils, the lack of resources within museums and the grip exerted by the art establishment generally maintained a stable, indeed unadventurous, approach in the provinces. For a number of reasons it was not surprising that scholarly, and innovative, exhibitions were so rare until the end of the century. There were few people in Britain, even in London or at the universities, capable of engaging in what would now be seen as art-historical research. Thoroughly researched exhibitions could scarcely be created by institutions possessing such small staffs and such limited resources as Victorian municipal galleries had. And as we have seen, the curators were generally artists rather than historians, and artists of the second or third rank at that.

In some cases, a mundane and opportunistic policy was followed. Once a municipal art gallery had finally been established at Leeds, the programme tended to feature displays of works for sale and South Kensington loan exhibitions, such as the 1889 display of English watercolours 'Illustrative of the Rise and Progress of the Art in England from 1710'.[59] The use of the space as a showplace for local artistic or commercial talent was supplemented by an 1895 display of posters, inspired by a similar show at the Westminster Aquarium. This commercial enterprise allowed a local firm to show the productions of 'some of the leading English and French Artists', which were available for sale.[60] In such a case the civic art gallery could hardly be differentiated from the commercial variety.

On the other hand, in some galleries a lively programme of exhibitions did develop, often concentrating on contemporary art. At Nottingham Castle Museum in 1894 G. H. Wallis organised an exhibition of the paintings of the Newlyn and St Ives schools, the first large-scale show devoted to their work.[61] Such an endeavour was considered worthy of comment, the *Western Daily Press* writing 'It is very creditable that a provincial town has been able to organize an exhibition which would certainly have attracted great attention in London.'[62]

In addition to these contemporary surveys, from the 1880s onwards a growing number of exhibitions explored a historic artist, assembling loans from various sources, sometimes concentrating on a particular aspect of their work, and often publishing a catalogue, though these tended to be on a small scale and not illustrated. Early in the nineteenth century British artists were particularly popular, notably Turner. His huge reputation owed much to the influence of his champion Ruskin, who in addition to his writings on the artist promoted him in such events as the exhibition of Turner drawings held at the newly founded Fine Art Society in London in 1878, to which he contributed a highly personal biographical introduction and critical discussion.[63] An exhibition in Birmingham in 1899 dedicated to the artist's paintings and watercolours had originated at the Guildhall in London.[64] 'The Engraved Work of J.M.W. Turner' in Leeds in 1896 was accompanied by watercolours and a catalogue, suggesting a focused academic approach, but it still relied on a single private collection, with the works arranged and the catalogue prepared by their owner.[65] Turner again featured, this time in relationship with Claude Lorrain, in an 1898 exhibition held at the Ashmolean Museum and drawn from the museum's collection, while the watercolours of Petworth were displayed at the Fitzwilliam in 1913. This succession of Turner monographic displays constituted a strong anticipation of the scholarly exhibitions of the twentieth century, with provincial galleries playing a prominent role.

An economical way of realising a scholarly exhibition was through an educational display using reproductions, an equivalent of the didactic displays of photographs and electrotypes that initiated many galleries. In an interesting parallel to Prince Albert's 1850s project to make a comprehensive survey of Raphael using reproductions of his work, the Walker in 1887 showed an 'exhibition of photographic and other reproductions of the works of Raphael…arranged chronologically, and (including) all the drawings, easel-pictures, and frescoes of the master which have as yet been reproduced. Thus all the studies for a picture are grouped with the picture itself, and a rare opportunity is afforded of watching the changes and development of the artist's style.' The catalogue listed 'all known existing works by Raphael of whatever kind, with references to the publications in which they were discussed, and, in the case of every work which has been photographed, the name of the photographer.'[66] The collection was formed and the catalogue drawn up by Martin Conway, the young Professor of Art at University College Liverpool. His faith in the value of systematic collections of photography as an art-historical tool led to his eventual presentation of 100,000 photographs to form the Conway Library of the Courtauld Institute of Art.

CONCLUSION

A modern viewer confronted by the kind of exhibition attacked by Harrison would no doubt react in similar terms. To our eyes such shows would seem ludicrously ill-designed, or not designed at all, accumulating great quantities of material with little regard for visual impact, and crushing the individual work. On the other hand, the size and confidence of these Victorian events, and the enormous audiences they generally attracted, make their more sophisticated modern equivalents seem pallid by comparison.

The robustness and variety of these exhibitions were underscored by an issue that is a recurring theme in this book, and that was never resolved. The pressure to avoid the taint of the marketplace, and to create didactic displays that would educate the whole population, was counterbalanced by the belief that an exhibition was a healthily commercial enterprise, to be assessed according to its financial success. Such events epitomised the conflict, implicit in the very notion of the exhibition, between financial objectives, instruction and entertainment. Only in the twentieth century did the curatorial sophistication and rigour that had been shyly emerging in the late Victorian years develop into a quite new phenomenon.

9

A NEW STYLE OF COLLECTING

To the influential group of art administrators revolving around the Department of Science and Art and the South Kensington Museum, it was ludicrous to suppose that provincial museums could aspire to collections that in any way resembled London's. In their view, provincial museums should primarily be educational, displaying collections suitable for training designers and manufacturers. Although J.C. Robinson was a passionate advocate of acquiring rare works of art for his own museum, this view did not extend to the regions. Citing a new museum in a cathedral city, he described in 1880 a debased cabinet of curiosities: a hideous new building in which was assembled

> [an] absurd *omnium gatherum*…the…dried head of a New Zealand chief and his moth-eaten old feather cloak, half a dozen clubs and paddles… snakes in bottles, a lamb with two heads, and a mummy; worthless pictures with high-sounding names, and several very conspicuous works of art on a large scale, such as a cork model of the cathedral three yards long, made by an ingenious but misguided shoemaker; big bulky curiosities, contributed by generous donors, evidently with an eye to…getting rid of worthless incumbrances,

and gaining a reputation for public spirit and liberality by so doing…the thing is a veritable incubus, not only useless, but offensive.[1]

Robinson's critical metropolitan mind objected to the survival of traditions nurtured by decayed versions of the cabinet of curiosities and the philosophical society, as well as the unseemly inclusion of ethnographical specimens. As his description suggests, many galleries and museums possessed no intellectually conceived programme for acquisitions, remaining passive recipients of whatever came their way.

It was a subject about which there was recurring disagreement. Many in the Department of Science and Art agreed with Robinson that provincial museums should not be collecting works of high art. It was an attitude that reflected a variety of viewpoints, not least the idea that older paintings were hardly worth acquiring in a modern age for a popular audience. As early as 1857, in an essay 'On the Gift of the Sheepshanks Collection' of modern British paintings, Robinson's colleague Richard Redgrave had expressed almost an institutional antipathy to the art of the past, at least in relation to popular education. Having praised the succession of British artists from the eighteenth century onwards, he enquired

> What is there in the *subjects* of the old masters, with all their beauties and all their excellencies…calculated to touch the mind of our own people like these I have named? What to our multitudes are fat Bacchuses and maudlin Silenuses?…To them Mercury and Venus are but mere names. Nor with the dreary saints and dark martyrs of the older church have they more sympathy…[2]

Mustering another argument, Robinson stressed the absurdity of municipal galleries attempting collections of Old Masters or major sculptures in face of the art market: 'Fine original works…are practically unattainable, and second-rate originals are of little value.'[3] If they must, they could buy affordable contemporary work, but this should not be a priority. He resisted the notion put forward by Henry Cole that national funding for purchases might go to provincial museums.

> Let us only suppose…what would happen if…a score or two of provincial committee men and curators, armed with funds to compete for works of art, were to enter the already narrow field of acquisition; inexperienced as such persons would be, helpless as against the innumerable frauds of dealers, falsifiers and forgers of art treasures, aiming at the unattainable, and uninformed as to the current value of really available matter, they would simply flounder about and perpetrate innumerable blunders – there would, in short, be a scandalous waste of public funds.[4]

Instead, provincial museums should assemble facsimiles.[5] It was a principle he later extended to the British colonies, a putative extension of the provinces: through 'the supply of copies and reproductions of the classic art treasures of the world…the State can most powerfully assist the great and ever growing centres of population of the empire'.[6]

Robinson did make two concessions, corresponding to what provincial museums did acquire. Firstly, there was no reason why their applied art collections (which were generally not regarded as high art) should not rival those in national museums. And secondly, the aim to 'attract and amuse the masses' might be 'safely left to provincial endeavour;

amusing rubbish, if amusing it really be, will accumulate fast enough without the assistance of the state'.[7] By 'amusing rubbish' he presumably meant everyday objects of the type that were, and are, regularly offered to museums, as well as easily understood contemporary paintings. His views remained, by implication, official policy well into the twentieth century. In 1911 it was still the practice of the Victoria and Albert Museum (as the South Kensington Museum had become) to dispense grants-in-aid 'to assist provincial museums in purchasing reproductions, in plaster or by electrotype or other process, of objects illustrating architectural, ornamental, and other decorative art', in preference to 'original objects of similar character'.[8]

Robinson's view of the dual status of museums and of the popular (and by implication, inferior) role of the provincial museum was applied in less polemical terms to scientific museums by W.H. Flower in *Essays on Museums* (1895). He identified two main purposes for museums: firstly, advancing scientific knowledge through collecting, research and displays aimed at specialists; secondly, arranging exhibitions for the general visitor. Museums were failing because they attempted to satisfy both audiences at once. It was the duty of curators in national museums to create comprehensive collections, alongside popular displays, on the lines of national establishments in Paris, Vienna, Berlin and Washington. At the local level the curator should not aim at scholarship, but 'develop the side of the museum which is educational and attractive to the general visitor'.[9]

A generation later, the situation had not greatly changed. In 1903 Charles Holmes, the recently appointed editor of the new *Burlington Magazine* and later Director of the National Gallery, published *Pictures and Picture Collecting*, a little guide to investment in art, graded according to the collector's means. After advising the 'Rich Man' that Michelangelo and Raphael drawings were still obtainable at fair prices, he launched into provincial galleries. 'Our provincial galleries are either too poor or too ignorantly administered to be able to delay in the least the constant drift of our art treasures to America and to Germany', he wrote, reiterating the contemporary sense of hopelessness as works of art were sold abroad by traditional owners, at first to Germany and from around 1900 to the United States.[10] The process was constantly lamented in the

147 *Councillor W. Edgar JP* by Richard Jack, 1919. Oil on canvas, 125 × 98.5 cm. Jack was a fashionable portraitist whose commissions included George V and Queen Mary. Such portraits of civic dignitaries were regular features of municipal collections into the twentieth century (Hartlepool Museums and Heritage Service).

art press – D. S. MacColl wrote of 'That hardy weed of debate, How to keep pictures in this country'[11] – and reached a climax in 1903 with the foundation of the National Art Collections Fund, a private society inspired by groups such as the *Société des Amis du Louvre*. Its founders felt that 'The art treasures of this country were rapidly passing abroad, prices were rising against the Museums and Galleries, the purchase grants were stationary or diminishing, the attitude of the authorities was one of helplessness or despair.'[12] They encouraged bequests to museums as well as gifts.

Holmes then engaged in a satirical account of provincial collecting. While acknowledging that 'In several places, such as Glasgow, Birmingham, and Norwich, the existence of a local school, the generosity of a private donor, or the intelligence and tact of a curator, has formed a nucleus of pictures' of quality, in many cases 'Councils are free to buy what pictures they please without any annoying responsibility to art or to tradition'.[13] Many Town Councils sent a 'special committee' to the Royal Academy to select

such pictures as they fancy will amuse their fellow-citizens. That no special taste or knowledge is needed to choose pictures is proved con-

clusively by the condition of some of our provincial galleries…the question of choice should be put on a business footing. Let the Council first ascertain by measurement the number of square feet of canvas and paper which the funds at their disposal have purchased year by year in the past…let them resolve that at least that average of art shall be bought annually. Then let the four senior members of their body travel up to London…provided with yard-measures, to procure the requisite quantity of material. The question of selection then becomes a mere matter of arithmetic, and can be settled by men of business [an echo of Dickens's phrase in *Hard Times*] in a single morning…[14]

Holmes suggested that any member unable to travel could 'show his public spirit, by spending part of the money on a portrait of himself…This portrait might then be presented to the local gallery as a memorial of the donor's services. In one provincial collection, at least, these presentation portraits have become the chief features of the place, with remarkable effect' (Fig. 147). Finally, echoing Robinson, he proposed the purchase of photographs of 'universally recognized masterpieces'.

Unkind as they are, Holmes's comments underline key aspects of provincial museums' art collecting. Acquisitions were indeed often steered by the taste promulgated by the Royal Academy, while accumulating images of local worthies and reproductions of famous works was a regular policy. In terms of Old Master or avant-garde nineteenth-century art, the most active collecting carried out by municipal galleries did not take place until after the Second World War. Didactic collections such as Thomas Roscoe's and Thomas Kay's (see below, pp. 209–10) did find their way into regional galleries, along with a number of Dutch paintings, and here and there seventeenth-century Italian pictures, but an overview of municipal collections in 1900 and even 1920 would reveal very few other works painted before 1700.

SOME DEFINITIONS OF ART

A prevailing theme in the nineteenth-century gallery was the nature and status of art, defined through expressions that today hardly carry the resonance they once had. The word 'art' did not have the (more or less) specific sense that it now bears: as in the distinction made in a cabinet of curiosities between art and nature, it was taken to mean anything created by the human hand, and to denote the process of creation, the human skill, rather than the artefact itself – in contrast to the work of nature, the creation of God. The loss of this meaning has made some of the old uses of the word hard to grasp today. For the nineteenth-century writer, the term 'art' was filled with potential alternative meanings. 'Fine art' did not only mean painting, sculpture or architecture; it could be applied (as by Henry Cole) to a variety of productions with pretensions to attractive design, including sculpture, which because of its regular use in an architectural setting occupied a liminal space between 'pure' art and practical art.

The 'polite arts' or 'liberal arts' distinguished the achievements of the intellectual artist – generally a history painter, for whom an intellectual framework and the delivery of a moral meaning were of predominant importance – from 'the mechanical arts', that is to say, work produced by manual and mechanical endeavour, and associated with the processes of trade. Later in the nineteenth century these terms give way to the current term 'fine art', a development that was deplored by some critics, notably Henry Cole.[15] For many commentators 'the mechanical arts' also embraced what was considered the inferior art of portraiture, which, defended by intellectually minded portraitists, also occupied an intermediate zone.

The terms 'industrial art' or 'the arts of industry', much used in the eighteenth and nineteenth centuries, present all sorts of confusion for the modern reader. They variously denote 'the skills involved in the processes of industry itself', art produced by industrial means and technical design (the term in current usage to which it perhaps most closely corresponds) and art aimed at the production of sellable commodities.[16] For Celina Fox, tracing the arts of industry through the eighteenth century and into the nineteenth, industrial art was a long and proud tradition, closely linked with the fine arts (in the modern sense) and with the development of technology. Only what she perceives as the baleful influence of the Royal Academy, and the stress laid by its first President on a high art divorced from

practicality and distinguished by its academic ambitions, contributed to a steady denigration of industrial art in artistic and academic circles. In nineteenth-century art galleries and exhibitions in Britain industrial art played a long-running role, demarcated by physical spaces and by semiotics from academic art but at the same time co-existing with it: sometimes the two could hardly be distinguished. Later in the nineteenth century the term was extended to describe objects of domestic or quasi-domestic use with artistic pretensions, if they were produced not by hand but by mechanical means. For Henry Cole, first director of the South Kensington Museum, industrial art was intimately associated with financial profit.

The arts of industry were widely collected by regional museums, through gifts or as purchases, and these acquisitions were supplemented until late in the twentieth century by loans from the South Kensington Museum through its 'Circulating Museum'. Initiated in 1853, what was to become the Circulation Department sent a very wide variety of objects, including textiles, engravings, oil paintings, bronzes, jewellery, and photographs of paintings and decorative arts to a growing number of towns that already possessed art schools, with the aim of encouraging the establishment of art museums.[17] The programme reflected a notable strand of the provincial art museum: its role as a centre for art education. At such a leading gallery as Birmingham, the holdings of metalwork and the gift of the Tangye collection of Wedgwood allowed the display of a wide range of material, while at Nottingham City Art Gallery, in a city famous for its tradition of lace-making, examples were acquired from an early date.

These were emphatically educational displays, intended to instruct the manufacturers and workers of the locality. They introduced to Britain and to the didactic galleries inspired by South Kensington all over Europe and the United States not only a new type of museum – the applied art gallery – but a peculiarly difficult one: row upon row of objects in South Kensington cases, divorced from their original context or any reflection of their original use. Later generations of curators have applied various solutions to this inheritance.

THE RULE OF BRITISH ART

Up to the First World War, the new galleries were heavily dependent on the gifts or bequests of private individuals. By the late 1860s art collecting was rapidly expanding: according to F.T. Palgrave, 'More money is probably spent on pictures in a year than was spent during the whole reign of George II.'[18] These individuals tended to be swayed by the ideals identified by Dianne Sachko Macleod as characteristic of Victorian bourgeois collectors: the rejection of long-standing classical and learned tradition, a passion for mimesis, an emphasis on patriotism and the moralistic.[19] They particularly admired technical proficiency: '"Finish" is an aesthetic element signaled tangible evidence of painstaking labour, pride in the work ethic, and corroboration of money well spent.'[20] Many of these new collectors had not been brought up to grasp classical mythology and history. They enunciated a new approach to collecting, celebrating narrative, geographical documentation, and civic identity.

It is remarkable how many of the newly rich of the first or second generation acquired works of art. On the whole they do not appear to have been the neurotic individuals in search of psychological reassurance and marked by 'an air of impoverishment and depleted humanity', identified by Jean Baudrillard as typical collectors.[21] Only a few, such as Joseph Shipley of Newcastle (discussed below), whose house was filled with a miscellaneous and everexpanding crowd of paintings, approximated to this definition. Rather, their collecting seems to have been comfortable and often pleasurable, conceived as an aspect of living appropriate for the rich, especially when guided by Sir William Agnew. Some collectors, such as Sir Merton Russell-Cotes, were on terms of sustained friendliness with artists. While many of these holdings were on a considerable scale, few of them contained major surprises.

By the last third of the century, contemporary British art reigned supreme in Britain (and often in the Empire), as critics frequently remarked. British paintings sold for huge sums – with the assistance of a good art dealer a work by a leading Royal Academician such as Millais might fetch over £5,000. Landseer achieved £8,000 for *The Monarch of the Glen* in 1892, and William Holman Hunt £11,000 for *The Light of the World* in 1874.[22] Many

built themselves in Holland Park and South Kensington palatial house-studios of a splendour few of their predecessors could have imagined. Historic British art was equally in demand, especially in the United States after 1900, with prices ranging from £9,000 for a Constable to a rumoured £20,000 for a Reynolds, or over £30,000 for a Turner.[23]

This reputation rested on the sustained polemic of apologists; on the numerous books on the subject that appeared from the 1830s onwards and particularly around the 1860s; on the display of British art in universal and in local exhibitions; and on the public-spirited acquisition of British art by such individuals as Robert Vernon, a London hackneyman hiring out horses and carriages, and the Leeds collector John Sheepshanks. From the 1820s to the 1840s Vernon collected eighteenth- and nineteenth-century British paintings and sculpture, which he exhibited in his Pall Mall house and presented to the nation in 1847.[24] Sheepshanks assembled a collection 'fully representing British art', which he gave to the recently formed South Kensington Museum in 1857, believing in its mission of reconciling the fine and the decorative arts. Sheepshanks's gift was only moderately successful, and to this day the museum has not succeeded in creating illuminating connections between the paintings and the applied arts: the impact of these works on the applied arts at South Kensington was apparently minimal. Nevertheless, his style of collecting – including works by Turner, Constable, Landseer, Mulready, Wilkie and Crome as well as more modern paintings – prefigured the collections that were to be made by provincial collectors and the art museums that they supported.

The Sheepshanks collection formed the basis of the National Gallery of British Art, as the paintings at South Kensington were known. In spite of its name, this was hardly recognised as an independent national art museum, being overshadowed by the National Gallery and the South Kensington Museum. Though (largely) modern, the National Gallery of British Art never emulated the creation of a national museum of contemporary art that was achieved in France. As Pedro Lorente has shown, Britain was one of the last major European countries to gain a state-funded museum of national or of contemporary art.[25] Britain achieved these objectives, together, only as late as 1897 in the Tate

Gallery, which for many years presented a confused marriage between British and contemporary art.

THE MORAL CHARACTER OF BRITISH ART

Painting (but not sculpture) came to be seen as a means of asserting the individuality and character of English or British artistic achievement. Some writers, as we have seen, granted English or British art an extended past life. In *The Picture Collector's Manual* of 1849 the engraver James Hobbes expatiated on the long history of art in these islands, claiming that oil was used as a medium 'in England even before the time of John van Eyck, the pretended discoverer of that mode of painting'.[26] Hobbes was characteristic of nineteenth-century writers in using the term 'English' for art created throughout the British Isles – a practice particularly engaged in by writers who were not themselves British.[27]

Much attention was given to defining the nation's art throughout the century, particularly in view of the agitating general recognition that the finest teaching derived from Paris.[28] For Palgrave, 'The best Art is that which best represents the mind of the race, and we may read ourselves as a nation in the independence and vigorous individuality of our artists'.[29] The notion of virtue was much in evidence, implying British superiority to the loose morals practised across the Channel. In the early days at least, the search for virtue in both the work of art and its creator encouraged a Vasarian biographical methodology: Allan Cunningham, poet and author of *The Lives of the Most Eminent British Painters* (1829–33), was described as 'our shrewd Scottish Vasari'.[30] Composing biographical dictionaries allowed writers to introduce a moralistic character to their narrative. Artists were discussed as moral beings, with their personal virtues and failings described and when necessary condemned. For Palgrave, the finest art was created by individuals with the finest characters: though Mozart, Shelley and Turner were geniuses, their moral flaws were reflected in their work. He wrote, 'Run over the list of first-rate men, and the impression will be that of sanity, of moderation; not by any means of "eccentricity", of "Bohemianism"; not even that of men who were not understood in their own age.'[31] Other

authorities concurred. George Morland's debauchery affected his creativity: 'The annals of genius', commented Cunningham, 'record not a more deplorable story than Morland's.'[32] Fortunately, it emerged that most British artists had proved to be not the loose-living improvident eccentrics of popular perception but virtuous and hard-working. This assertion of bourgeois normality was extended by S.C. Hall, editor of the influential *Art Journal*, to the desirability of depicting healthy subjects, and thence (by a curious train of thought) to the benevolent influence of the monarchy's respectability. In *Selected Pictures from the Galleries and Private Collections of Great Britain* (1863) – a set of four volumes that constituted a popular art gallery with appropriate commentary – Hall asked in relation to Augustus Egg's *The Life of Buckingham* (Fig. 148) whether 'an artist could not find a more worthy theme for illustration than a group of male and female bacchanals in the height of their saturnalia', but reflected at least that the painting offered 'a lesson of thankfulness that we live in times when the bright example of moral rectitude is reflected from the palace of the monarch into the cottage of the peasant'.[33] In keeping with this ideal of virtuous conformism, depictions of artists in such volumes as *Artists at Home* of 1884, which contained commissioned photographs by J.P. Mayall with commentaries by the *Athenaeum*'s art critic F.G. Stephens, show the sitters as well-dressed, seemly individuals, in some cases surrounded by references to their working practices but more prominently by signs of wealth and social success (Figs 149, 150).[34]

For these critics, one of the finest qualities of British art was its homeliness: as the Redgraves put it, 'pictures to suit the English taste must be pictures to live by'.[35] Since the English spent more time at home than any other nation, they loved to see 'cheerful and decorative' works of modest size and attractive colouring that would please the eye before the mind, by such artists as Wilkie, Mulready and C.R. Leslie. The humanity of British art was frequently emphasised, in association with its moral strengths. Just as, for Hobbes, Hogarth appealed to feelings of nature to teach 'a great moral lesson, that neither the poet nor the historian could depict with more truth, nor with greater effect',[36] so fifty years later the art critic Cosmo Monkhouse stressed the 'strong note of humanity' that had always character-

148 *The Life of Buckingham* by Augustus Egg, 1854. Oil on canvas, 74.9 × 91.4 cm. The Duke of Buckingham, magnificent favourite of James I and Charles I, was famous for the splendour of his art collection and his luxurious living. The paired picture shows his miserable death, murdered in an inn in Portsmouth. Egg was much influenced by Hogarth, and the moral of the paintings is clear (Yale Center for British Art).

ised the British school. This quality stood in contrast to much contemporary art, the 'landscapes of extreme "realists", "impressionists" and "iridescents"' having become 'almost inhuman (or at least unhuman) in their neglect of every aim beyond the imitation of phenomena'.[37] The argument that the prime purpose of art was to tell stories and offer morals, to touch a human nerve rather than study visual appearances, regularly featured in apologia for the native school.

The genius of English art was also seen to lie in naturalness and narrative skill. Instead of being perverted by sensuality and artifice and the study of previous art like the French, English artists had always been true to nature. In Palgrave's analysis, 'They are all unmistakably English, no doubt; they are generally alike in a certain neglect of figure drawing, and in a certain success in colour: – but they do not show signs of any systematic pursuit of art, they are not like students of any national Academy'.[38] That technical dexterity could be sacrificed in the interests of nature was a recurring theme for Allan Cunningham. The prints in his *The Cabinet Gallery of Pictures by the First Masters of the English and Foreign Schools* (1839) boldly juxtapose

Gainsborough with Guercino, Wilkie with Claude. The text stresses – almost to the point of caricature – the essential Englishness of leading artists, with Gainsborough praised for 'the homely nature and rustic truth' of his Market Cart...the stamp of Old England is impressed upon it every where'.[39] In contrast to the false teaching of the French system, 'his academy was nature; he imitated no one either in his conceptions, or his style of colouring'.[40] Wilkie's *Blind Fiddler* is 'of a class truly British' (rather than 'Scottish') since 'In simplicity it cannot well be matched'.[41] John Crome epitomises sturdy worth: 'All about him is sterling English; he has no foreign airs or put-on graces...nothing was mean, all was natural and striking.'[42] What many critics and many patrons sought was a non-intellectual, natural, fully English art: undemanding, heart-warming, lifelike, instructive, more notable for narrative than execution, which must nevertheless demonstrate painstaking proficiency.

This emphasis on English art's truth to nature was accompanied by assertions of its equality or superiority to foreign schools. National loyalty was a dominant theme, and as this patriotic discourse gathered strength, the national school came to be defined in terms of birth. A long-lasting tension (as well as mutual attraction) arose between the art of France and Britain. Although the Royal Academy instituted a category of Honorary Foreign Academician in the 1860s and in later decades did welcome foreign exhibitors, there was some prejudice against allowing artists from abroad to exhibit at the Summer Exhibitions. These barriers reflect those put up against women artists, as witnessed by the agonies experienced over the prospective election to the Academy of Lady Butler, the highly successful painter of military subjects.

The battle on behalf of English or British art was tenaciously fought. (Compounding the semantic confusion, Walter Thornbury explained in 1861 that his *British Artists from Hogarth to Turner* was intended as a forerunner to a history that would 'trace not merely the early sufferings and martyrdoms of our great English Artists, but also the growth and progress of English Arts, from the acorn to the oak'.)[43] For Thornbury, many collectors showed no sense of national loyalty. In a passage presumably directed at Eastlake's National Gallery, he thundered that 'men of feeble, antiquarian turn

149 Richard Redgrave, from *Artists at Home* (1884) by J.P. Mayall. A well-known photographer, Mayall produced twenty-seven photogravures of celebrated British artists (plus W.E. Gladstone) in their houses or studios. They were published as a set by Sampson Low, Marston, Searle and Rivington, accompanied by a text by the Pre-Raphaelite artist and art critic F.G. Stephens. Purporting to give an authentic view of the artist at work, the photographs were criticised by contemporaries for their staginess.

RICHARD REDGRAVE C.B
Hon Retired R.A

150 W.F. Yeames, from *Artists at Home* (1884) by J.P. Mayall.

W.F YEAMES R.A

of mind disregard our own brave Wilson and inimitable Hogarth, to buy absurd eccentricities of the early Italian school. Tame purism and cold religiosity waste money on those dead exotics, with a disloyalty disgraceful to the intellect as well as to the heart of our own great England.'[44] In other words, the National Gallery's survey of historic European art needed to be redefined in favour of native painting. Critics hailed the narrative tradition established by Hogarth as 'the first to abandon foreign models and foreign spirit, and to look to nature as the true source of art'.[45] They hailed 'the power of British landscapes and portraits, and the capacity of British pictures to satisfy 'the great aim of art – pure and lasting pleasure'.[46] Art too could represent the superiority of the native genius, and as a result almost all galleries aimed to collect works of art by British artists, both local and national.

For the private collector, and by extension for provincial galleries, the expanding literature offered a guide on how to form a collection. In *A Century of Painters of the English School*, of 1866, Samuel and Richard Redgrave issued a strong statement of the excellence of the native school. They claimed that the story had never been told; that though 'Hogarth, Wilson, Gainsborough, Reynolds, and Copley…upheld the high character of our art, and have left its records in their works, and its reputation to a race of painters by whom it has been well sustained; yet their works and their names remain at the end of another century without a history; and our English school is still scarcely recognized at home, much less on the Continent'.[47] The book identifies Hogarth as the first English artist of any merit and hails the three fathers of the English school: Reynolds for portraiture, Gainsborough for genre and 'fancy painting', Wilson for landscape. David Wilkie and Henry Raeburn, the truest of Scots, feature prominently.

The next generation was more difficult to assess for the Redgraves, as for Victorian collectors. The attempts at history painting made in the early part of the century by Northcote, Haydon and so forth, were condemned, since history painters had followed 'the old, heroic, absurd, incomprehensible unattainable rules', in defiance of what anyone actu-

151 *William Mulready RA*, a design for a mosaic by Frederick Bacon Barwell. In the 1860s a set of paintings for reproduction as mosaics were commissioned by Henry Cole for the South Court of the South Kensington Museum. They included applied artists as well as painters and sculptors, emphasising the importance of the applied arts in the museum's world view. Mulready was a friend of Cole and a supporter of the museum (Victoria and Albert Museum).

ally wanted.[48] Their approach seemed irrelevant in a society that lacked, as Thackeray put it, the 'government museums' and 'the painted chapels, requiring fresh supplies of saints and martyrs' that provided commissions in France.[49] In place of history painting, the Redgrave narrative saw the continuance of the eighteenth-century masters' achievement in Turner, regarded as a genius especially for his watercolours; Constable, increasingly admired as the century advanced; Wilkie, whose reputation did not flag; and many others.

Not all the artists acclaimed by the Redgraves were equally accepted by Victorian collectors, who found some of the artists they admired, such as Henry Fuseli, too bizarre.[50] More popular were early nineteenth-century artists such as George Morland, humorous and appealing and by the 1890s expensive; John Opie, praised for his triumph over humble origins; William Etty, considered heroically innovative for his painterly work; and William Müller, a Bristol artist working in the Turner manner, whose richly coloured landscapes sold well.[51] William Mulready enjoyed a high reputation, Thackeray exulting that the French 'have no painter like MUL-READY, above all, whose name I beg the printer to place in the largest capitals, and to surround with a wreath of laurels' (Fig. 151).[52]

In aspiration at least, the provincial galleries and the collectors associated with them followed the advice offered by Vernon, Sheepshanks and the Redgraves; but it was contemporary art that reigned supreme. Now that British paintings were regarded as tokens of wealth and national success, the public art museum became a forum for displays of civic and private virtue. The triumph of the visual arts shed lustre on the nation, on a donor of art, on an artist's birthplace, lustre that could not easily have been shed by geological or natural history or archaeological specimens – not least because such objects seldom achieved comparable prices. The painting enjoyed an aura that could not be emulated by the fossil.

❖

COLLECTING WITHOUT RESOURCES

Many of the new provincial art galleries opened with no collection at all, or at best a ragbag of objects left over from a previous institution. They were not helped by derisory or non-existent acquisition budgets. Various solutions were found. In Manchester, when the city took over Royal Manchester Institution in 1882, the condition was made that £2,000 per annum must be spent for twenty years by the city on the purchase of works of art.[53] This was a useful sum at a time when a Frans Hals could be bought for some £3,000 and works by Rubens for between around £1,700 and £5,000. Spending carefully, the Gallery 'concentrated on landscapes and figures studies, on truth to nature, on aesthetics rather than anecdote, and on serious moral tone'. It acquired works by Reynolds, Gainsborough and Wilson but primarily nineteenth-century art.[54] Usually, however, private donors provided the solution. In Birmingham a Public Picture Gallery Fund was endowed with its own Purchase Committee (resembling an American supporters' circle in the twenty-first century): with donations from private individuals, its endowment rose to £17,000 in 1881.[55] In the early years this Fund acquired works by such medium-priced artists as Briton Rivière and John Brett (a favourite, no doubt because he was admired by Ruskin), and later the Pre-Raphaelites.

When there was no acquisition budget, displays had to be patched together. In 1878 the Atkinson Art Gallery opened in the Lancashire seaside town of Southport. Given that the town owned no works of art, a circular was sent out to all the inhabitants requesting loans, as a result of which over a thousand paintings, watercolours, prints and photographs were displayed in the opening exhibition, hung four or five deep on the walls and extending into the reading room and entrance hall of the Library (Figs 152, 153).[56] It was, in its idiosyncratic way, a triumphant assertion of civic pride and indeed of what would now be called community art.[57] In a more orthodox instance, in its early days Birmingham City Art Gallery was given or lent portraits of prominent Birmingham citizens by the Midland Institute, as well as murals by Millais.[58] For needy galleries, London provided the bulk of the loans. Well into the twentieth century the Department of Science and Art was filling the halls of new galleries, particularly such educational ventures as the People's Palace in Glasgow, with reproductions as well as original works. The Glasgow museums acknowledged the Department's help: its 'very substantial' loans were 'of the utmost importance to the Corporation Museums and Art Galleries'.[59] In addition, in 1883 the National Gallery was empowered to lend paintings to British (though not foreign) galleries, with loans being made to the National Portrait Gallery, the National Gallery of Ireland and eleven British art galleries in the first year.[60] The powers were generously used, since they offered an answer to the perennial question of what to do with the growing national holdings, notably the huge Turner bequest for which there was no room at Trafalgar Square. The Walker was one among several recipients, being lent paintings by Turner, West, Lawrence and Etty as well as by other artists (Edward Villiers Rippingille, F. R. Lee) whose absence may not have been keenly felt in London.[61]

Pride in local artistic achievement was a powerful motive for acquisitions, which were often associated with a gallery's annual exhibition. E. K. Muspratt, a businessman and a loyal citizen of Liverpool, recalled that 'Although Liverpool cannot lay claim to having led the way in matters artistic, or proved itself an artistic centre, as Glasgow is, for instance, it has had its fair share of some who have come to honourable acceptance in the world of art'.[62] He listed names of varying degrees of celebrity, including 'many artists who are not native to the place, but whose work is associated with it'. Profits from the exhibition sales were regularly used to make acquisitions, and this system again encouraged local loyalties. At Liverpool in 1872 the modest surplus of £600 was spent on paintings by F.W.W. Topham and J.W. Oakes – locally significant in that Oakes hailed from Liverpool and was a member of the Liverpool Academy. On the other hand, it was not only local artists who were acquired in local exhibitions. After the 1879 exhibition the handsomer profit of £2,994 went on several works, including W.F. Yeames's 'And When Did you Last See your Father?', a picture that became hugely popular. Naturally, the scale of exhibition and profit influenced what could be bought. At the top end, Manchester acquired, especially from its 1880s Autumn Exhibitions, pictures by such established and expensive artists as Luke Fildes,

Edward Burne-Jones, Hubert von Herkomer and Frederic Leighton (Figs 154, 155).[63]

THE INFLUENCE OF THE ROYAL ACADEMY

The Royal Academy maintained its power to the end of the century and beyond, with its Summer Exhibitions attracting audiences of over 300,000 to Burlington House almost every year between 1869 (the first exhibition in this new venue) and 1896.[64] Its Private View became the opening event in the London social season, a commentator remarking caustically in 1897, 'Only within the past few years has what is called the 'private' view of the

Royal Academy become a fete day of fashionable society; – a promenade for the display of the latest devices in Parisian or Bond Street toilettes.'[65] The display of art, money and fashion became more intimately enmeshed than ever.

In many circles, however, the Royal Academy was despised for its conservatism and its corruption, notably in the administration of the Chantrey Bequest. The nineteenth-century sculptor Francis Chantrey had made a generous bequest to buy British art and works by foreign artists resident in Britain for the benefit of the National Gallery. It was widely considered that the funds were spent by the Royal Academy on second-rate works. As George Moore wrote, 'That nearly all artists dislike and despise the Royal Academy is a matter of

207

153 The Atkinson Art Gallery's opening exhibition 1878. Since the Gallery had no collection when it opened, the inhabitants of the town were asked to lend any work they possessed, and no proffered loans were rejected. The first bequest of works of art arrived in 1879.

common knowledge.'[66] Among the councillors who largely determined acquisitions in provincial galleries, however, it was revered. Works by successive Presidents – Leighton, Millais, Edward Poynter – were much in demand, as were paintings by other prominent members such as G. F. Watts. In Moore's view,

> Art in the provinces is little more than a reflection of the Academy. The majority of the pictures represent the taste of men who have no knowledge of art, and who, to disguise their ignorance, follow the advice which the Academy gives to provincial England in the pictures it purchases under the terms – or, rather, under its own reading of the terms – of the Chantrey Bequest Fund.[67]

Though provincial museums did not necessarily buy directly from the Summer Exhibition at Burlington House, many of their acquisitions had previously been shown there. The regular pattern was for a painting to be shown first at the Royal Academy and then, if unsold, in the Liverpool Autumn Exhibition or another large provincial event, where a purchase might be consummated.[68]

SIGNIFICANT OMISSIONS

A revealing aspect of municipal collecting was the type of work that was avoided. On the whole collectors, committees and curators did not favour Old Masters. Some were not considered desirable, notably the seventeenth-century Bolognese school beloved by earlier aristocratic collectors: the National Gallery of Scotland catalogue commented in 1859 on a work by Ludovico Carracci that 'The consequence of the excessive admiration in this country of the pictures of the late Bolognese School is, that among the Italian works imported, they far exceed anything like a due proportion, and so productions of a far superior kind have been excluded by them.'[69] Forty years later, J. C. Robinson noted the decline of interest in the artists venerated by an earlier generation when old collections were put on the market: Old Masters 'have greatly fallen from their high estate…Guido and Carlo Dolce, Salvator Rosa, Shibboleths and high-sounding Mesopotamias of the past, have lost their unction – democracy in art, as in other things, is pulling down these old idols.'[70]

Part of this hostility derived from a feeling that Old Master paintings represented fakery. The danger of forgery was a nineteenth-century commonplace, reflecting the insecurity of collectors and the quest for value for money. The Redgraves emphasised the ubiquity of forgeries and the doubtful quality of supposed Old Masters, enquiring 'Even when a picture comes direct from the studio of that artist, is it always certainly the work of his own hand?'[71] S.C. Hall congratulated himself on having 'destroyed, by conclusive evidence and continual exposures, the extensive and nefarious trade in "old masters"', and having 'lived to see such "old masters" valued accordingly to their worthlessness, and a thorough transfer of patronage to modern Art'.[72] This text postulates two forms of fakery: not only the fakes sold by the art trade, but the artistic falsity even of verified Old Masters in comparison to the genuine quality of the modern. With the modern British school, the purchaser could be confident of buying the genuine article.

It is true that some earlier works were donated by private collectors. Leeds in its early days was given paintings by such artists as Pietro da Cortona and Bergognone, while Birmingham acquired a Murillo and a Charles Le Brun, although these works had little meaning in the context of a primarily modern collection. The Walker benefitted from the long tradition of collecting in Liverpool, enjoying modest gifts and bequests of Dutch seventeenth-century paintings, alongside sculptures attributed to Canova.[73] Only in a few instances did industrialist collectors bequeath Old Master paintings to public institutions. Thomas Kay, a major philanthropist

who had made his fortune in patent medicines, gave the Heywood Reference Library in Rochdale a group of sixteenth- and seventeenth-century Netherlandish and Italian oil paintings (Fig. 156).[74] His intention was primarily didactic, 'showing the progress of Painting and the Decorative Arts from an early period', with an emphasis on the material

for full appreciation, also presented intellectual and social difficulties, neatly avoided by Lawrence Alma-Tadema or Albert Moore's costume dramas.

The strongest area of Old Master collecting lay in Dutch seventeenth-century painting. This was a school that had consistently influenced the development of British landscape painting and genre, was on the whole safely Protestant, was seen as richly humorous, meticulously crafted and concerned with the domestic interior, and maintained a comfortably small scale. All these qualities appealed to collectors in Britain late in the nineteenth-century, just as they did to their American contemporaries. In this genre, the works presented by Baron de Ferrières to Cheltenham concentrated on seventeenth as well as nineteenth-century Dutch painting.[77] One of the most striking groups of Dutch paintings to reach a municipal gallery belonged to Joseph Shipley, a rich Newcastle solicitor. In 1909 he bequeathed over 2,000 paintings, many of them Dutch and Flemish, to his city on condition that a new gallery be built next to the Laing Art Gallery (Fig. 158), although the unwillingness of the City Council and of the voters in general to accept responsibility for the collection led to Newcastle's refusal of the bequest.[78] It eventually formed the basis of the Shipley Art Gallery, across the Tyne in Gateshead (Fig. 159).

BRITISH PORTRAITS

A category that was only lightly represented in public collections was eighteenth-century British art. Paintings by Gainsborough or Reynolds were generally much too expensive by the late 1860s to be acquired by municipal galleries: the nobility were getting record-breaking prices for their family portraits from American collectors and also from banker-collectors based in Britain, such as the Rothschilds. A portrait (preferably a full-length) of a famous sitter by a major eighteenth-century English artist might fetch £10,000 or even more, particularly if it came from a great house and showed a beautiful female sitter: Charles Holmes used as the frontispiece for *Pictures and Picture Collecting* (1903) a portrait of Lady Louisa Manners by John Hoppner (Fig. 160) that had recently been sold for a staggering 14,750 guineas, at a time when a Rembrandt

156   *The Crucifixion* by Giovanni di Paolo, *c.* 1423–6. Oil on panel, 31 × 49.7 cm. A distinguished work from the educational collection of Thomas Kay, this was bequeathed to the Heywood Reference Library in Rochdale in Lancashire. The paintings were transferred to Rochdale Art Gallery in 1974 (Rochdale Arts and Heritage Service).

157   *Love Tunes the Shepherd's Reed* by Richard Jack, 1920. Oil on canvas, 121.9 × 224.8 cm. Bought by Sunderland Art Gallery in spite of moralistic reservations about the naked figures. (Sunderland Museum and Winter Gardens).

entity of works of art and the best means of restoring them.[75] This type of didactic collection recalls the acquisition of Roscoe's paintings by the Liverpool Royal Institution.

Highly unusual were religious paintings, historic or contemporary, reflecting a Nonconformist disapproval of sacred subjects and of Catholic art. Paintings depicting classical subjects that risked showing nudity were also avoided: as late as 1930, councillors in Sunderland objected to the acquisition of *Love Tunes the Shepherd's Reed* by the innocuous Richard Jack (Fig. 157) because the semi-nude figures made it 'unsuitable for display in the Gallery.'[76] The whole classical discourse, founded on paganism and requiring a classical public school and university education

158   *A Dutch Garden Scene* by Dirck van Delen, 1636. Oil on canvas, 67.3 × 81.3 cm. One of the finest works from Joseph Shipley's huge collection. (Shipley Art Collection).

159   The Shipley Art Gallery, Gateshead. The Gallery opened in 1917 with some 500 of the 2,500 paintings accumulated by Shipley, the others having been weeded out.

160   The frontispiece of *Pictures and Picture Collecting* by C.J. Holmes (1903). It depicts John Hoppner's *Lady Louisa Manners.* The painting had recently sold for an enormous sum (over £14,000), which made such a powerful impression that the amount was recorded differently by various authorities.

could be bought for less than £6,000. On the other hand, local associations might override such prejudices, as with the paintings by Joseph Wright of Derby bought by Derby Art Gallery after an exhibition of his work there.[79] Equally, the pictures and memorabilia associated with Joshua Reynolds given as part of the Cotton collection to the new Plymouth Art Gallery in 1915 came from a private owner interested in the city's history (Fig. 161).

Although this point of view is nowhere explicitly stated, it is also arguable that in contrast to such aristocratic patrons as the Marquesses of Hertford, municipal galleries and the private collectors from which they derived deliberately avoided works that referred to the traditional apparatus of power. The scorn heaped by Carlyle on 'the Idle Aristocracy, the Owners of the Soil of England; whose recognised function is that of handsomely consuming the rents of England, shooting the partridges of England and as an agreeable amusement…dilettante-ing in Parliament and Quarter-Sessions for England' would not have been lost on the 'Working Aristocracy; Mill-owners, Manufacturers, Commanders of Working Men'.[80] Not only the aristocracy's longstanding indifference to and contempt for industrial towns but what was seen as their moral degeneracy arguably made them unfit subjects for a people's gallery. Equally, as Jan Marsh has suggested, one reason why newly rich collectors avoided acquiring portraits of eighteenth-century aristocrats was that they preferred to avoid confusion in a context where a portrait on the wall of a private house might well be mistaken for a statement of ancestry.[81] In the case of the Queen, such reservations would not have applied, but even her image in a municipal collection (including public statuary as well as the art gallery) tended to take the form of a bust rather than a painting, and even then, in view of her unpopularity in mid-reign, probably post-dated the jubilees of 1887 and 1897.

THE PRE-RAPHAELITES

Under the influence of the Royal Academy and the aldermanic rule of taste, municipal collections tended towards the conservative. In general, although these galleries could be defined as galleries of modern art, they stretched the definition. It was

161 *The Artist's Father* by Joshua Reynolds, *c.* 1746. Oil on canvas, 75.7 × 63.1 cm. The Revd Samuel Reynolds, a Fellow of Balliol College, Oxford, and Master of Plympton Grammar school, is shown here in profile, a position traditionally associated with men of learning. The portrait was almost certainly painted soon after his death, as a personal tribute. Having descended through Reynolds's family, it was bequeathed to Plymouth with the Cottonian collection in 1853. (Plymouth City Museum and Art Gallery).

162 *Arrangement in Grey and Black, No 2* by J.A.M. Whistler, 1872–3. Oil on canvas, 171.1 × 143.5 cm. This portrait of Thomas Carlyle, a near-neighbour of Whistler in Chelsea, resembles in composition Whistler's portrait of his own mother (*Arrangement in Grey and Black, No 1*), 1871. Strong pressure was brought to bear on the city by Glasgow's artists to make this innovative purchase in 1891 (Glasgow Museums).

a condition that applied not only to the provinces but also to the capital, the Tate Gallery missing opportunity after opportunity to acquire fine contemporary works. Among provincial galleries, Glasgow was exceptionally far-sighted in its 1891 purchase of Whistler's portrait of Thomas Carlyle

(Fig. 162), following a petition by a large group of Glasgow artists. Even then the artists had to stress the sitter's Scottish associations, adding that 'the masterly execution, the dignity, and the simplicity rank it amongst the noblest works of art of our time'.[82]

The acquisition of works by the Pre-Raphaelites illustrates the difficulties over buying modern work. These artists had been greeted with suspicion and even hostility by critics and the public on religious and stylistic grounds. A fulmination in *Blackwood's Edinburgh Magazine*'s review of the Royal Academy Summer Exhibition of 1850 against 'the mountebank proceedings of a small number of artists, who, stimulated by their own conceit, and by the applause of a few foolish persons, are endeavouring to set up a school of their own' was characteristic of reactions to a movement whose members, with the exception of Millais and the sculptor Thomas Woolner, remained outside the Royal Academy's fold.[83] Nonetheless, their work was actively collected from the 1850s onwards, especially by Northern industrialists, and by the 1870s commanded considerable prices. In Newcastle, a dual pattern of collecting and exhibiting emerged. On one hand, the enterprising acquisition of Pre-Raphaelite pictures undertaken by businessmen in the city, as well as by such adventurous members of the landed gentry as the Trevelyans of Wallington Hall, extended to the loan of experimental works from private collections to the 1866 exhibition organised on behalf of the Newcastle Mechanics' Institute.[84] Yet these private tastes made almost no impact on the development of public collecting in the city, even after the Laing Art Gallery was set up in 1904. For financial reasons, as well as the caution of councillors, public collecting in Newcastle followed at least a generation behind private – just as it did in Glasgow, a city notable for private owners' bold acquisitions.[85]

In spite of all these obstacles, a determined and respected curator could form a distinguished collection. A striking contrast emerges between the confidence of the large galleries and the modesty of most of the smaller ones. At Birmingham, Wallis was active in buying or obtaining gifts of Pre-Raphaelite paintings from 1883 onwards, with the support of local collectors and the Public Picture Gallery Fund, including such stellar works as Millais' *The Blind Girl* and Hunt's *The Finding of the Saviour*

in the Temple (Fig. 163).[86] At Manchester, although the Pre-Raphaelites were initially greeted with distrust by local patrons, notable paintings were already being bought or given in the 1880s, and to brilliant effect from the 1890s onwards.[87] In 1899 the Curator wrote that Liverpool 'had reason to be proud of her early recognition and support of the little band of young men known as the Pre-Raphaelite Brotherhood…daring young men'.[88] All three galleries built up large, authoritative collections.

THE CHALLENGE OF FRANCE

The reputation of contemporary British art was not unquestioned. Even the most sympathetic foreign writers found it peculiar, remarking on the overpowering colour and the obsession with storytelling, particularly when stories had to be explained in the catalogue. Ernest Chesneau's doubts were expressed in his praise for the Scottish genre painter Erskine Nicol, whom he described as possessing 'the exceptional merit, for an Englishman [*sic*], of being a true artist and skilful in colouring'.[89] Equally, for the British, French art posed a perpetual challenge. It was, for a start, seen as superior to other European schools: the art historian Joseph Archer Crowe (who had studied in Paris) remarked in 1890 on 'a decided superiority of French artists over their competitors in most schools on the French side of the Channel'.[90] French art was regularly on view in London commercial galleries, such as the permanent gallery dedicated to the paintings and prints of Gustave Doré in Bond Street.[91] The enterprising dealer Ernest Gambart offered a succession of exhibitions of contemporary French art at his London premises, the French Gallery, and organised hugely successful tours of Britain for Rosa Bonheur in the 1860s.[92] French art was often praised at the expense of British art, even by British writers, with

shown in Victorian Birmingham. The foreign artists listed in museum catalogues from the 1870s to 1914 are relatively few and tend to have been acquired towards the end of the century or later: a Delaroche at Liverpool, a Fantin-Latour at Manchester and at Sheffield (in the Mappin collection), and some modern French, German, Dutch and Scandinavian works. The Barbizon school, and notably Corot (too bold in his artistic approach for the average alderman, according to George Moore, but much in demand in the United States and extremely expensive),[95] Daubigny and Millet, Díaz and Rousseau, all seen as quintessentially French, were much sought after for private collections, and it was there they mostly stayed (Fig. 164).[96] Even the National Gallery, though criticised for its timidity, was slow in acquiring Barbizon paintings.[97]

Some exceptions did of course occur. Among the leaders in this field, Glasgow acquired a mere five foreign contemporary pictures and the Walker twelve. At Liverpool, where foreign artists were welcomed to the Autumn Exhibitions, public purchases included Giovanni Segantini's *The Punishment of Luxury* (Fig. 165) and Henri Le Sidaner's *Saint Paul's from the River*. These acquisitions were made under the influence of Councillor Philip Rathbone, a radical in terms of taste, who when economy was urged at a council meeting would remark 'Damn the Ratepayers'. Only in such a cosmopolitan collection as the Bowes Museum, where Mrs Bowes was herself a landscape painter, could the nineteenth-century French school be found in any strength, with paintings by Valenciennes and Michallon, Granet and Corot, Boudin and Courbet acquired from Paris dealers or at auction in Paris.[98]

As attitudes changed in the first decade of the new century, Barbizon paintings began to find their way into public collections, with Glasgow receiving a number in the Donald Bequest in 1905. At best, modern French work might be shown in such sophisticated loan exhibitions as the inaugural display at the Laing Art Gallery, Newcastle, in 1904, which included a fine representation of established French taste, with loans from private collections of work by Corot, Isabey, Bonheur, Daubigny, Harpignies and Millet.[99] But although exhibitions of Impressionist art organised in London by the Paris art dealer Paul Durand-Ruel in the 1880s were well

164 *Going to Work* by Jean-François Millet (1850–1). Oil on canvas, 56 × 46 cm. Millet gained a major international reputation in the later nineteenth century for his realist paintings, particularly of peasant life in France. Although much admired in Britain, his works did not enter British public collections until the twentieth century and then went mostly to national museums. This bequest by James Donald to Glasgow in 1905 is an early example of his work entering a regional collection (Glasgow Museums).

the influential critic Harry Quilter commenting in the 1890s that French art was on a different plane, since 'Such painters as Harpignies, Díaz del la Peña…Flandrin…have no rivals at all at the present time in English art'.[93] This sense of inferiority in the face of the international capital of modern art never quite disappeared.

If public collectors were cautious in buying what might be broadly defined as British painting, they were even more careful about venturing into the field of foreign art.[94] French eighteenth-century art, though actively bought by the more dashing of the wealthy, the Hertfords and Rothschilds, was inaccessible, financially and otherwise, to provincial galleries – it is hard to imagine a Boucher being

165 *The Punishment of Luxury* by Giovanni Segantini, 1891. Oil on canvas, 99 × 172.8 cm. Acquired by the Walker Art Gallery in 1893 – the only work by this Symbolist painter in an English public collection – the painting typifies the adventurous collecting of Councillor Philip Rathbone (National Museums Liverpool).

166 James Aumonier's *A Breezy Day*, bought by Leeds Art Gallery in 1891. Oil on canvas, 71.1 × 101.6 cm (Leeds Museums and Galleries).

received, the British public in general were given almost no glimpse of their work until well into the twentieth century, in either national or municipal collections.[100] Modern German or Italian work was even less well represented.

Happily for contemporary audiences, the modern foreign artists found in the museum catalogues of the 1870s to 1900 on scrutiny frequently turned out to be honorary Britons. One name that recurs is Alphonse Legros, who was held to have made a wise

215

personal decision: born in Dijon in 1837, he had moved to London and become a British citizen. As Slade Professor of Art at University College, London, he exerted a powerful influence on art education in his adopted country. Where doubt might exist over an artist's nationality, a gallery's catalogue might well reassure the viewer. Visitors to Leeds City Art Gallery, confronted by *A Breezy Day*, which, for all its healthy subject matter, was painted by an artist named James Aumonier (Fig. 166), were assured that although he might sound like a Frenchman, 'He has never studied out of England, nor indeed has he ever been out of the country.'[101] A further bias can be detected: the near-exclusion of women artists. Though women's names do feature in municipal galleries, the proportion found at the Mappin Art Gallery in 1914 – nine women among a total of 217 artists – can be regarded as typical. With a few striking exceptions, women artists were habitually represented by works of a domestic or playful nature, or by the generally untroubling genre of landscape.

STYLES OF COLLECTING

In a few cases, an effort was made to set out what today would be called an acquisitions policy rather than to rely on the vagaries of the annual exhibition and the private donor. For Birmingham City Art Gallery, exceptionally expansive and ambitious, Whitworth Wallis published in 1904 an acquisitions policy in the form of a plea for donations:

> The Committee is not enabled to make any purchases at the expense of the ratepayers, the cost of the Gallery to the City being confined to expenses of maintenance. It is inevitable that a collection thus representing an aggregate of many individual gifts should be somewhat miscellaneous in character and less adequately representative...it is thought that it may be useful to specify directions in which it seems specially desirable to strengthen the collection. The Committee would heartily welcome fine examples of the eighteenth-century portrait painters, the landscape artists of the Norwich and Early English Schools, early water colours and those of later date, works of the English pre-Raphaelite painters, and drawings, engravings, and etchings

by Italian, Dutch, German, French, and English masters.[102]

This statement indicates the Gallery's aspirations. They were realistic, so that while the statement included older English paintings, only works on paper by foreign artists were mentioned, as though paintings by foreign artists could hardly be envisaged. Wallis's endeavour to make the Gallery's collecting into a shared public activity was only partially realised, since almost all the (numerous) donations were of nineteenth-century British works, with a focus on artists related to the city. That is what collectors owned, or at least were willing to give.

In many cases, acquisition policies (if such a name can be given to the process) concentrated on more narrative considerations. Documentation and topography often underlay the collecting. This aim was reflected in various ways. The collections were, firstly, statements of local pride and identity, made through depictions of the city and its hinterland; portraits of the city's most celebrated sons and (in a few cases) daughters; works created by artists born in the city or teaching or at least living there. Secondly, the collections recounted the history of England or Scotland, or of the region, especially through the historical picture depicting a rousing or moving episode and generally enshrining a straightforward moral. Thirdly, galleries showed (often on loan) sculptures depicting famous compatriots or fellow-townsmen. And finally, a few curators set about making systematic representative collections of modern, or at least recent, British art.

The purchasing policies of an art museum might be multi-faceted. At the Walker, Councillor Philip Rathbone exercised a dual acquisitions policy: to buy relatively innovative nineteenth-century painting and sculpture, and also works that would be pleasing to the public.[103] As Charles Dyall wrote in 1888 of the previous decade, it had not been 'lost sight of that the public, for whose edification and instruction the institution in a great measure exists, delight in subjects of a popular character, and with this end in view pictures have from time to time been added which, by appealing to common feelings and sentiments of our daily life, have afforded a fine moral lesson, and given great pleasure to the numerous visitors to the gallery who are uninitiated in the higher forms of art.'[104] In a later report he identified these pictures as ones that 'appeal to our common sympathies,…delineating domestic scenes, and every-day incidents of life'.[105] Such pictures encouraged the working classes to 'carry with them to their homes vivid impressions of a refining and elevating character'. This approach was reflected in the comments of Thomas Greenwood, who supported the idea that easily enjoyable paintings were appropriate for an uneducated audience: 'The "Village Wedding" of Luke Fildes, is worth more to them than all the works of Rubens in the National Gallery.'[106] Catering for a popular taste was a policy intended to address the moment rather than perpetuity, but it was a taste shared by many donors who 'brought to their judgement of a painting, not Lemprière's classical dictionary and the academic rules, but their own experience'.[107] This was a strikingly original policy, hardly paralleled in France, Germany or Italy.

Easy though it is to sneer at the acquisition policies of these galleries, what they were achieving was a form of folk art collection. Not folk art in the sense that its makers were uneducated or nameless, or that the works were not produced by professional artists, but in the sense that these acquisitions represented an attempt to create a collection that would be enjoyed by the broadest of audiences. It was a short-lived approach. Such a form of collecting has been denounced by critics and curators since at least 1900, and such dismissiveness persists. When the decision was made in the late 1990s to display a contemporary collection directed at a popular audience in the new Gallery of Modern Art in Glasgow it met with catcalls by the art establishment,[108] but it may be recalled that when after considerable hesitation the National Gallery of Art in Washington was persuaded in 1997 to show *The Victorians: British Painting, 1837–1901*, the result attracted almost a quarter of a million visitors, who could be observed enjoyably discussing the stories in the way that visitors to Victorian galleries had done.[109] Given the nature of the public in Victorian cities, and the way in which these galleries were visited, this was, and remains, an alternative canon.

The impact of the purchases at Liverpool can be studied through the list of paintings that the public chose to copy in the Walker's first ten years.[110] The artists presumably included art students and copyists producing pictures for sale as well as amateurs working for their own pleasure: these choices reflected popular taste, as well as the copyists' abilities. The most frequently selected paintings fell into three principal groups almost all concentrating on works executed in the later 1870s and the 1880s. The first group focused on landscapes, such as Peter Ghent's *Nature's Mirror* (Fig. 167), which was the most frequently copied picture overall, and John Fraser's *On the Moray Firth* (Fig. 168). The second concentrated on narrative or popular history painting, such as Topham's *The Fall of Rienzi* (Fig. 173), Yeames's *'And When Did You Last See your Father?'* and Herkomer's *Eventide* (Fig. 169), a study of the Westminster workhouse (the third most popular choice). A third, smaller, group, reflected the policy of pleasing the popular palette: humorous depictions of clerical self-indulgence, such as Walter Dendy Sadler's *Friday* (Fig. 170), the second favourite, in which Franciscans feast on fish on a fast day, or paintings of dogs, pretty women or children, in the style of John Morgan's *Dont'ee Tipty Toe* (Fig. 172) or J.C. Dollmann's *Table d'Hôte at a Dogs' Home* (Fig. 171). In this company it is hardly surprising that though they featured on the list, Leighton and Rossetti did not head it.

As might be expected, within these broad bands of taste each gallery showed individual preferences. At Leeds the committee and curator were particularly drawn to landscapes, often with a romantic or narrative association – the 1890s was a very active period for acquisitions. Catering for every climatic condition, they included *The Mouth of the Greta*; *The River, Bosham*; *Old Whitby*; *Eskdale*; *The Golden Valley*; *A Breezy Day*; *A Snow Storm*.[111] Landscapes – unusual in being often analysed in gallery catalogues in visual rather than narrative form – were supplemented by genre scenes. These ranged from the kitsch, such as Henriette Ronner's *A Literary Dispute*, which was 'above all happy in that instinctive rendering of kitten nature which characterises all Mme Ronner's works of the kind' (Fig. 174), to works by social realists such as Frank Holl and Herkomer.[112] Commentary on the poor social conditions of the time had become, through the medium of literature, a widely shared preoccupation.

One important message of the displays and the accompanying catalogues was the closeness of the art to the audiences' background. At Leeds, every opportunity was taken to point out that an artist

167 *Nature's Mirror* by Peter Ghent. Oil on canvas, 123 × 182.2 cm. Given to the gallery in 1882 (National Museums Liverpool).

168 *On the Moray Firth* by John Fraser. Oil on canvas, 66.5 × 127.5 cm. Painted in 1881, the picture was bought by the Walker Art Gallery the following year (National Museums Liverpool).

169 *Eventide: A Scene in the Westminster Union* by Hubert von Herkomer, bought by the Walker Art Gallery from the Liverpool Autumn Exhibition in 1878, the year it was painted. Oil on canvas, 110.5 × 198.5 cm. The artist's powerful social realist works were much esteemed by the Walker's public. Here he painted inmates of a London workhouse (National Museums Liverpool).

170　*Friday* by Walter Dendy
Sadler, 1882. Oil on canvas,
108 × 217 cm. Two Franciscans are
entertained by Dominican friars to
a sumptuous dinner on a fast day.
The painting, which exploited a
popular theme, was shown at the
Royal Academy and at the Walker's
Autumn Exhibition before being
presented to the Gallery by James
Pergam, a successful tea merchant
(National Museums Liverpool).

171　J.C. Dollman's *Table d'Hôte
at a Dogs' Home. Oil on canvas,*
75 × 129 cm. Painted in 1879, it
was bought the following year by
the Walker, where it exercised a
wide appeal (National Museums
Liverpool).

172　*Dont'ee Tipty Toe* by John
Morgan, 1885. Oil on canvas,
91.5 × 61 cm (National Museums
Liverpool).

173　*The Fall of Rienzi* by F. W.W.
Topham, 1872. Oil on canvas, 151.8
× 107.3 cm. Shown first at the
Royal Academy, where it did not
sell, the painting was bought by the
Walker Art Gallery from the
Liverpool Autumn Exhibition. It
tells the story of the rebellious
Cola di Rienzi, who briefly created
a new Roman state in 1334–7 and
again in 1354 before being killed by
the Roman mob. In the nineteenth
century he was seen as a forerunner
of Italian unity and freedom: his
life was the subject of one of
Wagner's early operas and a novel
by Edward Bulwer Lytton
(National Museums Liverpool).

174 *Cat Study* by Henriette Ronner, 1901. Oil on canvas, 15 × 20.5 cm. Ronner was famous for her paintings of cats and kittens – the kind of subject then often considered appropriate for a female artist. The painting by her in Leeds Art Gallery mentioned in the text was disposed of after the Second World War, an example of the abhorrence of Victorian painting then felt by many curators (Hartlepool Museums and Heritage Service).

came from the city or studied or taught there, or at least came from Yorkshire. The reader was frequently told that the artist was 'self-taught', suggesting that the determined spectator could instruct himself or herself. Though this message fluctuated from place to place, it emerges as one of the most consistent statements of civic identity. Thus at Birmingham the two principal native-born artists were David Cox and Edward Burne-Jones.[113] By 1912 the Gallery owned over 150 works by Cox, including 34 oils left by a local collector in the early days of the gallery, and numerous drawings and studies (Fig. 175).[114] Burne-Jones was represented by over 300 works, shown in a dedicated room. This absorption of artists in the discourse of civic self-assertion extended to assertions, in their biographies, of the stimulating educational and social effect exerted by the city. They had been inspired in various ways: by being taught by Cox, or encouraged to follow his example, through having exhibited at the Royal Birmingham Society of Artists, or at the very least, if a closer connection could not be claimed (as in the case of Ford Madox Brown), through having shown in the city's exhibitions.

WATERCOLOURS

The art of watercolour, already popular in mid-century as a cheaper alternative to oils, came to be seen as 'a school peculiarly English in its aims and character'.[115] Given that the English school was not internationally acclaimed, this medium proposed supremacy in at least one genre, and a healthy, natural, out-of-doors genre at that, appealing to

people from all social levels. Often painted in a highly finished style that was intended to match the achievements of oil painting, and ambitiously framed with broad mounts and heavy gold frames, watercolours were highly prized. They were often hung, as at the Whitworth in 1898, from floor to ceiling in semi-permanent displays with limited regard to their fragility (Fig. 176).[116]

In the Manchester Art Treasures Exhibition the genre was well represented, with an extended contextual history in the literature. The *Handbook to the Water Colours, Drawings, and Engravings, in the Art Treasures Exhibition* discussed the contemporary popularity of the genre among 'duchesses and dowagers, bishops and cabinet ministers, St James-street club-men and sober citizens, bilious barristers, overdone politicians and out-at-elbow artisans…in those pleasant rooms of the old and new watercolour societies in London'.[117] It appealed to all classes and ages, from 'the rosebuds of Belgravia' to 'hardened old harridans tough with the sun and storm of fifty seasons'. The author stressed that no one should suppose that 'the art which thus levels classes, callings, ranks, and ages, is of yesterday', tracing its development back to Cimabue, the illuminations of the early monks and Byzantine art. In the present age, watercolour had risen 'into a force and fertility of resource, which promise to make it the rival of oil in its age, as it was in its infancy'.[118] Watercolours were virtuous in that they were sanctioned by the antiquity of the medium and yet appealed to all (notably women) oblivious of social background. Presumably a contrast was being implied to Old Master paintings.

In later decades an even stronger pro-English agenda was applied. Under the influence of the South Kensington collection, the medium was viewed as a highly appropriate addition to a gallery. Though the most famous watercolourists were by no means cheap, their work tended to be pleasing and uncontroversial in style and subject matter, often instructively topographical, and inspiring to the amateur artist. For Monkhouse, the claims of these artists to be 'the founders of a truly National School of Art, peculiarly English in both feeling and method, distinguished by its sincerity and beauty, have been more widely recognised than ever'. He remarked that 'scarcely a Public Art Gallery in Great Britain' was without 'specimens of their

TOP 175 *Crossing the Sands* by David Cox, 1848. Oil on panel, 26.7 × 37.9 cm. Born in Birmingham and trained there as an artist, Cox spent his middle years in the South before returning to the area in 1841. This late painting was bequeathed to Birmingham City Art Gallery by Joseph Henry Nettlefold, one of the Gallery's most constant patrons (Birmingham Museums Trust).

BOTTOM 176 The watercolour gallery at the Whitworth Art Gallery, 1896. The dense, evenly spaced hang was typical of watercolour displays in the late nineteenth century. The Whitworth was from its early days especially strong in watercolours.

skill', singling out Liverpool, Birmingham and Manchester.[119]

At the Whitworth and Oldham, large donations or purchases of watercolours illustrated the entire history of the genre in England. At the Whitworth, watercolours were seen from the start as an essential element of the new collection: the Committee's first report on the new Gallery stipulated that along with sculpture, casts and portraits, two galleries would be dedicated to the medium.[120] This objective was realised. William Agnew made possible a handsome purchase grant from the proceeds of the Manchester Royal Jubilee exhibition of 1887 and presented numerous examples, while John Edward Taylor, a member of the Nonconformist family that founded the *Manchester Guardian*, gave over 150.[121] A similar spirit informed Charles Lees, who in 1888 gave Oldham a group of watercolours and drawing from his (much larger) collection, a gift 'intended to introduce Oldham people to British watercolour painting'.[122] The catalogue specified that the collection would show the whole history of the genre, since it 'illustrates very clearly the history and evolution of the art of painting in water-colour as practised in this country'.[123] Watercolour offered an ideal medium for creating an illusion of comprehensiveness of a type appropriate to a public gallery but hardly achievable through other media.

THE ROLE OF SCULPTURE

Sculpture – less physically convenient than painting, more demanding of space and often unsuited for the domestic settings from which many public collections derived – played a more complex role. On the one hand, its value as the principal adornment of architecture was an important message of the Great Exhibition, where the sculpture courts showed a wide-ranging selection, with early Italian works strongly represented in the Court of Monuments of Christian Art. The exhibition also offered numerous eighteenth- and nineteenth-century French, German and Italian pieces, with eighteenth-century sculpture represented by British artists such as John Bacon and by foreigners working in Britain such as Louis-François Roubiliac.[124] This tradition was maintained when the Crystal Palace was re-erected at Sydenham, where in the Greek

in English sculpture.[127] But the relative unpopularity of the medium, or at any rate the practical problems it created, was apparent at such a register of informed taste as the Manchester Art Treasures Exhibition, which included over a thousand Old Masters and almost 700 'Modern Masters' but only 160 sculptures (admittedly, occupying a visually prominent position).

Provincial galleries showed relatively little interest in developing historical sculpture collections. The traditional conjunction of classical sculpture and Old Master paintings could not be maintained in museums where the paintings were primarily modern, and at a time when classical sculpture was hard to obtain.[128] Displaying classical or Neoclassical sculpture presented problems in a culture in which nudity was regarded with discomfort, and in which the Neoclassical tradition, persisting in the work of such sculptors as John Gibson, was based on non-Christian precedents, which by mid-century were losing favour. British sculpture from the sixteenth century to the eighteenth had not achieved academic recognition, and being generally associated with funerary monuments, public sites of memory, or domestic settings was rarely available for purchase. Nor did later foreign sculpture necessarily attract much admiration. Even in the most sophisticated galleries, some early modern sculpture was viewed with disfavour: as *A Handbook to the Marbles, Casts, and Antiquities in the Fitzwilliam Museum* (1855), commented, 'The works of BERNINI and other Italian and French artists of the 17th century shew invention disfigured by affectation and bad taste.' The gift in 1867 to Liverpool of the possessions of the goldsmith Joseph Mayer, which included in addition to Greek and Roman antiquities important holdings of Egyptian and Etruscan objects, Wedgwood porcelain and Oriental objects, was highly unusual.[129]

Renaissance sculpture also played a minor role in the form of original pieces, even though it was regarded as a rich source of inspiration and was frequently shown in reproduction. Given the abstruse nature of Italian Renaissance sculpture and the difficulty after the 1860s of exporting works from Italy, municipal museums could hardly explore this field. Its status was complicated by the contemporary system of classification, which rated it primarily as a source of inspiration for designers. At

177 John Gibson's *Tinted Venus* (1851–6). Marble and wax. Gibson spent much of his childhood in Liverpool, where he was encouraged by William Roscoe, but for most of his career worked in Rome, where he achieved a major reputation. His *Tinted Venus*, at first extremely controversial, was intended to evoke the painted sculpture of classical times (National Museums Liverpool).

and Roman Courts, erected by Owen Jones and interpreted by George Scharf, the replica sculpture collection allowed visitors to 'see much that has hitherto been unattainable, except by laborious foreign travel'.[125] Similar thoroughness was applied to the Courts of Modern Sculpture, where Anna Jameson assembled an international array of modern work.[126] This she accompanied with a pungent commentary, which identified 'a poverty of invention, a want of fire and vigour in conception'

178 The sculpture gallery at Cartwright Hall, Bradford. With the advent of the New Sculpture in the late nineteenth century, sculpture collecting became increasingly popular among museums.

Birmingham, arranged at first on strictly South Kensington principles, the Italian Gallery contained a large decorative art collection, including chairs and *cassone*, brackets, doorways and chimneypieces, reproductions of Italian Renaissance specimens in the form of Della Robbia ware and 'Carvings in Marble', which belonged within Cole's definition of the Fine Art collection.[130] In the same spirit, in 1887 the Walker opened a 'Museum of Casts' to show medieval and Renaissance work, particularly for 'those of the industrial classes who are engaged in works where decorative forms are capable of being introduced.'[131]

Early in the nineteenth century, sculpture attracted some attention but for non-artistic reasons. Liverpool was a leader in this field. Its long-established interest in Neoclassical and later sculpture was fostered by private collections, such as Henry Blundell's at Ince Blundell, close to the city. Formed from the 1770s onwards and housed in a garden temple and a pantheon, the Blundell collections were open to the public and much visited.[132] In 1873, as the

Walker began to take shape, two statues by John Gibson, who had grown up in the city, were presented to the collection, and this tradition was maintained (Fig. 177).[133] In general, early in the nineteenth century, sculpture collections tended to be based on local associations, such as the pieces by the Sheffield-born Sir Francis Chantrey at the Mappin.

Contemporary British sculpture was regarded even by its practitioners as a restricted medium. It was in any case not a popular field: as Benedict Read has pointed out, until the last years of the century modern English sculpture tended to be dismissed by critics. In Palgrave's words, 'Our school has fallen lamentably low, and is the derision of foreigners.'[134] Only at the end of the century, with the advent of the New Sculpture with its naturalistic approach to the human figure, did interest revive. Galleries were included in some new buildings, such as the sculpture and cast gallery planned at the Whitworth Art Gallery, Manchester in 1889, and the magnificent purpose-built sculpture hall at Cartwright Hall in

Bradford of 1904 (Fig. 178).[135] Rodin, stylistically advanced but still safely figurative, was popular in Britain from the 1880s onwards: as early as 1888 the civic collection in Glasgow was given Rodin's *Victor Hugo*, while in 1911 Manchester acquired three works by him from Walter Butterworth, chairman of a successful glass-making company in the city and an enthusiastic patron of the artist. The Harris Art Gallery showed particular interest in modern British sculpture, acquiring works by several representatives of the New Sculpture, including Onslow Ford, W.G. John, Hamo Thornycroft and G.F. Watts (Figs 179, 180).[136]

Issues associated with Empire regularly featured in discussions around museums – whether at the practical level of the superiority of Indian textiles to anything created 'at home', or in the neo-colonial attitudes to exploring and taming the slums of great British cities as though they were tracts of some foreign continent. As for Western depictions of events taking place in the Empire or of landscapes or peoples, these appear to have been relatively few in spite of the increasing interest in India shown by the Queen and evident in particular at Osborne House. In many 'world exhibitions' Indian artefacts played an important part, with streets and pavilions dedicated to them. In some instances, a major object from overseas, discovered as a result of imperialist modernisation, played a role in the enunciation of the provincial museum: most notably, the 'Sultan-ganj Buddha', a bronze statue over two metres high and the largest known piece of Indian metalwork. Excavated in northern India in 1862, it was presented to the city of Birmingham, the centre of metalwork production, as the basis for its proposed museum, and attracted huge interest.[137] This was a particularly notable example of a wider trend: ethnographical collections, as they were known, developed in a number of regional museums, but the objects tended to be regarded as collections of historical or exotic interest in the style of the cabinet of curiosities, rather than as works of art.

In one respect, it could be argued that these collections were advanced in comparison to prevailing attitudes later in the twentieth century. The supremacy of Western art, as enunciated by high art collections, was not necessarily apparent to the regional curators of the period. It was standard practice to show ethnographical collections, in the same building and even in close proximity to modern paintings, an approach anticipating today's advocacy of world art. In 1881 at Liverpool the experiment of displaying prehistoric antiquities and ethnography from the recently acquired Mayer collection attracted over 610,000 people (rather more than the city's entire population). The event was considered 'so successful that the Committee determined on the erection of an annex behind the Walker Art Gallery...for the better display of the permanent collection of Ethnographical objects'.[138] Equally, archaeology was not necessarily segregated from fine art as it would be today. At Cartwright Hall in 1905 it was decided that in the Spring Artists' Exhibitions archaeological specimens should also be shown, including 'examples of man's handwork, which will illustrate the development of art, especially that of the North of England, from the earliest and rudest attempts to the most perfect expressions of design'.[139] Though the juxtaposition of art and archaeological collections was often rejected in the period following the Second World War, a holistic approach did sometimes emerge.

CONCLUSION

From their early days a schism existed in these galleries between the activities for which, by and large, they were founded – that is to say temporary exhibitions and educational work – and the creation of permanent collections. In particular, the period between 1890 and 1914 is marked by regular conflicts between the permanent collection and the exhibitions that required its removal from view. The prestige of acquiring works of art became important to these galleries, but the collections tended to be directed at immediate political rather than artistic purposes – particularly since so many of them came into existence in a short space of time, and operated with limited funds. Arguably, this problem has not been fully resolved to this day. It is significant that in many regional galleries now, the display of the permanent collection (other than a few key works) is spasmodic, and is seen as one curatorial option among several, rather than as a central purpose.

One question that arises is whether these galleries, particularly the smaller and poorer ones, really needed collections, whether the works of art served as much more than a totem of status; and whether these apparently obligatory acquisitions impeded the museums' original functions, functions that may, at least at the time, have been more valuable. For the modern visitor to smaller galleries where the permanent collection may not be on view, the question is particularly pertinent.

What the galleries did achieve, however, was a solid representation of the paintings and watercolours of their own time, notable collections being assembled by indomitable curators and collectors in such places as Liverpool, Glasgow and Norwich. In their own unusual way they were innovative in being collections of contemporary art. They sought to celebrate the art of their country and of their city, and to entertain and instruct the people of their own and other cities. In these objectives they succeeded.

10

EDUCATION IN THE VICTORIAN GALLERY

The Victorian provincial museum and art gallery was neither a palace nor a temple: essentially it was a schoolroom. Education – practical, artistic, intellectual (to a certain point) and moral (to a more advanced point) – was the driving force. However impressive the educational programmes offered in museums early in the twenty-first century may be, these achievements are not new. The majority of provincial museums were primarily seen from their earliest days not as the *loci* for important collections, but as didactic powerhouses, with the didacticism leavened by entertainment – rivalling and sometimes outdoing the national museums. Though the style of instruction took various forms, and changed in the run-up to the First World War, instruction remained a dominating theme. It is easier to present evidence of this work than to assess its success, though indications of how it was received do survive.

As we have seen, Steven Conn in his account of scientific museums in the United States argues persuasively that by 1900 the scientific museum had lost the battle for intellectual predominance. It was no longer in museums that major debates over contentious issues were conducted; they had shifted to universities. Museums had to seek a different role,

as sites for entertainment and the education of schoolchildren. The development of artistic discussion in Britain differed so greatly from controversy over the natural sciences that it is hard to make comparisons between the United States and Britain, particularly between art museums in Britain and scientific museums in North America. It is, however, valid to suggest that although the national museums, notably the British Museum and its offshoot the Natural History Museum, have never ceased to be involved in research and intellectual discussion, the role that was played by provincial learned societies in the country's intellectual life early in the nineteenth century had often declined by 1900 into the pursuit of local interests. And while the National Gallery and the university galleries engaged in connoisseurial activities, such ambitions seldom applied in the provincial art galleries, which made few claims to research in the history of art or the discovery of new artists – a situation that began to change in the twentieth century.

❖

PRACTICAL EDUCATION AND INDUSTRIAL ART

The provincial museums and art galleries set up from the 1860s onwards were, as we have seen, closely associated with the hegemony of South Kensington. One of the prime motives for their existence was the improvement of standards of design, in some cases through association with an art school. Given that educated audiences were provided for by national and university collections, the new galleries were aimed at an audience that, in Joshua Reynolds's words, had not begun 'to look for intellectual entertainments'.[1]

During the nineteenth century it came to be accepted that the working classes might be capable of appreciating some elements of art, if not the more intellectual elements, since it was felt that the full appreciation of art was something that had to be taught. The matter was addressed by Gustav Waagen. In his evidence to the 1850 Select Committee on the National Gallery he offered a view that was characteristic of thoughtful critics. Asked whether the uneducated public could benefit from the 'contemplation of pictures', he replied that 'in the ancient times of the Greeks, and during the middle ages, the monuments contributed a good deal towards the education of the lower classes, and I think that in our modern times it might be done a great deal the same way'. To the succeeding question of whether it required 'a considerable degree of habit and of education to appreciate the beauty of works of art of a high class', he replied that in his experience, 'the lower classes are not capable of appreciating them...but of enjoying them, and I think the poor have great pleasure in contemplating them'.[2] Here he distinguished between hard-won intellectual appreciation of a work of art and the instinctive sensual enjoyment that was seen as a lower, though still valid, reaction.

With the success of the Great Exhibition, and the foundation of the South Kensington Museum dedicated to the concept of applied popular education, the idea of general education in the arts expanded. The Redgrave brothers, pillars of South Kensington, stated in *A Century of Painters of the English School* (1866) that art 'gives an increased intelligence, a new pleasure, a truer love of Nature – the purest enjoyment we know'. In the spirit of South Kensington, they also affirmed that 'All have an interest in Art.' Even for them, however, this generous comment rested on an antithesis between the pure experience of art and the 'teaching of apprentices and mechanics'.[3]

The impact of such opinions was mixed. Waagen's views were implemented in the 1850s in Henry Cole's bold educational experiments at South Kensington. In 1860 a Select Committee recommended opening the National Gallery in the evening for the benefit of people who would otherwise be unable to attend, emphasising, as other committees had done, the value of art for all, and considering what was currently being done. Using the evidence of Cole's innovations at South Kensington, it commented approvingly on the working classes' appreciation of 'clear, legible labels in English, placed against specimens, and simple catalogues sold at a small cost, as well as occasional short popular lectures'.[4] The National Gallery and the British Museum were not to open in the evening for many years, but the Select Committee's pronouncements laid the way for a new, socially conscious approach to museums, in which encouraging general accessibility to works of art would be viewed as a means of educating, and bettering, the deprived.

As previous chapters have discussed, in their early days the *leitmotif* in the development of the new museums was the promotion of industrial art. This was not a new phenomenon. Technical exhibitions, showing products as well as machinery, had been regular events during the eighteenth century, notably at the Royal Society of Arts in London. Such displays maintained a vigorous life in the Mechanics' Institutes that flourished from the 1820s onwards, found a new strength in the Great Exhibition, and were maintained in the municipal museums. The early loans made to the Birmingham School of Design in 1855 by the Department of Science and Art introduced a purpose that was central to the Birmingham City Art Gallery in its early days as an industrial art museum showing technical exhibitions.[5] Yearly visits of around 200,000 were recorded, with the *Annual Report* for 1874 characteristically commenting that a large number were artisans.[6] What was offered to these aspiring individuals as well as to students at the Birmingham School of Art (also included in the targeted public) was a programme of exhibitions showing artefacts of the highest quality, making the museum a showplace for instructive design and technology.

At Birmingham the collecting of industrial art had always been a key objective, but by the early years of the twentieth century the Keeper was expressing disappointment at declining interest in this field. Though confident that many visitors were artisans, Whitworth Wallis remarked in 1911: 'It is to be regretted…that our art students and young workpeople do not make more use of our industrial collections, in the way that students do of the similar collections in London, Berlin and Paris' – as well as in other cities.[7] In spite of the quality and range of the Birmingham decorative art collections, learning from the art of the past, whether originals or fac-similes, no longer appeared to interest the young. Art and design were not as closely linked in the minds of artisans as the South Kensington pundits hoped, and once the novelty of visiting an art gallery had worn off they did not necessarily wish to spend their leisure hours improving their professional skills.

EDUCATION FOR THE MASSES

Concurrently with this decline, the aims of local museums and galleries gradually expanded. Attracting a wide audience, ideally from the local town, was certainly an objective for museum curators. In Liverpool in 1899 the Curator regretted that 'a larger number of the townspeople do not oftener pay a visit to the Gallery'; in spite of some 400,000 visitors per annum, 'by far the greater number of these are strangers passing through Liverpool [presumably on the way to or from ocean travel] or visitors from the neighbouring towns'.[8] At the end of the century, there was still a tendency among museum staff to regard their public as a form of low life susceptible of improvement: the Curator at Leeds City Art Gallery, commenting in 1898 on the increase in the number of free visitors, remarked that

> This latter circumstance is undoubtedly a healthy sign, and shows conclusively, I think, however unpromising many of these visitors may seem, that curiosity at least, even in these, is being aroused, while in others the Art leaven is already

fermenting and gradually increasing for good considerable numbers of the community. This is no idle or haphazard assertion, but a conviction founded on daily and hourly observation of the visitors themselves, and of the effects the various exhibits exercise upon them.[9]

His comments exemplify the idea of the museum as an agent for social change and as a means of encouraging moral improvements, even among the most apparently 'unpromising' visitor.

The ability of the public to appreciate what they were looking at remained an issue for curators well into the twentieth century (and indeed, remains one to this day). Wallis stressed the need to 'make [collections] interesting to the spectator' and offered a solution apparently justified by the huge number of visitors that the Gallery attracted. He noted that

> Three-fourths, or very nearly so, of the visitors to our National Museums possess, as a rule, but very scanty, if any, antiquarian and art knowledge. They wander through the superb Egyptian and Assyrian collections, the Greek treasures, the Mediaeval department, and elsewhere at the British Museum. At South Kensington they meander through the priceless collections of the industrial and decorative arts, and they leave each building with a crude notion that everything is very old, that people long ago used these things, that they possessed gold and silver in abundance, that their statues were very funny, and that the principal Assyrians cultivated very long beards and were adorned with wings. This is certainly not as it should be.[10]

This key problem could be addressed in various ways. One solution was the provision of detailed descriptive labels giving a range of information, including 'many little facts likely to awaken the interest of the reader', since these institutions were 'not kept up entirely for the benefit of antiquarians, artists, and scientists, but to foster a love of knowledge, and to promote the education of the uninformed in these matters'. Through apparently humble objects, extinct civilisations could be brought to life, and neglected branches of art revived. Birmingham was a pioneer in the production of cheap catalogues, having by 1911 sold over 300,000 penny catalogues and inspired other galleries to create similar sixpenny versions.[11] In addition, Wallis and his colleague had over the years given numerous public lectures: 'something like 100,000 people must have been talked to – poor souls'.[12] Wallis's approach was not solely instrumentalist: like German theorists of a century earlier, he felt that 'all museums ought to be places of noble instruction, where, free from the distractions of the outside world, one can devote a portion of secluded and reverent life to the attainment of divine wisdom, which the Greeks supposed to be the gift of Apollo or of the sun, but which the Christian knows to be the gift of Christ.'[13]

GALLERIES AND SCHOOLS OF ART

The associations between art school and museum, and the need for art students to have works of art to copy close at hand, pervade the discussion of Victorian art museums, not least because of the Department of Science and Art's control of national art education. Many provincial galleries were set up to serve jointly as museum and art school, including the Devon and Exeter Albert Memorial Museum at Exeter and the Art Galleries at Leicester and Wolverhampton.[14] This dual purpose gained strength internationally in the 1870s, notably in the United States: the Museum of Fine Arts in Boston, containing both art museum and academy, was founded in 1876, and the Chicago Academy of Fine Arts (now the Art Institute of Chicago) in 1879. Though originally conceived on a scale similar to their American counterparts, the British galleries failed to attract the lavish donations of works of art later seen in the United States, where 'The major enrichment [of museums] took place between 1900 and 1945'.[15] Nor did the close association between art gallery and art school flourish as in the United States, where such institutions as the Art Institute of Chicago and the Layton Gallery in Milwaukee (founded in 1888) were predicated on the notion of an intimate relationship between gallery and school.[16]

The Albert Memorial Museum at Exeter illustrates the didactic but somewhat muddled nature of these early art schools-cum-galleries.[17] Seen by its founders as 'an Art and Science Centre', the museum had been planned for almost a decade before its opening (Figs 181, 182). Sited at the centre of a rural county, it did not benefit from the largesse of industrialists, and money had to be scraped together from private individuals. It contained on two floors a museum, a Free Library and a school for Science, with the Art School (founded elsewhere and in need of more space) accommodated upstairs. The early accounts suggest that this co-existence was a matter of expedience rather than intellectual synthesis. Only four rooms out of at least a dozen were dedicated to exhibits: two rooms housed, respectively, antiquities and natural history, while two others contained a cast gallery and a print room. Paintings were at first hardly represented.

The early history of Leicester Art Gallery also suggests the doubtful effectiveness of such an alliance. There the art gallery was initiated 'under the auspices of the School of Art',[18] which had been set up in collaboration with the Science and Art Department, and by 1891 it was held to occupy 'the premier position in the country' in the Department's national competition for art prizes.[19] Particular care was, in theory, given to collecting. The acquisition policy stated that students would benefit from the study of major works of art, an aspiration that emphasised the development of training in art schools beyond the Dyce-Redgrave approach. Given that the Art Gallery Committee felt that discrimination (as well as economy) had to be employed in the selection of pictures, since 'The mere provision of furniture paintings by the cart load would soon lower the tone of public appreciation, and would disgust those who have any claim to artistic knowledge',[20] a regulation was made that 'the works accepted and purchased be confined to such as possess high artistic merit, some of which would be valuable as studies for Art students'.[21] These hopes were hardly realised. On being consulted, Ruskin merely commented gloomily that 'no-one nowadays can appreciate pictures by the old masters, and everyone can understand Frith's Derby Day'.[22] In the end, the acquisitions followed the usual programme of British oils and watercolours. The Art Gallery's records suggest that the link with the school was not very fruitful pedagogically: it was an idealistic rather than practical union, reflecting changing styles of learning, according to which copying from works of art was becoming less significant. The school moved out in the early 1890s.

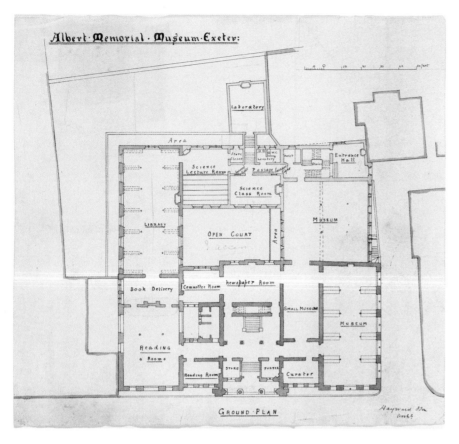

Albert·Memorial·Museum·Exeter:

GROUND·PLAN

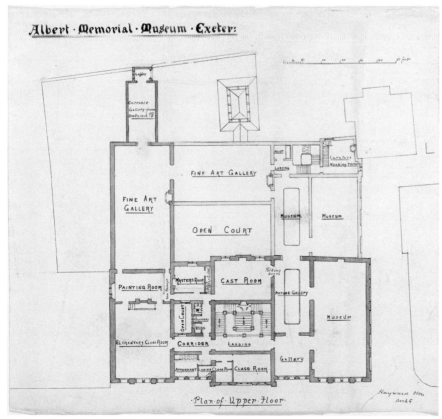

Albert·Memorial·Museum·Exeter:

Plan·of·Upper·Floor·

More usual was the creation of an art school as an independent entity with its own collections. At Manchester Municipal School of Art (descended from the Manchester Mechanics' Institute) a School Museum was founded which contained 'examples of everything but pictures – metal-work of all the best periods, coins and medals, pottery, sculpture, fine printing, stained glass, engraving of all kinds, woodcuts, etchings', with Gothic casts in one room and 'Renaissance work' in another, and a main court dedicated to textiles (Fig. 183).[23] These varied collections functioned in the tradition of South Kensington, but did not attempt to negotiate the gap between public and educational museum.

Instruction in technical proficiency did, however, underlie many of the pieces held in public collections. The ability of Alphonse Legros, a proponent of celerity in drawing, to draw a convincing portrait in an hour or less was regularly celebrated in gallery catalogues as an instructive ideal of practical virtuosity. The public was told that at Liverpool he had made a *Study of a Head* in a hundred minutes before 'a large number of art students at the Walker Art Gallery…[as] a practical lesson in art'.[24] In fact, as Edward Morris has shown, Legros' technique was based on an old-established academic tradition that was already long out of date in France, and among more advanced artists it aroused disquiet as a means of instruction.[25]

Galleries that were not linked to schools continued to be used by copyists through the century. Thus, the *Regulations for Students Copying Pictures in the Permanent Collection of the City of Manchester Art Gallery* of 1894 (Fig. 184) make it clear that though copying was permitted every weekday the pressure on places required strict regulation (as at the National Gallery).[26] Increasingly, however, galleries responded to the demands of a more general public. At Leicester in the 1890s the commentary on the conduct of visitors on the Sabbath (the gallery first opened on Sundays in 1891) conveys the public's thirst for instruction as well as the deference shown to official elucidation. Many catalogues having been sold, 'the pictures were inspected with great interest by many groups of men and women who frequently gathered round some one who had a catalogue, to hear the particulars read aloud…The utmost order and decorum prevailed.'[27] (The whole scene, and the word 'particulars', are significant,

indicating the essentially verbal, rather than visual, nature of this epistemological approach.) Curiosity, good order and respect were the ideal qualities to be found in such an audience (Fig. 185).[28]

THE CAST GALLERY

A further survival of old-established educational equipment was the cast gallery. From the early days of art schools and museums, casts of classical sculpture had served both as practical tools and as tokens of academic respectability, maintaining the ideal of the union of classical sculpture and paintings. In the 1820s establishments such as the Royal Manchester Institution asserted their academic credentials by

displaying casts in entrance halls and staircases, just as the National Gallery installed them on their lower floor for the use of artists (Figs 186, 187). At the Museum of Ornamental Art (a forerunner of the South Kensington Museum) in the 1850s, an early project sent the Keeper, Ralph Wornum, to France to study cast collections and assess the Government's holdings, with a view to improving their organisation and display. As part of the campaign to improve standards of design, agreements were made with foreign governments and museums to produce and exchange casts and reproductions of work that demonstrated skilled workmanship.[29]

In the university museums, collections of casts were also considered important. In 1850 the Fitz william Museum showed 'a set of Plaster Casts,

184 Regulations for students
copying pictures, from the City of
Manchester Art Gallery's *Catalogue
of the Permanent Collection of
Pictures in Oil and Water Colours*
(1894). Strict rules of this kind were
usual in nineteenth century
galleries, from the foundation of
the National Gallery onwards, and
testify to the heavy use made of the
galleries by students and copyists.

REGULATIONS

FOR STUDENTS COPYING PICTURES IN THE PERMANENT COLLECTION OF

THE CITY OF MANCHESTER ART GALLERY.

1. Each applicant for admission as a Student must obtain a form from the Curator, which must be signed by a Professional Drawing Master, or a Master of a School of Art, or any member of the Art Gallery Committee, certifying that the applicant is sufficiently advanced to profit by the privilege of copying. In cases where the applicant is a student under an Art Master, or is a pupil in any well-known School of Art, a letter of recommendation from such authority will suffice, and should be enclosed with the Form of Application.

2. Students are admitted to copy in the Art Gallery from 10 a.m. to 4 p.m. on any day, Saturday and Sunday excepted. Students attending at the Gallery are required to sign their names in a book kept for that purpose in the Entrance Hall.

3. In order to prevent inconvenient crowding, not more than two Students are permitted to copy from one picture at the same time.

4. Students desiring to copy from a picture, the places before which are already occupied, should leave their names with the Curator, who will assign them places in order of the date of their application.

5. Students engaged in copying a picture absenting themselves for an entire day, without giving notice in writing to the Curator, will forfeit their place if another application be made for it meanwhile, and must in that case await the next vacancy. In such notice the title of the picture should be distinctly stated.

6. Copies must not be of the same size as the originals, and in the case of works measuring above 12 feet superficial, not more than half the size ; under 12 feet, not more than two-thirds the size ; and all canvases must be legibly marked on the back as follows :—

   "Copied by permission of the Committee from the original picture in the Manchester Art Gallery, for improvement in study only, and not for sale."

7. Students infringing the above regulations will forfeit their privilege of copying in the Gallery.

185 *Students at work – Walker Art Gallery*, from the Walker Art Gallery's *Annual Report*, 1901. The education of artists through copying the masterpieces of the past (and in this case, contemporary works), was a key element in the nineteenth century art museum, and was still strong in the early twentieth century. By mid-century such teaching was more or less defunct. It has only recently been revived in a few art schools.

from the most celebrated statues in the world' alongside original classical sculptures, in the traditional eighteenth-century manner.[30] Instruction in the material culture of antiquity at the university was strengthened in 1884 by the creation of a Museum of Classical Archaeology on a separate site. The catalogue, written by the Director, indicates that the museum was seen as a handbook for the art and archaeology elements of the Classical tripos, offering 'an object lesson in the history of Greek art' by presenting the whole development of Greek sculpture through reproductions.[31]

At their most ambitious, provincial museums aspired to educate not only the artist but also the working man in classical art, a further shift from the imposition of merely technical education. It was in this spirit that in 1885, a year after it opened, the Committee of the Walker Art Gallery discussed forming a cast collection comparable to those at the British Museum, South Kensington and the Archaeological Museum at Westminster. 'It is scarcely fair', the *Report* comments, 'that little or nothing should exist out of London which can give to our artisans any insight into the progress of art, or furnish examples for their improvement in taste and skill.'[32] Even though classical architecture was losing ground, it was still felt that classical sculpture should be available to all, even if as reproductions. When the Museum of Casts opened, the official comments identified the usual target audience: the artisan.

At the same time, a change of emphasis at Liverpool reflected the movement at South Kensington towards a broad range of historical models. As an *Annual Report* put it, 'The beautiful Mediaeval and Renaissance work here brought to light and exhibited presents great attraction, and promises to be of great use in the promotion of taste amongst those of the industrial classes who are engaged in works where decorative forms are capable of being introduced.'[33] Classical art had come to be seen as only one element of the essential repertoire.

For some years the cast court retained a healthy life in municipal galleries, partly by force of tradition and partly because of a belief in the power of reproductions to tell the full story of art. Even when no art school shared the gallery's building, acquiring casts remained a frequent practice. The Harris Art Gallery in Preston was filled with casts, which embodied its impressive survey of the art history of the world (Fig. 188). Equally, when the Whitworth Art Gallery was being set up in the 1890s, it was equipped with a set of casts,[34] and on Aberdeen Art Gallery's reopening in 1905, its ground floor was entirely 'devoted to the illustration of sculpture by means of plaster casts representing all countries, styles, and period'. As Elijah Howarth approvingly commented, 'it is this complete, comprehensive, and thoroughly representative collection of the most expressive of the fine arts that gives to the gallery its great distinction'.[35] As late as 1909 a grant was made to Birmingham City Art Gallery for the provision of 'a collection of Casts, Models, Reproductions and Photographs, illustrative of the origin and development of Classical Art' (see Fig. 187).[36] This was installed after the First World War in a set of purpose-built side-lit galleries arranged on historical lines, with the casts supplemented by electrotypes of gold and other objects, reproductions of Greek vases, and photographs. Faith in a gallery of reproductions was asserted by the publication of a catalogue written by a prominent Professor of Archaeology from London University.[37] This was a late example of the type. As Alan Wallach has discussed with reference to cast courts in the United States: 'By the 1920s collections of casts were old-fashioned; by the 1930s they were obsolete.'[38] At a time when the original work of art was esteemed above all, casts were thought to be misleading, no substitute for the original work of art, symbols of the academic system of art training and fit only for the scrap heap. Where they did survive, as at the Victoria and Albert Museum or in university museums, they assumed a role as period pieces.

THE CHILD

The development of museum education is also apparent in the provision made for children. Positive attitudes to admitting children to national museums

186 A late nineteenth century photograph of the entrance hall of the Royal Manchester Institution.

187 The Cast Court, Birmingham City Art Gallery, in about 1920.

188 A cast of Michelangelo's *David*, in an upstairs gallery at the Harris Museum and Art Gallery, Preston. The Harris's collections represent one of the most ambitious attempts to create a museum of reproductions, using a variety of media as well as plaster casts. Its strongly didactic character was expressed in the building and its contents.

189 *T. C. Horsfall* by Frederick Samuel Beaumont, 1914. Oil on canvas, 106.5 × 87.6 cm. A philanthropist and believer in the beneficial powers of art, Horsfall was a leading figure in setting up the Manchester Art Museum in Ancoats. It was less an art museum than a charitable venture using the arts as its instruments (Whitworth Art Gallery).

190 Manchester Art Museum, Ancoats Hall, Manchester, in about 1900. The abandoned manor house of the Mosley family became the setting for T.C. Horsfall's Manchester Art Museum in 1886. Strongly influenced by Ruskin, Horsfall filled the museum with paintings, sculpture and architectural specimens, a Model Workmen's Room, a children's room, and spaces for craft activities.

were not new: at the National Gallery in London they had always been admitted, to the pained surprise of such foreign visitors as Waagen. A similar generosity of spirit applied at the National Gallery of Ireland. In 1864 a correspondent to *The Freeman's Journal*, the leading Irish newspaper at the time, complained about the experience of visitors (he meant middle-class visitors) to the recently opened gallery on a Sunday. In contrast to the 'order and decorum…they would have were they enabled to go there during the week days', they would suffer 'astonishment to find instead a set of ragged urchins wherever they go, and quite doing away with any pleasure they might otherwise derive from their visit'. Making a characteristic distinction between

the deserving and the undeserving poor, the correspondent disclaimed any desire to 'exclude the artizan or tradesman – who, however humble, can be respectable – from the gallery', but asserted that it was 'very ill-advised' to 'allow such parties into it, else, indeed, we will shortly see no respectable person there'. This is an unusually frank statement of the tension over the admission of people of all classes to what the correspondent clearly saw as a hieratic, or at least enclosed, space. The editor, in reply, supported unrestricted admission: 'If the poor youths alluded to misconduct themselves they ought to be turned out; but if not, the fact of being young, and not dressed in purple and gold, constitute no ground for exclusion.'[39] The exchange underlines the easy admission offered to young people who were evidently unconstrained by the setting, as well as the lack of any formal educational provision for them in this (or any other gallery) in mid-century.[40]

With the cautious extension of general educational provision in Britain and notably the assignment of responsibility for primary education to local government in 1870, museums began to welcome schoolchildren more actively, with Liverpool again at the forefront. As early as 1874 it was recorded that local schoolchildren had been brought to see the annual Art Exhibition, an opportunity considered important 'as fostering a love of art at a time when habits are being formed'.[41] Such visits became a regular event of the Gallery's programme.

By the beginning of the new century, offering museum education for children was a favourite theme of the *Museums Journal*, which regarded it as a prime duty.[42] This approach – which applied more often to natural history or scientific collections than to works of art – had been strengthened by the Manchester Art Museum at Ancoats, an altruistic venture set up in 1886 by the wealthy businessman, museum reformer and social agitator T.C. Horsfall in a particularly bad slum (Figs 189, 190). It was a forerunner of the modern children's museum aimed specifically at children in and out of school (and survived until the 1950s).[43] In museums generally, less attuned to educational programmes than Ancoats, the development of programmes depended on the dedication of individual curators, in the absence of specific education staff. In 1912 an innovatory system was introduced at Bradford City Art

Gallery by which schoolchildren visiting the Gallery received an introductory talk from the Director and a representative of the Municipal School of Art. It was evidently a successful experiment, since 30,000 children benefitted from it in the first year.[44] At Sheffield the school activities of the Mappin Gallery were organised with some care, the teachers being invited to specify what sort of instruction was required and to explain how this would relate to the work carried out later at school. Again, the curator found himself regularly giving half an hour's instruction to the visiting infants.[45] These efforts reflect a socially based approach in which the collection was seen as the servant of the population. Nevertheless, the role of the curator as teacher came to be questioned in the journal of the museum profession, with the suggestion that curators might be better employed doing the work for which they had originally been trained.[46]

PREACHING THE WORD: CATALOGUES AND LABELS

The printed catalogue has nowadays been almost totally abandoned as a way of instructing visitors within galleries, but in the early days of museums it was considered essential. In 1824 at the new National Gallery no labels, only numbers beside the pictures, were provided. The publication of a catalogue less 'diffuse' than those of the Louvre, and costing 'a Sum just *barely* to cover the Expence [*sic*] of them' was from the earliest days considered a necessity, offering information even to the poorest.[47] By the 1850s, under the influence of South Kensington and the new world exhibitions, labels were becoming increasingly popular, so that when the National Gallery of Scotland opened in 1859, 'Every work in the Gallery (was) distinctly labelled' (Fig. 191).[48] From their earliest days, catalogues were universal in regional museums, and one of the Curator's first duties was to compose one, that is if there was any collection. In his preface to the Leeds City Art Gallery catalogue, George Birkett explained his approach. Responding to visitors' desire for a short list of the works on view, normally including the artist's biography, he had produced a catalogue which 'was not intended for the learned in matters of the kind, nor does it lay claim to any literary

merit…simply a Handbook, embodying a few leading facts and observations which may perhaps enable ordinary visitors readily to understand and appreciate the works placed before them'.[49] These handbooks, which were extremely cheap (the Leeds one sold at a penny), were not usually illustrated. They simply offered, presumably in order of display, numerical lists of the objects on view, which were not categorised by artist or even medium. The Walker's 1902 catalogue indiscriminately listed oils, watercolours, plaster casts and statues, 'French vases' and a 'Berlin China Vase', engravings and paintings lent by the National Gallery.[50] These publications underline the early character of the provincial galleries, aimed at an audience requiring only the most basic instruction.

There were, however, more lessons to be gleaned from these little books. One of their purposes was to celebrate the help given to the fledgling institution through gifts or donations of money from private supporters as well as mayors and aldermen. The donor was mentioned in even the most perfunctory entries, while the philanthropy and excellence of the citizens involved in setting up the museum (or developing the town) were also underlined. Equally, the desire to inspire high standards of design and technique was reflected in the emphasis given to technical proficiency, and the stress on artists' training. If he (or, occasionally, she) had not been trained, this point was also underlined to save uninstructed visitors from feeling any artistic inhibition. The language of a drawing manual was often used, offering a formal technical analysis of a type appropriate to workers and manufacturers.

Moral improvement had for many years been one of the prime objectives of the catalogue. Thus an 1838 guide to the National Gallery discussed Correggio's *Venus, Mars and Cupid* in terms of the Victorian game 'Happy Families' (Fig. 192).[51] Though Venus was regrettably almost entirely naked, she was engaged in virtuous activity since, abandoning her usual tendencies, she 'presents herself, simply and meekly, in her maternal character, divested of amorous witcheries…In an attitude certainly of considerable elegance, and abounding in beauteous undulations of contour, but still calculated to attract us, *chiefly* by the interest which the goddess herself takes in the education of her son'.[52] This passage casts Venus as a well-behaved (if naked) English

191 Birmingham City Art Gallery. Hung on dark walls, presumably red, the paintings are arranged as though on the line at the Royal Academy, with a clear demarcation between the upper and lower level. The large label pays tribute to the gift by Sir John Gilbert RA, history painter and illustrator, of his own oils and watercolours to a group of museums, including the Guildhall Art Gallery in London as well as Liverpool, Manchester and Birmingham – a relatively rare act by an artist. Birmingham received a group of works in 1893. Gilbert's *Return of the Victors* hangs under the label.

192 A print after Correggio's *Venus, Mars and Cupid*, from *The National Gallery of Pictures by the Great Masters* (c. 1836).

193 *Motherless* by Arthur Stocks, exhibited in 1883 at the Royal Academy and then at Liverpool, where it was bought by the Walker. Oil on canvas, 112.7 × 87.3 cm. It shows 'a rustic labourer, with his baby, tending his wife's grave' (National Museums Liverpool).

lady, doubly admirable since, by implication, she derives from a social class that normally would not trouble itself with a child's upbringing. Such saccharine simplification was retained in later Victorian catalogues, though addressed to more appropriate pictures. Almost invariably, the catalogues of the municipal galleries offer improving explanations of the narratives within paintings, couched in terms that establish the virtue and potential for happiness of working people. The Walker's catalogue, written by George Dyall in simple language with undertones of the pulpit, points out the lessons to be gleaned. It is in this vein – similar to press descriptions of paintings in the Royal Academy – that Dyall discusses Arthur Stocks's *Motherless* (Fig. 193): 'A touching picture of sorrowing affection for the departed wife, – showing, with undoubted truth and power, that the finer feelings of human nature are shared by all classes'.[53] Equally, Stanhope Forbes's *A Street in Brittany* (Fig. 194) illustrates in Continental towns 'the contented and happy appearance of the humble classes; simple in their living, dressed in neat but inexpensive clothing, scrupulously clean, industrious, and sober, they show that real happiness is not confined to the powerful and wealthy'.[54] A series of little homilies was

194 *A Street in Brittany*, painted by Stanhope Forbes (1881). Oil on canvas, 104.2 × 75.8 cm. The picture was painted in Cancale, a small fishing village near St Malo, where the artist worked in the open air. Forbes was sure that 'it won't go down at all with the British public', but it was bought by the Walker the following year (National Museums Liverpool).

interspersed with accounts of the virtuous lives of prominent Liverpudlians and some others. It is reasonable to suppose that the talks given in municipal and philanthropic galleries for working people delivered similar lessons, directed at the immediate concerns and experiences of the local population, spiced with exhortations to virtue. Only a few examples, including Birkett's Leeds catalogue, tentatively suggest that the story need not be the viewer's only concern and that a more visual approach might also be of value.

These straightforwardly moralistic guides contrast with the publications produced by national and university museums. At the National Gallery, the mid-century catalogues prepared by Charles Eastlake and Ralph Wornum were also aimed at a general audience but contained the germs of art-historical information.[55] Predictably, a more academic approach is to be found in the publications produced for the university museums. In 1870 J.C. Robinson published *A Critical Account of the Drawings by Michel Angelo and Raffaelo in the University Galleries, Oxford*, which anticipated modern catalogues in providing information about the lives of the artists, provenance, dating, technique, reattribu-

tions, engravings after the drawings, the literature, and the watermarks on the leaves (though offering almost no aesthetic comment). Equally, the *Descriptive Catalogue of the Pictures in the Fitzwilliam Museum* of 1902 included research into signatures, stylistic analysis and comments by art historians such as J.P. Richter and Abraham Bredius, Director of the Mauritshuis.[56] This work was 'compiled largely from materials supplied by Sidney Colvin', the museum's Director and later Keeper of Prints and Drawings at the British Museum.[57] It is not easy to find analogous activity in regional galleries other than in the handful of well-organised collections that have already been identified: thus James Paton for his 1892 Glasgow catalogue consulted leading authorities of the time, including Bredius and Wilhelm Bode of Berlin.[58]

THE PUBLIC LECTURE

The classic style of imparting information to adults or children was the public lecture, a dominant and hugely popular mode of communication in the nineteenth century, at first in the scientific field and later in the arts (Fig. 195).[59] As we have seen, the failure of some of the earlier exhibitions to provide such lectures was deplored by some commentators, and the lesson was learned. The South Kensington Museum offered lectures from its earliest days, with blocks of seats reserved for working men. At the Liverpool Museum a programme of evening lectures was begun in 1865, followed by talks in the style of the Mechanics' Institutes on zoology, geology and mining, practical perspective, and the 'History and Practice of Decorative Art'.[60] The character of these occasions is apparent from G.H. Wallis's account of teaching at Nottingham Castle: 'I have lectured to 400 or 500 working men and women in our long gallery, afterwards gone round the various galleries, explaining the principal pictures; and since I have been enabled to adopt this system, there has been a marked increase of interest in the Museum.'[61] These winter evenings exemplify the South Kensington approach, the exhibits being seen to be fully understandable only through interpretation. In Glasgow in 1886 Francis Newbery, the celebrated Principal of the School of Art, gave a series of lectures at the museum on 'Historical Schools of Paintings' using

paintings from the collection to popular acclaim, and this style of lecturing was maintained.[62] Mentions of lectures on fine art increase around 1900, at a time when education for workers was moving onto a settled basis with the foundation of the Workers' Educational Association in 1903 and the growth of state secondary education for all from 1902 onwards. So successful were the exhibitions organised at the pioneering gallery for slum dwellers known as the Whitechapel Art Gallery that in 1901 Charles Aitken, the newly appointed Director, was invited to give a series of talks on Italian art for an eager audience, to advise on appropriate reading, and to arrange the loan of photographs of famous paintings.[63]

By the end of the decade, the organisation of non-vocational lectures on art had become widely popular. Frank Rutter introduced regular talks on art ('Is Art Essential to Life?' he bracingly enquired) at Leeds City Art Gallery as soon as he arrived there as Director in 1912. Leading art critic though he was, he did not hesitate to give frequent talks to Workers' Educational Association members as well as working men's clubs and school art societies.[64] At Leicester Art Gallery Saturday morning lectures attracted audiences of 400.[65] Even at the Fitzwilliam Museum, 'peripatetic lectures on the pictures' are recorded.[66] All of this took place long before the creation of the education departments that later became standard elements of museums.

The success of these ventures led to official recognition of the value of didactic programmes in high art museums. From around 1910, the fourth Lord Sudeley, late in a career involving quite other interests that had included a spectacular bankruptcy, devoted himself to creating education services for adults in national museums and galleries.[67] In the face of determined indifference, he persuaded various institutions to employ guide-lecturers: Kew Gardens, the British Museum, the National Portrait Gallery.

BEYOND THE GALLERY

In the last years of the century it became evident to a group of Ruskinians that the temples to the arts erected in great cities could not attract the poorest sectors of the population. Creating art galleries in the under-privileged areas of London had in fact been an aim of the Department of Science and Art from the 1850s onwards: the Department expressed the hope of establishing museums in the north, east, south and west of London, open in the evenings and on Sundays, to encourage visits by working people daunted by the idea of a visit to South Kensington. These museums would offer displays not only of fine and applied art but of natural and local history, as well as instructive material aimed at improving health and diet. Although the notion of these branch museums was largely superseded by the South Kensington Museum's Circulation Department, one was set up: the Bethnal Green Museum founded in 1872 in the East End of London.[68] Used for temporary exhibitions such as the display of the collection of Sir Richard Wallace, which was shown in 1872 to tremendous public interest (almost a million people visited in the first year), Bethnal Green was also convenient as a site to which to decant unwanted collections and even buildings, notably the Brompton Boilers from South Kensington.

The notion of branches of national museums in a capital that functioned on such powerfully centralised lines as London never really succeeded, and it was in the major provincial cities, notably Manchester, that the system was realised, largely in the twentieth century. The Queen's Park Museum was built in a northern suburb in 1883–4 and was to be one of five City Art Gallery outposts in the city's parks.[69] The new museum, designed by the City Surveyor on plain but efficient lines, stood in one of the city's earliest parks and was furnished with didactic displays and improving pictures on Ruskinian lines. Such a set of local museums aimed at their communities had become, at least in aspiration, an appropriate feature of a great city: the Queen's Park

Museum was by the mid-twentieth century one of a constellation of city museums in Greater Manchester, including Platt Hall and Wythenshawe Hall.[70]

For some social and educational reformers this was not enough. The poor living conditions in metropolitan slums were a topic of great concern and indeed fascination in Liberal circles. Urban poverty was investigated in popular fiction and journalistic accounts, in such romanticised narratives as Walter Besant's *All Sorts and Conditions of Men* (1882), which uses the language of colonisation to depict (favourably) the efforts of the well-to-do to assist poor neighbourhoods, and at an academic level in pioneering sociological studies such as Charles Booth's multi-volume *Life and Labour of the People in London* (1885–1902), a coolly detached yet alarming survey. The deprived proletariat, distanced by housing, education, clothing and accent from the middle and upper classes, were discussed like slum-dwellers inhabiting a remote land. The bourgeois explorers of the East End of London or the Manchester and Glasgow slums were struck by the dreariness, hopelessness and lack of opportunity they encountered.

Besant's rapturous evocation of a palace for the people that would transform such lives inspired two People's Palaces, in the East End of London and in Glasgow. The People's Palace in Mile End, established in 1887, offered the local population a concert hall and library, sporting facilities and a technical school, with a lively programme of events in which art almost always played a part (Fig. 196). The Glasgow People's Palace, opened in 1898, similarly provided a museum, picture gallery, winter garden and music hall, reflecting a recognition 'on the part of the authorities of the lofty function of Art, and an expression of their faith, that those whom they serve, are, or may become sufficiently cultured and refined to enter into the enjoyment of the kingdom of the beautiful'.[71] It flourished as an alternative centre of culture in the slum-ridden city, holding popular exhibitions of paintings and Glasgow history, fuelled by a strong reforming agenda. The two institutions had very different fates, the London example being soon transformed into Queen Mary's College, a university for the East End, while the Glasgow Palace retains much of its original purpose to this day (Figs 197, 198).

It was in this spirit of popular education and social change that the privately funded philanthropic museum developed in the slums. Social reformers recognised the existence of a dual working-class audience, comparable to but not precisely analogous with the accepted division between the deserving and the undeserving poor. A split was perceived between those who felt enabled to enter the imposing doors of their civic museum and those who would not venture into the city centre. The transforming power of art could, and should – it was felt – extend to all, and must be taken to those who would not leave their neighbourhood.

Several of these transformative enterprises were launched in the last years of the century in London and Manchester.[72] In addition to Ancoats, the most notable included the loan exhibitions at Whitechapel, in east London, arranged from 1881 onwards by Samuel Barnett, Rector of St Jude's, Whitechapel and his wife, Henrietta, whose success led to the construction of the Whitechapel Art Gallery; and the South London Art Gallery in Camberwell, south London (Fig. 199). After a prolonged gestation as a working men's college organised by a self-taught enthusiast called William Rossiter, the South London Art Gallery opened in 1891 in a purpose-built space, with the active participation of Frederic Leighton and a slate of powerful supporters.

None of these philanthropic galleries has lasted in its original form, undoubtedly because their finances were based on private donations and the enthusiasm of the organisers, and arguably because they became redundant. They represent an outstandingly sensitive subject, loaded with difficult issues. It is hard for the historian of today to consider them in a spirit of detachment, since the idea of imposing a simplified version of officially accepted culture on people less academically and socially privileged than the donor is alien to the modern sensibility. The language employed about the recipients of this largesse is even more jarring to the modern ear, more dependent on a concept of alterity, than the discourse around the Victorian municipal art museum. Late in the twentieth century these initiatives were subjected to fierce critical attention, not least because these histories must of necessity be presented almost entirely through the words of apparently condescending philanthropists rather than of contemporary visitors.[73] At the time,

The Ancoats Museum was particularly influential. Inspired and encouraged by Ruskin, Horsfall laboured on behalf of his museum from the 1870s until his death in 1932, collecting paintings and specimens of the decorative arts of a sort he thought suitable, and badgering artists and scholars to give objects, advice and lectures.[75] The decorative art reproductions were intended to educate the artisan on the model of South Kensington, while the paintings were generally easy contemporary works, featuring uplifting scenes of British history and pleasant landscapes. An innovative feature was the Mother's Room, intended for small children and their mothers and suitably furnished.[76]

Ancoats explored various agenda. In its early days it included among its supporters a number of leading socialists, such as William Morris. At first Morris believed that this little museum could help to break down the divisions between classes and effect a peaceful revolution, though he later became disillusioned, regarding it as manipulative and patronising. Certainly Horsfall was no advocate of revolution, peaceful or otherwise. What emerges most strongly from Ancoats and distinguishes it from Ruskin's museums is the essentially practical experience it offered. In an extreme version of the municipal gallery, it showed art that could tell an improving story, teach patriotic history and offer a glimpse of the best of British culture. There was no room for art for art's sake. Horsfall corresponded at length on these matters with Leighton, an enthusiastic advocate of the extension of artistic activities to a wide audience. Although Leighton admired the other man's energy, they could never agree over what he saw as Horsfall's excessively pragmatic objectives.[77]

The Ancoats educational programme brought many children from their schools to see the exhibits and to watch and act in plays and other entertainments arranged in the makeshift theatre. The museum initiated the idea of a school loans service, sending out miniature displays to local schools, an approach followed by the city ten years later when it launched a scheme for 'Circulating School Museums'. It was as a result of the success of Ancoats – for, like the others, it gained a considerable reputation – that in 1895 the Board of Education gave permission for school visits to museums to be counted as part of the curriculum, a decision

196 The People's Palace, Mile End, London. Inspired by Walter Besant's *All Sorts and Conditions of Men* (1882), which advocated a great cultural centre for the East End, the People's Palace opened in 1887. It contained a library, concert hall, lecture hall and more. It was visited by 1,500,000 people in its first year. The building was taken over by Queen Mary's College, part of the University of London, in 1934.

however, for those working in these galleries and their supporters, the idea of spreading an understanding of art and history among slum-dwellers who were deprived of almost every opportunity to improve their lives seemed part of a bold and enlightened effort, if not to destroy, at least to alleviate, the barriers between rich and poor. Relatively conservative in political terms though some of the leading players may have been, the Barnetts of Whitechapel were regarded by contemporaries as dangerously radical. And in terms of the educational agenda, it was within these energetic and non-bureaucratic enterprises that many of the most important initiatives in museum education were introduced.

In all these places, education was the key. At Whitechapel, Canon Barnett, though ignorant about art, composed improving little texts for the catalogues, while Mrs Barnett explained the paintings to visitors, sometimes to the derision of her sophisticated contemporaries. Throughout the brief period of the exhibitions, ladies and gentlemen were co-opted to give simple talks to the visitors. At Camberwell, the South London Art Gallery offered a working men's college, a free library for working people, and a wide-ranging lecture programme: the list for 1894 included 'Butterflies and Moths' and 'Mr Balfour's "Foundations of Belief"'.[74]

People's Palace, Glasgow   Valentines Series   31744

197 The People's Palace, Glasgow. Postcard. Built between 1893 and 1898, this was one of the most impressive buildings erected or adapted in Britain during the late nineteenth century in the belief that fine art and beautiful interiors would improve the lives and broaden the outlook of slum-dwellers. It originally contained a museum and picture gallery, with a library, reading and recreation rooms and a winter garden.

that radically affected the relationship between schools and museums in England.[78] It was in these adventurous little enterprises that the idea of museum education for all and especially for children, in contrast to the South Kensington definition of education for the artisan and manufacturer, was most vigorously developed. Though the philanthropic galleries' efforts to introduce new styles of teaching may appear naïve and simple to the modern eye, they demanded much originality and initiative, and exerted a wide influence.

CONCLUSION

This story is one of experiment, and, in the long term, frequently of failure. Of the varying educational approaches outlined in this chapter, the public lecture and the school museum visit are the only ones that flourish up to the present, or that even lasted much beyond the First World War. The displays of industrial art, the cast galleries, the survey of world art, even the printed catalogue for use during a museum visit, were all superseded within a few decades of the galleries' foundation. By the early years of the twentieth century, as the state education system became established and the idea of museums as training places for artisans lost its relevance, the educational programmes of Victorian provincial museums and galleries became, for the most part, anachronistic. What followed these programmes was something quite different: art galleries looking away from their original working-class audiences and towards the contemporary art world and an educated public.

Yet in spite of its provisional character, the educational work carried out in these museums expressed not only utilitarianism but lively experi-

244

ment. Their achievement was to create an exploratory way of thinking that is still active today. Unlike the high art museums initiated in the eighteenth century and early in the nineteenth, they focused less on the collections than on the impact that these collections would make on their public. The displays functioned as a means towards the end of 'improving' visitors, in whatever way was found to be suitable. In terms of the art that was put on view, its purpose was a new one, a purpose that was despised by the established order: to appeal to, indeed engross, an essentially uneducated public at a time when education was far from universal.

Evidently, for a while, this purpose succeeded, bringing in a public that was newly enabled to engage such an experience. And if such an endeavour is seen as an attempt to control its recipients, the same censure might be applied to any educational initiative, in which not only the physical but the intellectual movements of the students are directed, with varying degrees of overtness, by the potent pedagogue.

II

PATRONS, DONORS, COUNCILLORS, CURATORS, VISITORS

In 1953 Hans Hess, the German-born Curator of York City Art Gallery, satirically dismissed the creators of Victorian galleries: 'Our Victorian forefathers, having made their fortunes from the sweat, blood and tears of the working people, suddenly in their affluence discovered a conscience tempered by Christian virtues and proclaimed that the people – that meant the others – were in dire need of refinement and general improvement.'[1] It is certainly true that in the late Victorian period, founding a public art gallery became for the first time in Britain a prevailing mode of public philanthropy. This chapter considers the people who, in one way or another, created civic galleries, as well as the public that attended them, and by contrast the founders of museums based on private collections, and asks whether Hess's comments were justified.

The founders of private-collection museums were in a special category. The museums based on personal collections, often housed in their founders' former residence or private gallery, endowed by the founders, generally bearing their name and always stamped with their personality, were usually assigned to private trusts and excluded other benefactors (as at the Wallace Collection). The personal museums of the early period of the nineteenth century – notably Sir John Soane's Museum – had been distinguished by their learned and pedagogical qualities, inspired by their founders' researches into medicine, architecture, the classical world or fine art, and their desire to communicate this knowledge. The visitor might be invited to contemplate the passing of ancient civilisations and the brevity of life, and to enter a zone laden with associations. The collection museums of 1900 offered a very different phenomenon, from which such erudition and such admonitions were largely absent. If any admonition was offered, it was to admire the wealth and taste of those who had assembled such magnificence, and whose images presided in perpetual complacency. Unlike Cardinal Mazarin, who in his last illness wept to be parted from his works of art, the Wallaces and the Boweses were never to be subjected to such a separation, since in their museums they conversed with eternity. And they certainly did not seek to convey the message reiterated in municipal gallery catalogues, that by hard application ordinary people might achieve a status comparable to that of the artists or donors they were admiring.

The collection museum has received close attention in recent years, notably from Carol Duncan and Anne Higonnet (who devised the term).[2] Duncan paints a sharply critical picture of 'donor memorials', in which works of art are consigned 'to the purgatory of never again being used as art by anyone else, at least not publicly'.[3] Higonnet seeks to retrieve and reconstruct (citing Walter Benjamin) the 'ideas that animated the enchantments, the thrill, the magic' of these places, analysing the complex personal histories enshrined in, among others, that most egocentric of personal temples, the Isabella Stewart Gardner Museum in Boston. As these writers have discussed, the characteristic collection museum of the latter part of the nineteenth century and beginning of the twentieth served as a verbal and visual memorial to the founder or founders, and often to a deceased spouse or relation. The most important British examples received their first public visitors between 1892 and 1922: the Bowes Museum, founded by John and Josephine Bowes; the Holburne of Menstrie Museum, bequeathed to Bath by its creator's sister; the Wallace Collection, donated to the nation by Lady Wallace in 1897, and the Lady Lever Art Gallery in Port Sunlight, close to Liverpool, created by Lord Leverhulme in memory of his wife. The Russell-Cotes Art Gallery, granted to the borough of Bournemouth while its creators continued to live there, is an idiosyncratic seaside example of the type.

The style of collecting in these museums was cosmopolitan. Comparable museums, often associated with new money, were established in France, the United States and elsewhere, generally in major cities: among many others, in Paris the Musée Jacquemart-André (opened in 1913) and the Musée Cognacq-Jay (1929); in New York the Morgan Library and Museum (1924) and the Frick Collection (1935); and in California the Henry Huntington Library, Art Collections and Botanical Gardens (1919). These collections tended to resemble those assembled in the great Rothschild houses, their creators being highly conscious of what was being acquired by other private collectors at a comparable level of wealth and sophistication. They generally contained a variety of mediaeval artefacts; mediae-

val and Renaissance, but seldom classical, sculpture; pleasing Old Master paintings (Rubens rather than Poussin); the newly fashionable English and French eighteenth-century portraits and genre scenes; French and English furniture and ceramics, notably eighteenth-century, with Sèvres porcelain, Savonnerie carpets and Gobelins tapestries in particular demand; and often material associated with the founders, family portraits or (in the case of Josephine Bowes) their own paintings.[4] Contemporary art, if included at all, tended to be of the Salon type.

These museums could scarcely have been more different from municipal galleries in their collections, their displays, or their ambience of opulent privacy. The emphasis on personal ownership and use is habitual: at the Bowes Museum an apartment was provided for Josephine Bowes within the building, and most of the furniture on display had been in use at the family's French houses.[5] As Carol Duncan writes, 'the modern visitor, always under security surveillance, is not quite a guest…In Hertford House [the Wallace Collection] one visits *as if* calling on its donor and his ancestors, but hardly on equal terms.'[6] Such a gallery was to be seen as 'the artistic embodiment of a great personality', in which the donor assumed, by right of ownership and the highly visible sharing of such ownership, an artistic aura though not the socially dubious associations of artistic practice.[7] The galleries were intended, of course, to enhance the experience of viewing the work of art but also to underline the fine taste, the skilful wealth and the generosity of their owners. It has to be said that, easy though it is to question the motives of the founders, they appear (on anecdotal evidence) to have devised an exceptionally successful approach to display, since their museums – on a relatively small scale, stamped with individuality and offering an experience of refined sumptuousness – have become some of the most admired in the Western world.

Heightened quasi-domesticity is the linking theme. In the spirit of Wilhelm von Bode's pioneering displays created from the 1890s onwards at the Kaiser-Friedrich-Museum in Berlin, which combined various media in single galleries, these collection museums almost invariably assigned a key role to the decorative arts. These were and are shown in the same spaces as the paintings and sculpture, illustrating links between the media.

200 The Great Gallery at the Wallace Collection, London. The installation of the Wallace Collection, combining paintings, furniture and ceramics, was greatly admired when it opened to the public as a museum in 1900. The Great Gallery was an addition to the original building, made in 1872–5 when Richard Wallace decided to move the bulk of his collection from Paris to London.

201 *Joséphin Bowes* by Antoine Dury, 1850. Oil on canvas, 195.8 × 127.9 cm. Joséphin Coffin-Chevallier was an actress at the Théâtre des Variétés when she met its owner, John Bowes, the illegitimate son of the Earl of Strathmore. She became his mistress before they married in 1852. She was aged twenty-five at the time of this portrait. It shows her dressed with elegant informality, leaning on a fashionable Boulle *bureau* with a glimpse of a picture gallery in the background (The Bowes Museum).

In Britain, the Wallace Collection, opened to the public in 1900, was much imitated for its success in bringing together sculpture, furniture, ceramics, paintings and other media in a harmonious whole (Fig. 200). The creators of collection museums often investigated the relationship of works of art to their setting by installing (often invented) period rooms, particularly panelling, from houses that were being demolished or reduced.[8] These museums are of course redolent of wealth. Their sense of luxury and their blurring of divisions between private collection and public create a personalised, softened extension of the high art tradition.[9]

There was a social agenda to the collection museum early in the twentieth century, just as there is to its modern successors. Like the Jewish entrepreneurs who founded collection museums in Paris, or the railway magnates or robber-barons of the United States, British founders tended to derive not from the old aristocracy but from the fringes of high society or from new banking or industrial fortunes. The two most spectacular examples in Britain – the Bowes Museum and the Wallace Collection – were both created by married couples: in each case the husband was a nobleman's illegitimate son at a time when illegitimacy remained a disgrace for the child,

and the wife was a Frenchwoman of modest social background. (Fig. 201). The Bowes were under financial pressure for much of their lives, pressure that affected the character of the museum and notably its internal fittings.[10] It is hard not to see social self-justification – as well as the creation of a site of memory for two couples without surviving children[11] – as prime motives for the collections and their perpetuation, though it might also be suggested that the unusual social origins of the two men liberated them from the widely shared predilection for ignorant Philistinism then current in many aristocratic circles.[12] (Wallace's collection was based on a large inheritance of works of art from his cultivated father, whereas the Bowes collection was largely built up from scratch.) The concept of personal memorial is apparent in more than the museums' names. At the Wallace Collection, Lady Wallace's will insisted that the collection be kept intact, never loaned, never diluted by juxtaposition with other objects.[13] At Barnard Castle a French Renaissance *château* was erected to the designs of a

Entrance Hall, the Bowes Museum, Barnard Castle   2.

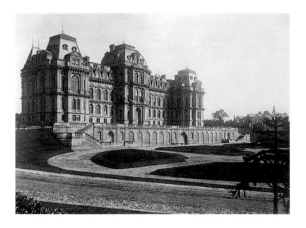

French architect, Jules Pellechet. The startlingly
incongruous building, surrounded by French
gardens, became the signifier of a new style of cultural shrine. The Bowes Museum asserts ancestral
links, being close to the centre of the (legitimate)
family estates while proudly stating its distinctive-
ness as a stately pile that is the epitome of otherness,
a Gallicised County Durham answer to Ludwig of
Bavaria's Herrenchiemsee (Figs 202, 203).

This tradition continued into the twentieth
century in Britain with the Russell-Cotes Museum
and the Lady Lever Art Gallery. Both sets of owners
paid tribute to Napoleon, hero of the self-made
man. The Russell-Cotes Art Gallery and Museum
was set up in 1908 in East Cliff Hall (Fig. 204), the
'spacious home of comfort and beauty' lately built
by Sir Merton Russell-Cotes, a hotelier who had
served as Mayor of Bournemouth.[14] Russell-Cotes
being primarily interested in paintings, his wife,
Annie, in ethnography and natural history, they
combined these interests in a dramatically planned
(yet somehow deeply suburban) house, complete
with mosaic hall and Moorish alcove and liberally
adorned with images of themselves. Conservative in
artistic matters, Russell-Cotes was praised for his
artistic taste as evidence of his wealth: 'After all, it
is certain there is not a great number of picture collectors who can afford to have such pictures as an
Alma Tadema and a Raffaeli in their collection at
the same time.'[15] In his memoir *Home and Abroad*
he quoted the view of his acquaintance Lord Rib-
blesdale that the museum was 'a miniature "Wallace"
Collection, and much more varied in its exhibits'.[16]
The Lady Lever Art Gallery, founded in 1922, is set
at the centre of Port Sunlight, the model village
created for his workers by Lord Leverhulme, brilliant businessman, creator of Sunlight Soap and
impassioned collector. A memorial to his wife, the
Gallery continued the tradition of grand patronage
in the Victorian style into the post-First World War
period, with its English eighteenth- and nineteenth-
century paintings, its representative collection of
English furniture and of Wedgwood, its classical
antiquities and Chinese art, its boldly selected
modern British and French sculpture, all housed in
a forcefully individual building by William and
Segar Owen. The Lady Lever represents the culmination of high Victorian taste and yet looks to the
future (Figs 205, 206).[17]

These collection museums, surviving more or less
intact in terms of installation and concept as well as
holdings (in spite of sales at various times), throw
into relief the municipal galleries: more modest, less
personal, less concerned with the concept of the
Gesamtkunstwerk, more pragmatic and flexible.
The numerous donors to municipal art galleries,
science museums and libraries seldom founded discrete institutions enshrining their own collections
and installations. A new style of donor emerged,
in keeping with a new age of widespread wealth

204 A postcard of the Russell-
Cotes Art Gallery and Museum,
East Cliff Hall, Bournemouth.

RUSSELL-COTES ART GALLERY AND MUSEUM. Bournemouth.   BALCONY

204 A postcard of the Russell-Cotes Art Gallery and Museum, East Cliff Hall, Bournemouth.

derived from commerce: dedicated to their city, in almost every case newly rich, outside the advanced art world and seeking counsel in such fortresses of wisdom as the Royal Academy. In comparison to the founders of collection museums, they tended to be less self-proclaiming, less closely related to the old social hierarchy, less confident in their purchases, less concerned to fill the museums they supported with coded personal messages. On the other hand, some of these new collectors arguably belonged to a new urban élite, celebrating or forwarding their rise to mayoralties and other emblems of civic distinction through their public patronage, and forming (as Carlyle suggested) a new aristocracy.

THE RULE OF ECONOMY

Municipal donors were often motivated by the reluctance of city fathers to fund a gallery or library. At Liverpool, the Library Committee, having considered the erection of a public gallery, concluded gloomily in 1869 that though 'a proper system of Art Education would be of essential benefit to all classes, especially the working classes, both intellectually and morally...[they] must relegate the subject to a

future period when there may be less indifference in the Council, and less apathy in the public.'[18] The Walker Art Gallery's first Curator recalled that in the early 1870s the erection of a building to accommodate the annual autumn art exhibition was 'so strongly opposed by a section of the ratepayers that it was not thought desirable to press the matter at that time'.[19] Only private generosity could resolve the problem. The prejudice that art galleries and collections should not be paid for from the rates led to a belief that such expenditure was inappropriate and possibly illegal. Even at Birmingham, a Curator found it necessary to confirm in 1913 that 'The whole of (the Gallery's) contents have been contributed by the generosity of private citizens, the only direct charge upon the public rates being that connected with maintenance and insurance.'[20] So strong was this shibboleth that when the Earl of Rosebery, Liberal politician and active supporter of public museums and galleries, inaugurated Towneley Hall in Burnley (Fig. 207) as 'the shell in which Burnley's future art treasures will be contained', he remarked that he did not 'suppose that the rates are applicable to the purchase of works of art for a gallery of this kind', to which the Mayor responded 'No'.[21] They were wrong, as the anonymous reporter in the

251

205 The Lady Lever Art
Gallery, Port Sunlight, Cheshire,
photographed in 1920s. Portraits of
Lord Leverhulme (painted in 1916)
and of his wife in court dress (1914)
hang in prominent positions in this
eclectic but classically symmetrical
arrangement of paintings, in which
fine pieces of furniture contribute
to the total effect. The black walls
were an unusual feature, reflecting
the taste of a passionate patron.

206 The Tudor and Stuart Room
at the Lady Lever Art Gallery,
photographed December 1922.
A fashionable London firm of
dealer-decorators installed and
adapted the seventeenth century
panelling from an Essex farmhouse.
The room was filled with a
miscellany of pieces, including the
state bed from Dyrham Park. No
attempt was made to create the
illusion of a once-inhabited room.

207 Towneley Hall, Burnley. This notable country house, originating in the fourteenth century and extensively extended and altered in the eighteenth and nineteenth centuries was until 1902 the seat of the Towneley family (notably the collector of Antique sculpture, Charles Townley). Acquired by Burnley for its intended art collections, it was at first used primarily for temporary exhibitions.

Museums Journal (presumably the Editor, the admirable Elijah Howarth) pointed out with some astringency:

> It may be as well to inform this eminent legislator, and also the civic ruler, that their opinions are not in accord with general practice, and if Lord Rosebery would consult some of the Law officers, or if the Mayor of Burnley would confer with his town clerk they would probably learn that works of art for an art gallery could be purchased out of the rates, just as lawfully as specimens for a museum, or books for a public library.

In view of this misconception and in the absence of any contribution from the state, regional galleries generally had to rely on private philanthropy. The self-induced bar against buying works of art from public funds reflects, it is suggested, a long-standing prejudice that art was frivolous and unworthy of serious consideration.[22]

When private donations did not materialise, some cities were reluctantly forced by public opinion to use public funds. Leeds, an old and wealthy city that in the 1850s had built one of the most impressive town halls in Europe, was notably mean in its treatment of the visual arts. After much campaigning for the creation of a gallery, including the organisation of major exhibitions, no private patron had come forward, and the city fathers were persuaded to pay for a civic art gallery. They managed to erect a building for a modest £10,000, about a tenth (at a time when inflation was negligible or non-existent) of what had been spent on the Walker in the mid-1870s and four per cent of what Glasgow was to expend some fifteen years later on its new museum. Leeds epitomised municipal frugality. The catalogue of the loan exhibition assembled for the opening of the new Art Gallery in 1888 opened with a bald announcement, redolent of defensive stinginess, that 'on the basis of a grant of £800 a year which the Council determined to set apart from the penny rate hitherto applied exclusively to the purposes of the Public library...it has become possible by a judicious administration of the penny rate fund, to spare what is absolutely necessary to start an Art-Gallery scheme without throwing any additional burden upon the ratepayers.'[23] The new building was partly paid for by donations celebrating the Queen's Golden Jubilee: the royal jubilee celebrations in 1887 and 1897 were a regular encouragement to civic largesse.

Leeds remained a national leader in miserliness, as successive Curators of the Art Gallery noted in annual reports in which they were obliged to justify the museum in financial, rather than cultural, educational or spiritual terms. Pointing out in 1899 that by expending £7,950 from the rates on its new gallery, the city had already in its first decade acquired a permanent collection worth 'upward of £24,000', George Birkett, the spirited first Curator, reminded the city fathers that 'the amounts granted for Art Gallery purposes by the other leading Corporations average within a fraction *six times* the amount of the Leeds grant, and yet our work is, in every sense, identical with theirs'.[24] Birkett returned to this theme in subsequent years, providing in 1900 a chart which demonstrated that while Manchester spent close to £7,000 per annum on its gallery, and Birmingham £4,000, 'In Leeds the corresponding grant is £800, or less than one-eighth of that in Manchester'.[25] Even though Leeds was exceptional, the assertion of economy was a *leitmotif* in justifications for public support: at Birmingham, Whitworth Wallis pointed out that in view of the fifteen million visitors who had attended the Gallery in the twenty-five years of its existence, 'there is no other Gallery in the United Kingdom of its size, with so large a number of visitors, with such valuable contents, and only closed to the public on two days in the year, which is worked more economically than that of the City of Birmingham'.[26]

The determination to spend as little as possible remained an abiding principle. This attitude was rehearsed in ironic terms by the museum educational reformer and social agitator T.C. Horsfall in 1894. At a time when so much needed to be done in terms of civic reform, he suggested in a letter to the *Manchester Guardian*, 'it seems ludicrous to ask that money shall be spent upon art. To many persons the payment of a high salary to a Director of Art Galleries by the Manchester City Council would seem as silly an act as the giving of a smart bonnet to a woman dying from want of food.' Horsfall did not agree: art was no luxury and needed support, just as better housing and public parks did. Truly healthy people, he claimed, 'all have another quality with which art has a great deal to do. They all find that life without any help from public-houses or low music halls is very interesting to them.'[27] In spite of these ideas, which gained strength during the period, the argument that the need to provide public health facilities disallowed expenditure on the arts was, and remains, a constant enemy of the civilised city.

THE TOWN COUNCILLOR

The meanness and ignorance of councillors in the context of the arts were for many years a source of metropolitan mockery. In his 1890s essay 'The Alderman in Art', George Moore attacked what he considered to be the absurd acquisition policies of Manchester and Liverpool, declaring 'that it should have ever come to be believed that twenty aldermen, whose lives are mainly spent in considering bankrates, bimetallism, and sewage, could collect pictures of permanent value is on the face of it as wild a folly as ever tried the strength of the strait waistcoats of Hanwell or Bedlam.'[28] The most blistering attacks were delivered at a time when the Victorian legacy was exposed to hostile scrutiny. Notably vocal were the art critic Frank Rutter, Curator of Leeds City Art Gallery from 1912 to 1917 (Fig. 208), and a generation later John Rothenstein, Director at both Leeds and Sheffield. Rutter's remarks underline the question mark hanging over the heads of a civic committee responsible for an art gallery or museum: their qualification for the position. In his memoir *Since I was Twenty-Five*, he retaliated for the frustrations he had suffered:

> Of the Leeds City Council I find it most difficult to speak in parliamentary language. Never before had I come into contact with the kind of men who become councillors and alderman, and – with remarkably few exceptions – I was appalled at their grossness, their ignorance and general lack of manners.[29]

He declared that in general 'the municipal art galleries of Great Britain are…a disgrace to the elected persons responsible for their maintenance, a laughing-stock to art-loving visitors from abroad,

208 *Frank Rutter* by Gerald Kelly, 1910. Oil on canvas. Art critic, exhibition organiser and museum curator, Rutter was exceptional in his knowledge of contemporary foreign art. In the insular cultural climate of early twentieth century Britain, he championed French Impressionist art as well as Brancusi, Epstein and Kandinsky, to each of whom he gave their first London showing. His polemical *Revolution in Art: An Introduction to the Study of Cézanne, Gauguin, Van Gogh, and Other Modern Painters* was published in 1910. With Michael Sadler he set up the Leeds Art Collections Fund to encourage exhibitions and purchases at the City Art Gallery; the Fund still flourishes (National Museums Liverpool).

and an offence as well as a burden to the average ratepayer.' Given as they were to hampering their curators, 'With our municipal committees composed as they usually are, what chance is there of a provincial art gallery being efficiently and intelligently administered?'[30]

The history of the councils is not as black as Rutter and others suggested. Some nineteenth-century councillors were men of wealth and standing, and in many cases – such as the Rathbones in Liverpool and the Chamberlains and Kendricks in Birmingham – members of old-established families with a tradition of public service. Kate Hill has analysed the constitution of various councils later in the nineteenth century, concluding that they were often dominated by merchants until early in the twentieth century, when professional men began to play a larger role, and that membership of the museums and libraries committee might be seen as an honour.[31] Running through these metropolitan criticisms is a strong element of animosity and condescension, social (in that the councillors were seen to be exercising power for which their backgrounds did not equip them), geographical and intellectual. This animosity reflected a deep distrust among the London élite of attempts by people from other backgrounds to create a new type of museum, containing a new type of collection, and directed at a new public. In the frequently uninspired and cost-conscious environment of Victorian local government, a number of men stand out for their dedicated service and insistence on civic patronage, examples of the impact that could (and can) be made by impassioned individuals willing to fight for their beliefs.

Criticisms of local councils, equally, were sometimes unfair. In many cases, the councils could call on only very limited resources. The creation of new art galleries in Victorian cities was impeded by the small units of government set up in many districts, which created a narrow basis for taxation within the city centre, as well as by the tendency for richer families to move into the suburbs or the countryside, ceasing to be ratepayers or supporters of civic institutions.[32] In this respect the 1840s seem to have been a transitional period. Whereas the progressive social reformer Charles Rowley (born in 1839) recalled that in the Manchester of 'The Hungry Forties', 'the communal spirit was alive…The richer men all lived at their businesses and provided for the town a fine Art Gallery, Concert Hall, Assembly Rooms, Theatre, Natural History Museum, Town Hall, Infirmary',[33] Léon Faucher commented that in the same decade the merchants and manufacturers abandoned Manchester as soon as work stopped, for their 'detached villas, situated in the midst of gardens and parks in the country'.[34] By the 1870s the abandonment of the city centres by the prosperous was apparently complete, although later the extension of city boundaries often brought the suburban wealthy back within the cities.

In spite of these financial difficulties, the spirit of public philanthropy was a powerful incentive. Many of the most forceful advocates of public galleries were actively involved in supporting other causes, associating intellectual and cultural life with physical health and by extension moral well-being.[35] For them, Ruskin's belief in the ability of art to transform and elevate the lives of everyone – as opposed to the concept of art as a luxury for the few – was a guiding principle, as was his belief in the power of art to transform and elevate industry. At Oldham it was the determination of James Yates, a medical doctor and at the time Mayor of Oldham, 'a valiant champion of physical, mental and social health',[36] that pushed through a public library and an art gallery in the face of the indifference or hostility of fellow-councillors who dubbed his scheme 'Yates's Folly'.[37] In Leeds the arts were championed by Colonel T. Walter Harding, Chairman of the Art Gallery Committee from its foundation to his death in 1914, who in a Ruskin-inspired campaign to embellish the city pressed for the erection of a public gallery.[38] In Sunderland, a wealthy coal-trading port on the River Wear, an existing geological collection was developed into a civic museum and art gallery by Robert Cameron. Cameron (Fig. 209) was an archetypal civic hero: a headmaster and Nonconformist preacher, he served for many years as a town councillor and alderman before becoming a Liberal MP, campaigned for the prohibition of alcohol, and acted from 1868 to 1913 as the museum's Honorary Curator.[39]

Collecting at the Walker Art Gallery was fostered by the single-mindedness of Philip Rathbone, for many years (Liberal) Chairman of the Art and Exhibitions Sub-Committee. A member of a family 'celebrated in Liverpool for their high principles, intellect and philanthropic activities', who had retired early from a career in insurance, Rathbone, inspired by Ruskin, was a passionate lover of art.[40] Although Rathbone was obliged by his fellow-councillors to buy more conservatively than he might have wished, he spent modest sums on works by artists of the Newlyn school such as Stanhope Forbes, the New English Art Club and the Glasgow school that otherwise would not have entered the collection. After his death the *Annual Report of the Art Galleries and Museums* commented that 'His wide and catholic art-culture and taste, and his strong individuality, were so woven into the history, daily work, and life of the institution, that it seemed as if the ruling spirit of inspiration and guidance had gone for ever.'[41]

In Birmingham, the City Art Gallery was fostered by enthusiastic local businessmen who supported the Public Picture Collection Fund. William Kendrick MP, member of a prominent Birmingham family, a manufacturer of hollowware but at the same time a poet and painter, patron of William Morris and friend of Burne-Jones, served as Chairman of the Museum and Art Gallery Committee for thirty years.[42] He presented Millais' *Blind Girl* to the Gallery and 'headed the list' in the 1904 and 1906 appeals for the purchase of Pre-Raphaelite drawings.[43] Other leading donors included members of such powerful local families as the Chamberlains; their cousin Joseph Nettlefold, industrialist and engineer, who bequeathed a large collection of works by David Cox; Frederick Elkington, from the pioneering firm of metalwork manufacturers that developed the electroplate and the electrotype; and, from a wholly different background, the ubiquitous collector, art dealer and patron Charles Fairfax Murray.[44] This was a tightly knit, successful, hard-working nucleus of men from a variety of backgrounds, who used the emergent apparatus of local government to express their civic pride in a similar style to the city fathers of Boston, Pittsburgh or Chicago. It would be impossible to unravel the motives of these various men. No doubt they were bound up with personal and corporate agendas but one may not unreasonably credit them with energy, intelligence and a degree of altruism rather than the patronising self-justification attributed to them by Hess or the desire to control the lower orders which might be ascribed to them today.

THE CIVIC GOSPEL

The faith in the public value of art was to develop further towards the end of the century at a time of powerful social change and a questioning of traditional patterns of ownership. The belief in the need to provide libraries, museums and art galleries available to all became a central element in the concept of civic government, notably in two Liberal-controlled cities, Birmingham and Glasgow. These ideas were articulated by a leading Glasgow councillor, Robert Crawford (Fig. 210), in a lecture 'The People's Palace of the Arts For the City of Glasgow', given in 1891, when the city, though filled with confidence, did not yet possess a full-blown museum or art gallery. Crawford was another creative city father: Chairman of the Health Committee and of the Committee on Art Galleries and Museums, he was interested not only in such practical issues as the purification of the Clyde, the treatment of sewage, the housing of the poor and the creation of a tramway system but also in the promotion of international exhibitions and art.[45] It was he who persuaded the Art Gallery committee to buy Whistler's *Thomas Carlyle*. He differed from his American counterparts in believing that such initiatives should

emerge from the public sphere rather than private initiative.

While stressing that his views were a layman's, Crawford presented a passionately idealistic concept of the importance of art to everyday living. Recalling that 'For more than a generation, the promotion of Museums and Art Galleries has been urged on communities as an essential for the technical education of the working classes', he affirmed that 'This view of Municipal Art is important, but not the highest.'[46] It had aimed merely to ensure 'that our calicoes may be more acceptable to the Hindoos, and our crockery more pleasing to the South Sea Islanders'.[47] Craw-

ford declared his faith in the transformative power of art as something 'more and higher than a mere agent for developing trade and stimulating commerce'. The pursuit of beauty could lead to 'pure enjoyment of the loftiest order', an enjoyment hardly definable in words. For a municipality, what could be achieved might be limited but 'it is still very great, and if exerted to the fullest it is mighty indeed'.[48] If the members of a Town Council were 'endowed with an artistic sympathy and an earnest zeal to make the life of a city fuller, brighter, and happier...a warmer, fuller, richer stream of communal blood...would sweep before it all narrow prejudice and class isolation, and unite all its citizens in a common desire to make that city distinguished for all that makes a city's life noble, good, and happy'. He did not set the old aim of unifying the classes as the prime objective of a gallery: its essential purpose 'should be pure and elevating pleasure of the best and highest kind',[49] offered in the most attractive setting attainable. Crawford concluded with a statement that reflects the imminent rise of the Labour Party (the first three independent working men were elected to Parliament in the following year): 'Such...is the notion I have formed of one path by which the municipality may facilitate the great socialistic and communal march of our time. The path will be an ever-broadening one as time rolls on, but...it is a path which leads to light and life.'[50]

THE PRIVATE DONOR

Outside the confines of the council chamber, the shortage of public money precipitated a new breed of personal donor. In many cases they were newly rich, often self-made, generally not university-educated (though the Scots were more likely to have attended university), Liberals and Nonconformists. They found in the municipal museum and gallery an attractive supplement to the long-standing British tradition of self-commemoration through philanthropy. In Paisley, the donation of a building appealed to such wealthy men as Sir Peter Coats, a leading figure in J. & P. Coats, the family thread-making business, which was the largest in the world. The Coatses were distinguished for their strong religious beliefs and for their erection of churches for the United Free Church; from their faith

211 The Crown Hotel, Lime Street, Liverpool, 1905. This is one of the flamboyant public houses set up by Walkers Warrington Ale, the business owned by Andrew Walker, patron of the Walker Art Gallery. These pubs, with their boldly decorative exteriors and sumptuous interiors, were intended to offer a seductively enjoyable experience. The attention paid to the physical environment for consuming alcohol parallels the attention given to creating attractive settings for works of art.

emerged a sense of mission to the socially deprived. Although Peter Coats was not notably interested in art, he was, like the rest of his family, a Liberal and an active philanthropist who supported the city's Infirmary, Government School of Design and Philosophical Institution.[51] In 1867 he founded a new museum and library in Paisley and assisted it financially for the rest of his life.[52]

Giving one's name to a museum conveyed the highest respectability. At a time when alcohol was seen as a social menace and the temperance movement was at its height, alcohol and the desire to escape the implications of its production funded several new museums. Alderman Andrew Walker of Liverpool, a brewer known for the glamorous public houses he erected (Fig. 211), on being elected Lord Mayor in 1873 'nobly came to the rescue' of the beleaguered cause of a civic art gallery to the tune of £20,000.[53] This brought him a knighthood 'in recognition of his public spirit and generosity',[54] in spite of opposition in some (Liberal) quarters on the grounds of his association with alcohol, which pro-

voked caricatures suggesting that the gallery was built on drink (Fig. 212).[55] In Derby the brewer (and Liberal MP) Michael Bass founded the town's museum in the 1870s. In Sheffield another brewer, J.N. Mappin, bequeathed a monument to his taste and generosity in the form of his own collection, on condition that a building was erected to house it;[56] while Newcastle's Laing Art Gallery derived from Alexander Laing's success in bottling beer and purveying wines and spirits (he is politely described in an early history of the Gallery merely as 'an enlightened and public-spirited business man').[57] Tobacco, which had made the Wills family rich, and was regarded as less reprehensible than alcohol, funded the construction of Bristol City Art Gallery.

Sources of wealth were, inevitably, very mixed. Since so many of these patrons flourished in Lancashire (Fig. 214), cotton inevitably provided the fortunes of many, including Charles Lees of Oldham Art Gallery and J.F. Cheetham, founder with his wife, Beatrice Astley, of the Astley Cheetham Art Gallery, Stalybridge, to which he bequeathed Italian and

212 *A Fresco for the Walker Art Gallery*, after Harry Furniss, *c.* 1877. This satirical print depicts the dangers of alcohol at the height of the temperance movement. Presided over by a figure of Death, men in a public house toast the contribution that their drinking makes to the Walker Art Gallery. They end up on the gallows or throw themselves into the sea, while wife and children enter the workhouse, crying 'Curse the Drink'.

A FRESCO FOR THE WALKER ART GALLERY.

"DRINK—DRINK—DRINK!"
FILL UP, MEN, AND PLEDGE THE GOOD HEALTH
OF HIM WHO ASCENDS, AS WE FALL,
AND MOUNTS BY OUR SHOULDERS TO WEALTH

"THE BREWER!" A RIGHT CLEVER SOUL—
A LEGALIZED VAMPIRE IS HE
WHO SUCKS (AS WE DRAIN THE HOT BOWL)
THE LIFE-BLOOD FROM YOU AND FROM ME!

213 Sir Joseph Whitworth, Bt, photographed by McLean and Haes in the 1860s.

Flemish Renaissance paintings. Textiles and textile machinery enriched James Guthrie Orchar, patron of the Victoria Galleries in Dundee; the wool trade, numerous individuals in Bradford and notably Samuel Cunliffe-Lister, patron of Cartwright Hall. In some cases, new fortunes derived from industrial sources at a time of huge expansion in the North and the Midlands, so that engineering created a fortune for the Tangye brothers in Birmingham and for Sir Joseph Whitworth, founder by bequest of the Whitworth Art Gallery in Manchester (Fig. 213). Characteristically, Whitworth was concerned with moral and physical health as well as sound business, inventing in 1842 a street-sweeping machine that 'was reported to have changed [Manchester] from one of the dirtiest into one of the cleanest of the large English towns'.[58] The building trade enriched Philip Horsman, builder at his own expense of the Gallery at Wolverhampton to which he gave his British pictures; the heavy steel industry, and the Sheffield Gas and Light Company, Sir Freder-

259

ick Mappin in Sheffield; the creation of the Irish railway system benefitted William Dargan, instigator of the Dublin exhibition of 1853, which led to the foundation of the National Gallery of Ireland. More domestic products also provided wealth: the jewellery trade provided the wealth of James Ward Usher of the Usher Gallery at Lincoln; jam and marmalade, James Keiller, a Dundee patron; the manufacture of household goods, Thomas Ferens of the Ferens Art Gallery in Hull. Some donors derived their riches from a diversity of interests, such as Thomas Wrigley, whose British paintings, watercolours and ceramics formed the basis of Bury Art Gallery and who had profited from paper, banking and railways (Fig. 215). Though relatively few donors had made their fortunes in the professions, they included the lawyer James Clark, who left a substantial legacy to Aberdeen; the Newcastle conveyancer and manic collector Joseph Shipley, whose paintings entered the eponymous gallery at Gateshead; and the banker Richard Newsham, donor to the Harris Museum in Preston. Donations by artists were rare other than in Glasgow, renowned for the vigour and brilliance of its private collecting, where the gallery received handsome donations from the widow of the Glaswegian portraitist John Graham-Gilbert – including Rembrandt's *A Man In Armour* (Fig. 216) and

Giovanni Bellini's *Virgin and Child* (Fig. 217) – the children of the artist James Reid and many other donors. In contrast to France, where the practice was much more common, the only artist sufficiently convinced of his own genius to set up a gallery in self-commemoration was G.F. Watts, at Compton in Surrey, in 1904.

THE ROLE OF WOMEN

It is notable how few of these donors were women, even after the Married Women's Property Act of 1882 gave married women greater control of their own property: only in the case of collector museums, where the donors tended to come from older-established social backgrounds, did such women as Josephine Bowes act as equals to their husbands. The relatively few major women collectors in the nineteenth century were remarkable individuals such as Lady Charlotte Guest (better known in museum circles as Charlotte Schreiber), who ran her husband's ironworks in Wales – an extraordinary achievement for the time – and later made a notable collection of ceramics, which went to South Kensington Museum. The essential problem was that, in comparison to men, women very seldom had access to the large sums required for active patronage.

This exclusion of women from positions of power extended into many fields of museum activity, and was paralleled in national museums.[59] In terms of City Councils, women could not become borough or county councillors until the passing of the Qualification of Women Act in 1907. Very few women employees are recorded in museums until early in the twentieth century, other than in the stereotyped subsidiary roles of typists and housemaids, and their fitness for professional employment was much debated. As Jordanna Bailkin has discussed, women were in many cases not regarded as suited to work in scientific museums in Britain (other than in a domestic capacity) even early in the twentieth century.[60]

From some areas, women were not excluded. Some of the most important writers on museums and the visual arts – notably Anna Jameson – were female. This limited inclusion extended to the visitor: for a middle- or upper-class woman to be seen in a museum, albeit normally under the protec-

215 *The First Voyage* by William Mulready (1833). Oil on panel, 52.5 × 63.5 cm. The painting was part of the substantial collection of paintings, watercolours, prints and ceramics assembled by the paper manufacturer Thomas Wrigley and presented to Bury Art Gallery by his children in 1897 as its founding collection (Bury Art Museum).

tion of a man or a servant, was perfectly acceptable, even though such places might bring the visitor into contact with 'undesirable' members of the public. Bailkin has also demonstrated that a number of upper-class women, particularly in the late Victorian period, did become involved in philanthropic enterprises associated with museums, if against some resistance. The sites where women appear to have been most active tended to be on the fringes of the official museum world, in the 'philanthropic museums' set up in slum areas, where quasi-charitable activity offered such women a form of liberation. At the Ancoats Museum middle-class women played an important voluntary role,[61] while one of the founders of the Whitechapel Art Gallery was the formidable Henrietta Barnett, supported by hosts of ladies (as well as gentlemen) acting as guides. Money, and a powerful intellect, could with great difficulty breach male bigotry.

OLD AND NEW MONEY

A few major donations derived from old money. In Chester, the Grosvenor Museum, opened in 1886, was supported by the first Duke of Westminster, whose principal seat, Eaton Hall, was nearby. Very unusual in this narrative was Stafford Northcote, a politician and notable as the reformer of the Civil Service, and a member of an old Devon family, who was a leader in the foundation of Exeter Art School and Museum in the 1860s. In this county and cathedral town the patronage of the new institution had a distinctive character, the new art school and museum being promoted by two separate groups of 'city and county gentlemen': Northcote headed the latter group and undertook to raise the necessary funds, though this proved difficult given the resistance of the landed gentry to supporting the activities even of such non-industrial cities as Exeter.[62]

216 Rembrandt van Rijn's *A Man in Armour*, painted in about 1655. Oil on canvas, 137.5 × 104.4 cm. Bequeathed to Glasgow by Jane Graham-Gilbert in 1877, it is an example of the outstanding wealth of Glasgow's private collections. Her late husband, John Graham-Gilbert, a prominent Glaswegian portraitist and collector, is a rare example of a professional artist being a donor to a municipal collection (Glasgow Museums).

217 *Virgin and Child* by Giovanni Bellini, 1480–5, bequeathed by Jane Graham-Gilbert to Glasgow in 1877. Oil on panel, 62.2 × 46.4 cm (Glasgow Museums).

By and large, the major collectors belonged to the considerable segment of the newly rich who remained faithful to their roots and did not choose to merge into the landed gentry. Cunliffe-Lister was relatively unusual in taking the title of Lord Masham and buying over 30,000 acres in Yorkshire, which placed him firmly among the landed aristocracy.[63] In a few cases a family that had made a fortune in one generation maintained a tradition of patronage in the next generation, though such sustained benevolence may have applied particularly in southern, non-industrial, towns. Thomas Brassey, Liberal MP for Hastings in the 1860s and 1870s, used his inheritance from the £5,000,000 amassed by his father, a successful railwayman, to found the Brassey Institute in Hastings, to which he left the Durbar Hall he had bought from the Indian and Colonial exhibition of 1886.[64] In another rare example, an inherited copper fortune enabled the aesthetically minded Richard Glynn Vivian to found Swansea's Glynn Vivian Gallery.

On the whole, though, these were new fortunes, often created by men who had embarked on a working life at an early age without higher education. Ferens became a clerk in the mineral department of the Stockton and Darlington Railway at the age of thirteen Whitworth entered employment as a mechanic at eighteen. The principle of hard work from youth upwards linked Samuel Cunliffe-Lister, who chose business over the Church, and William Dargan, a farmer's son and already at twenty the leader of major engineering projects.

As one might expect, strong personal attachment to a place of birth was a recurring motive. When in 1899 the Beaney Institute, a handsome building in the Tudor style, opened in the High Street of Canterbury, tributes were paid to the founder, 'the erstwhile Canterbury chemist's boy, who quitted life as one of the most eminent surgeons in Australia, and a member of the New South Wales Legislature'[65] (Fig. 218). James Beaney's bequest was motivated by fondness for his native town and a belief that such an institution could assist the young: 'A poor lad himself, it was his desire to give others a better chance than he himself enjoyed'[66] (Fig. 219). His approach parallels Andrew Carnegie's. Born in Dunfermline, Carnegie made a huge fortune in the United States from steel and railways, much of which he devoted to establishing free libraries there

262

218 Monument to Dr James Beaney, a native of Canterbury, who made a fortune as a surgeon in Australia and died in 1891. Though considered vulgar and grasping by enemies in Australia, he was celebrated in his native town, where he gave £1,000 to the cathedral on condition that a monument be erected there. Grand in scale and alluding to his character as a Good Samaritan, it was criticised as inappropriately massive; later monuments were reduced in scale.

219 The Beaney Institute, Canterbury. It was designed by the City Surveyor, A.H. Campbell, in a wild eclectic style, with a half-timbered façade and a rich variety of ornamentation, including reference to the principal cities of the Empire. The interior was more conventional.

and in Britain (particularly Scotland). A eulogistic biography published during his life quotes him as saying '"What Benares is to the Hindoo, Mecca to the Mohammedan, Jerusalem to the Christian, all that and more Dunfermline is to me."'[67] On the other hand, many philanthropic businessmen were relatively recent arrivals in the city they supported, such as the German-born Andrew George Kurtz, owner of a chemical works, patron of Agnew's and donor to the Walker Art Gallery.[68] Like many American donors – such as the British-born Frederick Layton, founder of the Layton Art Collection in Milwaukee – these men expressed their gratitude to their new homeland through works of art.[69]

Political affiliations were almost entirely Liberal, and often active (Fig. 220). These sympathies were generally associated with Nonconformist beliefs, though very few if any of these donors were Jews. Thomas Ferens, a Methodist and Liberal MP for Hull East from 1906 to 1918, was an advocate of the rights of women and of the poor and orphans, and a champion of University College Hull: he regarded the opportunity to give as 'one of the greatest blessings of my life'.[70] Ferens (Fig. 221) more than once refused a title, presumably unwilling to make any concession to the traditional social hierarchy. Baron de Ferrières, donor of paintings to Cheltenham Art Gallery, served as the local Liberal MP, as did Sir William Wills, donor of Bristol City Art Gallery (and a Congregationalist), for Bristol. Frederick Mappin was Liberal MP for Sheffield from 1880 to 1905. Variously radical though these men were, their political activities and the variety of their philanthropic work suggest that support for the civic art museum was part of a larger political agenda, which – if not as progressive as the ideals of the emerging Labour Party – was set against old privilege and espoused the interests of working people. This pattern of philanthropy did not prevent such men from being aggressive business figures: Mappin, to take one example, was well known as a strikebreaker and an opponent of trade unions, much like Mr Frick of the Frick Collection.

One collector may exemplify the connection between social ideals and the growth of municipal museums: Henry Willett of Brighton (Fig. 222). This town, traditionally devoted to pleasure but latterly grown more staid, already possessed in the Royal Pavilion one of the earliest publicly owned

263

220 W.E. Gladstone's Meeting, at the Coloured Cloth Hall, Leeds, 1881. When the Liberal Prime Minister visited Leeds to address party members, an enormous structure was erected in the courtyard of the eighteenth century Coloured Cloth Hall to accommodate a banquet for 2,000 – testimony to Liberal strength in the city. The hall no longer stands.

historic buildings when, around the middle of the century, Willett set about collecting. An ardent Liberal, a disciple of Ruskin and an advocate of the public ownership of land, he was given to reading aloud political literature to 500-strong audiences of working men, and donated his political pamphlets to Brighton Reference Library.[71] Willett was unusual among Victorian patrons in the clarity of his vision for his collection and seems to have been, like Joseph Mayer of Liverpool, a frustrated curator. He bought early Italian and German paintings selected on historical principles and followed Ruskin in acquiring fossils and natural history specimens, but it was ceramics that constituted his most original contribution to Brighton Museum and Art Gallery. His collection was organised 'to illustrate the principle

that the history of a country could be read in its domestic homely pottery; to this end everything else, such as the names, dates and places of manufacture, were sacrificed'.[72] The objects were arranged in such enjoyable and easily grasped categories as crime, kings and queens, or British victories. They were intended to appeal to and instruct a broad audience, the museum receiving the ceramics on the understanding that they would be displayed according to his original typology.

Only occasionally was the advocate of a gallery a self-proclaimed working man. At Sunderland one of the champions of the Art Gallery (and many other causes) was Thomas Dixon, a self-educated cork-cutter (Fig. 223). A passionate advocate of universal education and the transformative power

264

221 *Thomas Ferens*, a bromide print of 1917 by Walter Stoneham.

222 Henry Willett with a grandchild. One of the leading socially motivated collectors of the late Victorian period, Willett concentrated on Brighton Art Gallery but also lent and gave generously to other museums.

223 *Thomas Dixon* by Alphonse Legros, 1879. Oil on canvas, 48.3 × 38.1 cm. An example of the rapid execution of a portrait by Professor Legros of the Slade School of Art for the instruction of watching students. It was given by the artist to Sunderland (Sunderland Museum and Winter Garden).

of art, he was in regular correspondence with Ruskin, who published his letters to Dixon as *Time and Tide* (1867).[73] As a member of the Sunderland Libraries and Museums Committee, Dixon was active in setting up local libraries and a School of Design. Through his friendship with the artist William Bell Scott, he entered into correspondence with artists, including Millais, Burne-Jones and Rossetti, and writers such as Tennyson, Carlyle and Dickens. Rossetti was persuaded to give two drawings to the Gallery; Ruskin, to create a scheme of decoration. Idealised by Ruskin as the supremely virtuous and aspiring working man, Dixon was exceptional.[74]

'AN AGNEW-OCTOPUS EMBRACE'

The shaping of municipal collections tended to be a local business, dependent on modest purchases and the tastes of individual donors. As Pamela Fletcher and Anne Helmreich have argued, from the mid-nineteenth century London gained international importance 'as the site for the development of the modern retail market in fine art'.[75] This development exerted relatively little influence on the provinces, since art dealers did not generally sell to municipal collections, though they had dealings with many regional collector-donors.[76] This metropolitan bias among collectors had a discouraging effect on local artists and dealers.

The notable exception was the firm of Thomas Agnew and Son, initially based in Manchester and active in the North of England and in London. As Dianne Sachko Macleod has written, 'It would be no exaggeration to say that every Lancashire collection of note was served, in one way or another, by this influential firm of art dealers',[77] to the extent that a councillor involved in commissioning Ford Madox Brown's paintings for Manchester Town Hall wrote of his hope that the artist would relieve them 'from the possibility of an Agnew-octopus embrace'.[78] William Agnew (Fig. 224), who managed the firm from 1861 until 1895 (and served briefly as a Liberal MP) repeatedly features in the development of municipal collections and institutions, as well as dominating sales of art to Northern collectors. Described by a contemporary as 'pre-eminently a creation of the new wealth',[79] he advised such supporters of municipal galleries as Charles Lees and Thomas Wrigley, and private collectors, such as the successful businessman George Holt of Sudley House in Liverpool (Fig. 225), to whom he supplied paintings from the 1860s onwards.[80] It was through gifts rather than sales that Agnew helped the nascent galleries to develop collections. He bought for the enormous sum of £10,500 Holman Hunt's *Shadow of Death*, which he exhibited and engraved for sale (a highly profitable process) before presenting it to Manchester City Art Gallery, a shrewd combination of motives.[81] He also played a prominent part in encouraging and shaping new institutions in Manchester and neighbouring Salford, where he served as Alderman and Mayor and presented thirty-six oils to the new Museum and Art Gallery.[82] When in 1893 the Whitworth Art Gallery was set up as part of the new Whitworth Institute, with funds left by Joseph Whitworth, Agnew was involved from the earliest days. With his friend Charles Lees – their joint support for the Institute typifying the close-knit world of Lancashire patronage – he served as Council member and then Governor, developing the institution beyond its original role as a technical education college into a more complex organisation that embraced the visual arts. His numerous donations to the Whitworth included paintings and watercolours by celebrated artists, including William Dyce, B.W. Leader, Clarkson Stanfield and John Linnell.[83] The choice of artists and the loyalty to the watercolour typified the style of collecting he fostered.

Few other names of dealers occur in the annals of regional galleries, which seldom commanded budgets interesting to the art trade. On the other hand, the most important private collections were formed through the trade or at auction, if not directly from artists. In Glasgow, the dominating dealer was Alexander Reid, friend of Vincent and Theo van Gogh and of Toulouse-Lautrec, and champion of the Glasgow Boys and later of the Scottish Colourists, but though he sent an Impressionist exhibition to Kelvingrove in 1923 it was to private collectors, not public galleries, that he sold.[84] Merton Russell-Cotes in Bournemouth bought directly from artists he knew personally, such as Edwin Long, but also from Christie's, the fashionable New Gallery in London, Agnew's and the Dowdeswell and Dowdeswell Gallery in Bond Street. He loved to buy 'when the artists' reputations were on the wane' and their works were dropping in price, a notable example of the misguided bargain-hunting that often marked the creators of collection museums.[85]

THE UNCERTAIN RISE OF THE CURATOR

The character of the new galleries was partly shaped by the curators. They ranged in status from such men as the highly respected James Paton, Curator and then Superintendent of Museums in Glasgow from 1876 until his death in 1921,[86] to the obscure curator working in a museum in a small town, characterised by the *Burlington Magazine* as 'a mere servant who has no voice in the selection or arrangement of the things under his control, the management being left entirely in the hands of a committee of the Town Council, sometimes with ludicrous results'.[87] In some cases a determined individual transferred his interests from the sciences to the arts. At Norwich, as it moved from learned society to municipal museum, the Castle Museum was

224 *William Agnew in his Gallery* by Edward Salomons, 1877. Pen and ink with watercolour, 31.1 × 58.7 cm. Agnew is seen in his Bond Street gallery, completed the previous year. He was painted by his architect, who regularly exhibited paintings as well as architectural designs at the Royal Academy. A Manchester-based architect with an extensive practice, Salomons also designed a gallery for Agnew in Liverpool (National Gallery, London).

225 The verandah at Sudley House, Liverpool, photographed in 1961. Built in the early nineteenth century in a prosperous Liverpool suburb, the house was bought by George Holt, a cotton-broker, in 1883. He enthusiastically collected British paintings of the eighteenth and nineteenth century, largely domestic in scale and including many famous names. Bequeathed to the city of Liverpool by Holt's philanthropic daughter Emma in 1944, the house is a rare intact example of the residence of a Victorian merchant.

enriched by the activities of James Reeve, Curator from 1851 to 1910 (Fig. 226). Trained in the natural sciences, Reeve became a champion of the early nineteenth-century Norwich school, which had been somewhat forgotten, curating an influential Cotman exhibition in Norwich and London in 1888 and writing the accompanying *Memoir of John Sell Cotman*.[88] From 1863 he served as adviser to J.J. Colman, wealthy manufacturer of mustard, who bought the museum a choice group of Norwich school works. Reeve was exceptionally dedicated, and his collaboration with private collectors suggests the enterprising spirit of the American curator.[89] More typical was his willingness to spend an extended career in the service of one institution: once in post, curators of regional museums and galleries tended to remain until retirement or death.

It is characteristic of the polymathic nature of the museum profession at this period – a residue of the old belief that one person could gain an understanding of every branch of human knowledge – that Elijah Howarth at Sheffield, prominent as an astronomer, was also an enthusiast for art. The phenomenon of crossing intellectual borders was later to become more difficult, as art history raised barriers against easy access, and converse movement

from the visual arts to the natural sciences does not seem to have occurred, but in the nineteenth century art curatorship was apparently a skill easily acquired.[90] In general, curatorship (particularly in the arts) was not considered a profession requiring expert training until well into the twentieth century: the tradition of artists (generally less successful ones) working as curators was maintained throughout the nineteenth century, in the largest and the smallest institutions. Successive appointments at the National Gallery epitomised the artist's hegemony: the first Keeper, William Seguier, was succeeded by a line of painters, including Charles Eastlake PRA and Sir Edward Poynter PRA, a succession broken only by the appointment of Kenneth Clark, art historian, in 1934. In Dublin and Edinburgh, senior posts were considered the prerogative of artists such as G.F. Mulvany, the first Director of the National Gallery of Ireland, or W.B. Johnstone, the first Principal Curator and Keeper of the National Gallery of Scotland.[91] Few of these officials could rival the expertise of scholar-directors in Continental Europe, such as Wilhelm Bode of the Kaiser-Friedrich-Museum or Abraham Bredius, Director of the Mauritshuis: among nineteenth- and twentieth-century British museum directors and curators, only Eastlake, Robinson and Sir William Armstrong, Director of the National Gallery of Ireland from 1892 to 1914, commanded comparable respect.[92] This dispiriting record reflected the long British tradition of amateurishness in the visual arts, in both the academy and the art gallery. By contrast the British Museum contained from the early years of the nineteenth century a cadre of scholarly curators, often leading experts in their fields – though even there it was apparently considered that all that was needed at least to initiate the appropriate duties was a trained mind.[93]

In the major provincial galleries, the tradition of appointing artistic amateurs persisted, though with some innovations. George Birkett, Curator of the Leeds City Art Gallery from 1887 to 1911, and Charles Dyall, Curator of the Walker Art Gallery from 1877 to 1904, illustrate the diversity of attitudes. Birkett belonged loosely to the artist tradition, having studied under Rossetti and Burne-Jones and become friendly with Ruskin. According to his obituary, he was distinguished as an art expert and a linguist whose unusual career had also included

227 The Hanging Committee for the Autumn Exhibition, the Walker Art Gallery, 1891. Seated from left to right are the artist J.M. Whistler, Councillor Rathbone, and the artists Arthur Melville and W. Boadle. Behind them stands the Curator, Charles Dyall, in the centre, flanked by the two Gallery Assistants.

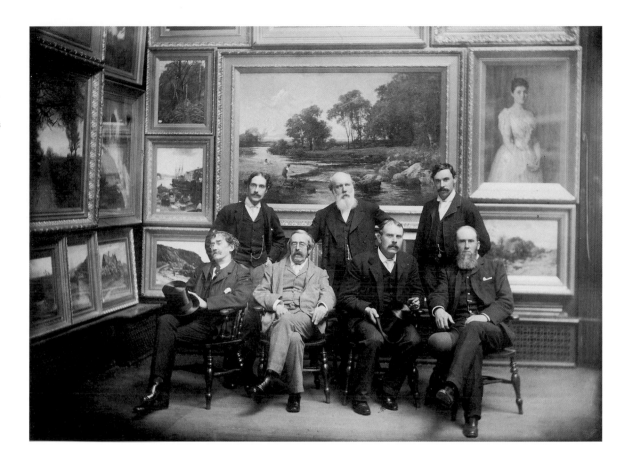

'an important position on the Peruvian railways' and twelve years as manager of a London art dealers.[94] His appointment exemplifies the lack of trained applicants. In Dyall, Liverpool chose a man with no background in the visual arts, his relevant experience being limited to the publication of some verses and the secretaryship of a literary club, the Liverpool Lyceum. Though Dyall published annual reports and a short history of the collection, observers regarded him as exerting limited influence: the critic R.A.M. Stevenson wrote to Whistler at a moment when Liverpool was considering buying one of Whistler's paintings that having spoken to Dyall, 'a sort of weather-cock of the Art Committee', he supposed him 'to be the voice of the Art Committee'.[95] Such figures perpetuated the tradition of the Curator as upper servant (Fig. 227).

A new style of professionally trained curator was, however, developing. In this process the South Kensington Museum played a major part. George Wallis, Senior Keeper of art collections at South Kensington and intimately involved with regional schools of design and exhibitions of industrial art,

trained up two of his sons, who distinguished themselves in regional museums. George Harry Wallis was appointed Curator at Nottingham Castle Museum in 1878, while his brother Whitworth was appointed Keeper at Birmingham in 1884 at a moment when the Birmingham City Art Gallery Purchase Committee wanted a curator from South Kensington. A traveller in his early years to Egypt and Italy to buy specimens for the Gallery, responsible for building up the outstanding collection of Cox and Burne-Jones and the remarkable Pre-Raphaelites, Wallis followed the South Kensington tradition of learned and adventurous curatorship.[96] Serving until 1927 and known popularly as 'The Gallery Knight', he was pre-eminent in his profession, admired for his ability to create, with no direct funding from the city, a collection worthy of the city. As an obituarist pointed out, 'It is an indisputable fact that the city owes many of its finest treasures to the persuasive powers of the Keeper. What art he used to persuade wealthy owners to part with some of their most desirable possessions for the public delight cannot be stated.' He was also admired for

269

228 The immensely distinguished Sir Whitworth Wallis, seated in the model of a museum curator's office, combining erudition with efficiency.

history and (perhaps) archaeology than in the fine arts. When Sir Frederic Kenyon named the Victorian curators who had made the greatest contributions to the overall appreciation of museums, it was Flower, Edward Bond and Edward Maunde Thompson, successive Principal Librarians of the British Museum, that he mentioned, rather than directors of art galleries.[100] One result of changing attitudes was the formation in 1889 of the Museums Association, which paralleled increasing professionalism in other fields and aimed through annual conferences to give curatorship a professional status.[101] Much as the National Trust for England and Wales emerged at this period as a communal response to the lack of Government support for historic buildings and land, so the Association was the first professional body for curators in the world, created with no Government backing. Instrumental in its creation was a group of men who made major contributions to their museums and to their cities: Paton, Reeve, Howarth, Whitworth Wallis. It was, however, natural history curators who were primarily responsible for the Association's foundation, curators of art museums being initially loath to join. The associated launching in 1901 of the monthly *Museums Journal*, a publication which in its early days often showed remarkable vivacity and humour, allowed the exploration of theoretical as well as practical issues – not least museum education – in a way that the fragmented profession had not previously encouraged.

Many of the founders of the Museum Association dedicated their careers to their chosen city. They were allowed to advance their museums without excessive interference from council officials or civil servants, or the need to analyse outcomes, outputs or how each hour was spent. Trusted, they were esteemed for their professional abilities and their creativity, and brought energy, determination, expertise and imagination to their museums. They sought to assemble collections of high quality, whether artistic or scientific, as well as initiating exhibitions and research – and many of them succeeded.

Many of these curators and librarians must have worked in the spirit expressed by A. Capel Shaw, Librarian of the Birmingham Central Lending Library from 1879. His words of 1911 express idealistic fervour and generosity of spirit:

his tact and rigour in refusing unsuitable donations. 'To make these refusals without offence would tax the powers of most people, but Sir Whitworth allowed nothing to stand in the way of the honour and reputation of the city collection' (Figs 228, 229).[97]

By the 1880s leading figures in the museum world were pressing for the better organisation of the curatorial system. W. H. Flower, Director of the Natural History Museum and a distinguished zoologist, believed passionately in the importance of the curator. 'What a museum really depends upon for its success and usefulness is not its building, not its cases, not even its specimens, but its curator', he declared in 1889. 'He and his staff are the life and soul of the institution, upon whom its whole value depends; and yet in many – I may say most of our museums – they are the last to be thought of.'[98] Flower deplored the chaotic organisation of almost all museums in Britain and advocated better training and better pay for the staff.[99] Though he was primarily interested in the importance of curators of scientific collections, his remarks on curatorship applied equally to the visual arts. They remain just as pertinent today.

As we have seen, the development of the curatorial profession was much more advanced in natural

229   The young Whitworth Wallis posing in an imaginative version of the dress of what would then have been described as a Red Indian, photographed on 29 February 1884 by Searle Brothers of Brompton Road, London.

SEARLE BROS.   191, BROMPTON RD, S.W.

We are glad that they [the Birmingham libraries] assist in the culture and education of the people; we are glad also that by the provision of wholesome fiction and great poetry they open to all the lofty realms of imagination, and enable the sorrowful and weary to escape for a time from the sordid cares and trials of life.[102]

THE PUBLIC

Enough has been said in these pages to establish the popularity of these galleries in their early years. Visitors were observed, reported on, and generally approved of by officialdom; their desire for instruction and their gratitude when it was offered were frequently noted. Popular reactions to museums and especially to exhibitions are also vividly (if perhaps misleadingly) evoked in the popular fictitious genre of the comic museum visit by the 'common man and woman'. But the actual experiences of working-class visitors seldom emerge from their own mouths;

their witness has largely vanished. We must rely on the observations of the observer for a sense of the feelings of the nineteenth-century gallery public – although as Lara Kriegel has urged, 'The working man…in his many incarnations was no passive recipient of the [South Kensington] museum's efforts. During the middle years of the nineteenth-century, working men played an active role in the making of museological London.'[103] In the provinces, the impact of 'the working man' on the development of museums is even less clearly defined than at South Kensington. The impressions left by contemporary commentators are mixed, sometimes jaundiced, sometimes (in the earliest days) joyfully optimistic.[104] The contrast between the metropolitan vision and regional attitudes is striking.

In an article beginning 'Oh! The dullness of museums!' the natural historian J.G. Wood, who had castigated the experience of visiting scientific museums for people with no understanding of what they saw, suggested in 1887 that art museums offered equally little by way of pleasure or instruction:

> Even in art galleries, much of the same indifference persists. Go to the National Gallery, or to the sculpture galleries of the British Museum, and watch the people as they wander among the priceless treasures of brush and chisel. The general visitors stroll listlessly through the building, utterly failing to appreciate a single beauty of canvas or marble, and sometimes openly avowing that they wonder why people should make such a fuss about faded pictures and battered statues.[105]

The tone used in discussing provincial galleries tended to be less jaundiced. In 1910 E.R. Dibdin, Curator of the Walker, reported on his recent visit to Oldham. While he found the town 'smoke-stained, ugly, uninviting', a place that was 'all town and no country', he was impressed by the Art Gallery, much superior to collections in Southern towns.[106] He found the gallery 'well planned, well kept, and full of things potent to charm you into a happier frame of mind', including modern paintings acquired from the artist, including such local figures as William Stott of Oldham.[107] For Dibdin, the role of such a gallery was clear, as were the opinions of the public, who expected to be entertained, much as their children were entertained by the cinema (or, as it was revealingly known, the 'picture palace'). The story was king:

> Oldham does not forget it is the function of a popular gallery to make its attractions suitable to the community for which it is provided. We may still, even now, have some lingering belief in the heresy Whistler imported from Parisian studios – that subject does not matter in art, and, indeed, is inimical to it – a fallacy very comfortable to many painters, too lazy of mind or too little educated to achieve anything beyond good design, interesting colour, and "good paint." The public, however, doggedly sticks to its old opinion, and prefers a picture that has something beyond merely sensuous qualities, which, while it delights the eyes, has charms also for the mind and the heart. The Oldham authorities, mindful of this, have bought pictures that have something to tell us about history, myth, life, and morals, though they have leaned especially to landscapes, which have a special value, since, in a town so remote from Nature's happier moods, they attract the public of an English operative centre almost as certainly as a "story" picture – not consciously for their art, but for the stimulus given to the love of natural beauty latent in all. In the "story" picture the art is merely, for the unlearned, a latent unperceived factor in their enjoyment; but if they look because of the subject, they are, if the art be good, acquiring something towards the development of their standard of taste.[108]

Dibdin's sturdy evocation of popular untutored taste, less patronising than realistic, accords with an account of a lantern slide lecture given in Manchester in 1908. The writer evokes the acquiescent and enthusiastic audience, the presentation of contemporary British painting, the thirst for recognisable narrative:

> Picture after picture was shown on the screen, and [the lecturer] in homely language, told their histories and explained why they were good pictures and what were the things to look for in them. His audience, plain folk for the most part, listened most attentively, and every now and then when especially pleased by some picture or other warmly clapped approval. It was easy to see that the pictures with a human 'story' appealed to them most.

Rossetti's big-lipped women were looked at reverently enough and let go quietly by; but Herkomer's 'Hard Times' evoked loud applause.[109]

And at the Nottingham Castle Museum a former Curator recalled the impact made in the 1870s by the new museum, the sense of novelty and excitement:

> They [the citizens] were looking at art for the first time and they were delighted. It was a completely new world for most of them. Now-a-days, remember, even a person who never sees an original picture, sees reproductions of pictures all over the place – they surround him, he cannot evade them. But it wasn't so in 1878, reproductions as we know them, did not exist – art was something new, and swards of people climbed to the top of the Castle rock to see it…[110]

Novelty, narrative, a wholesome escape from urban ugliness – those were the qualities in demand. And when another medium was able to offer these diversions more potently, the basis of the popular gallery was undermined.

CONCLUSION

This chapter has aimed to indicate the variety of people who created the regional art museums of Victorian Britain. A striking difference emerges between the founders of the private collection museums, usually determined and self-confident in their self-perpetuation, and the councillors, donors and curators who shaped the municipal art galleries in a more haphazard and extended manner.

The philanthropists of the late Victorian period are sitting ducks for the modern revisionist critic, and have been sprayed with shrapnel on many occasions. There is no doubt that this style of philanthropy operated as paternalistic control. To take one example, it was almost impossible – as a recent historian has noted – for a worker in Paisley to escape from the domination of the leading thread-making families, the Clarks and the Coatses: 'Their imprint was placed on practically every educational, recreational and medical development in the town.'[111] However Peter Coats may have supported good causes, his family, depending as it did on the labour of the young, opposed any legislation to limit the hours of youth labour.[112] These great industrialists were hardly angels. But, however they were derided by their contemporaries or by later commentators, they had particular qualities. They were closely involved, materially and emotionally, with their cities. They were often inspired by the writings of John Ruskin, by a belief in not just the instrumentalist benefits of art but also its ability to transform people's lives, and often by strong religious faith and a belief in the possibility of improving the human condition. Though many of them were culturally unsophisticated, they believed that no civilised city could properly exist without an art collection. And by one means or another they did equip the provincial cities and towns of Britain with museums and collections. Hess was unjust in his derision.

I2

ADDRESSING
THE PAST

At one level, Victorian art galleries were heralds of the modern age. They represented a novel genre, the gallery of contemporary art. Their buildings explored pioneering approaches to construction, heating and lighting; their displays offered a range of newly made objects, including works of art, for study or for sale; they developed an innovative attitude to the public and in particular to less privileged members of society. But, as Philippa Levine has written, 'Paradox lay at the heart of Victorian culture and nowhere was it more apparent than in their simultaneous adulation of their own age and their reverent fascination for the past.'[1] While extolling the present, galleries and museums purveyed the past, not only because the objects in their collections acted as metonyms for human and natural history, but because these collections were often seen as signifiers of positive past values in a debased present.

This chapter suggests that the presentation of the past – almost always, the British past – was a key element in the nineteenth-century art gallery, as it was in the museum. This approach emerged from various sources, generally derived from the antiquarian tradition but encouraged by the growth in academic historical studies, and fed by patriotism

and regional pride as well as excitement over the modern. In their physical embodiment the new galleries were equally ambivalent towards the past. In temporary exhibitions, national museums and regional museums, narratives around the country's or the locality's past greatness were spelled out in iron and glass halls designed on the most modern principles, and in galleries lit by the most advanced technology, but with classical, Gothic or 'Renaissance' façades. Conversely, when a historic building did become available for museological displays, its ancientness was, by and large, ignored.

THE ANTIQUARIAN APPROACH

The multi-faceted tradition of antiquarianism in England has offered a potent approach to investigating and assessing the past from the Middle Ages to the present. With the exception of early chronicles by such figures as the twelfth-century Geoffrey of Monmouth, whose *Historia Regum Britanniae* relied on invented sources, antiquarian studies represented the earliest attempts to explicate the nation's history. Antiquarianism, as Graham Parry suggests, is easier to describe than define: it was (and

OPPOSITE P.H. Delamotte, *Crystal Palace, Sydenham: Nineveh Court* (detail of Fig. 233).

275

is) concerned with the origins of societies, languages, laws and institutions, and in the search for these origins its early proponents tended to compile a mass of documents and other objects known as 'collections' (the equivalent of the modern local studies collection).[2] Although the aims of research changed, the central typology of antiquarian studies remained topographical, directed at the analysis of locations, often through individual counties – in the spirit of Pliny the Elder, whose *Naturalis Historia* had used natural and artificial evidence of the past and present to define a location. William Camden's *Britannia*, published in 1586, and aiming on the basis of empirical evidence to record the present condition of the country as well as the remains of the past, provided 'a starting point and a base of reference' for all the later work in the field.[3]

This tradition was intimately linked with the development of the museum in Britain, as elsewhere. Several of the long line of antiquaries who followed Camden became the creators or curators of early museums. Robert Plot, the first Keeper of the Ashmolean Museum, studied things 'very remote from the present Age', seeking to understand the roots of English culture and the beginnings of English artistic creativity.[4] The use of antiquities to define one's nation was to become a commonplace among scholars and collectors in Britain (just as it was, for example, in contemporary Prussia). The sharp division that would now be made between such antiquarian pursuits and the study of the natural sciences did not apply: seventeenth-century private museums, such as Ralph Thoresby's, contained numerous British antiquities, while the Royal Society also engaged in antiquarian studies. In a similar spirit, the archaeological and local history collections that developed from antiquarianism co-existed with natural history and art collections in nineteenth-century galleries and museums, so that a dual artistic/historical tradition developed, much as it did at the National Portrait Gallery.

In the antiquarian narrative, national or local self-assertion was a constant motif. Camden was inspired by a desire to establish Britain not as a barbaric Northern nation but 'as a member of the fellowship of nations who drew their strength from roots struck deep in the Roman Empire'.[5] In the mid-eighteenth century researchers addressed new problems, notably the nature of the ancient (that is, pre-Roman) Britons and the Celts, the early history of Wales, Scotland and Ireland (all rich and heavily loaded subjects of investigation), or the character of the Anglo-Saxons (conquerors of the Celts) and of the Norman invaders who in turn displaced the Anglo-Saxons.[6] A recurring aim was to establish the superiority and antiquity of the culture to which the scholar was attached. Saxon history in particular developed into a nationalist, even racist, expression of the idea that the Anglo-Saxon English, derived from a strong Germanic race, were of superior stock to the Celts or ancient Britons, the earliest inhabitants of the British Isles, while the Irish (descended from the Celts) were caricatured as a low breed, dissolute, almost animal.

Later in the nineteenth century, antiquarian studies carried out by individuals or societies were rivalled by the development of archaeology, directed by an increasingly professional body of experts and seated in universities. While antiquarianism became 'an increasingly amateur approach to the past', it flourished within the museum.[7] As Lara Perry has pointed out, at the National Portrait Gallery (founded in 1856), 'picturesque history [developed] within antiquarian discourse, which provided a specialist and quasi-scientific context in which procedures for the authentication of portraits were developed and justified'.[8] The Gallery's historical aims took priority over its artistic ambitions, so that in official assessments a portrait's historical importance outweighed its artistic quality. From the beginning, a major aim was to provide accurate historical information, notably on dress, the display of portraits being accompanied by manuscripts and other relics for the benefit of artists, writers and historians. Information rather than ideas was the desideratum. In Edinburgh, the Scottish National Portrait Gallery shared a building with what was seen as an appropriate neighbour, the Society of Antiquaries of Scotland.[9] A similar approach was adopted in the large-scale historical exhibitions organised at Glasgow and elsewhere (see Chapter Eight), which asserted the value of historical relics as statements of national pride and as modes of instruction. In their ruthless presentation of mountains of material, such exhibitions descended directly from seventeenth-century antiquaries' 'collections'.

In several ways the antiquarian tradition shaped the new galleries and museums. The interest in local history and geography was perpetuated in the Victorian gallery with its emphasis on local achievement and topography and on home-grown artists or inventors. The old style of ethnic competitiveness found modern expression in the rivalries of regional Victorian museums and their determination to establish the British, and if possible regional, antecedents of artists represented on their walls. And in the print rooms developing in some larger art galleries, many of the contents, notably the local topographical views, belonged in the same tradition.

In the museums linked to art galleries, antiquarianism also exerted a strong if uneven influence. The practice of assembling evidence of material culture became disorganised: according to a recent account, 'by the First World War, provincial museum collections relating to local or regional human history were a jumble of oddments, frequently called bygones'.[10] Having survived the recurrent risk of assembling disparate bits and pieces, more than a century later local history collections, archaeological studies and local studies libraries flourish, or at least survive, in municipal museums. Though separated from the fine and decorative arts by traditional taxonomical systems, this cohabitation reflects a long-standing development.

As the nineteenth century developed, works of art came to occupy an enticing space between art and history: notably the novels of Walter Scott, beginning with *Waverley* in 1814, and the poems of Thomas Macaulay. As Stephen Bann has discussed, the historian in the early part of the nineteenth century was confronted with the need 'to situate somewhere, even if not in the historian's practice, the possibility of using the rhetoric of recreation to dubious ends. And a notorious culprit is there to be arraigned: the author of *Waverley*.'[11] Bann traces the 'perturbation' that the romantic inventions of Scott – plausible because well researched, popular but historically inaccurate – caused to the growing profession of academic historians. In reaction, historians aspired to 'recovering the mythic wholeness of the historical *disjecta membra*', that is to say the body of information for which reliable evidence existed, without recourse to the rhetoric of fiction.

This new genre of romanticised history influenced historical presentation in British art, and by extension the presentation of history in Victorian museums and exhibitions. The invitation to the reader or spectator to become absorbed in the Romantic past made depictions of historical events peculiarly palatable, notably when people were invited to identify with the heroic protagonist: what patriotic boy would not thrill to Horatius Cocles' defence of the bridge and aspire to emulation? Whereas academic historians might aim for colourlessness,[12] the historical novels, plays and paintings of the nineteenth century were anything but colourless: they offered in exciting form messages about citizenship, courage, self-sacrifice, qualities appropriate for the island race that ruled an empire (as they did for other countries emerging as imperialist nation-states).

In this discourse, national greatness was naturally a dominant theme. The stress on British art and still more the choice of subject matter repeatedly asserted the achievements of leading characters in Britain's history, characters who could offer inspiration to the humbler citizens of modern times or arouse pity and fear for royal or noble victims. A painting was no less enjoyable than a novel or than a film would soon be. In municipal collections, themes from foreign history were much rarer than British ones. At Sheffield, the Mappin donations contained, in addition to the inevitable Waterloo subjects, portrayals of favourite moments from British history in the tradition of Delaroche: Lady Jane Grey, John Knox reproving Mary Queen of Scots, Charles I after his trial. By 1894 Manchester City Art Gallery's historical paintings included both titillating scenes of child murder, notably *Prince Arthur and Hubert*, which shows the little prince about to be killed by his gaoler on the orders of King John (Fig. 230) and stirring national narratives. The catalogue text for *A Hundred Years Ago* by the Manchester artist George Sheffield (Fig. 231) tells us that 'the artist has sought to commemorate the memory of the great days when England asserted her sovereignty of the sea',[13] while Albert Goodwin's *Invincible Armada* is accompanied by an extended account of the English victory. Most famously, perhaps, W. F. Yeames's *'And When Did You Last See your Father?'*, acquired by the Walker the year after its opening (Fig. 232), captivated the public with its historical accuracy, the stage-like arrangement of the figures, the sympathetic portrayal of representatives of both

230 *Prince Arthur and Hubert* by W.F. Yeames, 1882, acquired by Manchester City Art Gallery from the Autumn Exhibition of 1883. Oil on canvas, 201.3 × 125.8 cm. Hubert, the jailer, has been ordered by King John to blind the young prince with a hot iron. (Manchester City Galleries).

231 *A Hundred Years Ago* by George Sheffield Junior, painted in 1890, when it was bought from the Autumn Exhibition by Manchester City Art Gallery. Oil on canvas, 117.3 × 166 cm (Manchester City Galleries).

sides in the Civil War and above all the thrilling dilemma it posed: to save one's father or tell the truth?

THE UNIVERSAL SURVEY

The historical approach extended to the taxonomy of works of art, which were frequently treated as specimens in the history of art. A historical perspective was applied from the beginning of the century onwards to the display of art, in contrast to the old-established idea that an art collection should focus on master works. The idea that medieval and earlier art, created in whatever medium, should be presented as part of a continuous narrative had been expressed by various pundits from early in the nineteenth century onwards. John Flaxman had suggested in his Royal Academy lectures that the earliest civilisations, as then defined, were worthy of study, citing the Jews of the Old Testament (even though almost no material culture survived from that period), the ancient Egyptians, and of course the Greeks.[14] William Dyce gave these ideas an institutional character by advocating a single great repository of art containing paintings, sculptures, architectural and archaeological fragments, together with a library.[15] For Gustav Waagen, one of the most important issues in his Select Committees' testimonies was the creation of an extended historical display, covering world art from the 'earliest days' to the present: this objective was to be triumphantly realised on the Museums Island in Berlin. He represented a point of view that was contemporaneously being debated in Britain with reference to national museums. In the same spirit, Eastlake advocated the arrangement of public art collections on historical principles rather than through the taxonomy of the physical medium, meaning that sculptures, works on paper (housed, then as now, at the British Museum) and a reference collection of engravings would be gathered in the National Gallery.

The concept of a universal survey of the past leading to a superior present was sporadically but vigorously reflected in the Victorian art gallery and in the great exhibitions. It was an interest characteristic of a period marked by a profusion of dictionaries and encyclopaedias: the *Dictionary of National Biography*, issued in sixty-three volumes between

1885 and 1900, George Grove's *Dictionary of Music and Musicians*, published in 1878, and Banister Fletcher's *History of Architecture on the Comparative Method* in 1896, with the first attempt at a comprehensive encyclopaedia of art being initiated by Ulrich Thieme and Felix Becker in 1907. The lack of such a publication before that date was to an extent compensated for by the three-dimensional encyclopaedias offered by permanent and temporary exhibitions. And in this field the Department of Science and Art was predictably active, producing in the 1870s for its own use and for Government schools a *Universal Art Inventory: Consisting of Brief Notes of Works of Fine and Ornamental Art Executed Before A.D. 1800*, and later a *Universal Catalogue of Books on Art*.

The first major attempt in Britain, and perhaps internationally, to create a survey museum was made at the Crystal Palace, as reinstalled in 1854 at Sydenham, south of London. The interiors of the new Palace, semi-commercial, semi-educational, were wholly different from those in the Great Exhibition, even though experts such as Owen Jones, the German architect and theorist Gottfried Semper, and the archaeologist Henry Layard were involved

in both.[16] The ten Architectural Courts – Egyptian, Assyrian (known as 'Nineveh'), Greek, Medieval, Italian and so forth – (Fig. 233) used scaled-down replicas of buildings to offer a 'complete historical illustration of the arts of sculpture and architecture from the earliest works of Egypt and Assyria down to modern times'.[17] As the *Crystal Palace Expositor* put it, the courts were intended to lead to 'a comprehensive view…of the rise, the advancement, and the perfection of art'.[18] As at the British Museum, ancient Assyria was represented in a display organised by the historian James Fergusson, assisted by Layard, with a guidebook stressing the sensational rediscovery of a lost civilisation. Not only the public's taste but their sense of history and the passage of time would be elevated, while guidebooks emphasised the relationship between the aesthetic quality of the art and its moral excellence.

The desire to illustrate the development of great art was a motivating force at the National Gallery of Ireland, which offered a didactic catalogue by the Director, G.F. Mulvany.[19] The casts in the Sculpture Hall representing the historical development of sculpture were intended to relate each period or school to those closest to it, drawing out

233 *Crystal Palace, Sydenham: Nineveh Court* by P.H. Delamotte. Photograph. The ten architectural courts at the reconstructed Crystal Palace, designed by Owen Jones and Matthew Digby Wyatt, aimed to educate the public in the highest artistic principles. For this Court, Henry Layard, who had recently excavated Nineveh, acted as an adviser, archaeological accuracy being considered essential. As a vanished 'monument to imperial power and pride', Nineveh was intended to offer a lesson to modern visitors at the heart of the British Empire.

'the principles and practice of these early sculptors', and to offer comprehensive instruction for practising artists (Fig. 234).[20] But the most spectacular example of a grand historical survey was created at the Harris Art Gallery at Preston. This ambitious Neoclassical structure, designed by a local architect, James Hibbert, was adorned externally with a sculpture representing the School of Athens and other classical themes. The four-storeyed and 120-feet-high central hall, decorated between 1882 and 1893 with columns and mosaic floors, offered a bold survey of world art. Using casts in bronze and plaster including the Elgin Marbles and sculptured reliefs from Nineveh, numerous photographs and a series

of wall paintings depicting Greek and Egyptian themes, the narrative descended from Assyrian art on the top floor, through Egypt, Greece and Rome, to the Italian Renaissance casts on the ground floor.[21] The process of creation of ancient civilisations was invoked as a lesson to fine artist, artisan and employer (Fig. 235).

THE ROLE OF PORTRAITURE

Portraiture, always regarded as a particular achievement of the British, played a crucial role in the enunciation of a historical narrative with con-

temporary relevance. Effigies, in painted or sculpted forms, were central to many of the early collections, whether in the set of effigies of departed monarchs exhibited at Westminster Abbey, the images of famous men that adorned the walls of the Bodleian Library from its rebuilding early in the seventeenth century, or the portraits of eminent persons accumulated in the early British Museum and originally seen as a basis for the new national collection of pictures. Numerous publications from the sixteenth century onwards in Italy and Germany celebrated famous men and stressed the importance of an individual's likeness for an understanding of their achievements.[22] This approach was adapted in

Britain by the compilers of sets of prints depicting famous people.[23] In all these cases the images were matched by explanatory texts and arranged in categories to appeal to a wide public. The prevailing message was that images of great men (with women emerging in later publications, sometimes in a category of their own) should stir the beholder to emulation.

As Marcia Pointon has discussed, the idea of a portrait gallery in the form of a British Valhalla was central to the emerging theme of a national gallery early in the nineteenth century: in some texts the two were almost synonymous.[24] The artistic agitator Prince Hoare demanded in 1813 to know why the

281

ENTRANCE HALL, HARRIS FREE LIBRARY
AND MUSEUM, PRESTON

235 The interior rotunda of the Harris Art Gallery and Museum, Preston. Originally library users entered the building at ground-floor level, while visitors to the museum used a grand staircase to the portico, a stately approach that was later abandoned. In architectural and museological terms the most innovative element of the Harris was its large central hall, rising the height of the building and offering a panoramic overview of the development of world culture, comparable to the displays at the Crystal Palace at Sydenham.

country possessed 'no Gallery of Portraits, either of the kings who have swayed, or the Statesmen who have administered their Realm'.[25] It was a campaign that was reflected in the commissioning of memorials in St Paul's Cathedral,[26] while in the 1820s King George IV installed in the Grand Corridor at Windsor Castle a gallery of the great Britons of his time, a shrine to friendship. But such monuments remained largely confined to religious buildings and in the view of the new Palace of Westminster's architect, Charles Barry, these were unsuited to the purpose: the monuments should be moved to Westminster Hall and Parliament should commission statues of 'a certain number of the most eminent of its public characters and benefactors of bygone times, in order that a collection of monuments, to the memory of all whom the country delights to honour, may be at once commenced'.[27] Later discussions offered a list of suitable figures, including monarchs,

historians, writers, scientists, architects and artists, admirals and generals, statesmen and churchmen.[28]

The fascination early in the nineteenth century with the period variously defined as Olden Times and as Merrie England – 'a construction based on the later years of the reign of Elizabeth, lasting until the 1680s but with gaps' and offering the image of a wholly English and pre-capitalist society as a healthy alternative to the present – stimulated the role of portraiture in museums.[29] This fantasy of an English golden age was a site of imaginative memory fuelled by contemporary paintings, prints and portraits, enthusiasm for Tudor architecture, and the popularity of historical fiction. In this spirit, Anna Jameson passionately advocated the public display of historical works:

How would it keep alive in the mind of the people all the chivalrous, and patriotic, and historical associations connected with the families of our old nobility, to see from these walls [of public galleries] the effigies of our Stanleys, Howards, Cecils, Percies, Russells, Cavendishes, Whartons, Villierses, with their noble dames and daughters, the Lady Margarets and Lady Dorotheas, looking down magnificent and gracious, as they have been immortalised by the pencil of Van Dyck.[30]

Van Dyck's works, which had to be sought out at Windsor, Chatsworth or Wilton, would, she suggested, be more suitable exhibits for public galleries than some of the paintings currently on view. Jameson posited an interpretation of English history couched in terms of famous families and names, and the houses associated with them. She anticipated the ambivalent status of portraiture that was to be embodied in the National Portrait Gallery. When the Gallery finally opened in 1856, it offered a view of English history based largely on the style of portrait that Jameson described, and was closely linked with the legacy of the English country house, as recorded by the Gallery's first Director, George Scharf.[31] This concern with the noble past did not, however, represent a preoccupation with rank. Like the antiquary John Britton and other contemporaries, Jameson advocated antiquarianism in terms of the education of 'the people': these great aristocratic portraits would, like the historic buildings that contained them, offer both historical narrative and artistic education. As Lara Perry has shown, Jameson expanded the relevance of the historical portrait into the field of morality, discussing in *The Beauties of the Court of Charles IInd* (1833) the moral implications of portraits, with the ladies of the court divided into 'the nineteenth-century currency of genuine and false, virtuous and vicious, beauty'.[32]

The possibilities of portraiture on a large scale, that is to say the depiction of scenes involving numerous characters, were developed in the official commissions for murals in public buildings that formed a crucial element of Victorian public art, notably in the rebuilding of the Palace of Westminster after its destruction by fire in 1834. The reports of the Fine Arts Commissioners set up to define the character of the new Palace were filled with reflections on the role of art. The first report stated that the rebuilding offered scope for 'promoting and encouraging the Fine Arts in the United Kingdom',

so that the competition for the paintings within the Palace stipulated that the artist should 'select his subject from British History, or from the works of Spenser, Shakspeare [sic] or Milton'.[33] Only British artists were eligible and the subjects had to 'express the manners, the general taste and, to a certain extent, the intellectual habits of the nation in which they are cultivated'.[34]

The programme at Westminster anticipated the commissioning of murals and sculpture in Victorian town halls and to a lesser extent in museums. One of the most notable civic examples was the mural sequence by Ford Madox Brown for Manchester Town Hall, painted from 1879 to 1893 and a revealing document in the *Gründerzeit* of municipal art provision. The programme for the twelve paintings demanded prolonged discussion and illustrated the adaptation of the Westminster ideal to local requirements. Not that Brown's murals were routinely celebratory of the established order – just as at Westminster, the iconography expressed a sustained ambiguity between loyalty to Crown or Parliament. In Manchester the choice of subjects reflected such themes as the city's Nonconformist leanings, in *The Trial of Wyclif* (Fig. 236); economic initiative, in the establishment by fourteenth-century Flemish weavers of the city's source of wealth in textiles; and the spirit of scientific observation and technical inventiveness – *Crabtree Watching the Transit of Venus* (Fig. 237); *John Kay, Inventor of the Fly Shuttle* – which had made Manchester the city it was. These heroes were not military figures or noblemen but primarily inventors and practical men, 'local, or near local men of genius risen from the ranks of the people'.[35] The tradition of history painting was tempered by Madox Brown's humour and sense of humanity, appealing to the large popular audiences that were expected to use the Great Hall. In the words of one of the councillors involved in the commission, the murals would 'in this dull business world of ours…[teach] the people that Manchester had a history of which they might be proud, that there was, and is, something to brighten the age, and quicken the pulse'.[36]

The influence of the Palace of Westminster was ubiquitous. It anticipated the statue galleries (and to a lesser extent the picture galleries) that adorned the streets, the parks, the town halls and the museums of Victorian Manchester and

236 *The Trial of Wyclif AD 1377.* One of the twelve Manchester Town Hall murals by Ford Madox Brown, this especially ambitious work was completed in 1886. The reforming cleric John Wycliffe, brought for trial before the bishops, was passionately defended by his patron, John of Gaunt. As an advocate of church reform and the translator of the Bible into the vernacular, Wycliffe may be seen as a forerunner of Protestantism, and notably of the Nonconformism that helped to shape Manchester.

237 Ford Madox Brown's *Crabtree Watching the Transit of Venus AD 1639.* The Manchester linen-draper observes an astronomical phenomenon, in a scene that evokes both 'the excitement of scientific discovery' and the potential for people of modest background to participate and lead.

Birmingham. Municipal galleries too would serve as shrines to national, and local, history, arousing in British breasts pride in what Lord Mahon, a promoter of the National Portrait Gallery, described as 'a race who, from a low and humble origin…have, gradually, in the course of ages, attained perhaps the very first place among the nations'.[37] As Benedict Read has noted, a city such as Manchester 'proclaimed its historical, industrial and political iden-

tity in sculpture in a series of statues and busts of national heroes, national heroes of local significance, and local heroes, by a wide variety of artists'.[38] In the magnificent Town Hall one of the most prominent public spaces, the Sculpture Hall, was filled with images of eminent sons of the city, notably radical politicians such as Richard Cobden and John Bright, former MP for Manchester and Cobden's ally in fighting the Corn Laws. National figures

such as the Duke of Wellington, and Sir Robert Peel, the Lancashire-born Prime Minister who repealed the Corn Laws, were also represented (Fig. 238). In such a hall the separation between art gallery and ceremonial space dissolved.

A similar approach to commemorative sculpture marked museums. Robert Vernon had anticipated the role of a British art collection as a historical shrine by owning portrait busts of Samuel Johnson, Isaac Newton, George Canning and Wellington, mostly commissioned by him as part of a pro-

gramme of British worthies for his personal collection, which he bequeathed to the nation. Most displays included local figures alongside national heroes, the latter dignifying the former. In the inaugural exhibition for its new art gallery in 1885 Birmingham displayed statues of the writer Oliver Goldsmith and the politician and writer Edmund Burke. Wellington and Peel featured at Birmingham, at Manchester, and in numerous other collections.[39] At Liverpool the permanent collection numbered favourite figures such as Charles James

illustrates how the pattern of development laid down by South Kensington and supported by an abundance of advice and loans was tempered by an idiosyncratic historical agenda. The city of Nottingham was distinguished for its links with the traditional apparatus of civil power. It had been a major centre in the Midlands for close to a thousand years, built around the fortress established there by William the Conqueror. It was distinguished creatively by its medieval cloth-making and its famous alabasters, romantically as the headquarters of Robin Hood's enemy the Sheriff of Nottingham, historically as the place where Charles I raised his banner in 1642 as the symbolic declaration of the opening of the Civil War (Fig. 239). Its relative proximity to the Dukeries, a district named from four huge ducal estates, associated Nottingham more obviously with traditional structures of power than most Midlands or Northern cities of comparable status. At the same time, by the early years of the nineteenth century it was poverty-ridden and during the anti-aristocracy Reform Bill riots of 1831 the Castle, rebuilt by the first Duke of Newcastle in the seventeenth century and by the 1830s a highly visible symbol of the power of the notoriously reactionary fourth Duke of Newcastle as it towered over the city, had been attacked by angry crowds and burnt out. The choice of its shell as the site for the new museum was therefore peculiarly potent (Figs 240, 241).

The museum was an important element in the emerging national museum system emanating from South Kensington and the Department of Education and Science. In 1872 the city was lent, for its provisional gallery, a large exhibition of artefacts from South Kensington, primarily intended for students at the School of Art, where the quality of work gained Cole's approval. The objects were intended to demonstrate 'the application of design to the Lace trade as the great staple of Nottingham; as also to give some idea of the history of the origin, progress and development of lace making, as practised in the various countries of Europe from the end of the 16th century'.[44] Since lace was a relatively new mainstay of the Nottingham economy, the Department's aim of improving standards of design was particularly applicable to the School of Art, which was offering training in lace-making. The new institution was seen as a trade museum, where craftsmen and manufacturers could study work of a standard

Fox, along with the inevitable Wellington. It also included recent writers, such as Dickens, Scott and the historical novelist Harrison Ainsworth, whose books regularly provided subjects for paintings of the type admired by municipal galleries at a time when, as Richard Altick has pointed out,[40] literature was seen as respectable in a way that painting had traditionally not been.[41] Birmingham showed a varied collection of portraits of figures with local associations, including images of the engineer Matthew Boulton and his business partner James Watt, both closely connected with the city, of David Cox, and of Cardinal Newman, who though not a son of Birmingham had as the founder of the Birmingham Oratory become a prominent citizen, while Manchester City Art Gallery in 1894 celebrated Charles Swain, writer and engraver, and Edwin Waugh, 'the most distinguished poet of Lancashire'.[42] In many cases the published catalogues offered biographies, stressing when appropriate the sitters' humble origins and scant education, and stimulating the reader to emulation. Such famous figures were accompanied by mayors and philanthropists, Manchester displaying likenesses of such worthies as Charles Richards, Guardian for the Poor of Manchester for twenty-seven years, and Alderman P. Goldschmidt, twice mayor of the city, whose 'Zeal for charitable works was one of his chief characteristics'.[43]

NOTTINGHAM CASTLE MUSEUM

In some municipal museums and galleries the historical tradition played a particularly strong part. Nottingham Castle Museum, which opened in 1878,

240 *Nottingham Castle on Fire, 10 October 1831* by Henry Dawson, 1875. Oil on canvas, 47 × 67.9 cm. By the 1830s the city of Nottingham could be described as 'the worst slum in the Empire apart from Bombay'. Its inhabitants participated enthusiastically in the riots over the Reform Bill. The Castle was ransacked and gutted – its owner, the fourth Duke of Newcastle, was extremely unpopular and opposed parliamentary reform – and remained empty until restored as a museum in the 1870s (Nottingham City Museums and Galleries).

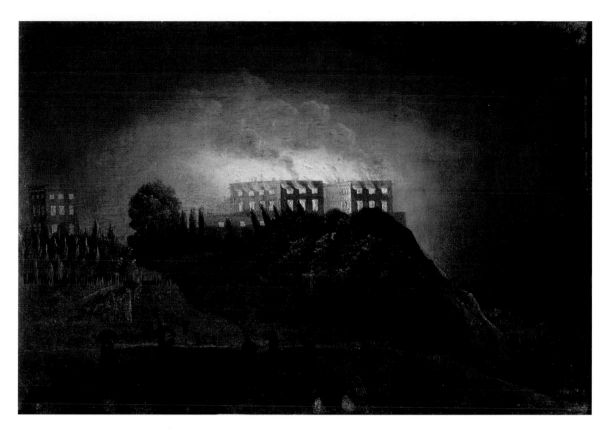

241 Nottingham Castle Museum. The former medieval castle was rebuilt as a Baroque palace by the Duke of Newcastle in the 1670s. Its principal façade boldly faced the town, a symbol of aristocratic dominance. Following its gutting in 1831, it was rebuilt by the Nottingham architect T.C. Hine as the city's museum and art gallery.

higher than anything they were normally exposed to. At the same time it was felt that 'the taste of the purchaser and consumer' must also be educated, requiring the inclusion of more varied exhibits such as old and new ceramics, glass and metalwork, with pictorial art represented through paintings, watercolours and photographs of Old Master drawings.[45] In a speech delivered to the students of the School of Art in January 1873 before the museum opened, Cole outlined his expectation of the day when every town with a population of more than ten thousand would have its own museum of science and art, just as in the thirteenth-century churches filled with works of art were spread far and wide through England.[46] The Castle would act 'as a beacon to all the Midland counties'.[47] For Cole and his colleagues, the museum would initiate and form a major part in a national network of commercial exhibition spaces, raising standards of design in every town where profitable industry was carried out. His role was fully acknowledged in the *Official Catalogue*, published when the museum opened in 1878. The new rooms, which contained paintings and drawings as well as the applied arts, were planned with the advice of Cole and George Wallis, Senior Keeper of the South Kensington art collection. In addition to making numerous loans, the Department assisted in practical arrangements, such as moving the exhibits.

In much of the display, however, the museum went its own way, and showed a marked individuality. Since it had no permanent collections of any substance, one of the new curator's principal tasks was to assemble sufficient loans: as listed in the *Statement of the Objects of this Institution*, presumably in order of desirability, these were firstly paintings, then lace, then tapestry, furniture, pottery and other objects, and finally sculptures and bronzes.[48] This was achieved through the formation of an Honorary Council of 'gentlemen of influence and art knowledge', and through letters of solicitation sent to the local nobility, famous collectors such as Lady Charlotte Schreiber, learned institutions such as the Bodleian Library, and city corporations.[49] Owners were almost as generous as they had been at Manchester in 1857.

So far, the new institution followed the expectations of the Department, and its South Kensington affiliations were strengthened by the appointment in 1878 of the first Curator, G.H. Wallis, son of George and brother of Whitworth Wallis of Birmingham. From its earliest days, however, one can detect ideas that drew the new museum away from the South Kensington ideal. The museum developed to an exceptional extent the element of nationalistic historical pride in acquisitions and displays. (Unlike almost all the industrial cities of the North and the Midlands, Nottingham elected Conservative MPs throughout the 1870s.)[50] The paintings sought by the Corporation for the opening exhibition included not only British, and (in smaller numbers) foreign, paintings, but three additional categories: 'Old pictures of ancient seats and mansions in Midland Counties', 'Old English Sea Fights', and 'Portraits of English Celebrities'. At the suggestion of the Bishop of Nottingham, the historical element included the display on the walls of the principal staircase of portraits depicting leading participants in the Civil War. Externally, the museum's traditional and local allegiances were emphasised by the restoration of the Castle to its seventeenth-century appearance. The internal planning included an enfilade of rooms with details loosely reminiscent of Jacobean architecture on the ground floor, and a pair of staircases to north and south leading to an imposing long gallery for the bulk of the paintings. The plan and scale of the ensemble recalled a great aristocratic house – as though expiating the incendiary memories of 1831.[51]

Local pride, directed at the city rather than at the whole of the East Midlands that Cole had in mind, pervades official accounts: 'It is universally admitted that the alterations when completed will supply the finest Art Galleries, considered in relation to situation, size, and proportion of rooms, lighting, and general suitability, to be found in the United Kingdom outside the metropolis.'[52] In celebration of these happy events, a 'Historical Ode' was composed by one P.J. Bailey on the opening of the castle:

> But lift up now thy head,
> Art-fortress! Let no dread
> Of lawless hosts, nor fenceless floods
>   affright;
> Full glorious dost thou stand,
> 'Mid strong-holds of our land;
> An intellectual beacon burning bright.

Much admired for its contrast between riotous past and peaceful present, the ode was officially printed at the request of Mayor and Corporation.

Unusual in its whole-hearted approach to the presentation of history among contemporary civic art galleries, Nottingham Castle Museum exhibited in a particularly well-developed form the pragmatic use of a historical site, the invocation of past greatness, and the blending of historical themes with artistic or technological innovation.

THE HISTORIC BUILDING

In creating a sense of national pride as well as a heightened artistic awareness, a peculiarly potent instrument is the historic building. This potency was much discussed in the early part of the century by Parliamentary Select Committees, with various reports advocating that old buildings, including churches, should be made easily available to the public. In 1824 the Painted Hall at the Royal Hospital for Seamen at Greenwich, in itself a celebration of British maritime greatness, was converted into a National Gallery of Naval Art containing portraits and relics (Fig. 242). These trophies were rendered more interesting by their inclusion in a building that proclaimed royal patronage and national triumph, doubly affecting in that it offered living testimonies to past achievement in the pensioned sailors who inhabited the buildings. The hall was seen as especially interesting to 'the naval service', offering invocations to virtue much as the paintings of the municipal art museums were to do [53] A further sign of the growing respect for the public value of historic buildings was the restoration of Hampton Court Palace, impelled by Queen Victoria's decision in 1838 to open it to the public, free of charge and even on Sundays. Laden with associations, it became one of the most popular places of resort for Londoners, a powerful statement of the popular appetite for the past and especially a romanticised Tudor past

289

243 A nineteenth century postcard of the Queen's Gallery, Hampton Court. The late Stuart period exerted a strong attraction in Victorian England, evident in Thackeray's *The History of Henry Esmond* (1852) and in architecture emulating Wren.

B.5. HAMPTON COURT PALACE.
The Queen's Gallery.

H·M·Office of Works

expressed in the historical novels of Harrison Ainsworth (Fig. 243).[54]

The antiquarian tradition had always been marked by a streak of nostalgia, notably for monastic life, even though the Roman Catholicism of the monastery made this a delicate subject. Such studies assumed, as early as the seventeenth century, a strong symbolic resonance: 'The very process of casting off the past generated nostalgia for its loss. And with nostalgia came invigorated historical activity.'[55] Ruins, in particular, came to evoke a pleasurably melancholy musing over the transience of human life and achievements, along with a growing willingness to perceive artistic quality in fragments of the past. The genre of the Romantic museum was an international phenomenon, developed in Paris at the Musée des Monuments Français (1795–1816) and the Hôtel de Cluny (1830s). Such museums offered the visitor the opportunity to sense the past phenomenologically in spaces, particularly interiors, where the exhibits formed an affective and united impression rather than existing as individual items for inspection. Such a persuasive reworking of the past could be seen in Britain at such houses as Walter Scott's Abbotsford, where a passion for the past was refracted through the mind of an imaginative re-creator of history, the whole building becoming an expression of his character and the culture he personified. In Sir John Soane's Museum, the holistic spectacle of archaeology, painting, art and architecture represented the owner's personality and creativity. *Description of the House and Museum…*, written under his influence, illustrates the diversity of the reflections that such a museum could arouse:

On every side are objects of deep interest alike to the antiquary, who loves to explore and retrace them through ages past; the student, who in cultivating a classic taste, becomes enamoured of their forms; and the imaginative man, whose excursive fancy gives to each "a local habitation and a name"….Yes! These are all feathers shed from the wings of Time, reminding us of the glories of days that are past, and of countries comparatively sunk into oblivion.[56]

To an extent this theme was recalled in Victorian displays. At the Crystal Palace in Sydenham, the displays were interpreted with a consistently moralistic undertone. In viewing a 'complete history of civilisation' the visitor would be reminded of the

245 *Landscape in the Dukeries, Nottinghamshire* by Henry Dawson, 1850. Oil on canvas, 121.9 × 182.9 cm (Nottingham City Museums and Galleries).

transience of past eras and empires, and by implication their own.[57]

This form of nostalgia could extend beyond architecture. Increasingly in an urbanising age a sense of nostalgia was expressed for the countryside by such figures as Edwin Waugh (Fig. 244), whose *Poems and Lancashire Songs* express his longing for the countryside: as he confided to his diary, 'My heart saddened as I saw the moors and fell of Blackstone Edge recede, and the clangour and corruption of this great sooty city [Manchester] advance upon us.'[58] Paintings could express the same feelings. The innumerable idyllic landscapes to be found in Victorian galleries (such as the works of the Nottingham artist Henry Dawson) express a fondness for an imagined Arcadia, however far it was from the actuality of the countryside from which many of the visitors to municipal galleries derived (Fig. 245).

On the other hand, this fascination with the historical embodiment of the past hardly extended to the restoration of historic houses: the 'Romantic' museum is not a genre found within the municipal discourse. It is true that many of the earliest municipal acquisitions took the form of historic buildings, donated or purchased for public enjoyment. In some instances an old building was converted into a museum, adding an air of antique respectability to the collections (and, at least in theory, saving money). Although Britain, unlike France, had few palaces and no convents available for this purpose, obsolete town houses in London were found to offer adaptable spaces, as at Montagu and Hertford Houses.[59] Similar conversions were made in the regions. At Norwich the keep of the twelfth-century castle, converted into a prison around 1790, was reconverted into Norwich Castle Museum between 1889 and 1894.[60] Historic houses were similarly adapted at Maidstone, where Chillington Manor, an Elizabethan house, was bought by the town and opened to the public as early as 1858 (Fig. 246), and at Carlisle, where the seventeenth-century Tullie House was bought by public subscription in 1893 as the town's museum and art gallery. Generally, however, other than at Nottingham the new installations made few concessions to the building's previous character. Only a ruin offered few problems of interpretation: when Kirkstall Abbey was presented to the city of Leeds in 1889, it was subjected to a major programme of restoration and opened to the public in the setting of a landscaped park.

Historic houses generally entered the public sphere with no clear idea of their future function other than a general sense that an old building ought to be preserved. The early history of Aston Hall, Birmingham in public hands expressed a conundrum: an appropriate style of display that reflected and enhanced the house's historic character

246 The Great Hall of Chillington Manor, Maidstone, from *Maidstone Museum (Chillington Manor House): Its History and Epitome of the Collections* (1919). Built in 1562, Chillington Manor was occupied in the early nineteenth century by an antiquarian doctor, Thomas Charles, who in 1855 bequeathed the collection to Maidstone. The town bought the house two years later and opened it as a museum. The Bentlif Art Gallery was added as an annexe in 1890.

247 Aston Hall, Birmingham. Postcard. This large and notable house was built between 1618 and 1638 by Sir Thomas Holte, whose family lived there until 1817. Having been bought by James Watt Junior, Aston Hall was acquired by the city of Birmingham in 1864.

could apparently not be devised, even though the house dated from a period admired for its architectural qualities and had experienced a siege during the Civil War, that most popular of periods. Set up as a museum in 1858 by a private company to save the building from demolition, Aston passed into the city's ownership in 1864. Though described 'as undesirable a place for a museum as can be well imagined', the house was for many years used as a container for the city's growing collections, with little effort made to enhance its historic character.[61] Even when the purpose-built museum and art gallery opened in the centre of Birmingham in the 1870s, Aston Hall remained a storehouse for secondary objects. The incongruity of using this historic building as a repository for incongruous bits and pieces was raised in the 1890s by the *Art Journal*, which remarked that though some rooms were furnished as though the house were inhabited, such displays as the oriental objects were 'hardly in harmony with the historic traditions of the old mansion'.[62] Although in 1925 it was agreed that the building should be furnished as a historic house,

little progress was made until after the Second World War (Fig. 247).

During the later years of the century a rising interest in social history and the preservation of ancient buildings under the influence of the Society for the Protection of Ancient Buildings (founded in 1877) was reflected in the National Trust's acquisition of the Clergy House at Alfriston (in 1896), the foundation of *Country Life* in 1897, whose discussions of country houses introduced a newly scholarly approach to architectural history, and the advancement of serious research into old English furniture.[63] Public authorities became more active in acquiring old houses, particularly from the sixteenth century and early in the seventeenth. The process continued well into the twentieth century as the traditional owners of country estates situated on the edge of growing industrial cities abandoned their properties and moved further into the countryside. The numerous examples included Christ Church Mansion in Ipswich, a Tudor (and later) house, which was given to the town in 1894; Towneley Hall in Burnley, bought by the Corporation in 1902; and Astley Hall, near Chorley in Lancashire, a Tudor house given to the town in 1919 by its family. Manchester acquired the eighteenth-century Heaton Hall as early as 1902, although, as at Aston Hall, the city's principal interest was the parkland.[64] In their approach to these buildings the public authorities were uniformly ambivalent. They did not seek to restore the interiors to any facsimile of their original appearance, instead devising solutions that partially invoked some historic character while concentrating on other purposes. The public history of two historic houses in Northern England – Bolling Hall on the outskirts of Bradford and Hall i' th' Wood near Bolton – exemplifies this equivocation.

Both buildings date from the favoured period: Hall i' th' Wood is a sixteenth-century half-timbered yeoman's house, Bolling a grander building erected from the late Middle Ages to the eighteenth century. Both houses were preserved for their local town by locally based businessmen. Following a period of near-dereliction, Hall i' th' Wood was bought by Lord Leverhulme (then W. H. Lever) in 1899 and after restoration was presented to Bolton Corporation, while Bolling was given to the town in 1912 by George Paley of the long-established and philanthropic Bowling Iron Company, and opened

HALL-I'TH'-WOOD, BOLTON.   *Official Series*

THE MAIN HALL

to the public in 1915. In neither case was the house furnished with appropriate furniture and paintings; rather, a mixture of approaches was adopted (Fig. 248).

The main reason for the acquisition of Hall i' th' Wood was its association with Samuel Crompton, the eighteenth-century weaver-spinner, who had lived there for many years. As the *Museums Journal* explained, 'it was this fact of it being a former residence of Crompton that induced the donor of the building to purchase it for Bolton'.[65] His invention of the spinning mule – which revolutionised the cotton industry by spinning yarn more rapidly and efficiently than any manual worker could achieve – was a principal reason for Lancashire's development as a centre for cotton production, able on account of its humid climate to establish a clear lead over the Midlands from the 1780s onwards. Like Cartwright Hall, ostensibly built to commemorate Edmund Cartwright, Hall i' th' Wood became a shrine to an individual who has since been described as fulfilling 'all the criteria appropriate to the heroic theory of invention, whereby new devices are produced by individual minds and not by impersonal social forces'.[66] As one of the founders of Lan-

cashire's wealth, and indeed of the Industrial Revolution, relatively humble in origin, hardworking and creative, Crompton was an ideal model for the people of Bolton, and the presentation extended the principle of the improving didactic collection into a historic building. The attempt was not universally praised, the *Museums Journal* praising 'the attempts...to restore some of the rooms to the habitable condition of the periods in which they were built', but considering that the 'illustrations of the modern processes of dealing with cotton, some of these exhibits savouring of advertisements' were 'not in keeping with the character of the building'.[67]

At Bolling Hall a different approach was taken, but again historical accuracy was not a priority. The *Museums Journal* reflected on the value of the house as an illustration of social history: 'As each addition to the original building represented a more secure condition of life and property and a greater perception and desire for a larger measure of elegance and domestic convenience and comfort, they [the antiquary and the historian] noted the gradual and marked development in this direction'.[68] This relatively large gentry house was treated as 'the museum

293

249 Bolling Hall, Bradford, West Yorkshire, from *Museums Journal*, November 1915.

of the Bradford people'.[69] In other words, it was a museum of social history, reflecting a new appreciation of the traditions and values of working people under the influence of Skansen, the greatly admired open-air museum of folk life created by Artur Hazelius near Stockholm in the 1890s. In such social history museums, visitors could relish the extended history of their town and appreciate modern progress. Although the house also offered historic interiors containing furniture and historical artefacts, these were arranged without regard for historical accuracy. Visitors were not encouraged to consider in any depth what the house had meant at the different stages of its past, or how its formerly privileged owners had inhabited it. House and display were in permanent disjunction (Fig. 249).

In both these houses, a similar policy was pursued. Both, threatened by urban expansion, were preserved at a time of growing concern about saving relics of the past. Surprisingly enough, however, at a time when the Victoria and Albert Museum and the Bowes Museum were busily acquiring period rooms, they avoided historic installations even in

rooms that survived *in situ*. As with the acquisition of historical portraits, the re-creation of gentlemen's and ladies' dwellings was not a *desideratum* for a Liberal City Council. The study of British history was an admirable activity, as long as it was restricted to the realm of fictitious imaginary paintings or kept within the bounds of the temporary exhibition. Civic museums could use history to present the exemplary hero, to give a sense of national or local identity, to create a sense of patriotism. But the evocation of nostalgia for a baronial past, or of sympathy for an inimical way of life, was not an objective of the city fathers. Their version of history was limited, instructive and aimed at a modern audience.

CONCLUSION

This is a complex and sometimes contradictory narrative, shot through with a fascination with the past that was loaded with difficult issues. Most of the new museums and galleries were sited in new indus-

294

trial towns where a knowledge of history was hardly relevant to the present, particularly since the history that was officially presented at the time enshrined associations with the established Church or with the landed classes that were inimical to the ideals of the museums' founders. Any attempt to understand the past underlay a present that found these histories both alluring and inimical, and that was only partially willing to address the issues that such a study might raise.

PART THREE

THE AFTERMATH

13

A NEW ORDER

With the new century, the steady growth of art museums and art collections continued up to the First World War. There was indeed some sense of innovation. At a national level, the energy of building construction contrasted with the lethargic miserliness that had dogged much of the previous century, with museums making an energetic effort to modernise themselves. A free-standing gallery of British art in the form of the Tate Gallery was finally established in 1897, though in its early days it was hardly a beacon of innovation. Major expansion and modernisation took place in some of the oldest museums: the British Museum opened its noble Edward VII Galleries, designed by John Burnet, in 1914, while the Victoria and Albert Museum (as the South Kensington Museum was renamed in 1899) demolished or concealed its Victorian interiors in favour of a clean, stripped-down look.[1] In a modest but revealing campaign, the National Portrait Gallery removed 'the old, dirty, green wall-paper' from its walls to reveal panelling, which, painted white, made a sympathetic background for the re-hung paintings and broached the idea of an atmospheric setting.[2] The old universities took an equally vigorous approach: the Ashmolean Museum was transformed by its new archaeology galleries 'from an enchanting junk shop into a most important and up-to-date institution',[3] while the Fitzwilliam Museum under Sydney Cockerell

became one of the most elegant and innovative art museums in Britain (Fig. 250). And Wales finally gained a National Museum in Cardiff, founded in 1905 but not opened to the public until 1922.[4]

These expressions of confidence were reflected in regional cities. Superficially, at least, the torrent of museum foundations and new public collections that had marked the late Victorian period seemed to be unchecked. While the larger cities almost all possessed public galleries by 1900, smaller towns that lacked them remained anxious to acquire this mark of civic good breeding. In the North these included mill towns in the vicinity of Manchester, as well as Bradford and Newcastle upon Tyne. In the South, new galleries were set up in the biscuit-manufacturing town of Reading, in old-established pleasure resorts such as Worthing and Bath, and in the naval city of Plymouth, while the ancient but by this time somnolent city of Bristol finally acquired a gallery. Nor was there any halt in donations and bequests. In 1912, for example, a large collection of paintings, including many nineteenth-century French works, was bequeathed to Barnsley by the philanthropist S. J. Cooper, son of a local industrialist, who was faithful to the old values of civic loyalty and narrative painting. In Birmingham a flood of gifts and bequests, mostly traditional in character, arrived at the Gallery, including English watercolours, Pre-Raphaelite works and paintings by Ford

250 The Upper Marlay Gallery
at the Fitzwilliam Museum,
Cambridge, in about 1931, arranged
in the aesthetic manner with
paintings hung on the (surviving)
gold-toned fabric, and furniture
and carpets chosen to create a
harmonious interior.

Madox Brown, Lawrence Alma-Tadema and B.W. Leader (whose *February Fill Dyke*, bequeathed in 1914, was to be seen by radical critics as the epitome of false Victorian art).

In architectural terms, the old order still ruled in the museum world. Much of this new construction retained the eclectic conservatism that had marked earlier generations, with an imperialistic agenda informing national buildings. The Victoria and Albert Museum's assertive new entrance front on the Cromwell Road, designed by Aston Webb in an indefinable style, was embellished with statues of the royal family flanked by a pantheon of British artists. The British Museum's Edward VII Galleries, adorned with crowns and royal coats of arms, were conceived of as the focal point for a victory parade route, with a saluting gallery above the new entrance – a remarkably militaristic statement for a museum. Equally, the architecture of the Tate Gallery expressed national pride rather than any wavering new ideas. No commissions for museums went to Charles Rennie Mackintosh or the leading Arts and Crafts designers. Only a few museum buildings used a new language, notably a trio of galleries completed between 1901 and 1904 and situated outside national or local government: the Whitechapel Art Gallery in east London and the

Horniman Museum in south London, both by Charles Harrison Townsend, and the Watts Gallery in Compton, Surrey, by an amateur architect, Christopher Hatton Turnor (Fig. 251). Respectively urban, suburban and rural in setting, the three buildings were broadly influenced by the Arts and Crafts movement. They allowed the needs of the interior to shape the elevations, experimented with materials (the Watts Gallery is constructed completely in concrete, the Whitechapel was designed to be richly decorated in mosaic) and externally and internally avoided symmetry or overt reference to past architectural styles (Fig. 252). The buildings were admired by contemporaries, the Watts being praised as 'that almost ideal gallery',[5] while the *Studio* wrote of the Whitechapel that 'While eschewing any positive historical style, Mr Townsend has succeeded in being thoroughly architectural, not to say monumental, in his design.'[6] But this was a small, eccentric group of commissions, resulting from the licence associated with private and non-statist patronage: the main stream of regional galleries tended to be traditional in design and modern in technology.

MUSEUMS AND THEIR PUBLICS

In many respects, however, the ideal of a philanthropic Liberal-inspired gallery for the improvement of simple people was under threat. The early years of the new century were marked by a new egalitarianism in regional galleries, notably in their attitude to ownership, reflecting the Fabian Society's belief in the gradualist shift of the national economy and public services towards collectivism. Regarded in the past in Britain as politically insignificant, museums came to be seen as symbolising the transference of property from the few to the many (a transference reflected in the gradual increase in the rate of taxation, greatly deplored by the rich). This point of view was variously expressed. Educationally, it was reflected in the move away from training artists and artisans towards the non-vocational enjoyment of art for the public at large. When exhibitions of contemporary British art were organised at the Whitechapel in 1910 and 1914, middle-class critics expressed scepticism over the validity of showing avant-garde work to a working-class

251 The Horniman Museum, London. Designed by Charles Harrison Townsend to house the collections of the tea trader Frederick Horniman and opened in 1901, the Horniman exemplified innovative thinking in museum architecture that aimed to make them as welcoming and enjoyable as possible. It abandoned the classical and 'Renaissance' language of much museum architecture in favour of a free style of design.

252 Whitechapel Art Gallery. The Gallery originated in a series of loan art exhibitions organised by Canon Samuel Barnett and Henrietta Barnett for the inhabitants of Whitechapel. The success of the exhibitions led to the erection of a permanent Gallery in 1897–9.

253 'Nippers' photographed at the Whitechapel Art Gallery by Horace Warner in about 1901.

audience, but the events attracted crowds, suggesting that it might no longer be necessary to offer sweetened, facile interpretations of art for people with a limited formal education, in the way the Barnetts had done (Fig. 253).[7]

On a more political note, the people's ownership of their galleries and museums was a much-repeated trope at a time when, as Jordanna Bailkin has shown, the status of art as property was a sensitive field.[8] Just as Robert Crawford in 1891 asserted the Glasgow public's ownership of the city's galleries, this position was resoundingly affirmed in 1902 by the mouthpiece of the emergent curatorial profession. For the *Museums Journal*, 'Museums are now-a-days the most democratic and socialistic possessions of the people. All have equal access to them, peer and peasant receive the same privileges and treatment, each one contributes in direct proportion to his means to their maintenance, and each has a feeling of individual proprietorship.'[9] Such plainly stated hostility to the old order and desire for change had seldom been heard in a decorous professional journal, at least within the museum world. No

longer were the public, and particularly the working classes, to be admitted as an act of generous patronage and then benevolently surveyed; now, the galleries were theirs.

Ironically, while the people's ownership was being affirmed, the public appeared, if not to shun the curator's embrace, at least to view it with scepticism. With the new century, the number of visitors began a steady decline, even though by the 1890s most galleries were open on Sundays. In Bradford, annual attendances fell from 800,000 at the opening to 600,000 in 1910, and a mere 400,000 in 1913. When a new art gallery opened in the relatively small town of Bury in 1901 it attracted 142,000 people in the first year but by 1910 the Public Library and Art Gallery Committee was regretting 'the steady fall in the attendances which has been so evident during the past few years' and was experimenting with various ways, notably temporary exhibitions, of sustaining interest.[10] A large gallery such as Birmingham which had the resources to mount ambitious temporary displays kept its attendances at a relatively high level, but even there

302

254 The Great Western Arcade, Birmingham. Built in 1876, the arcade and its surrounding streets reflect the city's increasing wealth and the creation of attractive environments for shopping in regional centres.

picture developed rapidly, via showings of short comic films at vaudevilles and fairgrounds to permanent picture palaces. By 1917 there were 4,500 cinemas in the country, often providing entertainment for young people who no doubt enjoyed the freedom of darkness to engage in non-cultural activities (much as art galleries were often the site of amatory encounters).[12] But cinemas were not the only popular attraction. Music halls, more decorous than in the past, were 'at the height of their popularity, providing clean family entertainment for all classes, every age group, and both sexes'.[13] The dates suggest that the climax of the Victorian galleries' popularity fitted neatly between the early period of the nineteenth century, when the theatre exerted a strong appeal for all social levels before becoming socially disreputable, and the age of the moving picture.

Two years after the Bradford conference, the Liverpool Art Gallery's *Annual Report* echoed the earlier presidential statement, attributing the steady fall in attendances at the Autumn Exhibition to both 'the attractions of the numerous picture palaces' and 'the tendency on the part of many to spend their leisure time motoring'.[14] It was hoped that the 'shrinkage' would be 'merely transitory'. Throughout the country, increased mobility and greater affluence encouraged sophisticated urban shopping (Fig. 254) and such new crazes as cycling. A further challenge came from the mounting popularity of spectator sport, generally regulated on class lines and symbolised by the inauguration of the Football Association cup in 1871 and the first visit to Britain by an Australian cricket eleven, in 1878.[15] The football teams in major cities had been established at the same period as the art museums: Glasgow Rangers in 1873, Aston Villa in Birmingham in 1874, Manchester United (under another name) in 1878. Small-scale at first, by the 1880s they were increasingly professional and attracting huge crowds (almost exclusively male) who evidently found a match between Aston Villa and Woolwich Arsenal more exciting than a repeat visit to the local collection of narrative paintings. The erection of Manchester United's stadium in 1910 at Old Trafford on the site of the Manchester Art Treasures Exhibition may be construed as a symbol of the passing of mass cultural education in favour of mass sporting entertainment (Fig. 255).

in the decade before the First World War these averaged slightly over 400,000 compared to over a million in 1888.

In the view of prominent museum figures, this decline was the fault of new, competing, attractions. As the President of the Local Government Board told the Museums Association in Bradford in 1910, people were more quick-witted and under greater stress than in the past. Repeating a key Victorian message, he said that museums retained a vital role in the education of the people, both intellectual and moral: 'Museums were absolutely essential if they were to provide for the great mass of the people a nobler way of spending their leisure time than the public-house.' The current threat to the local museum was only a temporary one: 'The new craze was the cinema picture palace, but the art gallery was better still. One picture by Watts, or a tapestry by William Morris, was better than a whole field of panorama picture palaces.'[11] Like this worthy official, most commentators ascribed the drop in popularity to competition rather than to any failings in the museums themselves. The competition was certainly strong. After the first screening of a film in Britain in 1896 the popularity of the motion

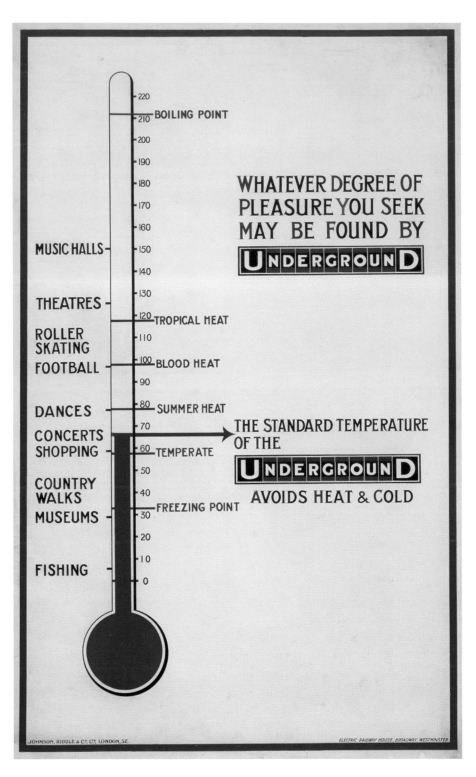

220
210 BOILING POINT
200
190
180
170
160
MUSIC HALLS 150
140
130
THEATRES 120 TROPICAL HEAT
ROLLER SKATING 110
FOOTBALL 100 BLOOD HEAT
90
DANCES 80 SUMMER HEAT
70
CONCERTS
SHOPPING 60 TEMPERATE
50
COUNTRY WALKS 40
FREEZING POINT
MUSEUMS 30
20
10
FISHING 0

WHATEVER DEGREE OF
PLEASURE YOU SEEK
MAY BE FOUND BY
UNDERGROUND

THE STANDARD TEMPERATURE
OF THE
UNDERGROUND
AVOIDS HEAT & COLD

JOHNSON, RIDDLE & Cº Lᵀᴰ LONDON, S.E.

ELECTRIC RAILWAY HOUSE, BROADWAY, WESTMINSTER

255 *The Temperature of the
Underground* by an unknown artist,
1912. Museums feature low on this
chart, suggesting that by then they
were losing their allure.

the status of women, and Scottish and Irish public identity, the Liberalism that had fuelled the creation of provincial galleries seemed increasingly less valid, just as the hallowed writings of John Ruskin were losing their appeal. The idea that art enshrined a set of moral and political values that could be used for the improvement of society no longer persuaded.

In other ways, public art galleries did not seem the sources of reassurance they had once been. The sense of anxiety in the public arena was expressed in various ways in the field of art museums and art collecting, which remained the subject of continuing press interest. The problem, for a country that prided itself on its superiority to other cultures, was the threat of being outdone by foreign nations. For the specialist press, what might be interpreted either as a failure of confidence or as a new open-mindedness was apparent in a change of outlook towards the United States. In 1876 the *Art Journal* had commented on the construction 'in several of the chief cities, [of] museums on a comprehensive scale' and recommended patronisingly that they should 'study the experience of the Old World'.[17] A generation later, a growing sense of inferiority was apparent over the organisation and collections of art galleries in Britain in comparison with France, Germany or America: as Bailkin has written, 'The national sense of failure in artistic matters was overwhelming by the end of the nineteenth century.'[18] A critic commented in 1898 that 'though neither Boston, nor Washington, nor even New York are yet art centres in any way comparable to London, or Paris, or Munich, the time is not far distant when the inevitable must happen', and suggested that in terms of their art treasures 'the great cities of the States are already beyond our own provincial cities and towns'.[19] By this date American museums were regularly pointed to as models of how art museums should develop: in 1899 the *Art Journal* described the new Carnegie Art Gallery in Pittsburgh (Figs 256, 257) as 'one of the finest of the many noble buildings in the United States, and vastly superior to our "pepperbox" National Gallery'.[20] This was only one among many encomia. After the First World War, Sir Frederic Kenyon, Director of the British Museum, writing a retrospective account of libraries and museums, concluded that 'In America the technique of the museum has reached its highest level. The spread of museums has coincided in time with that of our own country,

Perhaps, however, the most potent, though least visible, factor in the decline of the Victorian museum and art gallery was the phenomenon that Jordanna Bailkin has defined as the crisis of Liberalism.[16] Over many issues, notably definitions of ownership,

256 Plan of the Carnegie Institute, Pittsburgh from James D. Van Trump, *An American Palace of Culture: The Carnegie Institute and Carnegie Library of Pittsburgh* (1907).

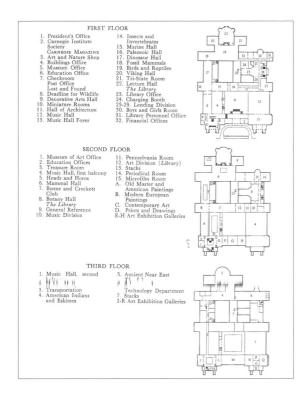

FIRST FLOOR

1. President's Office
2. Carnegie Institute Society
   CARNEGIE MAGAZINE
3. Art and Nature Shop
4. Buildings Office
5. Museum Office
6. Education Office
7. Checkroom
   Post Office
   Lost and Found
8. Deadline for Wildlife
9. Decorative Arts Hall
10. Miniature Rooms
11. Hall of Architecture
12. Music Hall
13. Music Hall Foyer

14. Insects and Invertebrates
15. Marine Hall
16. Paleozoic Hall
17. Dinosaur Hall
18. Fossil Mammals
19. Birds and Reptiles
20. Viking Hall
21. Tri-State Room
22. Lecture Hall
    The Library
23. Library Office
24. Charging Booth
25-29. Lending Division
30. Boys and Girls Room
31. Library Personnel Office
32. Financial Offices

SECOND FLOOR

1. Museum of Art Office
2. Education Offices
3. Treasure Room
4. Music Hall, first balcony
5. Heads and Horns
6. Mammal Hall
7. Boone and Crockett Club
   The Library
8. Botany Hall
9. General Reference
10. Music Division

11. Pennsylvania Room
12. Art Division (*Library*)
13. Stacks
14. Periodical Room
15. Microfilm Room
A. Old Master and American Paintings
B. Modern European Paintings
C. Contemporary Art
D. Prints and Drawings
E-H Art Exhibition Galleries

THIRD FLOOR

1. Music Hall, second
3. Transportation
4. American Indians and Eskimos

5. Ancient Near East
6. Technology Department
7. Stacks
I-R Art Exhibition Galleries

257 The Hall of Sculpture, 1907, at the Carnegie Institute, Pittsburgh.

but with greater space, more liberal pecuniary support, and wider public interest, it has attained a scale with which no other country can compete.'[21] Many years had passed since an observer of the museum scene could imply the inferiority of the United States – not least because the regional art museums of Britain, as critics regularly pointed out, were not developing with the vigour and success of their American equivalents.

The art market mirrored the threat created by foreign economic and military competition. A loss of confidence was created from the 1880s onwards by the sale of works of art from private collections, to Germany and later to the United States.[22] It was a development agonised over by the press. When the National Art-Collections Fund was founded in 1903 to raise money for buying works of art for British galleries, this was a characteristically private initiative in the face of dithering indifference from Government, and persisted a series of hand-wringing lamentations over the incapacity of a once boldly acquisitive nation to retain its artistic possessions. This incapacity came to symbolise a broader national decline.[23]

A NEW SPIRIT?

The threat to the Victorian art museum did not come only from the changing tastes of the public. With the new century and the death of Queen Victoria in 1901, it was felt 'that the end of a great epoch has come upon us'.[24] This was a period of national self-questioning as the optimistic teleology of the latter years of the nineteenth century was shaken by the revelation that over half the volunteers for service in the Boer War were physically unfit for military service.[25] The new century was marked by the election of radical Liberal Governments, which introduced state pensions and fiscal reform, including higher taxation for the very rich, and curbed the powers of the House of Lords. The period also saw mounting trade union militancy, with violent strikes in 1911 and 1912; the steady rise of the Labour Party, which in the January 1910 election won forty seats; and the campaign for female suffrage.

At a national level, these turbulent years witnessed extreme conservatism and xenophobia. An extended campaign was fought on behalf of public purity by such bodies as the National Vigilance Association, which set itself up as 'England's moral watchdog'.[26] Censorship of the stage and of books was enforced with practical if not intellectual rigour: England was the last European country to permit public staging of Ibsen's *Ghosts*. In the field of the visual arts this form of conservatism was rampant. The famous 1910 exhibition *Manet and the Post-Impressionists* elicited violent reactions even from such cultivated men as Robert Ross, art critic for the *Morning Post* and editor of Oscar Wilde's works: 'if the movement is spreading...it should be treated like the rat plague in Suffolk. The source of infection [the pictures] ought to be destroyed.'[27] Many of the early reviews suggested that the Post-Impressionists were childlike, impostors or mentally deficient. On the other hand, Britain was exposed to many artistically revolutionary influences from overseas, notably the Ballets Russes, and within the field of the visual arts, attitudes did shift. Between 1910 and Fry's *Post-Impressionist Exhibition* of 1912 the early contempt softened into a willingness to consider the possibilities of this new style of art. And, as we shall see, regional galleries had an important role to play in these developments.

A new spirit is apparent in publications, which amplified the coverage already offered for many years by the *Art Journal* and the *Magazine of Art*.[28] From 1893 the *Studio* acted as a champion of Arts and Crafts design and contemporary painting and sculpture. More academic in character was the *Connoisseur*, set up in 1901 and intended as a 'magazine for collectors', unprovided for even though their numbers had increased 'by leaps and bounds'.[29] The most influential new publication was probably the *Burlington Magazine*, launched in 1903. Although the art press had been active in the nineteenth century, Britain had had no scholarly equivalent to the *Gazette des Beaux-Arts*, launched in France in 1859, or the *Zeitschrift für bildende Kunst*, published in Germany from 1866.[30] The *Burlington* aimed to publish academic articles on the received canon of Western art, to investigate other cultures or to discuss current issues in frequently trenchant editorials. In the first issue the editor bemoaned the 'sameness' of modern life and art, including among his strictures the works shown at the Academy, which 'all emit the same odour of false sentiment...For the most part...our artists... deal in fatuities, mild parlour jests, tit-bits of curiosity, "A baby crab," "A merry jest," "Where there's a will there's a way".'[31] Coolly dismissive of the recent past, the *Burlington* offered Britain a newly rigorous approach to art history that was to bear fruit in

the foundation of the Courtauld Institute in 1932 and the establishment of the Warburg Institute in London in 1934. It did not ignore provincial galleries, publishing a series of articles on their modest achievements and lack of purpose.

Certain names recur in the exhibitions and publications of Britain early in the twentieth century: the smallness of this world was reflected in the discussions about the directorships of national museums, which considered a very restricted number of candidates. Apart from Clive Bell and Roger Fry, the most prominent figures included Michael Sadler, Vice-Chancellor of Leeds University from 1911 to 1923, champion of contemporary art, friend of Wassily Kandinsky and closely linked with Germany; Frank Rutter, art critic, promoter of Impressionist painting and museum director; Charles Holroyd, artist, the first Keeper of the Tate Gallery and later Director of the National Gallery; D.S. MacColl, critic and Holroyd's successor at the Tate Gallery; Charles Holmes, artist, critic, Director of the National Portrait Gallery and Holroyd's successor at the National Gallery; and Sydney Cockerell, Director of the Fitzwilliam Museum. Though these men did not always agree (Cézanne was a particular subject of contention), they knew one another well and regularly collaborated. Several were members of the New English Art Club, Fry and Holmes were both closely involved with the *Burlington Magazine*, while Rutter and Sadler worked together to promote contemporary art in Leeds. They were responsible for introducing a new approach to the visual arts, an approach that extended to the *Museums Journal* and thence to regional museums. Most relevantly, several worked as directors or curators in national or regional museums, where they applied a breadth of knowledge unavailable to the Dyalls or Birketts of the previous generation. As the twentieth century advanced, directors and curators became increasingly well-trained and well-informed, with power passing from council committees to staff.

THE REJECTION OF VICTORIAN ART AND PATRONAGE

Within municipal galleries, the attitudes of a new generation of art critics and artists towards Victorian art struck a fatal blow. For such leaders of taste

258 *The Doctor* by Luke Fildes, 1890–1. Oil on canvas, 166.4 × 241.9 cm. Sir Henry Tate commissioned a painting on any subject from Fildes. Fildes recalled the devoted care shown by the doctor looking after the artist's first son, who died, aged one, in 1877. The painting is a celebration of the medical profession (Tate Galleries).

(as they proved to be), the collections in municipal galleries were, by and large, objects of derision, the collectors had been damagingly misguided, and the context for creating works of art had become distorted. If what is admired by the élite generally comes in course of time to be admired by a broad audience, then the rejection in Britain of Victorian narrative art in favour of Impressionism and Post-Impressionism is a notable instance. Although critics might not always agree on the new schools of art, they did agree about Victorian popular-academic art (that is to say, the kind of naturalistic art that obeyed the basic principles of academic art but was aimed at a popular audience). For Clive Bell, writing in 1913, 'the mass of painting and sculpture had sunk to something that no intelligent and cultivated person would dream of calling art'.[32] He singled out Luke Fildes's *The Doctor* (Fig. 258): it was 'not a work of art…it is worse than nugatory because the emotion it suggests is false…It is sentimental…the state of mind to which it is a means, as illustration, appears to me undesirable'.[33] The distinguished museum curator and connoisseur Sidney Colvin developed the theme.[34] While he

allowed some credibility to late Pre-Raphaelite painting, he dismissed popular-academic narrative art as a superficial version of narrative writing:

In the then state of English painting, the appeal…to the sense of visible beauty or significance in things…was made almost exclusively in the representation of remote or romantic subjects…But from the average popular art depicting scenes and figures of ordinary life the attempt to appeal to such sense had almost entirely passed away, and people had got used to looking at pictures not for any truly pictorial value they might possess, but simply for the sake of the story they more or less expressively told or the scenery they more or less accurately reproduced. The result was a kind of shallow reflection of obvious aspects of life and nature, leaving out all the character which more finely attuned senses could discern in daily things or a more active power of selection and arrangement impose on them.[35]

For these critics, true art had nothing to do with narrative: a formalist approach, applied through the appreciation of 'significant form', was the only valid one. The essential message of these attacks was that so-called Victorian art was no such thing, that art was not about subject-matter or social improvement but about looking and developing an intensity of vision that allowed one to see the world differently. For most young artists, eager to experiment, Victorian art offered nothing.

One of the faults of the Victorian system was seen to be the system of patronage. In Fry's opinion the plutocratic patron of the nineteenth century had encouraged 'a race new in the history of the world, a race for whom no name has yet been found, a race of psuedo-artists [sic]'.[36] In strong language for the time, Fry continued, 'As the prostitute professes to sell love, so these gentlemen professed to sell beauty, and they and their patrons rollicked good-humouredly through the Victorian era.' MacColl enlarged on the theme, suggesting that 'the taste of the new community [the newly rich Victorians] was much of it raw and artless. The best artists have often suffered neglect, while the wealthy spent their money on shallow and ephemeral art'.[37] In this climate, the 'work of the truly creative artist…appears to be noxious and unassimilable'.[38] These were the patrons and the works of art that had shaped the provincial art gallery.

Art museums were culpable in other ways, notably their encouragement of false erudition. In the spirit of the Italian Futurists, whose diatribes against museums were being published contemporaneously, Fry and Bell were sceptical of all museums, which were seen to foster misleading reactions to works of art. For Fry, they encouraged an ignorant love of 'patina', rather than inspiring a feeling for the new.[39] For Bell, museums led experts (and by extension, the public) to approach works of art in an irrelevant way; they turned works of art into specimens. In an attack on the irrelevant criteria of the art market and the cult of the subject painting, Bell declared that anyone who had had the misfortune to be 'led into the haunts of collectors and experts' would have been exposed to such questions about a painting as:

By whom was it made? For whom was it made? When was it made? Where was it made? Who paid for it? How much did he pay? Through what collections has it passed? What are the names of the figures portrayed? What are their histories?

What the style and cut of their coats, breeches, and beards? How much will it fetch at Christie's? All these are questions to moot; and mooted they will be, by the hour. But in expert conclaves who has ever heard more than a perfunctory and silly comment on the aesthetic qualities of a master-piece?[40]

Bell did not restrict himself to advocating 'blowing out of the museums and galleries the dust of erudition and the stale incense of hero-worship', which diverted observers away from the essence of a work of art through 'irrelevant' circumstantial information (though later generations, reacting against this formalist approach, would find such information compelling).[41] The 'aesthetic emotions' must be released from the 'pernicious nonsense' of believing that a work of art could be understood only when interpreted through artificial scholarship. He attacked the style of art interpretation that had been built up late in the nineteenth century and was being developed in museums and galleries 'by the schoolmasters and the newspapers, by cheap text-books and profound historians, by district visitors and cabinet ministers, by clergymen and secularists, by labour leaders, tee-totallers, anti-gamblers, and public benefactors of every sort'.[42] It is a revealing list, throwing together education, the press, politicians and social improvers, a juxtaposition that associated the purveyors of well-meaning popular instruction not only with 'public benefactors' but with established systems of power. The information offered by such people made it impossible for the public to 'approach works of art courageously and to judge them on their merits', in other words to respond naturally to the visual image.[43] Particularly to blame were those who sought to instruct children:

Who is not familiar with those little flocks of victims clattering and shuffling through the galleries, inspissating the gloom of the museum atmosphere? What is being done to their native sensibilities by the earnest bear-leader with his (or her) catalogue of dates and names and appropriate comments?…In the guise of what grisly and incomprehensible charlatan is art being presented to the people?[44]

In such a context there was no place for the 'genuine emotion' that art should inspire.

Such attacks exploded the foundations of the Victorian gallery, dismissing not only its works of art but its modes of instruction. For these critics, art was not an instrumentalist device for improving the lives of the poor and uneducated: its aims were quite different, harder to attain but eventually open to all.

VICTORIAN SURVIVAL

To an extent, these attacks exploded the hopes of the old guard. It was true that vested interests, financial and psychological, in maintaining old-established values did ensure some continuity. The Victorian giants were not immediately toppled in ӏ̤er̥ large am̤ounts were still paid well i̤nto the new century for mainstream artists such as Leighton and Millais by wealthy collectors such as Lady Tate and Lord Leverhulme, buying for the Tate Gallery and the Lady Lever Art Gallery respectively. For such a stalwart champion of the old values as Charles Rowley, a former Manchester councillor, looking back from 1910 over fifty years of municipal improvements, the new art appearing in London and elsewhere was an outrage:

> Slade professors, Mr. Ruskin himself, have let loose a lot of jabbering about Art which has become a flood of blatant, nauseous, misleading rhetoric. Recent examples of this baneful tendency have been the terrible gushes about "impressionism," and that lowest phase of human impudence, post-impressionism.[45]

His views, no more extreme than those of critics in the national press, must have been echoed in many council chambers. Equally, the old guard entrenched in Burlington House did not surrender easily. In a test case, in 1903 the trustees of the Chantrey Bequest were accused by critics, including MacColl, of having misappropriated its funds. The issue was contested publicly and at length, not least by a committee of the House of Lords, but the trustees refused to budge.

In spite of these rearguard actions, the financial value of Victorian works of art did begin to waver, a reliable indication of failure in a context where the worth of collections had regularly been stated in terms of pounds, shillings and pence. When a Landseer that had sold for £7,350 in 1883 made only £2,520 in 1909 – and a drop of this sort was characteristic of the fate of many oils, though not yet watercolours – 'safe' investments in nineteenth-century art were clearly safe no longer. This process reached its climax after the First World War. Writing about his directorship of Leeds City Art Gallery in the early 1930s, John Rothenstein (later Director of the Tate Gallery) remarked that members of his committee, while remaining fond of the Victorian paintings they had grown up with, 'could not remain unaffected by their fate in the sale-room and by the evident determination of persons not always otherwise distinguished by civic spirit to present or bequeath them to civic institutions'.[46]

EXHIBITIONS IN THE REGIONS – A CHANGE OF ATTITUDE

As it grew evident that the old style of collecting was losing its appeal, municipal galleries attracted the attention of the proponents of the new forms of art.[47] As Camille Pissarro wrote to his son Lucien in 1891, 'The provinces in England are more sympathetic to innovators – it is just the opposite in France, where the provinces are so bourgeois and pusillanimous.'[48] It is revealing that the Honorary Committee for Fry's *Manet and the Post Impressionists* included, along with the Directors of the National Gallery and the Wallace Collection, Parisian art dealers and such eminent critics as Harry Graf Kessler of Berlin, both James Paton and Whitworth Wallis, a testimony to their reputations.

Led by a small group of enterprising curators, regional art galleries assumed a role as venues for exhibitions of contemporary art, both British and international. They played an important part in making it better known, particularly since the leading London art museums showed no enterprise in this direction. Exhibitions were on the whole the province of curators, who were able to experiment more adventurously than they could over acquisitions. The leading examples appear to have been the result of the work of enterprising avant-garde curators, often battling against aldermanic reaction. At Brighton Museum and Art Gallery, Henry Roberts, the energetic Chief Librarian and Curator

259 A page from the catalogue of the innovative exhibition *Modern French Artists* held at Brighton Art Gallery in 1910.

Gaston Prunier
85 Le Parlement, Londres—The Houses of Parliament, London ... 32 0 0
Water-colour.

Jean Boldini
86 Portrait d'homme—Portrait of a man
Lent by Comte Robert de Montesquiou-Fezensac.

Abel Truchet
87 Nature morte—Still life ... 40 0 0

Charles Milcendeau
88 Famille sarde—A Sardinian family ... 200 0 0

Gaston Prunier
89 Paysage de montagne, Pyrénées—Mountains in the Pyrenees ... 32 0 0
Water-colour.

Henri Caro-Delvaille
90 Fleurs dans un vase—Flowers in a vase ... 32 0 0
Lent by M. Georges Bernheim.

Lucien Simon
91 Les foins—Haymaking. ... 240 0 0
Lent by MM. Bernheim-Jeune et Cie.

Edmond Aman-Jean
92 Portrait d'enfants—Portraits of the artist's children.

Charles Milcendeau
93 Coup de filet corse—A Corsican haul ... 120 0 0

Henry Caro-Delvaille
94 Étude de femme nue—Study ... 120 0 0
Lent by M. Georges Bernheim.

Paul Madeline
95 Port Breton—A Breton port ... 28 0 0

20

Gustave Colin
96 Rêverie ... 60 0 0
Lent by M. Jacques Moleux.

Claude Monet
97 Le verger—The orchard ... 800 0
Lent by M. J. Hessel.

Eugène Boudin
98 Bénerville ... 400 0 0
Lent by MM. Bernheim-Jeune et Cie.

Jean-Baptiste-Camille Corot (1796-1875)
99 Sunset
Lent by W. B. Chamberlin, Esq.

Monticelli
100 Fête Champêtre.
Lent by Miss Chamberlin.

Camille Pissarro (1830-1903)
101 La charrette de foin—The hay cart ... 120 0 0
Lent by MM. Durand-Ruel et Fils.

Jean-François Raffaëlli
102 La Seine à Paris—The Seine at Paris ... 200 0 0

Henri Morisset
103 Portraits de Madame S. et de son fils.
Lent by M. A. T. Swann.

Alfred Sisley (1839-1899)
104 La route de Verrières ... 480 0 0
Lent by MM. Durand-Ruel et Fils.
105 Le coteau de Bois des Rochers ... 400 0 0
Lent by M. J. Hessel.

André Dauchez
106 Kerandran, Bretagne—Kerandran, Brittany ... 60 0 0

Jean-Baptiste-Camille Corot (1796-1875)
107 Woody landscape.
Lent by the Corporation of Glasgow.

21

appointed in 1906, inaugurated a series of exhibitions intended to introduce advanced foreign art to the British public.[49] He outlined his policy in the *Museums Journal*, deploring the 'rut' into which exhibitions had fallen in Britain on account of the general ignorance of artistic activities overseas.[50] One of the most innovative of his exhibitions was *Modern French Artists* (1910), curated by Robert Dell, previously the first editor of the *Burlington Magazine*, who was living in France as Paris correspondent of the *Manchester Guardian*. It presented 120 artists, many of them unknown in Britain, including the major Impressionists and Post-Impressionists as well as later artists such as Matisse, Vlaminck and Rouault (Fig. 259). The exhibition attracted primarily local interest (and censure), but Roberts followed it with other shows, including in 1913 *English Post-Impressionists, Cubists and Others*. As with other exhibition organisers, he sought to absorb British artists in the enunciation of an international movement.

Such innovation was not limited to Brighton. Leeds had already been distinguished by the creation in 1903 of the Leeds Art Club, a small and active group led by the remarkable figures of Alfred Orage, a Leeds schoolmaster, and Holbrook Jackson,

then working in the Leeds lace trade. The club brought together professional people (including many teachers) to attend lectures by such figures as W.B. Yeats, G.K. Chesterton and Bernard Shaw and become acquainted with contemporary developments in European art and thought. Though both Orage and Jackson soon left Leeds for careers as writers and journalists in London, the club continued. It represented a new version of the learned societies of the eighteenth and early nineteenth centuries, included many women members, studied developments overseas, and showed 'an intense antipathy to nineteenth-century Liberalism, with what they believed was its moral hypocrisy, its smug belief in perpetual progress but mostly its philistinism'.[51] Liberal values were seen to reduce art to a cretinous instrumentalism. The club's influence extended to such notable figures from Yorkshire and elsewhere as Herbert Read and William Rothenstein. It was active in the visual arts, especially after Frank Rutter's arrival at the City Art Gallery and the installation of the distinguished educationalist Michael Sadler as Vice-Chancellor of Leeds University. Rutter and Sadler initiated a series of contemporary art exhibitions.[52] These included in 1912

Modern Paintings and Drawings: in a spirit of aggression towards everything represented by the Academy, the catalogue made a violent attack on the Chantrey Bequest. They followed with a *Loan Exhibition of Post-Impressionist Pictures and Drawings* organised in 1913 at the Leeds Art Club, which showed Toulouse-Lautrec, Cézanne, Van Gogh, Gauguin, Picasso and Kandinsky, lithographs by Matisse and photographs by Picasso, and work by advanced British artists such as Charles Ginner and Spencer Gore.[53] Such activities were not to the taste of Rutter's municipal committee, which refused to give him even the £30 he requested towards the cost of an exhibition of models and designs by the avant-garde theatrical designer Edward Gordon Craig.[54]

Rutter recorded in his memoirs that as a young man his artistic life had been transformed by an exhibition at Wolverhampton in 1902, one of the 'two exhibitions of modern art which have most deeply stirred me'.[55] This was the Fine Art section of an Industrial Art Exhibition, curated by Laurence Hodson, a local scholar, collector and associate of William Morris – and also a brewer and business-man – who was described by Rutter as 'one of the most enlightened and far-seeing patrons of the art of his own time'. Rutter was delighted to find that 'popular Academicians' had given way to such advanced painters as Philip Wilson Steer, William Orpen, Charles Conder, William Nicholson, William Rothenstein and Augustus John, along with sculptors including Rodin. The catalogue's 'Remarks on the Greater Movements in English Art' explained that many of the artists had been taught by Alphonse Legros, and concluded that the visitor who had traced the development of English art to the final room 'cannot…leave this last Room without feeling that England's artistic outlook was never so full of splendid promise as it is to-day'.[56] According to Rutter, this display 'dealt a very severe blow to the prestige of the Royal Academy' in that having 'meekly followed wherever the Academy chose to lead', the provincial galleries came to realise that outside the Academy existed 'a number of painters of very high distinction'.[57]

Rutter and his colleagues were not interested only in contemporary art: they also studied historic artists and notably British ones. A revealing example of the new scholarly approach was a Constable exhibition organised at Leeds in 1913.[58] It included 132 oils as well as twenty etchings after Constable, reflecting a sophisticated interest in the broader impact of the artist. Loans were secured from the National Gallery, Manchester and Glasgow, the Royal Academy, and private owners. The exhibition was made possible by a network of supporters, including Holmes, who was thanked for sharing his knowledge and experience. The catalogue remarked on the difficulties of such an enterprise: many of Constable's pictures had been exported to the United States, the numerous forgeries were hard to detect, and owners were unwilling to have their pictures moved at a time of international unrest. While this was a relatively cautious enterprise in the choice of artist, it indicated the development within enlightened provincial museums of an informed approach to art and art history, based not on the easy availability of works of art or their commercial potential, but on scholarship. It represented a great advance on the pell-mell selection of works lent more or less indiscriminately from local collections.

Even though many of these exhibitions offered works for sale, they made relatively little impact on public collecting, reflecting the customary caution of art galleries faced with works by an untested artist. At Brighton, the Fine Arts Sub-committee could have bought from *Modern French Artists* a Monet, Renoir or Sisley for less than £500, but they preferred *Swans at Play* by Gaston La Touche, an artist on the fringes of the Impressionist circle who was producing pretty pastoral scenes. At Leeds, Rutter's committee insisted on accepting a sixth painting by Atkinson Grimshaw but refused a Charles Shannon drawing offered by the National Art-Collections Fund. When Rutter remonstrated, his Chairman 'indignantly snorted, "We don't want bits of things like this in the gallery: we only want important pictures".' Although a public lecture by the novelist and collector Michael Sadleir (son of Michael Sadler) in June 1913 urged the purchase of works from the exhibition, nothing was acquired.[59] In reaction, Rutter and Sadler founded the Leeds Art Collections Fund to allow the purchase of works without interference from councillors. It is not surprising that Rutter felt that provincial galleries should 'cut adrift from municipal politics' in favour of boards of trustees.[60]

This abandonment of the old tradition of buying from one's own exhibitions reflected the unwillingness of municipal galleries (as of the Tate Gallery) to acquire work with the faintest claim to modernity until some time after the First World War: the first paintings by W. R. Sickert, a symbolic leader of the new British art and already prominent in the 1890s, were not to enter municipal collections until the early 1920s, and the same applied to other members of the Camden Town Group.[61] Even at Birmingham few acquisitions reflected contemporary British achievement. The two Augustus John portraits presented in 1920 were both associated with the recent war, while one of the rare 'modern' works to enter the collection during the early years of the century – *Autumn Sunlight* by Laura Knight, presented in 1922 – hardly expressed advanced taste. As late as 1930 the *Catalogue of the Permanent Collection of Paintings* scarcely listed any recent work. Equally in Glasgow the thrust of acquisitions was towards traditional Scottish art as well as French art. The Art Gallery took the relatively bold step in 1913 of buying *Pauvre Favette* by the social realist painter

Jules Bastien-Lepage, and received the notable James Donald Bequest of French nineteenth-century paintings, but from all the innovative Scottish artists of the time only works by the fashionable portraitist John Lavery and the technically ambitious Edward Hornel were acquired.

THE OPENING OF CARTWRIGHT HALL

The opening exhibition at Bradford's Cartwright Hall in 1904–5 gives an impression of the character of public art galleries early in the twentieth century. The ambitious new museum opened with minimal holdings, even though several private individuals in the city already owned substantial art collections.[62] A multi-stranded agenda emerged in this highly successful event, which daily attracted audiences of some 10,000 people (Figs 260, 261). On one level the Cartwright Hall offered an exhibition of the fine and decorative arts, arranged on principles influenced by the Aesthetic Movement as well as by the ideas

applied in national museums. The importance of a sympathetic hang was enunciated by the Curator, Butler Wood, who explained the principles behind the display. He commented on the 'formalised and irritating effect of the prevailing method of picture exhibitions…crowded unspaced paintings…exhibits (that) crush and jostle each other…very much the counterpart of a mob'. 'Everywhere', he wrote, efforts were being made to remedy this problem by 'the grouping and spacing of pictures'. The exhibition committee had sought the 'fitting association and geniality of effect when displaying art objects…to move towards something less formal; and have the collection wear the air of being at home in a somewhat natural combination'.[63] Much attention was given to integrating furniture and porcelain, since porcelain has 'graced the whole with the lighter touches of piquancy, flutter and capriciousness in these flower-like things'. Acknowledging the influence of the metropolis, he explained that the scheme that they were aspiring to had been 'splendidly and

completely realised in the Wallace Collection' as well as the Jones Collection at the Victoria and Albert Museum. It was to be hoped 'that arrangements of this character may be more persisted in, and a less "cast iron" type of display become general'.[64] Wood's willingness to be guided by the quality of the works of art rather than historical or indeed industrial principles was of the moment: the *Art Journal* commented approvingly on the hang of a single row of paintings in almost all the rooms (see Fig. 261) for 'lend[ing] itself admirably to an effective display of the various works'.[65]

So far, so modern, and Butler Wood's style recalls the reinstallation being carried out at the Fitzwilliam. But the situation was more complicated. For one thing, a somewhat parochial agenda still guided the display, with the history of British art being unfolded in a survey of painting from the eighteenth century onwards. It was also traditional in its overt didacticism in the South Kensington style: the historical display included 'a series of

262, 263 The Somali Village at the 1904 Bradford exhibition. Postcards. The settlement of Somali villagers installed in the park around Cartwright Hall was one of the high points of the opening exhibition for the public.

INTERIOR of SOMALI VILLAGE, BRADFORD EXHIBITION

FIRST LESSONS IN SPEAR THROWING, SOMALIS.

drawings and studies intended to give students and the general public some idea of the way in which our most notable British Artists prepare and build up their finished pictures'.[66] Other aspects recalled

the earliest days of regional art galleries, notably the displays of industrial art. Exhibits of the fine silks and other expensive dress materials increasingly being manufactured in Bradford formed a promi-

314

nent part of the installation, as though in tribute to the old Department of Science and Art.

The mixture of genres did not end here. In the new park that surrounded the museum, temporary buildings housed a range of industrial exhibits. And more complex attractions were organised in the style of the great international fairs. One of the principal entertainments offered in the gardens was a settlement of Somali villagers who were instructed to lead a version of their ordinary lives, to the fascination of Bradford – it was a tradition stretching back at least to William Bullock's display of Laplanders at the Egyptian Hall in Piccadilly in 1822. The quaint barbarism that the Somalians were held to exemplify made, of course, a striking contrast to the glories of civilisation expressed by the arts of peace and industry elsewhere on view (Figs 262, 263).

In the determination to instruct at many levels, to show industrial art, to illustrate the progress of English art, to celebrate local achievement, to offer a refined aesthetic display, to borrow the techniques of the international exhibition, the displays epitomised the various and sometimes contradictory nature of the Victorian art museum and exhibition. And they represented, also, its swansong.

CONCLUSION

The first decade and a half of the twentieth century represented a fascinating period in the history of these galleries, a period when the old forms of power and display were being subverted, when the ideals of a previous generation were being abandoned, and when some of the most advanced figures in the art world found in regional galleries a stage where – modestly but persuasively – new ideas about art could be explored. At the same time, a Victorian ideal was being gradually abandoned. The people's art galleries experienced a reversal of role. They became, gradually and partially but unmistakably, galleries devoted to art for its own sake, rather than to art as a vehicle for popular entertainment and instruction.

14

THE AFTERMATH

1914 marked the final stages of the type of art gallery discussed in this book. With the advent of war, the museums in London ceased to function normally, but the history in the provinces was more individual. In some cases, exhibition policy tended to be directed at the war effort, in a way that hardly reflected the galleries' original aims. At Leeds City Art Gallery, to take one example, the demands of war were taken especially seriously, with the modest wartime programme including such displays as *What German Invasion Means...An Exhibition of Photographs, Proclamations, Relics &c.* Inspired by two war correspondents, this event aimed 'to help people to more fully realize what invasion means, and to appeal for their help for the Belgian sufferers'.[1] It also included *The Glory of Rheims Cathedral*, which illustrated through photographs the effects of German bombardment. Other galleries were less bellicose; indeed, they went so far as to offer, as an alternative to preoccupation with the war, a sense of continuity, and the provision of instruction and delight for the military and for civilians. At Bradford, the programme at Cartwright Hall was hardly affected by the conflict, the *Annual Report* for 1917 commenting that 'In spite of the altered conditions brought about by the war the activities of this Department have not been curtailed to any appreciable extent.'[2] At the Ashmolean, the Keeper poignantly recorded that although two-thirds of the staff

had been called away by the war, the museum had remained open and 'has constantly served a good purpose', with numerous visits by 'soldiers in uniform or hospital dress and of nurses'.[3] Although at such an actively collecting museum as Birmingham City Art Galley acquisitions inevitably diminished during these years – they consisted primarily of coloured reproductions of historical paintings and of electrotypes – regional galleries do seem to have enjoyed a considerable degree of independence from institutionalised conflict.

After the First World War things were not quite the same. The annual reports and other official accounts do not convey the earlier sense of excitement and mission. To start with, the spate of new foundations diminished: the old style of patron was on the wane; Victorian art was derided, and not only by the fashionable; and most towns of any size already possessed an art gallery building and at least the rudiments of a collection. Equally, the economic situation in Europe and the United States in the aftermath of war, and following the Great Depression, hardly favoured the foundation or growth of museums and galleries. It is true that a few new galleries were founded, usually on the basis of old-established private fortunes. The Barber Institute 'for the study and encouragement of art and music' was set up as part of Birmingham University in 1932 with funding for a new building from Sir Henry

Barber, a Birmingham solicitor and property developer (Fig. 264). A variant of the collection museum movement, the Institute provided for the acquisition of works of art, though artistically the bequest consisted only of twenty-four portraits of Lady Barber. In the municipal sphere, several new gallery buildings were erected, generally adapting a modernist variation of classicism to house relatively traditional collections, such as the Graves Art Gallery in Sheffield, funded by a Victorian-style collector, the businessman and alderman J.G. Graves. The most spectacular of these traditional collections in new buildings was the Lady Lever Art Gallery, already discussed.

The new style of absorbing historic houses into the fabric of municipal patronage also continued in such places as Temple Newsam, near Leeds, and Torre Abbey at Torquay. The debate over whether such houses should be shown as neutral spaces for the display of extraneous museum specimens or as

historical interiors with their original fittings persisted, and it was only late in the 1930s that the National Trust for England and Wales launched its Country Houses Scheme to preserve intact historic houses with their contents and grounds. Though for many years the National Trust did not acknowledge that its country houses were in any respect 'house museums' in the American manner, the Country Houses Scheme represented a novel concept of presenting the great house, in that the history of its past owners was seen as an essential element in the narrative. It was an approach that was ultimately to influence the presentation of historic houses in local government care.[4]

Acquisitions also changed. Some galleries remained traditional in their acquisitions, with Birmingham continuing to accumulate British watercolours and woodcuts, as well as works by Cox, Burne-Jones and Ford Madox Brown.[5] On the other hand, acquiring more advanced art became increasingly feasible, in spite of a lack of leadership from the Tate Gallery. This development was assisted by the rejection of much of the art of the previous century. Thus, in Liverpool in 1931 Vere E. Cotton, a partner in the old-established firm of Rathbone Brothers, and later Lord Mayor of Liverpool and a prominent local figure, launched a public attack on the Walker's collection.[6] Cotton described it as 'utterly unworthy of the second city of the Empire, because it has been formed without any definite purpose or plan', and advocated 'the ruthless pruning of the redundant, the indifferent and the meretricious'. His comments were taken up by numerous furious correspondents – 'one described [the permanent collection] as "sugar plums and glucose" and another…pointed out that thousands of pounds had been spent on pictures which had become almost valueless'.[7] A new acquisitions policy was eventually formulated during Cotton's chairmanship, from 1939 to 1951, of Liverpool's Libraries, Museums and Arts Committee. While avoiding anything unhealthily foreign, the policy 'gradually to build up a new collection illustrating every period and phase of British painting' was triumphantly vindicated.[8]

It was in this period that two notable new galleries were established, at Southampton and Hull. Thanks to the foresight of Councillor Robert Chipperfield, who paid for the building and established a purchase fund, and of a succession of art advisers (including two Directors of the National Gallery, Kenneth Clark and Philip Hendy), Southampton Art Gallery was to become one of the most notable regional collections in Britain. At the Ferens Art Gallery, rehoused in a jewel-like building in 1927, Thomas Ferens presciently endowed an acquisitions fund, allowing the Gallery – even in the days of Hull's economic decline after the Second World War – to assemble an outstanding collection of Old Master and modern painting and sculpture.

In spite of these successes, the interwar period hardly represented the finest hour of the British art museum, or of museums in general. In 1928 the eminent mineralogist and university administrator Sir Henry Miers submitted to the Carnegie United Kingdom Trustees *A Report on the Public Museums of the British Isles*. This document analysed the dismal state of the 507 museums (excluding national institutions, and galleries dedicated solely to works

of art) that Miers and his colleague had identified and visited. He found the museums on the whole badly housed (often in unsuitable old buildings), ill displayed, chaotically stored, deficient in their education policies, and almost universally drastically underfunded. He also delivered some pithy reflections on the subject of art galleries, noting that apart for the more modern ones these too were poorly housed and badly lit, with excessively crowded displays and art collections that administratively were inappropriately combined with museums and libraries. He regretted 'a total absence, in general, of any arrangement which would help to explain such things as the history of art, the development of a particular school, or the different periods of any given artist'.[9] His comments appear not to have had any immediate effect: as the Carnegie trustees pointed out, 'it is not to be expected, in the present state of public finance, that public authorities will for some time be able to spend large sums on museum development'.[10] Miers's comments were embodied in the much-quoted but irresistibly vivid memoirs of John Rothenstein, published in 1965. At Leeds City Art Gallery in the early 1930s he found that 'The building, squalid itself, had fallen into an incredible state of disrepair', and that the interiors were as dismal as the general character of the collection, where even the good pictures 'had taken on protective colouring and become all but indistinguishable from their drab or meretricious companions'.[11] The Art Gallery was 'a place disgusting to enter'.[12] Though Rothenstein did his best, the period encouraged little consolidation of the creativity of earlier generations.

The Second World War was more galvanising in its effects. When museums did not send their collections away to safety they risked the fate of the Liverpool Museum, where the Egyptian collections were eliminated in a bombing raid in 1940. The Walker Art Gallery had prudently put its collections into storage, but the building was turned over to the Ministry of Food and not reopened as a gallery until 1951. Bristol Museum was also gutted, with the loss of thousands of natural history specimens, in November 1940, though the neighbouring Art Gallery suffered less badly (Fig. 265). As in the First World War, however, some galleries continued their exhibition programmes in a context that encouraged the presentation of contemporary

265 Bristol Museum after
bombing in November 1940.

the history of English art'.[14] As Hendy wrote in December 1939, the leaflet available at Temple Newsam 'exhorts the visitor to urge his friends to forget the war sometimes at Temple Newsam but never to forget the civilization for which the war is being fought'.[15] The municipal gallery had assumed a new guise as a haven of peace and artistic appreciation.

The history since the Second World War has been a roller coaster of alternating prosperity and unhappiness, a narrative that recalls all too clearly the lack of a national policy that William Dyce attacked in the 1850s. Whereas national museums and galleries have steadily increased in scale and activity, the municipal galleries have had strikingly mixed fortunes. The handful of galleries founded or rebuilt in the years after the Second World War were modest in comparison with those in Germany or France or the United States, and it was primarily the new collector museums – notably the Sainsbury Centre for the Visual Arts at the University of East Anglia, Norwich, and the Burrell Collection in Glasgow – that offered any architectural quality or originality of concept.[16] Additionally, the university museums, both old and new, flourished in the twentieth century, gradually expanding in terms of buildings, and dramatically in terms of collections, under a series of inspired directors.

In another respect the post-war period was highly positive. The art-historical establishment in Britain had been transformed in the 1930s by the arrival of fugitives from the German-speaking world: Nikolaus Pevsner, Johannes Wilde, Rudolf Wittkower, Edgar Wind, Ernst Gombrich, men of great distinction who played a major role in developing the study of art history, notably through the establishment of the Courtauld and Warburg Institutes in the early 1930s. After the Second World War their influence extended to art museums all over the country, often through their students.[17] A new style of director and curator emerged, who did not briefly work in a provincial setting (like Frank Rutter and John Rothenstein) but devoted themselves for life or at least for long periods to their regional galleries. These people – including Hans Hess at York, Hans Schubart at Bristol, Fred Grossmann at Manchester, Trenchard Cox and 'Mighty Mary' Woodall at Birmingham, Frank Constantine at Sheffield – were able, with modest funding and some generous lega-

art for practical as well as intellectual reasons. At Leeds the Art Gallery Committee resolved 'that the functions of the Gallery should continue to be performed in all circumstances'.[13] While the Director, Philip Hendy, was obliged to evacuate the City Art Gallery, he organised an active programme of contemporary exhibitions at Temple Newsam, which was supposedly less vulnerable to air raids. There he exhibited Sickert, Jacob Epstein and Matthew Smith, Paul Nash and Barbara Hepworth, Ben Nicholson and many others, while his display in 1941 of works by Henry Moore, John Piper and Graham Sutherland was greeted by Kenneth Clark, Director of the National Gallery, as 'a very great landmark in

cies and gifts, to build up important Old Master and modern collections. Their successes refuted J.C. Robinson's patronising notion that the purchase of major works of art was an impossible and inappropriate aspiration for the municipal gallery.

This activity was assisted by the relative cheapness of works of art, at least in comparison to the situation at the end of the twentieth century. To take one of many possible examples, Birmingham City Art Gallery bought numerous works of art from the late 1940s onwards. Exploiting the unfashionable status of Baroque painting, the curators acquired notable seventeenth-century paintings, including Orazio Gentileschi's *Rest on the Flight into Egypt* (paying £500 at Christie's in 1947) and Guercino's *Erminia and the Shepherd* (which cost only £4,000 as late as 1962).[18] In the 1950s alone they bought works by Simone Martini, Jan van Scorel, Claude Lorrain, Jean-François Millet, Joshua Reynolds and Thomas Couture. They also acquired paintings of the emergent modern British school by, among others, Nash, Hepworth, Moore and Nicholson, while works on paper by Eric Ravilious, Edward Bawden, Stanley Spencer and many others including Diego Rivera were snapped up, often for very small sums.[19] Comparably discriminating and energetic collecting, assisted by the National Art-Collections Fund and the Contemporary Art Society, was pursued in Manchester, Glasgow and Liverpool.

Purchases were not the only achievement of this generation. The Walker Art Gallery was pioneering in setting up its own conservation department in the 1950s. It also housed such ambitious events as the John Moores Liverpool Exhibition. This series began in 1957 and aimed 'to give Merseyside the chance to see an exhibition of painting and sculpture embracing the best and most vital work being done today throughout the country', and 'to encourage contemporary artists, particularly the young and progressive';[20] in the Victorian tradition, it was funded by John Moores, a local businessman who had made his fortune in football pools and department stores. Manchester City Art Gallery maintained its active wartime exhibition programme, exploring for example such (then) relatively unfamiliar names as Lovis Corinth (in 1967) and Georges Rouault (in 1974). Instead of the sharp division that exists today between curatorial staff in national or university museums and their relations

in the regions, staff moved easily between national and regional museums: Philip Hendy went from Leeds to be Director of the National Gallery, Cox from Birmingham to the Directorship of the Victoria and Albert Museum. Behind this approach was a conviction that the regions deserved no less than the capital, that high art should be made available to everyone, and that acquiring major works of art should be central to the work of a regional gallery. It was accepted that 'if the authorities supported the arts people would realize what intense joy the greatest works of man could bring to their lives'.[21] Even though a shortage of funding remained a problem and was constantly raised by the writers of reports advocating funding from central government, a new type of regional gallery was unanointed, operating on a par with galleries in the capitals of England and Scotland.[22]

This halcyon period did not last long. In the 1980s the dream that regional art galleries run by local authorities could become museums of national and international calibre faded, sometimes abruptly. With the rapid reduction of funding for local government, municipal galleries were especially vulnerable at a time when many of the great Victorian cities were in a state of serious economic decline. Expert curatorial staff retired and their jobs were frozen; acquisition budgets disappeared; branch museums closed. When galleries were seen to be competing with social services (however illusory the competition might be) it was clear which would lose. By the early 1990s the situation began to seem desperate. And in some cases – the evidence here is anecdotal but recurrent – gallery staff lacked the time or expertise to make substantial purchases or to publish their collections, or even disapproved of what was sometimes perceived as the elitist activity of making acquisitions.[23]

With the advent of the Heritage Lottery Fund, with a self-appointed brief to revive and extend the museums of Britain, the volatility and versatility of the provincial museum re-emerged. From 1994 onwards the Fund distributed hundreds of millions of pounds to museums throughout Britain, restoring and extending not only national museums but many of the regional institutions discussed in this book: Exeter, Kelvingrove, Manchester, the Mappin, Norwich, Swansea and many others.[24] Following much agitation over the condition of regional museums, given a platform in a Royal Academy exhibition, *Art Treasures of England* (1998), for the first time ever in England central government provided funds to support regional museums through the programme 'Renaissance in the Regions'. The reduction in staff numbers was to some extent reversed. Several galleries were set up as trusts (as at Sheffield and York) in the hope that independent trustees would be better able to raise funds than councils. Most notably, numerous contemporary art spaces were opened all over Britain, reflecting the huge increase in interest in contemporary art in Britain since the 1980s.[25] It was an international trend, greatly influenced in Britain by the creation of Tate Modern, which opened in 2000. Learning and access became, under Labour administrations from 1997 to 2010, central to museums, strongly influenced by the report *A Common Wealth: Museums in the Learning Age* (1999), edited by David Anderson, then Director of Learning at the Victoria and Albert Museum. Museums worked hard to make themselves appealing: whereas the decision by Michael Jaffé, Director of the Fitzwilliam, in the 1970s to introduce an attractive shop and café had shocked his more conservative colleagues, such facilities came (under the influence of the United States) to be accepted as essential features of any fair-sized museum.[26] It seemed that the problems might be over and that in a new form regional galleries would realise their potential (Fig. 266).

No longer. At the time of writing the situation seems worse than ever, as local councils, forced to cut budgets, again turn to non-statutory expenditure. While as yet few museums or galleries have actually closed, the future looks black: curatorial expertise dwindles or disappears, opening hours diminish, the fine new buildings and extensions paid for by the Heritage Lottery Fund can be hard-pressed to operate. Museum services are merged, or are placed under joint directorships.[27] The ugly prospect of the sales of works of art by local councils has reopened. Historic houses in local authority care sometimes find themselves almost without professional staff, and reduced to functioning as wedding venues. Many municipal galleries remain stubbornly active and the great university museums and galleries flourish, while some independent museums – Pallant House in Chichester, the Holburne Museum in Bath – have by superhuman efforts raised money to build extensions and make themselves central to the artistic lives of their communities. But in general this is a troubling period in the history of these institutions.

THE VICTORIAN LEGACY

This book is not intended as a polemic, or at least that is not its prime purpose. A more significant motive has been to explore the individualist, opinionated, competitive, insular, yet in a sense heroic museum movement described in the preceding chapters. What can be viewed as the legacy of the municipal gallery movement that flourished from the 1860s to the 1910s? In terms of collections, an interesting but unusual array of objects (leaving aside acquisitions made post-1914): innumerable British nineteenth-century paintings, a thin array of earlier British works of art, quantities of watercolours, a few pieces of sculpture, numerous casts, photographs and electrotypes, a diverse representation of the decorative arts, and a smattering of Old Masters. The Victorian paintings, as we have seen, became an embarrassment to later curators for many years, though since the 1970s they have gradually regained critical and popular esteem, so that works by such artists as Burne-Jones and Lord Leighton are now greatly admired. Many of the pedagogical collections, notably the plaster casts, were considered in the inter-war period no longer fit for use and were disposed of. One of the mainstays of these galleries, the once-mighty Summer or Winter Exhibition, gradually disappeared: galleries such as Brighton and Sheffield, which remained faithful to the practice until well after the Second World War, eventually abandoned them. The publications of the Victorian galleries consisted primarily of slender catalogues of permanent collections. Their educational programmes were largely obsolete.

The most substantial inheritance offered by this period of hyperactivity was threefold. Firstly, a set of gallery buildings that were architecturally varied but in almost all cases reliably planned, and that have since determined the nature of the art museum (and arguably, the nature of artistic experience) in many British cities. Sometimes criticised as out-of-date early in the twentieth century, when their architectural features were often disguised, the prac-

266 The Hepworth Wakefield. Opened in 2011, this spectacular building by David Chipperfield was named after Barbara Hepworth, who was born and grew up in the city and whose work is richly represented in the collection. Funded by the Heritage Lottery Fund and many other sources, the Hepworth replaced the older Wakefield Art Gallery.

ticality and grandeur of these buildings was increasingly recognised from the 1980s onwards, with major building restorations taking place not only in London but also in Manchester, Glasgow and elsewhere. And, secondly, the creation of the network of institutions throughout the United Kingdom that have survived bombs and funding cuts and generations of contempt and dismissal, but which, like their cousins the public libraries, remain (on the whole) a physical presence and an item within the collective consciousness.

Perhaps the most important contribution made by the regional galleries may be too easily overlooked. What was especially new about them was that they were so popular, in the sense that they reached out to the whole people and that people responded. In attracting, and for many years satisfying, this broad audience, they were outstandingly successful, appealing to audiences that in relative and even actual terms were often much larger than those drawn to their contemporary equivalents. However strange they may seem to our eyes, they offered a good deal to their publics: a vision of countries that few of their visitors would ever see

for themselves, a sense of the past, a chance for people who could not afford to collect for themselves to behold rare and precious objects, a feeling for the historic identity and the present achievements of their city or town. Altogether these concepts formed a worthwhile cultural vision, different though it was to the Enlightened style of collecting and displaying art that inspired the national and university galleries. Though museums in the United States, in Italy and France, and in Germany had comparable aspirations, the presentation of these possibilities seems to have been a peculiarly British achievement. What makes it remarkable is that the process flourished with such energy for fifty or so years and then diminished.

Today, this ideal of popular inclusion has re-emerged, and offers a repudiation of Bourdieu's association of art with cultural capital. In many of the galleries that this book has considered, the idea of the family gallery, of the gallery that belongs to all and appeals to all regardless of social or educational background, has become dominant. This idea, or indeed ideal, may be the most important legacy left by the Victorian art museum: truly, a people's gallery.

DATES OF THE FOUNDATION OF ART MUSEUMS IN BRITAIN, 1684–1939

This list is intended as a guide, not a definitive statement. Some museums – such as the British Museum – have a clearly defined date of foundation, even though they may have opened at a later date. The Ashmolean, which heads this list, has a long and complex prehistory, but it opened in its new building as an official university museum, rather than a private one, in 1684. In many cases, municipal museums or galleries existed in earlier versions long before they were re-embodied in their present forms. The list aims to outline the development of art museums in the United Kingdom, whatever omissions or errors may be detected by zealous supporters of particular institutions.

National museums are shown in italics. 'Museum and Art Gallery' is abbreviated to 'M & AG', and 'Art Gallery' to 'AG'.

❖

1600s
1684 Oxford: Ashmolean Museum (university)

1700s
1753 London: British Museum, London

1800s
1807 Glasgow: Hunterian M & AG (university)

1810s
1811 London: Dulwich College Picture Gallery (trust)
1816 Cambridge: Fitzwilliam Museum (university)

1820s
1824 London: National Gallery

1830s
1837 London: Sir John Soane's Museum

1850s

1851 Brighton: Royal Pavilion (purchase of historic building – municipal)

1852 London: South Kensington Museum (from 1899, the Victoria and Albert Museum)

1854 Glasgow: bequest of McLellan collection (municipal)

1856 London: National Portrait Gallery

1858 Birmingham: Aston Hall (commercial; becomes municipal property 1864)

1858 Maidstone: M & AG (in Chillington Manor) (municipal)

1859 Edinburgh: National Gallery of Scotland

1860s

1862 Blackburn: M & AG (municipal)

1864 Dublin: National Gallery of Ireland

1865 Northampton: Central M & AG (municipal)

1867 Birmingham: M & AG (municipal)

1868 Exeter: Royal Albert Memorial Museum (municipal)

1870s

1871 Paisley: M & AG (municipal)

1872 Blackburn: M & AG (municipal)

1873 Brighton: M & AG (municipal)

1873 Dundee: M & AG (municipal)

1873 Liverpool: Walker AG (municipal)

1877 Carlisle: M & AG (municipal)

1877 Warrington: AG, extension to older building (municipal)

1878 Derby: M & AG (municipal)

1878 Nottingham: Castle Museum (municipal)

1878 Southport: Atkinson AG (municipal)

1879 Sunderland M & AG (municipal)

1880s

1881 Inverness: M & AG (municipal)

1882 Edinburgh: Scottish National Portrait Gallery

1883 Egham: Royal Holloway College Picture Gallery (university)

1883 Manchester: City AG (municipal, replacing Manchester Royal Institution)

1883 Oldham: AG (municipal)

1884 Crawford: Municipal Gallery (municipal)

1884 Wolverhampton: AG (municipal)

1885 Aberdeen: AG & M (municipal)

1885 Leicester: AG (municipal)

1886 London: Guildhall AG (Corporation of London)

1886 Manchester: Ancoats Art Museum (trust)

1887 Sheffield: Mappin AG (municipal)

1888 Leeds: City AG (municipal)

1888 Newport: M & AG (municipal)

1889 Manchester: Whitworth AG (university)

1890s

1890 Bath: Holburne of Menstrie Museum (trust)

1890 Belfast: AG for Ulster Museum

1890 Bolton: M & AG (municipal)

1891 London: South London AG (trust)

1892 Barnard Castle: Bowes Museum (trust)

1892 Preston: Harris AG (municipal)

1892 York: City AG (municipal)

1894 Bournemouth: Russell-Cotes AG & M (municipal)

1894 Falmouth: AG (municipal)

1894 Ipswich: Christchurch Mansion and AG (municipal)

1894 Norwich: Castle Museum (municipal)

1895 Portsmouth: M & AG (municipal)

1896 London: Leighton House (trust)

1897 Halifax: Bankfield House (municipal)

1897 London: Tate Gallery

1897 Reading: AG extension (municipal)

1897 Worcester: AG (municipal)

1898 Huddersfield: AG (municipal)

1898 Plymouth: City M & AG (municipal)

1899 Canterbury: Beaney Institute (municipal)

1899 Cheltenham: AG (municipal)

1900s

1900 Bath: Victoria AG (municipal)

1900 London: Wallace Collection

1901 Bury: AG (municipal)

1901 Coniston: Ruskin Museum (trust)

1901 London: Whitechapel AG (trust)

1901 Stalybridge: Astley Cheetham AG (municipal)

1902 Bolton: Hall i' th' Wood (historic house; municipal)

1902 Burnley: Townley Hall (municipal)

1902 Glasgow: Kelvingrove AG (municipal)

1903 Compton: Watts Gallery (trust)

1904 Bradford: Cartwright Hall (municipal)

1904 Newcastle: Laing AG (municipal)

1905 Bristol: City AG (municipal)
1905 Hastings: M & AG (municipal)
1905 Keswick: AG, added to existing Museum (municipal)
1906 Walsall: M & AG (municipal)
1907 Brighouse: Smith AG (municipal)
1905 Cardiff: National Museum of Wales – foundation
1908 Doncaster: M & AG (municipal)
1908 Dublin: Hugh Lane Municipal Gallery of Modern Art (municipal)
1908 Worthing: M & AG (municipal)

1910s
1910 Beverley: AG & M (municipal)
1910 Hull: Ferens AG (municipal)
1911 Blackpool: Grundy AG (municipal)
1911 Swansea: Glynn Vivian AG & M (municipal)
1912 Birkenhead: M & AG (municipal)
1912 Hereford: AG (addition to existing Museum)
1912 Rochdale: AG (municipal)
1913 Kettering: Alfred East AG (municipal)
1914 Barnsley: Cooper Gallery (municipal)
1915 Bradford: Bolling Hall (municipal)

1915 Gateshead: Shipley AG (municipal)
1919 Hartlepool: Gray AG (municipal)
1919 Manchester: Fletcher Moss Museum (municipal)

1920s
1921 Accrington: Haworth AG (municipal)
1922 Leeds: Temple Newsam (municipal)
1922 Port Sunlight: Lady Lever AG (trust)
1923 Eastbourne: Towner AG (municipal)
1923 Lancaster: City M & AG (municipal)
1927 Hove: M & AG (municipal)
1927 Lincoln: Usher AG (municipal)
1928 Birkenhead: Williamson AG (municipal)
1928 Leamington Spa: AG & M (municipal)

1930s
1930 Torre Abbey, Torquay (municipal)
1932 Birmingham: Barber Institute of Fine Arts (university)
1933 Darlington: AG (municipal)
1934 Sheffield: Graves AG (municipal)
1935 Perth: M & AG (new building: municipal)
1939 Southampton: AG (municipal)

NOTES

INTRODUCTION

1 The studies of individual institutions that have been written – as well as the increasingly voluminous socio-economic literature on the regional city – have been richly valuable to the writer, whether in the form of (often unpublished) theses or in monographs.

2 For a broad discussion of South Kensington's influence, see Morris 1986.

3 Notable examples include, for Britain, Taylor 1999; for France, Daniel Sherman's *Worthy Monuments: Art Museums and the Politics of Culture in Nineteenth-Century France* (Cambridge, MA, 1989); for the United States, Duncan 1995; and, internationally, Bennett 1995.

4 Conn 1998, pp. 11–12.

5 Ibid., p. 12.

6 The modern sense of 'science' and 'scientific' was seldom applied until early in the nineteenth century.

I: BRITAIN AND THE VISUAL ARTS

1 Opened respectively in 1830, 1836 and 1855 (the Dresden gallery had existed in another building since the eighteenth century).

2 In addition, an alternative system for founding museums developed in German cities in the nineteenth century that was closer to the creation of Victorian city collections. In such cities as Bremen a group of citizens formed a *Kunstverein* or 'Art Union' to encourage contemporary art by organising lotteries of paintings and sculpture from which the subscribers would win a prize. The profits from the lottery funded new museum buildings and collections.

3 The forerunner of the Louvre.

4 See Andrew McClellan, *Inventing the Louvre: Art, Politics, and the Origins of the Modern Museum in Eighteenth-century Paris* (Cambridge, 1994).

5 On his accession in 1760 George III surrendered to the Government's Aggregate Fund the royal income from tax and from the Crown lands in exchange for a fixed annual sum of £800,000. The King remained responsible for much civil expenditure and the allowance soon proved inadequate. The impact of this kind of economy extended into the twentieth century and an age when the monarch would not be expected to fund public causes: the National Theatre was founded, against considerable public opposition, only in 1963.

6 National Gallery archives, NG/1/1823 (2).

7 George IV did, however, give generously to the National Gallery of Naval Art, the forerunner of the National Maritime Museum, founded at Greenwich in 1824, just before the National Gallery.

8 Such men as Matthias Österreich at the Electoral Gallery of Saxony, and Gerhard Joseph Karsch at the Elector Palatine's Gallery in Düsseldorf. See Plagemann 1967 and Sheehan 2000.

9 They were appointed in 1765 and 1778 respectively.

10 Numerous manuscript inventories were prepared for internal use.

11 Law 1881, p. vii.

12 For a detailed bibliography of the royal inventories, see Oliver Millar, *The Later Georgian Paintings in the Collection of Her Majesty the Queen* (London, 1969), pp. xlv–lii.

13 The first guidebooks for Windsor Castle were George Bickham, *Deliciae Britannicae; Or, the Curiosi-* *ties of Hampton-Court and Windsor-Castle* (London, 1742) and Joseph Pote, *Les Délices de Windsore; Or, A Description of Windsor Castle, and The Country Adjacent* (Eton, 1755).

14 Law 1881, p. xxxi.

15 See Frank Prochaska, *Royal Bounty: The Making of a Welfare Monarchy* (New Haven and London, 1995).

16 Holger Hoock, *The King's Artists: The Royal Academy of Arts and the Politics of British Culture, 1760–1840* (Oxford, 2003) discusses the political role of the Academy and its relationship with the Crown.

17 Leigh 1818, pp. 57–8.

18 Norman Gash, *Aristocracy and People: Britain 1815–1865* (London, 1979), p. 51.

19 Ibid., p. 44.

20 For discussions of this issue, see Minihan 1977, Nicholas M. Pearson, *The State and the Visual Arts: A Discussion of State Intervention in the Visual Arts in Britain, 1760–1981* (Milton Keynes, 1982) and Peter Mandler (ed.), *Liberty and Authority in Victorian Britain* (Oxford, 2006).

21 Valentine Green, *A Review of the Polite Arts in France, at the Time of their Establishment under Louis the XIVth, compared with their Present State in England In a Letter to Sir J. Reynolds* (London, 1782), p. 20.

22 Ibid., p. 34.

23 Hoare 1813, p. 16.

24 Minihan 1977, p. 18.

25 Letter from Office of Woods and Forests to William Seguier, 7 January 1834, National Gallery archives.

26 J.D. Passavant, *Tour of a German Artist in England* (two vols, London, 1836), vol. I, p. 23.

27 See Liscombe 1980, Chapter Twelve, for a full account of the building campaign.

28 Haydon 1844–6, vol. 1, pp. 101–2.

29 The Liberal politician William Coningham, quoted in Select Committee Report, National Gallery 1850 (751).

30 Lord Seymour, quoted in Select Committee Report, National Gallery 1853 (8047, 8048).

31 Edward Edwards, *The Administrative Economy of the Fine Arts in England* (London, 1840), p. 121. Edwards discusses the National Gallery on pp. 118–31.

32 *The Turner Gallery: A Series of Sixty Engravings from the Principal Works of Joseph Mallord William Turner. With a Memoir and Illustrative Text by Ralph Nicholson Wornum* (London, 1861), pp. xxii–xxiii.

33 Francis Haskell, *Rediscoveries in Art: Some Aspects of Taste, Fashion and Collecting in England and France* (London, 1976), p. 20.

34 J.J. Volkmann, *Neueste Reisen durch England, vorzüglich in Absicht auf die Kunstsammlungen, Naturgeschichte, Oekonomie, Manufakturen und Landsitze der Grossen* (two vols, Leipzig, 1781–2), vol. 1, p. 2.

35 Simond 1815, vol. 2, p. 65.

36 Published as *Kunstreise durch England und Belgien* in 1833 and as *Tour of a German Artist in England* in 1836.

37 The only universities in England until the foundation of University College, London in 1826.

38 Whiteley 1997, p. 619. 'University Galleries' was the name originally given to what is now the Ashmolean Museum, the building by C.R. Cockerell in Beaumont Street, built from 1841 to 1845 to house the growing art collections of the university, as opposed to the original seventeenth-century museum building on Broad Street. Fox-Strangways also made a substantial donation of works of art to Christ Church, Oxford.

39 Quoted in Minihan 1977, p. 85.

40 See Chapter Three, especially pp. 57–61.

41 Linda Colley, *Britons: Forging the Nation 1707–1837* (London and New Haven, 1992), p. 177.

42 Similar arguments emerged late in the twentieth century around the preservation for public ownership of such houses as Kedleston Hall and Calke Abbey.

43 Barry 1799, p. 9.

44 Ibid., p. 10.

45 Sir George Beaumont to Charles Manners-Sutton, Archbishop of Canterbury, 31 July 1823, National Gallery archives, NG/1/1823.

46 Jameson 1842, Part 1, p. 6.

47 Such as the ideas of the engraver Valentine Green ARA, the painter John Opie RA, Prince Hoare, who acted as the Royal Academy's Secretary for Foreign Correspondence, and Noel Desenfans, art dealer and close friend of Francis Bourgeois.

48 The President of the Royal Academy takes the initials PRA after his name, Royal Academicians RA; ARA denoted an Associate of the Royal Academy, the position to which aspiring Academicians were initially elected (no longer in existence).

49 Whether for artists, architects or, in the case of the Hunterian Museum in London, as a centre for the study of the sciences and the arts.

50 See Paul 2012 for an extended discussion of the influence of the Capitoline Museum.

51 'Keeper' was the term generally used in many British museums well into the twentieth century.

52 J.T. Smith, *A Book for a Rainy Day; Or, Recollections of the Events of the Years 1766–1833*, ed. W. Whitten (London, 1905), p. 224.

53 *The Gentleman's Magazine*, n.s. 21 (January 1844), p. 97.

54 *The Athenaeum*, 18 November 1843, p. 1028.

55 Quoted in Conlin 2006, p. 57.

56 *The Athenaeum*, 18 November 1843 p. 1028.

57 For the early development of the art market, see Iain Pears, *The Discovery of Painting: The Growth of Interest in the Arts in England, 1680–1768* (New Haven and London, 1988) and Brewer 1997, Chapter Five.

58 The process continues today.

59 Brewer 1997, p. 453.

60 Barry 1799, pp. 56–7.

61 On Boydell, see Sven Bruntjen, *John Boydell (1719–1804): A Study of Art Patronage and Publishing in Georgian London* (New York, 1985) and Rosie Dias, *Exhibiting Englishness: John Boydell's Shakespeare Gallery and the Formation of a National Aesthetic* (New Haven and London, 2013).

62 This apartment, like the staircases and the shop, was gas-lit – a novelty that attracted 'crowds of the nobility, gentry and artists' to weekly *soirées* attended by 'the most eminent artists and men of science of our own and of foreign countries': John Britton, *Autobiography* (three vols, London, 1850), vol. 1, p. 311.

63 See Richard Altick, *Paintings from Books: Art and Literature in Britain, 1760–1900* (Columbus, 1985), pp. 28–32 and Chapter Eighteen.

64 Leigh 1818.

65 Mainardi 1993, p. 27 and *passim*.

66 For details of their foundation, see Appendix.

67 See Ronald K. Huch and Paul R. Ziegler, *Joseph Hume: The People's M.P.* (Philadelphia, 1985).

68 Haydon 1960–3, vol. 4, 19 January 1833.

69 For a recent account, see Roger Tittler, 'Portrait Collection and Display in the English Civic Body, c.1540–1640', *Journal of the History of Collections*, 20, no. 2 (2008), pp. 161–72.

70 Ralph Thoresby, *Ducatus Leodiensis, Or the Topography of the Ancient and Populous Town and Parish of Leedes…*, ed. Thomas Dunham Whitaker (2nd ed., 1816), title page. The catalogue of his collection was added to this study of Leeds 'at the request of several learned persons'.

71 'Life of the Author', in ibid., p. xii.

72 See Peter Brears, 'Commercial Museums of Eighteenth-Century Cumbria', *Journal of the History of Collections*, 4, no. 1 (1992), pp. 107–26, at p. 107; and A.J. White, 'Early Museums in Lakeland', in *Transactions of the Cumberland & Westmoreland Antiquarian & Archaeological Society*, 89 (1989), pp. 268–75.

73 *Catalogue of a Series of Pictures, Illustrating the Rise and Early Progress of The Art of Painting, in Italy, Germany, &c. – Collected by William Roscoe, Esq. and now Deposited in the Liverpool Royal Institution* (Liverpool, 1819).

74 Edward Morris, 'The Formation of the Gallery of Art in the Liverpool Royal Institution, 1816–1819', *Transactions of the Historic Society of Lancashire and Cheshire*, 142 (1992), pp. 87–98, at p. 88.

75 Ibid., p. 96.

2: JUSTIFYING THE MUSEUM

1 See the first volume of Johannes Dobai, *Die Kunstliteratur des Klassizismus und der Romantik in England* (Bern, 1974).

2 Attributed to Bainbrigg Buckeridge.

3 Jameson 1842, Part 2, p. xxxiv (footnote).

4 Reynolds 1975, p. xxiii.

5 See Mainardi 1987, pp. 151–3.

6 Conlin 2006, p. 49.

7 *Hansard*, quoted in Liscombe 1980, p. 183.

8 Jameson 1842, Part 2, p. 6.

9 For an eloquent exposition of German ideas on museums, see Sheehan 2000.

10 Sheehan 2000, p. 73.

11 David Hume, 'Of the Rise and Progress of the Arts and Sciences' (1741–2), in *Essays and Treatises on Several Subjects* (London, 1758 edition), pp. 70–86, at p. 85.

12 Barry 1799, pp. 129–30.

13 John Opie: Lecture 3, 'On Chiaroscuro', in Wornum 1848, pp. 289–313, at p. 292.

14 Hazlitt 1856, pp. 226–7.

15 Flaxman 1838, p. 78.

16 See Carol Gibson-Wood, *Jonathan Richardson: Art Theorist of the English Enlightenment* (New Haven and London, 2000), p. 144.

17 Jonathan Richardson, *An Essay on the Theory of Painting* (London, 1725), p. iii.

18 Ibid., p. 2.

19 Ibid., pp. 5–6.

20 Reynolds 1975, p. 171.

21 Originally published in 1824 as one of a series of reflections on picture galleries.

22 Hazlitt 1856, p. 1.

23 Possibly referring to William Bullock's 'Liverpool Museum', which had opened in Piccadilly in 1812.

24 Hazlitt 1856, p. 1.

25 Ibid., p. 2.

26 Reflecting this spirit at a popular unofficial level, John Landseer's *A Descriptive, Explanatory, and Critical Catalogue of Fifty of the Earliest Pictures Contained in the National Gallery of Great Britain* (London, 1834) quoted on its title page John Keats's 'A thing of beauty is a joy for ever'. Though visitors to the crowded, polluted gallery may not have found it a joy, the concept is clear.

27 Haydon 1844–6, vol. 2, p. 94.

28 Haydon 1960–3, vol. 2, 18 May 1824.

29 Haydon 1844–6, vol. 1, p. 9.

30 Louis Viardot, *Les Musées d'Espagne, d'Angleterre et de Belgique…guide et mémento de l'artiste et du voyageur* (Paris, 1843).

31 Ibid., pp. 280–2.

32 Wey 1935, p. 24.

33 See Mainardi 1987, p. 103.

34 Wey 1935, pp. 24–5.

35 Ernest Chesneau, *Les Nations rivales dans l'art* (Paris, 1868), pp. 1–3.

36 For a discussion of this issue, see especially Mainardi 1987, pp. 163–4.

37 It was immediately translated into English as *The Present State of the Arts in England* (London, 1755).

38 Rouquet 1755, pp. 71–2. He refers to Anna Maria Garthwaite (1689/90–1763), a major designer in Spitalfields, the centre of the silk-weaving trade in London, who produced designs for silk for thirty years up to 1756.

39 Ibid., pp. 93–4. The allusion must be to the Huguenot Nicholas Sprimont, who founded the Chelsea porcelain factory in 1744.

40 Ibid., p. 133.

41 Fox 2009, p. 521.

42 Ibid., p. 496.

43 Ibid., pp. 496, 501.

44 Richardson 1719, pp. 3–4.

45 Ibid., p. 4.

46 Simond 1815, vol. 1, p. 177.

47 Haydon 1960–3, vol. 1 (1960) 23 July 1808, pp. 4–5.

48 Hugh Brigstocke (ed.), *William Buchanan and the 19th Century Art Trade: 100 Letters to his Agents in London and Italy* (London, 1982), p. 89.

49 Ibid., p. 43.

50 Barry 1799, p. 13.

51 Hazlitt 1856, p. 235.

52 *Quarterly Review*, December 1824, p. 212.

53 Ibid., p. 211.

54 *Travels, Chiefly on Foot, Through Several Parts of England, in 1782 by Charles P. Moritz, A Literary Gentleman of Berlin. Translated from the German by a Lady* (London, 1795), p. 68.

55 W.H. Quarrell and W.J.C. Quarrell (eds), *Oxford in 1710, From the Travels of Zacharias Conrad von Uffenbach* (Oxford, 1928), p. 31.

56 Select Committee Report, National Gallery 1850, p. iv.

57 Quoted in Wilson 2002, p. 67.

58 Notably in Bennett 1995.

59 Farington 1978–98, vol. 5, p. 1847 (11 September 1802).

60 Ibid., p. 1856 (17 September 1802).

61 Ibid., p. 1819 (1 September 1802).

62 Ibid., p. 1854 (15 September 1802).

63 Reynolds 1975, p. 169.

64 Ibid., p. 169.

65 Peter Black (ed.), *'My Highest Pleasures': William Hunter's Art Collection* (London, 2007), p. 168.

66 Farington 1978–98, vol. 5, p. 1851.

67 The small but fine collection of pictures in William Hunter's bequest to Glasgow University included portraits by Allan Ramsay and Reynolds, with studies of animals by George Stubbs.

68 Some of the British paintings – by Fuseli, for example – were omitted from the selection of works for the gallery.

69 British art is still only grudgingly admitted to the National Gallery, where a single room contains works by the masters recognised as leaders of the British school a hundred years ago, and it is to that room that they are largely confined.

70 Richardson 1719, p. 51.

71 Ibid., p. 53–4.

72 Horace Walpole, *Anecdotes of Painting in England, With Some Account of the Principal Artists;…Collected by…G. Vertue and now Digested and Published from his original mss* (four vols, London, 1762), vol. 1, p. xii.

73 John Opie, Lecture 1: 'On Design', in Wornum 1848, pp. 237–68, at pp. 239–40.

74 Haydon 1844–6, vol. 1, p. 37.

75 Paul Barlow, for example, has vigorously stated this position. See Barlow and Trodd 2000.

76 M.T.S. Raimbach (ed.), *Memoirs and Recollections of the late Abraham Raimbach, Esq* (London, 1843), pp. 57–8.

77 *Hansard*, House of Commons, 23 July 1832, series 3, vol. 14, column 645.

78 Ibid.

79 Sheehan 2000, p. 46.

80 Select Committee Report, Arts and Manufactures 1836 (1356).

81 Select Committee Report, National Gallery 1850, p. iv.

82 Ibid., p. 393.

83 *Report from the Select Committee on Public Institutions*, 1860, pp. 439, 501.

84 *Report from the Select Committee on Extending a Knowledge of the Arts*, 1836, p. iii.

85 Ibid., p. iv.

86 John Barrell, *The Political Theory of Painting from Reynolds to Hazlitt: 'The Body of the Public'* (New Haven and London, 1986).

87 Reynolds 1975, pp. 169–71.

88 *Hansard*, House of Commons, 2 April 1824, series 2, vol. 11, column 102.

89 This notion had been discussed by Richardson and Reynolds, in discussions around the British Institution, and by Sir George Beaumont in his National Gallery campaigning.

90 *Hansard*, House of Commons, 13 April 1832, series 3, vol. 12, column 468.

91 Select Committee Report, Arts and Manufactures 1836 (245–61).

92 National Gallery archives, Board Minutes, 14 February and 10 May 1848.

93 William Dyce, *The National Gallery: Its Formation and Management* (London, 1853), p. 6.

94 Ibid., p. 39.

95 Ibid., p. 27.

96 Ibid., p. 25.

97 Ibid., pp. 51–2.

3: STRUGGLING FOR A VOICE

1 See *Städtische Sammlungen für Geschichte und Kultur Görlitz, Kunst und Wissenschaft um 1800: Die Sammlungen der Oberlausitzischen Gesellschaft der Wissenschaften zu Görlitz* (Görlitz, 2011).

2 For a recent account, see Marjan Scharloo (ed.), *Teylers Museum: A Journey in Time* (Haarlem, 2010).

3 James Raven, *London Booksellers and American Customers: Transatlantic Literary Community and the Charleston Library Society, 1748–1811* (Columbia, 2002), p. 26.

4 See Daniel Roche, *Le Siècle des Lumières en province: académies et académiciens provinciaux, 1680–1789* (two vols, Paris, 1978).

5 Ibid., vol. 1, p. 20.

6 *An Account of the British Institution for Promoting The Fine Arts in the United Kingdom* (London, 1805), p. 3.

7 *Prospectus of the Plan to Establish a Museum of Natural History, Antiquities &c in Norwich* ([Norwich], 1825). There is a copy in Norwich Castle Museum archives (No. 1, Committee Proceedings 1824–36).

8 See, for example, Gunn 2000.

9 The Royal Cornwall Institution in Truro and the Canterbury Philosophical and Literary Institution were founded in 1818 and 1825 respectively.

10 The Philosophical Society of Birmingham, 1800; the Liverpool Royal Institution, 1817; the Leeds Philosophical and Literary Society, 1818; the Yorkshire Philosophical Society in York, 1822.

11 John Brewer has illustrated this position with reference to the lively intellectual life of eighteenth-century Lichfield. See Brewer 1997, especially Chapter Fifteen.

12 Sydney Middlebrook, *The Advancement of Knowledge in Newcastle upon Tyne: The Literary and Philosophical Society as an Educational Pioneer* (Newcastle upon Tyne, 1974), p. 7.

13 See Brears and Davies 1989, pp. 17.

14 See *The History of the Literary and Philosophical Society of Newcastle upon Tyne,* vol. 1 by Robert Spence Watson (London, 1897), vol. 2 by Charles Parish (Newcastle upon Tyne, 1990). It is now the second oldest surviving society of its type in Britain.

15 Many Manchester Unitarians were also linked through education, having been taught at the Dissenting Warrington Academy, which from 1756 to 1782 offered an alternative to the Anglican universities under the tuition of such men as Joseph Priestley, and was the direct ancestor of Manchester College, Oxford.

16 See Vic Gatrell, 'Incorporation and the Pursuit of Liberal Hegemony in Manchester 1790–1839', in Derek Fraser (ed.), *Municipal Reform and the Industrial City* (Leicester, 1982), pp. 15–60, at p. 28.

17 Chris Makepeace, *Science and Technology in Manchester: Two Hundred Years of the Lit. and Phil.* (Manchester, 1984), p. 15.

18 The Society still exists.

19 Seed 1982, p. 5.

20 D.C. Stange, *British Unitarians against American Slavery 1833–65* (Rutherford, 1984), p. 13.

21 The first five mayors of Leicester were all Unitarians.

22 See Seed 1982.

23 Barker 1906, p. 28.

24 *Norwich and Norfolk Annual Report, 27th Annual General Meeting, 1851* (Norwich 1851).

25 See J.C. Barringer, *Norwich in the Nineteenth Century* (Norwich, 1984).

26 *Prospectus of the Plan to Establish a Museum of Natural History, Antiquities & in Norwich* ([Norwich], 1825). See Note 7, above.

27 Ibid.

28 *Norfolk & Norwich Museum Annual Reports 1826–1869* (bound volume in Norwich Castle Museum archives), *Report, 25 November 1829.*

29 Ibid., *Report of 37th Annual General Meeting,* 1861. For an extended discussion of this issue, see Yanni 1999, notably in the account of the Oxford University Museum.

30 A.J. Turner, 'A Forgotten Naturalist of the Seventeenth Century: William Cole and his Collections', *Archives of Natural History,* 11, no. 1 (1982), pp. 27–41.

31 See Crane 1983.

32 John Evans, *The New Guide or Picture of Bristol* (Bristol, c. 1823).

33 *Bristol Mercury,* 1824, quoted in Fawcett 1974, p. 185.

34 Its official name was the Bristol Institution for the Advancement of Science, Literature and the Arts.

35 The Very Revd. Beeke, quoted in Barker 1906, p. 16.

36 Michael Neve, 'Science in a Commercial City: Bristol 1820–60', in Inkster and Morrell 1983, pp. 179–204, at p. 187.

37 *Laws and Regulations of the Bristol Institution for the Advancement of Science, Literature and the Arts* (Bristol, 1825), p. 18.

38 David Watkin, *The Life and Work of C. R. Cockerell* (London, 1974), pp. 145–6.

39 He had rediscovered the order and was to use it again at the University Galleries in Oxford.

40 See Crane 1983.

41 The building survives but the interiors were rebuilt in simplified form after severe bomb damage in the Second World War.

42 These were given by E.W. Rippingille, a leading member of the Bristol school.

43 Barker 1906, p. 21.

44 Cockerell presented casts from the Pan-hellenium at Aegina in 1823, and in 1827 the Committee bought casts of the finest statues from the Vatican.

45 See Fawcett 1974, pp. 44–50, 63–4.

46 *Report of the Bristol Institution,* 1828.

47 *West of England Journal of Science and Literature,* January 1835.

48 See Haskell 2000, Chapter Three.

49 Ackermann et al. 1808–10, vol. 1, p. 98.

50 See British Institution exhibition catalogues, for example, British Institution 1814.

51 British Institution 1805, pp. 23–4.

52 *Regulations of the British Institution,* quoted in Ackermann et al., 1808–10, vol. 1, p. 100.

53 British Institution 1805, p. 24.

54 British Institution 1814, p. 13.

55 British Institution 1805, p. 3.

56 British Institution 1814, p. 2. They regained some income by selling prints after the painting to their subscribers.

57 Carey 1810, p. 39.

58 Ibid., p. 41.

59 Carey 1829, p. 24.

60 Ibid., p. 17.

61 Carey 1810, p. 36.

62 Carey 1829, p. 2.

63 Ibid., p. 3.

64 Stuart Macdonald, 'The Royal Manchester Institution', in Archer 1985, pp. 28–45; and John Seed, '"Commerce and the Liberal Arts": The Political Commerce of Art in Manchester, 1775–1860', in Janet Wolff and John Seed, *The Culture of Capital: Art, Power and the Nineteenth-Century Middle Class* (Manchester, 1988), pp. 45–81.

65 *The Eighth Exhibition of the Royal Manchester Institution* (Manchester, 1832), p. 3.

66 R.G. Wilson, *Gentlemen Merchants: The Merchant Community in Leeds 1700–1830* (Manchester, 1971), p. 216.

67 Quoted in ibid., p. 157.

68 Macleod 1996, pp. 110–11.

69 John Money, *Experience and Identity: Birmingham and the West Midlands* (Manchester, 1977), p. 2.

70 Birmingham Society of Arts, *Exhibition, Modern Works of Art* (Birmingham, 1832).

71 See Fawcett 1974.

72 Generally a shilling with a further shilling or sixpence was charged for the catalogue, and season tickets sold at five shillings, as in the Birmingham Society of Arts exhibition of 1832.

73 *The Exhibition of the Northern Society for the Encouragement of the Fine Arts* (Leeds, 1824). See Fawcett 1974, p. 60–1.

74 Carey 1829, p. 3.

75 Raeburn showed a portrait of John Rennie that was not for sale.

76 There were 46 portraits; 42 genre scenes; and 43 animal/still life paintings.

77 The Scottish Academy of Painting, Sculpture, and Architecture stated that 'no Copies of any kind' were to be allowed: *The Exhibition of the Scottish Academy of Painting, Sculpture, & Architecture* (Edinburgh, 1839).

78 See Fawcett 1974, pp. 85–9, for a discussion of Benjamin Gott.

79 *Exhibition of the Northern Society* (Leeds, 1824).

80 *Catalogue of the Exhibition of Paintings, Curiosities, Models, Apparatus and Specimens of Nature and Art, at the Music-Hall, Leeds, for the Benefit of the Mechanics' Institution; with the Names of the Contributors* (Leeds, 1839).

81 See Luckhurst 1951.

82 *Catalogue of the Ninth Exhibition of the Liverpool Academy* (Liverpool, 1832), p. 5.

83 *Catalogue of the Eighth Exhibition of the Liverpool Academy* (Liverpool, 1831), p. 5.

84 Fawcett 1974, p. 113.

85 Carey 1829, pp. 20–1.

86 Fawcett 1974, p. 115.

87 For a more extended account of this body, see Atkins 1996.

88 Carey 1829, p. 53. See the account of the Northern Academy of Arts in the *Newcastle Magazine,* 6 (1827), p. 568.

89 For a detailed account, see Usherwood 1984.

4: UNPROMISING SOIL

1 George Eliot, *Felix Holt* (1866), ed. Fred C. Thomson (Oxford, 1980), pp. 7–8.

2 Waugh 2008, p. 15.

3 Wallis 1911, p. 519.

4 J.B. Priestley, *English Journey* (London, 1934, repr. 1984), pp. 69, 198.

5 This history has been eloquently discussed in Hunt 2004.

6 Engels 1958, pp. 16 and 50.

7 Faucher 1844, p. 16.

8 Ibid., p. 24.

9 Tocqueville 1958, p. 96.

10 Kay 1832, p. 8.

11 Ibid., pp. 23, 59.

12 Ibid., p. 64.

13 Faucher 1844, p. 55.

14 Charles Dickens, 'Sunday under Three Heads: As Sabbath Bills Would Make It', in Charles Dickens, *Collected Papers* (London, 1903), p. 170.

15 Kay 1832, pp. 10, 49.

16 Ibid., p. 12.

17 Engels 1958, pp. 54, 31.

18 Ibid., p. 26.

19 See Chapter Twelve.

20 H. Gawthorp, *Fraser's Guide to Liverpool* (Liverpool, 1855), p. 33.

21 Ibid., p. 45.

22 Benjamin Love, *Hand-Book of Manchester; Containing Statistical and General Information on the Trade, Social Condition, and Institutions, of the Metropolis of Manufactures: Being a Second and Enlarged Edition of "Manchester As It Is."* (2nd ed., Manchester, 1842), pp. 273, 49.

23 *Morning Chronicle*, 18 October 1849, quoted in Reach 1972, p. v.

24 Reach also served for more than ten years as art, music, theatre and book critic for the *Morning Chronicle*.

25 Reach 1972, p. 1.

26 Ibid., p. 1.

27 Faucher 1844, pp. 82–3.

28 Ibid., p. 46.

29 P. Gaskell, *Artisans and Machinery: The Moral and Physical Condition of the Manufacturing Population Considered with Reference to Mechanical Substitutes for Human Labour* (London, 1836), p. 103.

30 Ibid., p. 111.

31 Reach 1972, pp. 8, 36, 2, 33.

32 Rowley 1911, p. 33.

33 Reach 1972, p. 16.

34 Ibid., p. 18.

35 Ibid., pp. 38–9.

36 Waagen 1854–7, vol. 3, p. 286.

37 For a recent account, see Robert Wenley, 'Masterpieces of a Merchant City', *Apollo*, 169 (July 2006), pp. 40–8.

38 Bell and Paton 1896, p. 352.

39 John Morrison, 'Victorian Municipal Patronage: The Foundation and Management of Glasgow Corporation Galleries 1854–1888', *Journal of the History of Collections*, 8, no. 1 (1996), pp. 93–102.

40 Bell and Paton 1896, p. 353. For an account of Paton and the early history of his museum, see Andrea McKeating, 'Kelvingrove Art Gallery and Museum', MA dissertation, University of Glasgow, 1990.

41 Bell and Paton 1896, p. 353.

42 *Report of the Parliamentary Select Committee on Arts and the Principles of Design*, 1836, p. iv.

43 Ibid., p. vii.

44 Ibid, p. v.

45 Ibid.

46 For a summary of the legislation and its implementation, see G. Lewis, 'Collections, Collectors and Museums in Britain to 1920', in J.M.L. Thompson et al. (eds.), *Manual of Curatorship: A Guide to Museum Practice* (Oxford, 1984), pp. 23–37.

47 It survives as a fine example of the period in its 1850s building.

48 The service had been planned since 1850. See W.A. Munford, *Penny Rate: Aspects of British Public Library History 1850–1950* (London, 1951).

49 Tocqueville 1958, p. 94.

50 Edwards 1877, pp. 70–1.

51 Ibid., p. 72.

52 Ibid.

53 Ibid., p. 91.

54 Ibid., p. 75.

55 Hartnell 1996, p. 39.

56 Conway 1991, p. 16.

57 See Mark Girouard, *The English Town* (New Haven and London, 1990), Chapter Eight.

58 Conway 1991, p. 21.

59 Ibid., p. 49.

60 Now closed, though still standing.

61 Manchester had five branches of the City Art Gallery set in parks.

62 Edwards 1877, p. 75.

63 Sharp 1898, p. 360.

64 Gill and Grant Robertson 1938, p. 45.

65 Alfred St Johnson in *Magazine of Art* (1887), quoted in Hartnell 1996, p. 1.

66 Armstrong 1895, p. 248.

67 Alexander Ireland, *Recollections of George Dawson and his Lectures in Manchester in 1846–7* (Manchester, 1882), p. 22.

68 Armstrong 1895, p. 248.

69 Ibid., pp. 259–60.

70 Gill and Grant Robertson 1938, p. 48.

71 Armstrong 1895, p. 249.

72 Charlotte Gere, 'Gilding the Corporations: Victorian Mayoral Chains', *Country Life*, 21 August 1986, pp. 572–4.

73 Bell and Paton 1896, p. v.

74 Ibid.

75 Ibid., p. xxii.

76 Ibid., pp. xxii–xxiii.

77 See John Dinkel, *The Royal Pavilion, Brighton* (London, 1983), pp. 131–2.

78 *Report of the Fifty-Seventh Meeting of the British Association for the Advancement of Science, Held at Manchester in August and September 1887* (London, 1888), pp. 101–13.

79 Greenwood 1888, p. 3.

80 I am grateful to Edward Morris for this suggestion, and for his guidance on the following paragraph.

81 A detailed account of the development of art museums in Birmingham, Liverpool and Manchester is given in Woodson-Boulton 2012.

82 Greenwood 1888, pp. 369–77.

83 Ibid., p. 43.

84 *British Association Report*, 1887, p. 118.

85 Howarth and Platnauer 1911, pp. 130, 156.

86 Greenwood 1888, p. 2.

5: THE UNIVERSAL EXHIBITION

1 For an extended discussion of this history, see Greenhalgh 1988.

2 Ibid., p. 15.

3 Walter Benjamin, 'Paris, Capital of the Nineteenth Century: Exposé [of 1939]', in Walter Benjamin, *The Arcades Project*, trans. Howard Eiland and Kevin McLaughlin (Cambridge, MA, and London, 1999), pp. 14–26, at p. 17.

4 Richards 1990, pp. 3–4.

5 Ibid., p. 5.

6 Auerbach 1998.

7 Fox 2009, p. 494.

8 Davis 1999, p. xvii.

9 Kriegel 2007, pp. 90, 89.

10 *Gems of the Great Exhibitions, London 1851, New York 1853* (London 1853), verso of title page.

11 Speech at the Royal Academy, 3 May 1851, in Helps 1862, p. 112.

12 The *Crystal Palace Exhibition Illustrated Catalogue* [special issue of the *Art Journal*] (London, 1851), pp. 105, 184.

13 Ibid., pp. 202–4.

14 Ibid., p. 233.

15 *The Art-Treasures Examiner* (1857), p. i.

16 Macleod 1996, p. 91, points out that this notion was a cliché, reflected in such novels as Thackeray's *The Newcomes* of 1855.

17 Faucher 1844, p. 21.

18 Pergam 2011, pp. 103–4.

19 Ibid., p. 137.

20 *Catalogue of the Art Treasures of the United Kingdom, Collected at Manchester in 1857* (London 1857), p. 151.

21 Palgrave 1862, p. 63.

22 The catalogue of the Paris exhibition was entitled *Notice des estampes exposées à la bibliothèque du Roi*, ed. Jean Duchesne (Paris, 1819). Information from Antony Griffiths.

23 Manchester 1859, p. 4.

24 Shaffner and Owen 1862, p. iii.

25 *The Record of the International 1862 Exhibition* (Glasgow, 1862).

26 Ibid., p. 588.

27 Ibid., p. 585.

28 Illustrated Exhibitor 1851, p. 27.

29 *Modern London* (1887), quoted in Alison Adburgham, *Shopping in Style: London from the Restoration to Edwardian Elegance* (London, 1979), p. 144.

30 Ibid., p. 156.

31 *Report of the Library and Museum Committee to the Town Council, of the Borough of Liverpool, October 1853* (Liverpool, 1853), p. 7.

32 *Charter of Incorporation of the Manchester Whitworth Institute* (Manchester, 1890), Whitworth Art Gallery archive.

33 See Conn 1998, Chapter Four, pp. 115–50.

34 *Charter of Incorporation of the Manchester Whitworth Institute* (Manchester, 1890), p. 12, Whitworth Art Gallery archive.

35 Quoted in Piggott 2004, p. 28.

36 Ibid., p. 13.

37 Ibid., p. 61.

38 Illustrated Exhibitor 1851, p.1.

39 Mayhew 1851, pp. 1, 3.

40 Davis 1999, p. 108.

41 *The Record of the International 1862 Exhibition* (Glasgow, 1862), p. 1.

42 Ibid., p. 64.

43 Ibid.

44 Ibid., p. 63.

45 Mayhew 1851, p. 129.

46 The quotation is from *Encyclopaedia Britannica* (8th ed., Edinburgh, 1853–60), p. 705.

47 Cole 1884, vol. 1, pp. 103–5.

48 *A Guide through the Great Exhibition Containing a Description of Every Principal Object of Interest* (London, 1851), p. 3.

49 Illustrated Exhibitor 1851, p. 2.

50 See Davis 1999.

51 'Proposal Presented to the General Council for the Exhibition of Art Treasures of the United Kingdom, 23 June 1856', cited in Manchester 1859, p. 5.

52 *What to See* 1857, pp. 6, 7. The bed had been inspired by the Great Exhibition.

53 Ibid., p. 6.

54 Barringer 2005, p. 28.

55 Kriegel 2007, p. 179.

56 A similar display had been held shortly before in Battersea.

57 J.F. Wilson (ed.), *Illustrated Memorial of the North London Working Classes Industrial Exhibition of 1864* (London, 1864), p. 11.

58 Carlyle 2005, p. 195.

59 Ibid., p. 21.

60 *The Times* dedicated two articles to the event.

61 Carlyle 2005, p. 52.

62 Ibid., p. 23.

63 Ibid., p. 50.

64 'W.W.', 'Workmen's Industrial Exhibitions', *The Art Journal*, 42 (1880), p. 24.

65 Manchester 1859, p. 1.

66 Helps 1862, p. 180.

67 *A Handbook to the British Portrait Gallery in the Art Treasures Exhibition, From the Manchester Guardian* (Manchester, 1857), p. 4.

68 'The National Gallery', *Art Journal* (1857), pp. 236–8, at p. 237.

69 They were assembled by such men as the Revd William Bromley Davenport at Capesthorne Hall, Cheshire, and the Revd Henry Wellesley of Oxford.

70 *A Handbook to the British Portrait Gallery in the Art Treasures Exhibition, From the Manchester Guardian* (Manchester, 1857), p. 4.

71 Illustrated Exhibitor 1851, p. 2.

72 Letter from Prince Albert to Lord Ellesmere, 3 July 1856, printed in Manchester 1859, p. 17.

73 *A Walk through the Art-Treasures Exhibition at Manchester, Under the Guidance of Dr. Waagen* (London, 1857), Foreword.

74 See Samuel Redgrave (ed.), *Catalogue of the Special Exhibition of Portrait Miniatures on Loan at the South Kensington Museum* (London, 1865).

75 Ernest Chesneau, *The English School of Painting* (London, 1885), p. 167.

76 Discussed further in Chapter Nine.

77 Gibbs 1887, p. 110.

78 Ibid., p. 118.

79 Ibid., p. 120.

80 Special Collections, Getty Research Institute, Los Angeles.

81 Information from the website of Brian Payne, Chairman, John Peck Society, Wisbech St Mary, accessed 26 April 2011 (website no longer available).

82 Hawthorne 1941, p. 355.

83 Ibid.

84 Ibid., p. 371.

85 Ibid., p. 376.

86 See Archer 1985, p. 125.

87 Hawthorne 1941, p. 551.

88 Ibid., p. 376.

89 Charles Dickens, 'The Manchester School of Art', *Household Words*, 10 October 1857, p. 350.

90 Ibid.

91 Ibid.

92 *The Record of the International Exhibition 1862* (Glasgow, 1862), p. 587. John Agnew suggests that this benevolent pedagogue may be either Robert Hunt (1807–87), chemist and photographer with a developed interest in the education of working miners, or (more likely) Thomas Romney Robinson (1793–1882), astronomer and physicist, and 'in great demand as an erudite and entertaining public speaker on scientific subjects' (ODNB). Both were officially involved in the exhibition.

93 As in *What to See* 1857, p. 17, Appendix.

94 Mark Haworth-Booth and Anne McCauley, *The Museum and the Photograph: Collecting Photography at the Victoria and Albert Museum, 1853–1900* (Williamstown, 1998), p. 10.

95 Manchester 1859, p. 20.

96 *International Exhibition of 1862, Catalogue of the Photographs Exhibited in Class XIV* [London, 1862], p. ii.

97 Shaffner and Owen 1862, p. vi.

98 *Manchester Guardian Handbook, Prefatory and General…to British Paintings* (Manchester, 1857), p. 12.

99 In the context of displaying the visual arts in Victorian Britain such consumption had been sanctioned only at the annual Royal Academy dinner.

100 Physick 1982, p. 30.

101 *Victorian Nottingham*, 8 [n.d.], p. 81. In spite of vigorous objections from the temperance lobby, the licence persisted until 1904.

102 Davis 1999, pp. 160–1.

103 I am grateful to Charlotte Gere for pointing out this detail.

104 *The Exhibition of Art-Industry in Dublin* (Dublin and London, 1853), p. vi.

105 Manchester 1859, p. 20.

106 Conway 1991, pp. 127–31.

107 Kennedy 1960, p. 4.

108 Ibid., Chapter Five.

109 Manchester 1859, p. 20.

110 Gibbs 1887.

111 It remained under his direction until his death in 1895.

112 W.S. Jevons, *Methods of Social Reform* (London, 1883), quoted in Conway 1991, p. 131.

113 Faucher 1844, p. 49.

114 Ibid., p. 49, note.

115 Reach 1972, pp. 57–9.

116 Kennedy 1960, p. 23.

117 For a detailed account, see Musgrave 1995.

118 Much as a hall for music had formed an important feature in earlier civic buildings, such as the first Birmingham Town Hall, built in the 1830s.

119 *Corporation of Glasgow, Report for the Year 1897* (Glasgow, 1897), pp. 7–8.

120 Musgrave 1995, p. 73.

121 Quoted in Kennedy 1960, p. 68.

122 As at Liverpool.

6: FOR INSTRUCTION AND RECREATION

1 Greenwood 1888, p. v.

2 Murray 1904, vol 1, p. v.

3 *Nature*, 31 May 1877, p. 78.

4 These views were reflected by A.C.L.G. Gunther, Keeper of Zoology at the Natural History Museum, writing three years later (*Nature*, 26 August 1880, pp. 393–6).

5 J.A. Crowe and G.B. Cavalcaselle, *A History of Painting in North Italy* (two vols, London, 1871), vol. 1, title page.

6 See Robertson 1978, pp. 435–7, for a discussion of

illustrations. The book provides a masterly summary of the earlier Victorian literature on the visual arts.

7   Emile Molinier, *The Wallace Collection* (London and New York, 1903), p. xi.

8   Hippolyte Taine, *Notes on England*, trans. Edward Hyams (London, 1957), p. 234.

9   Matthew Arnold, *Culture and Anarchy* (1869), in Noël Annan (ed.), *Matthew Arnold, Selected Essays* (London, 1964), pp. 233–319, at p. 296.

10   Bailey 1998, Chapter One (pp. 13–29), 'The Victorian Middle Class and the Problem of Leisure'.

11   T.H.S. Escott, *Social Transformations of the Victorian Age: A Survey of Court and Country* (1877), p. 14, quoted in ibid., p. 16.

12   Best 1971, p. 3.

13   Thompson 1988, p. 291.

14   Wallis 1911, pp. 477–8.

15   *Report of the Library and Museum Committee to the Town Council, of the Borough of Liverpool*, 1853, p. 7.

16   Ibid., p. 6.

17   *Report of the Library and Museum Committee to the Town Council, of the Borough of Liverpool*, 1854, p. 3.

18   *Report of the Library and Museum Committee to the Town Council, of the Borough of Liverpool*, 1856, p. 3.

19   Greenwood 1888, pp. 173–4.

20   The population of Bradford was 228,000 in 1909; 288,000 in 1911.

21   Howarth and Platnauer 1911.

22   Sir Benjamin Heywood, *Addresses Delivered at the Manchester Mechanics' Institution* (London, 1843), p. 41.

23   Edmund Swinglehurst, *The Romantic Journey: The Story of Thomas Cook and Victorian Travel* (London, 1974), p. 13.

24   *Report of the Committee of the Free Public Library, and The Derby Museum of the Borough of Liverpool*, 1854, p. 3.

25   *Report of the Library and Museum Committee to the Town Council, of the Borough of Liverpool*, 1856, p. 3.

26   Report presented to the Council, 23 June 1856, cited in Manchester 1859, p. 11.

27   Quoted in Johnstone 1859, p. 6.

28   Supplement to the *Bury Times*, 12 October 1901 (copy in Bury Art Gallery archives).

29   *Report of the Library and Museum Committee to the Town Council, of the Borough of Liverpool*, 1896, p. 59.

30   Russell-Cotes 1921, p. 54.

31   *The National Gallery of Pictures by the Great Masters* (London, 1838), p. iii.

32   Greenwood 1888, p. 125.

33   Bell and Paton 1896, p. 350.

34   Quoted in Muirhead 1911, p. 511.

35   *The Fine Art Collection of Glasgow, with an Introductory Essay by James Paton FLS Curator of the Gallery* (Glasgow, 1906), p. 43.

36   Davies 1985, p. 22.

37   Notably, 'Picture Galleries – Their Functions and Formation: Evidence given by Ruskin to the National Gallery Site Commission, April 6, 1857' (1857), in Ruskin, *Works*, vol. 13, pp. 539–53; 'On the Present State of Modern Art, with Reference to the Advisable Arrangement of a National Gallery' (1867), ibid., vol. 19, pp. 197–229; and 'A Museum or Picture Gallery: Its Functions and Its Formation' (1880), ibid., vol. 34, pp. 247–62.

38   Ruskin, *Works*, vol. 19, p. 226.

39   Ruskin 1880, p. 162.

40   For the most recent account of the museum, see Barry Jackson, *Cawthorne 1770–1990: A South Yorkshire Village Remembers its Past* (Cawthorne, 1991), pp. 118–25. Always intended to serve the local community, it survives as a unique example of a Ruskin-inspired rural museum.

41   Henry Cole, 'Introductory Address on the Functions of the Science and Art Department', in Cole 1884, vol. 2, p. 286.

42   See Quentin Bell, *The Schools of Design* (London, 1963), p. 67.

43   Henry Cole, 'Address at the Opening of an Elementary Drawing School at Westminster', in *Department of Practical Art. National Art Training Schools. Elementary Drawing Schools* (London, 1853), p. 3.

44   For a summary of the teaching programme, see Casteras and Parkinson 1988, pp. 53–6.

45   *Department of Science and Art* [DSA] *Annual Report*, 1854, p. xxvi.

46   DSA, *Annual Report*, 1858, p. 55.

47   DSA, *Annual Report*, 1862, p. 122.

48   Ruskin 1880, p. 249.

49   He served as curator of the Museum of Ornamental Art (the forerunner of the South Kensington Museum, sited at Marlborough House) from its foundation in 1852, and then as curator and from 1863 as Art Referee at the South Kensington Museum.

50   J.C. Robinson, *An Introductory Lecture on the Museum of Ornamental Art of the Department* (London, 1854), p. 31.

51   Ibid., p. 8.

52   Cole 1884, vol. 2, p. 293.

53   DSA, *Annual Report*, 1855, p. vi.

54   Ibid.

55   Cole 1884, vol. 2, p. 288.

56   DSA, *Annual Report*, 1859, p. 23.

57   DSA, *Annual Report*, 1867, pp. 192

58   Henry Cole, 'National Culture and Recreation: Antidotes to Vice. An Address Delivered at the Liverpool Institute', in Cole 1884, vol. 2, pp. 357–69, at p. 368.

59   DSA, *Annual Report*, 1858, p. 79.

60   Ibid., p. 80.

61   Ibid.

62   DSA, *Annual Report*, 1865, p. 177.

63   DSA, *Annual Report*, 1864, p. xv.

64   Howarth and Platnauer 1911.

65   For a full discussion of this debate, see Geoffrey N. Swiney, '"The Evil of Vitiating and Heating the Air": Artificial Lighting and Public Access to the National Gallery, London, with Particular Reference to the Turner and Vernon Collections', *Journal of the History of Collections*, 15, no. 1 (2003), pp. 83–112.

66   Hudson 1851, p. 62.

67   See Davies 1985.

68   J.C. Robinson, 'On Our National Art Museums and Galleries', *The Nineteenth Century*, 32 (1892), pp. 1021–34, at p. 1022.

69   *Catalogue of the Objects of Art and Art Manufacture in the Corporation Free Art Gallery* (Birmingham, 1870).

70   *Birmingham City Art Gallery Annual Report*, 1874, p. 3.

71   Whitworth Wallis, 'Contributions from the South Kensington Museum', in Wallis and St Johnston 1885, p. 64.

72   Wallis and St Johnston 1885, p. 22.

7: ART ON SHOW

1   Yanni 1999, p. 1.

2   Ibid., p. 43.

3   This issue is developed by Whitehead 2005a, especially at pp. 194–7.

4   Baretti 1781, p. 3.

5   Select Committee Report, Works of Art 1848, pp. 3–4.

6   Wey 1935, p. 19.

7   Ibid., p. 20.

8   'J.W.', 'The New Museum, or Picture Gallery, at Dresden', *Art Journal* (1855), pp. 214–15, at p. 215.

9   Whiteley 1997, p. 615.

10   Waagen 1853, p. 102.

11   Wyatt Papworth was a distinguished historian, editor with his brother of the eleven-volume *Dictionary of Architecture* (1853–92) and Curator of Sir John Soane's Museum from 1892 to 1894.

12   'Art-Gallery and Museum for Manchester', *Art Journal* (1860), p. 72. He had originally published these ideas in a local newspaper.

13   Summerson 1955, p. 35.

14   Pennethorne's most important museum building was the Museum of Practical Geology in Jermyn Street, London, of 1847 (demolished).

15   A term proposed by Whitehead 2005.

16   McClellan 2008 ably summarises the recent controversy.

17   Baretti 1781, p. 31.

18   Jean-Nicolas-Louis Durand, *Précis of the Lectures on Architecture*, translation by David Britt (Los Angeles, 2000), p. 160.

19   *Report of the Select Committee on the National Gallery 1847–8*, 1848 (124–5).

20 Waagen 1853.

21 Ibid., p. 102.

22 Ibid., p. 101.

23 'The New Scottish National Gallery', *Art Journal* (1850), p. 308.

24 Redgrave 1857, pp. 25–6.

25 Robinson 1880, p. 260.

26 Ibid.

27 Ibid., p. 261.

28 The debate through the ages has recently been discussed in McClellan 2008.

29 Wilson 1851, p. 207.

30 Greenwood 1888, p. 5.

31 Ruskin 1880, p. 161.

32 Ibid.

33 Ibid.

34 Harry Quilter, 'French and English Pictures', *Cornhill Magazine*, 40 (1879), pp. 92–106, at p. 93.

35 'The New National Gallery', *Art Journal*, 38 (1876), pp. 333–4, at p. 333.

36 G. Shaw Lefevre, 'The Public Buildings of London', *The Nineteenth Century*, 24 (1888), pp. 703–18, at p. 710.

37 'Autumn Exhibitions' in *Art Journal* (1884), pp. 317–18, at p. 317.

38 Walker Art Gallery, *Annual Report*, 1895, p. 15.

39 McGibbon 1901, p. 131.

40 Robert Ruschenberger, *Academy of Natural Sciences of Philadelphia* (1876), quoted in Conn 1998, p. 41.

41 Greenwood 1888, p. 75.

42 See Hill 2005, p. 107; and for issues of ornament in science museums, see Yanni 1999.

43 Charles Cornish, *Sir William Henry Flower: A Personal Memoir* (London, 1904), p. 148.

44 The Yorkshire Museum belonged to the Yorkshire Philosophical Society and was erected 1827–30.

45 The Hancock Museum of Natural History in Newcastle is now known as the Great North Museum: Hancock.

46 *The Builder*, 4 February 1888, p. 84.

47 Greenwood 1888, p. 170.

48 John Summerson, *The Architecture of British Museums and Galleries*, in Chapel and Gere 1985, pp. 9–19, at p. 16.

49 Ingrid A. Steffenson-Bruce, *Marble Palaces, Temples of Art: Art Museums, Architecture and American Culture, 1890–1930*, Lewisburg, 1998.

50 Ibid., pp. 132–3.

51 For a notable recent analysis of the South Kensington Museum style and its implications, see Whitehead 2005, pp. 38–68.

52 Summerson 1985, p. 15.

53 By contrast, in the United States in mid-century Ruskin exerted a powerful influence on buildings, from the Pennsylvania Academy of Fine Arts to the original Metropolitan Museum of Art.

54 Donisthorpe 1868, p. 23.

55 H.M. Cundall, 'Our Provincial Art Museums and Galleries: IV – Sheffield and Wolverhampton', *Art Journal* (1892), pp. 282–3, at p. 282.

56 Sparke 1907, p. 2.

57 Atkinson Art Gallery, Southport, broadsheet (n.d).

58 Lewis F. Day, 'Decorative and Industrial Art at the Glasgow Exhibition', *Art Journal* (1901), pp. 237–43, at p. 237.

59 Nikolaus Pevsner, revised Enid Radcliffe, *The Buildings of England: Yorkshire: West Riding* (Harmondsworth, 1979), p. 315.

60 Written communication to the author, 3 October 2012.

61 Davis 1999, p. 87.

62 Saint 2007, p. 140.

63 Ibid., p. 134.

64 Wilson 1851.

65 Nottingham Castle 1878, p. 6.

66 Sparke 1907, p. 2.

67 *Glasgow Museums and Galleries of Art, Report*, 1894, p. 5.

68 *Report of the Library and Museum Committee to the Town Council, of the Borough of Liverpool*, 1897, p. 67.

69 David Scruton, *The Victoria Galleries: Art and Enterprise in Late Nineteenth Century Dundee* (Dundee, 1989), p. 10.

70 Nottingham Castle 1878, p. 6.

71 Flower 1898, p. 31.

72 Ibid., p. 33.

73 The Museums Association's Dublin conference, 1912, reported in *Museums Journal*, 12 (1912–13), pp. 39–46, at p. 43. For Armstrong's time at the National Gallery of Ireland, see Somerville-Large 2004.

74 'English Provincial Museums – III', *The Burlington Magazine*, 10, no. 43 (December, 1906), pp. 141–3, at p. 141.

75 Ibid., p. 142.

76 'The Birmingham Art Gallery', *Burlington Magazine*, 8, no. 34 (January, 1906), p. 285.

77 Sparke 1907, p. 2.

78 James Ward, 'The Relation of Schools of Art to Museums' (a paper read at the Museums Association conference, Dublin, 1912), *Museums Journal*, 12 (1912–13), pp. 229–42, at p. 237.

79 'New Art Galleries, Birmingham' in *Birmingham Daily Post*, partly reprinted in *Museums Journal*, 12 (1912–13), pp. 81–3, at p. 82.

80 *Museums Journal*, 4 (1904–5), p. 199.

81 'Notes and News', *Museums Journal*, 10 (1910–11), pp. 185–6.

82 Charles L. Eastlake, 'Picture-Hanging at the National Gallery', *The Nineteenth Century*, 22 (1887), p. 823.

83 *A Record of the Collections in the Lady Lever Art Gallery* (London, 1928), foreword by C.R. Grundy, p. 5.

84 Ibid.

85 See Bennett 1995.

86 Hill 2005, pp. 103–4.

87 Forgan 1994, pp. 143–4.

88 The Founder's Building of the Fitzwilliam Museum, Nottingham Castle Museum and the Wallace Collection are examples.

89 James Paton, 'An Art Museum: Its Structural Requirements', *The Proceedings of the Royal Philosophical Society of Glasgow* (1891), pp. 128–38, at p. 130.

90 Ibid., p. 137.

91 See T.J. Honeyman, *Art and Audacity* (London, 1971).

92 James Paton, 'Glasgow Art Gallery and Museum', *Museums Journal*, 1 (1901–2), pp. 314–24, at p. 315.

93 McGibbon 1901, p. 131.

94 See Church and Lawson 1987.

95 Priestley 1902–3, p. 6.

96 Church and Lawson 1987, p. 9.

97 Ibid., p. 13.

98 'The New Art Galleries of Glasgow', *Museums Journal*, 2 (1902–3), pp. 93–4.

99 A separate Science Museum was not created until 1909.

100 In Dublin, the relationship between science and art was paralleled in the design for the new museum buildings: the National Gallery of Ireland, which opened in 1864, was housed on one side of Leinster Lawn, facing and duplicating the façade of the Natural History Museum (completed in 1857) on the other side. The juxtaposition emphasised the relationship between old art (and history) and new, asserting the place of Irish culture as part of a broader historical tradition.

101 Information on Oldham was generously provided by Sean Baggaley, Gallery Oldham.

102 *Museums Journal*, 2 (1902–3), p. 60.

103 Corporation of Nottingham, *Official Catalogue of the Pictures and Objects in the Midland Counties Art Museum, The Castle, Nottingham* (Nottingham, 1878).

104 Forgan 1994, p. 144.

105 See Thomas Markus, *Buildings and Power: Freedom and Control in the Origin of Modern Building Types* (London and New York, 1993), pp. 19–25.

106 Greenwood 1888, p. 3.

107 For discussions of this issue, see Lorente 1998, Chapter One, and Sheehan 2000.

108 *Report from the Select Committee on Trafalgar Square*, 1840, p. 10 (191).

109 A recognition of the role of cultural buildings in a grand urban setting was apparent in Edinburgh and Dublin, and later in Cardiff. The National Gallery of Scotland and the neighbouring Royal Scottish Academy were conceived in boldly scenic terms in the Classical revival tradition. In Dublin, a fine central site was provided for the National Gallery of Ireland (1864), while

in Cardiff the new National Museum (1912–27) gained a notable setting in Cathays Park.

110 Saint 2007, p. 37.

111 This problem has recently been addressed in a reworking of the building.

112 Bruno Foucart, 'Le musée du xixe siècle: temple, palais, basilique', in Chantal Georgel, *La Jeunesse des musées: les musées de France au xixe siècle* (Paris, 1994), pp. 122–51, at p. 125.

113 McClellan 2008, pp. 70–1.

114 John Newman, *The Buildings of Wales: Glamorgan* (London, 1995), p. 220.

115 Select Committee Report, National Gallery 1853 (7996), cited by Whitehead 2005, p. 63.

116 *Manchester Guardian*, 13 October 1887.

117 Greenwood 1888, p. 170.

118 Priestley 1902–3, p. 7.

119 Crawford 1891, p. 17.

120 Eyre-Todd 1934, p. 82.

121 Canon Samuel Barnett, *The Ideal City* (Bristol, n.d.), in *Tracts of Social Questions, 1894–1908* (British Library compilation, 08275.de.25). The essay was reprinted in a compilation, *The Ideal City*, edited by Helen N. Meller and published by Leicester University Press in 1979, where the date given for it is 1894.

122 Armstrong 1895, p. 261.

8: THE TEMPORARY EXHIBITION

1 For a recent assertion of this approach to museums, see Cuno 2004.

2 The entrance fee and the cost of the catalogue were refundable if a purchase was made (information from Charlotte Gere).

3 As Patricia Mainardi has discussed at length: Mainardi 1987 and Mainardi 1993.

4 Caroline New, 'The Old Master X-rayed, Examined and Exhibited: The Display and Interpretation of Technical Material at the National Gallery, London', MA dissertation, Courtauld Institute of Art, London, 2009.

5 See Leonée and Richard Ormond, *Lord Leighton* (London, 1975), p. 66.

6 *Royal Academy of Arts Annual Report*, 1870, p. 20.

7 Royal Academy archives, Correspondence File, Box 796A.

8 *Royal Academy of Arts Annual Report*, 1869 quoted in Sidney C. Hutchison, *The History of the Royal Academy 1768–1968* (2nd ed., London, 1986), p. 114.

9 With the exception of Ruskin, almost all the lenders belonged to the high aristocracy.

10 See p. 194 below.

11 Henry James, 'The Old Masters at Burlington House' (1877), in John L. Sweeney (ed.), *The Painter's Eye: Notes and Essays on the Pictorial Arts by Henry James* (London, 1956), pp. 124–9, at p. 124.

12 Ibid.

13 Quilter 1892, p. 281.

14 Leeds City Art Gallery, *Official Catalogue, Loan Exhibition* (Leeds, 1888), p. 6.

15 Walker Art Gallery, *Liverpool Autumn Exhibition of Modern Pictures, in Oil and Water Colours* (Liverpool, 1888).

16 *Report of the Library and Museum Committee to the Town Council, of the Borough of Liverpool*, 1885, p. 3.

17 Dyall 1888, p. 17.

18 Ibid., p. 19.

19 Ibid., advertisement opposite p. 1. The 'Art History and Museums' section was organised by Sidney Colvin and Lionel Cust, both to become notable art historians and curators.

20 Ibid., p. 6.

21 *Report of the Library and Museum Committee to the Town Council, of the Borough of Liverpool*, 1895, p. 65. They may have been visiting the open studios, which were arranged before the opening of the Royal Academy Summer Exhibition.

22 Oldham Reference Library, minutes of Oldham Free Library and Museum Committee No. 1.

23 [City of Glasgow], *Report on the City Industrial Museum, Kelvingrove Park, and the Corporation Galleries of Art*, 1877, p. 10.

24 From 162,000 in 1892 to 420,000 in 1898.

25 *Leeds Art Gallery Annual Report*, 1911, p. 8.

26 Verbal information from Edward Morris.

27 Glasgow Museums and Galleries of Art, *Guide to the Collection of Indian Presents Lent by His Royal Highness The Prince of Wales to the City of Glasgow for Public Exhibition* (Glasgow, 1879), pp. 6–7.

28 Glasgow Museums and Galleries of Art, *Oriental Art Loan Exhibition 1881–2* (Glasgow, 1881).

29 [City of Glasgow], *Report on the City Industrial Museum, Kelvingrove Park, and the Corporation Galleries of Art*, 1881, p. 7.

30 Ibid., 1882–3, p. iii.

31 Report by J.C. Robinson, quoted in [City of Glasgow], *Report on the City Industrial Museum, Kelvingrove Park, and the Corporation Galleries of Art*, 1882, p. 5.

32 [City of Glasgow], *Report on the City Industrial Museum, Kelvingrove Park, and the Corporation Galleries of Art*, 1883, p. 3.

33 Glasgow Museums and Art Gallery, *French Art Loan Exhibition 1883–4* (Glasgow, 1883), p. 56.

34 The Walker Art Gallery, *Fourteenth Autumn Exhibition of Pictures in Oil and Watercolour, and inauguration of the Extension of the Walker Art Gallery* (Liverpool, 1884), p. 2.

35 The Walker Art Gallery, *Liverpool Naval Exhibition* (Liverpool, 1892), p. xxxvi.

36 Leeds City Art Gallery, *Official Catalogue, National Exhibition of Works of Art, at Leeds* (Leeds, 1869) and Leeds City Art Gallery, *Early Days at Leeds City Art Gallery* (Leeds, 1974).

37 Leeds City Art Gallery, *Official Catalogue, National Exhibition of Works of Art, at Leeds* (Leeds, 1869), p. 87.

38 Ibid., pp. v–vi.

39 Manchester City Council took over the Royal Manchester Institution's Gallery in 1882 and converted it into the Manchester City Art Gallery in 1882–3.

40 Leeds City Art Gallery, *The Yorkshire Fine Art Society* (Leeds, 1880), p. 2.

41 Leeds City Art Gallery, *The Yorkshire Fine Art Society* (Leeds, 1886), p. 3.

42 Oldham Reference Library, press cutting reporting a speech by the Mayor of Oldham, 8 November 1882.

43 Oldham Reference Library, minutes of Oldham Free Library and Museum Committee, 8 November 1882.

44 Oldham Art Gallery, *Official Catalogue of the Fine Art and Industrial Exhibition, In Connection with the Opening of the Free Reference Library & Museum, 1 August 1883* (Oldham, 1883).

45 British Institution, *An Historical Catalogue of Portraits...* (London, 1820).

46 Ibid., p. 14.

47 For a detailed account of this and other Glasgow exhibitions, see Kinchin 1988, p. 26.

48 Not including some 1.5 million schoolchildren, for whom no charge was made: ibid., p. 93.

49 Kelvingrove Museum and Art Gallery, *Old Glasgow* (Glasgow, 1894).

50 Eyre-Todd 1934, p. 177.

51 According to ibid., p. 175, 'museums and private mansions throughout Scotland were ransacked for relics'.

52 Kelvingrove Museum and Art Gallery, *Scottish Exhibition of National History, Art and Industry* (Glasgow, 1911).

53 Eyre-Todd 1934, p. 172.

54 Frederic Harrison, 'A Few Words about Picture Exhibitions', *The Nineteenth Century*, 24 (1888), pp. 30–44, at pp. 30–1.

55 Ibid., p. 43.

56 Richard Altick, *Paintings from Books: Art and Literature in Britain, 1760–1900* (Columbus, 1985), pp. 408–9.

57 W. Archer Shee, 'Painters and their Patrons', *The Nineteenth Century* 14 (1883), pp. 243–56, at p. 245.

58 Quilter 1892, p. 202.

59 Leeds City Art Gallery, *Historical Series of Water-Colour Paintings, Illustrative of the Rise and Progress of the Art in England from 1710* (Leeds, 1889).

60 Leeds City Art Gallery, *Exhibition of Posters... December 1894–January 1895* (Leeds, 1894).

61 Williams 1981, p. 62.

62 *Western Daily Press*, 7 August 1894.

63 The Fine Art Society, London, *Notes by Mr. Ruskin on his Collection of Drawings by the Late J. M. W. Turner, RA., Exhibited at the Fine Art Society's Galleries: Also a List of the Engraved Works of that Master Shown at the Same Time* (London, 1878).

64 Birmingham City Art Gallery, *Catalogue of the Loan Collection of Pictures and Drawings by J. M. W. Turner, R.A.: With Descriptive and Biographical Notes* (Birmingham, 1899).

65 Leeds City Art Gallery, *Catalogue [of] the Engraved work of J. M. W. Turner, R.A. 1896–97, With an Introduction by George Birkett* (Leeds, 1896).

66 'Art Notes and Reviews', *The Art Journal* (1887), pp. 286–8, at p. 288.

9: A NEW STYLE OF COLLECTING

1 Robinson 1880, p. 250. At the time of writing it had not proved possible to identify the museum Robinson had in mind, but a cork model of Lincoln Cathedral was held by the Lincoln Mechanics' Institute collection late in the nineteenth century (information from Sara Basquill, Museum of Lincolnshire Life).

2 Redgrave 1857, p. 13.

3 Robinson 1880, p. 262.

4 Ibid., p. 252.

5 Ibid., p. 250.

6 J.C. Robinson, 'The Reorganization of our National Art Museums', *The Nineteenth Century*, 44 (1898), pp. 971–9, at p. 974.

7 Robinson 1880, p. 253.

8 Howarth and Platnauer 1911, p. 18.

9 Flower 1898, p. 40.

10 Holmes 1903, p. 6.

11 MacColl 1931, p. 356.

12 Sir Robert Witt, 'Introduction', in *Twenty-Five Years of the National Art-Collections Fund* (London and Glasgow, 1928), p. 5.

13 Holmes 1903, p. 61.

14 Ibid., pp. 62–3.

15 Fox 2009, pp. 501–2, quotes Sidney Colvin's entry 'Art' in the *Encyclopaedia Britannica* (1875 edition) as identifying a recent change in the use of the word to denote the arts 'which exist only or chiefly for pleasure' and in particular 'only architecture, sculpture, and painting by themselves, or with their subordinate and decorative branches'.

16 Fox 2009, p. 1.

17 See Morris 1986, pp. 56–63.

18 F.T. Palgrave, 'How to Form a Good Taste in Art', *Cornhill Magazine*, 18 (1869), pp. 170–80, at p. 171, quoted in Macleod 1996, p. 255.

19 Macleod 1996, pp. 1–17.

20 Ibid., p. 16.

21 John Elsner and Roger Cardinal (eds.), *The Cultures of Collecting* (London, 1994), p. 24.

22 Both works were sold by Agnew's. Artists and dealers received comparable sums for the engraving rights. The dealer Joseph Gillott bought the reproduction rights to *The Light of the World* and made a fortune out of them (information from Jeannie Chapel).

23 These figures are taken from Gerard Reitlinger, *The Economics of Taste: The Rise and Fall of Picture Prices 1760–1960* (London, 1961).

24 Hamlyn 1993.

25 See Lorente 1998 for an extended discussion of these issues, especially pp. 97–139.

26 Hobbes 1849, p. xvii.

27 Equally, the term *Engländer* was widely used in Germany to mean a Briton.

28 Morris 2005, p. 29

29 Palgrave 1862, p. 8.

30 Mrs C. Heaton, 'Editor's Preface', in Cunningham 1879–80, vol. 1, p. v.

31 Palgrave 1869, pp. 4–5. This approach had been criticised by Luigi Lanzi, whose *History of Painting in Italy* was translated into English by Thomas Roscoe in 1828: 'due regard should be paid to that very respectable class of readers, who, in a history of painting, would rather contemplate the artist than the man; and who are less solicitous to become acquainted with the character of a single painter, whose solitary and insulated history cannot prove instructive, than with the genius, the method, the invention, and the style of a great number of artists, with their characteristics, their merits, and their rank, the result of which is a history of the whole art.' These reservations did not prevail. (L.A. Lanzi, *The History of Painting in Italy, from the Period of the Revival of the Fine Arts to the End of the Eighteenth Century. Translated from the…Italian by T. Roscoe*, six vols, London, 1828, vol. 1, Preface, p. iv.)

32 Cunningham 1879–80, vol. 2, p. 25.

33 S.C. Hall, *Selected Pictures from the Galleries and Private Collections of Great Britain: A Series of Engravings from the Best Works of the Best British Artists* (four vols, 1862–8), vol. 2, n.p. (13th engraving).

34 For a full discussion of the habitats of such artists, see Charlotte Gere, *Artistic Circles: Design and Decoration in the Aesthetic Movement* (London, 2010).

35 Redgrave 1947, p. 288.

36 Hobbes 1849, p. xviii.

37 Cosmo Monkhouse, *British Contemporary Artists* (London and New York, 1899), p. x.

38 Palgrave 1869, p. 26.

39 Allan Cunningham, *The Cabinet Gallery of Pictures by the First Masters of the English and Foreign Schools* (two vols, London, 1836), vol. 1, p. 15.

40 Ibid., p. 19.

41 Ibid., p. 23.

42 Ibid., vol. 2, p. 23.

43 Thornbury 1861, vol. 1, p. v. Daniel Maclise, an Irishman, was considered part of the British/English school.

44 Ibid., vol. 1, p. vi.

45 Ibid., vol. 1, p. 6.

46 Palgrave 1869, p. 26.

47 Redgrave 1947, p. 2.

48 W. M. Thackeray, 'Letters on the Fine Arts. No 3. The Royal Academy' (from *The Pictorial Times*, 13 May 1843), in Lewis Melville (ed.), *Stray Papers of William Makepeace Thackeray, Being Stories, Reviews, Verses and Sketches (1821–1847)* (London, 1901), pp. 214–17, at p. 214.

49 W. M. Thackeray, 'An Exhibition Gossip by Michael Angelo Titmarsh in a Letter to Monsieur Guillaume Peintre', in *Ainsworth's* magazine, 1 (1842), pp. 319–22, at p. 319.

50 Swiss by birth, Fuseli was one of many foreign-born artists who were more or less subsumed in the British school.

51 Over £3,000 around 1890.

52 W. M. Thackeray, 'May Gambols' (from *Fraser's Magazine*, June 1844), in *The Biographical Edition of the Works of William Makepeace Thackeray* (thirteen vols, London, 1897–1900), vol. 13, pp. 419–45, at p. 429.

53 Royal Manchester Institution, Sub-committee, 9 February 1881, Manchester City Archives, M6/1/8/3.

54 Elizabeth Conran, 'Art Collections', in Archer 1985, pp. 65–80, at p. 79.

55 Davies 1985, p. 22.

56 Broadsheet, Atkinson Art Gallery, n.d.

57 The first paintings arrived with a bequest the following year.

58 City of Birmingham Museum and Art Gallery, *Illustrated Catalogue* (Birmingham, 1912).

59 *Glasgow Corporations and Art Galleries, Report for the Year*, 1898, p. 6.

60 This was made possible by the passing of the National Gallery (Loans) Act. See National Gallery archives, *Reports &c. Director of the National Gallery* [10 April 1883]. The National Gallery was not empowered to make overseas loans until 1954 (information from Alan Crookham, National Gallery).

61 Dyall 1888, p. 4.

62 Muspratt 1917, p. 255.

63 Stanfield 1894.

64 Nicholas Savage, 'The Royal Academy and Regional Museums, 1870–1900', in the Royal Academy of Arts, *Art Treasures of England: The Regional Collections* (London, 1998), pp. 67–73, at p. 73, note 1.

65 T.H.S. Escott, *England: Its People, Polity and Pursuits* (London, 1879), p. 358.

66 George Moore, 'Our Academicians', in Moore 1898, pp. 97–127, at p. 97.

67 George Moore, 'The Alderman in Art', in ibid., 160–74, at p. 164.

68 See Morris 1996 for a full account of these histories.

69 Johnstone 1859.

70 J.C. Robinson, 'English Art Connoisseurship', *The Nineteenth Century*, 36 (1894), pp. 523–37, at pp. 525–6.

71 Redgrave 1947, pp. 17–18.

72 S.C. Hall, *Retrospect of a Long Life: From 1815 to 1883* (two vols, London, 1883), vol. 1, p. 344.

73 [Walker Art Gallery, Liverpool], Charles Dyall, et al., *Descriptive Catalogue of the Permanent Collection of Pictures* (Liverpool, 1901).

74 See Kay 1911 and Bolton Museum and Art Gallery, *Presents from the Past: Gifts to Greater Manchester Galleries from Local Art Collectors* (1978), pp. 23–4. The paintings were subsequently transferred to Rochdale Art Gallery.

75 Kay 1911, p. 5

76 Jessop and Sinclair 1996, p. 11.

77 Similar taste was evident at Norwich and Liverpool.

78 It went instead to Gateshead, across the Tyne. For its history, see Christopher Wright, *Dutch and Flemish 16th and 17th Century Paintings from the Shipley Collection* (London, 1979), pp. i–xiii; and 'Shipley Bequest (Gateshead Council)', on-line resource, accessed 30 May 2010. An analysis of the complex patterns of collecting and patronage in Newcastle is made in Atkins 1996.

79 *The Art Journal* (1892), p. 123.

80 Carlyle 2005, p. 178.

81 Written communication to the author, 2 November 2011.

82 Minutes of the Town Council of Glasgow, 1890–1, in University of Glasgow, 'The Correspondence of James McNeill Whistler' (www.whistler.arts.gla.ac.uk, accessed 16 February 2012).

83 *Blackwood's Edinburgh Magazine*, 68 (1850), p. 82.

84 See Macleod 1989.

85 Some of the finest holdings of Pre-Raphaelite work in modern regional collections – for example at Tullie House, Carlisle – were assembled in the twentieth century.

86 See Wildman 1995.

87 See Treuherz 1993. On the initial distrust, see Macleod 1996, p. 139.

88 *Report of the Library and Museum Committee to the Town Council, of the Borough of Liverpool*, 1899, p. 83.

89 Chesneau 1885, p. 273.

90 *The Nineteenth Century*, 27 (1890), p. 582.

91 Morris 2005, pp. 129–30.

92 Jeremy Maas, *Gambart: Prince of the Victorian Art World* (London, 1975); and Morris 2005, pp. 131–2.

93 Quilter 1892, p. 293.

94 Edward Morris, 'Philip Henry Rathbone and the Purchase of Contemporary Foreign Paintings for the Walker Art Gallery, Liverpool, 1871–1914', *Walker Art Gallery, Liverpool, Annual Report and Bulletin*, 6 (1975–6), pp. 59–67.

95 Moore, 'The Alderman in Art', in Moore 1898, p. 165.

96 Morris 2005, p. 231.

97 See Sarah Herring, 'The National Gallery and the Collecting of Barbizon Paintings in the Early Twentieth Century', *Journal of the History of Collections*, 13, no. 1 (2001), pp. 77–89.

98 See [Bowes Museum], Howard Coutts, *The Road to Impressionism: Joséphine Bowes and Painting in Nineteenth Century France* (Barnard Castle, 2002).

99 [Laing Art Gallery], C. Bernard Stevenson, *Catalogue of the Special Inaugural Exhibition of Pictures by British and Foreign Artists, Collections of Decorative and Industrial Art...* (Newcastle upon Tyne, 1906).

100 On Durand-Ruel in London, see Morris 2005, p. 134. The slender Impressionist holdings in regional collections were almost all acquired after the Second World War.

101 Birkett 1898, no. 9.

102 Whitworth Wallis and A.B. Chamberlain, *Illustrated Catalogue (with Descriptive Notes) of the Permanent Catalogue of Paintings and Sculpture, and the Pictures in Aston Hall and Elsewhere* (Birmingham, 1904), 'Prefatory Note', p. v.

103 Morris 1996. For Rathbone, see Chapter Eleven below.

104 Dyall 1888, p. 5.

105 *Walker Art Gallery Annual Report*, 1899, p. 82.

106 Greenwood 1888, p. 176.

107 Raymond Watkinson, *Pre-Raphaelite Art and Design* (London, 1970), p. 165, cited in Richard Altick, *Paintings from Books: Art and Literature in Britain, 1760–1900* (Columbus, 1985), p. 93.

108 The Gallery opened in 1996.

109 Malcolm Warner (ed.), *The Victorians: British Painting, 1837–1901* (Washington, DC, 1997).

110 Dyall 1888, p. 20. This attention to the choices made by copyists was a standard museum practice, also followed at the National Gallery.

111 Birkett 1898.

112 Ibid., no. 23.

113 City of Birmingham, Museum and Art Gallery, *Illustrated Catalogue* (Birmingham, 1912).

114 Ibid., nos. 144–298.

115 Samuel Redgrave, *Catalogue of the Historical Collection of Water-Colour Paintings in the South Kensington Museum* (London, 1877), p. 1.

116 Charlotte Gere points out that whereas the British Museum holds the national collection of watercolours, the Victoria and Albert Museum has the 'National Collection of Watercolour Painting', an old definition that reflects this emulation of oil painting.

117 *A Handbook to the Water Colours, Drawings, and Engravings, in the Art Treasures Exhibition* (London, 1857), p. 3.

118 Ibid., p. 4.

119 Cosmo Monkhouse, *The Earlier English Water-Colour Painters* (London, 1890), p. vii.

120 *Galleries and Museums Report to Whitworth Committee*, 16 January 1889, Whitworth Art Gallery archives.

121 *Manchester Whitworth Institute Report*, 1893–1902, Whitworth Art Gallery archives, and C.R. Dodwell (ed.), *The Whitworth Art Gallery, The First Hundred Years* (Manchester, 1968), pp. 4–5.

122 Trevor Coombs, *Watercolours: The Charles Lees Collection at Oldham Art Gallery* (Oldham, 1993), p. 4.

123 [Oldham Art Gallery and Museum], E.A. Parry, *Catalogue of the Charles E. Lees Collection of Watercolour Drawings and Engravings* (Oldham, 1889), p. 3.

124 *The Fine Arts' Courts in the Crystal Palace* (London, 1854).

125 *The Sculpture of the Crystal Palace – being the Handbooks to the Greek Court, the Roman Court, and the Courts of Modern Sculpture* (London, 1859), *Greek Court*, p. iv.

126 Anna Jameson, *A Hand-book to the Courts of Modern Sculpture* (London, 1854).

127 Ibid., p. 12.

128 If Victorian museums did acquire original classical sculptures, it was generally by bequest, other than at the British Museum and the university museums at Oxford and Cambridge.

129 Margaret Gibson and Susan M. Wright (eds), *Joseph Mayer of Liverpool 1803–1886* (London, 1988). See Cole 1867, p. iii. Only occasionally did a collection of antiquities reach a corporation. At Sheffield Thomas Bateman, who had inherited Celtic and Romano-British objects excavated by members of his family, lent them to the city in 1876 and eventually sold them to it.

130 Birmingham Handbook 1885, p. 19.

131 *Report of the Library and Museum Committee to the Town Council, of the Borough of Liverpool*, 1887, p. 3.

132 The Liverpool Royal Institution also assembled a cast collection.

133 *Report of the Library and Museum Committee to the Town Council, of the Borough of Liverpool*, 1873, p. 8. See Martin Greenwood, *European Sculpture 1750–1920 from the Permanent Collection, Walker Art Gallery* (Liverpool, 1988).

134 F.T. Palgrave, *Essays on Art* (London and Cambridge, 1866), p. 87.

135 On the Whitworth's gallery, see Whitworth Committee, Manchester, 16 January 1889, Whitworth Art Gallery archive.

136 The Preston Corporation Art Gallery, *Illustrated Catalogue* (Preston, 1907).

137 For a discussion of the continuing meaning

and force of this statue, see Chris Wingfield, 'Touching the Buddha: Encounters with a Charismatic Object', in Sandra Dudley (ed.), *Museum Materialities: Objects, Engagements, Interpretations* (London, 2010), pp. 53–70.

138   *Report of the Library and Museum Committee to the Town Council, of the Borough of Liverpool*, 1881, p. 4.

139   [City of Bradford], *Annual Reports of the Libraries, Art Gallery and Museum Committee*, 1905.

10: EDUCATION IN THE VICTORIAN GALLERY

1   Joshua Reynolds, *Discourses on Art*, ed. Robert Wark (San Marino and Oxford, 1975), p. 170.

2   Select Committee Report, National Gallery 1850 (606–7).

3   Ibid.

4   *Report from the Select Committee on Public Institutions*, 1860, p. iii.

5   See pp. 136–8.

6   *Birmingham City Art Gallery Annual Report*, 1874, p. 3.

7   Wallis in Muirhead 1911, p. 496.

8   *Report of the Library and Museum Committee to the Town Council, of the Borough of Liverpool*, 1899, p. 81.

9   *Leeds Art Gallery Annual Report*, 1898, p. 4.

10   Wallis in Muirhead 1911, pp. 486–7.

11   Ibid., p. 502.

12   Ibid.

13   Ibid., p. 491.

14   This was the original title of the museum.

15   Nathaniel Burt, *Palaces for the People: The Social History of the American Art Museum* (Boston, 1977), p. 228.

16   See ibid. for an extended account of the development of American museums.

17   See Donisthorpe 1868 and W.M.S. D'Urban, *History and Description of the Devon and Exeter Albert Memorial with a Synopsis of the Contents of the Museum* (Exeter, 1877).

18   [Leicester Art Gallery], *Annual Report of the Art Gallery Committee*, 1882, p. 5.

19   [Leicester Art Gallery], *Conversazioni On the Occasion of the Opening of the Museum and Art Gallery Extension Buildings May 19th and 20th 1892* (Leicester, 1892), p. 46.

20   [Leicester Art Gallery], *Annual Report of the Art Gallery Committee*, 1882, p. 6.

21   [Leicester Art Gallery], *Annual Report of the Art Gallery Committee*, 1891, Regulations.

22   Leicester Archives Department, *City of Leicester 1849–1949*, Leicester Art Gallery archives, p. 10.

23   Rowley 1911, pp. 73–4.

24   [Walker Art Gallery], Charles Dyall, *Descriptive Catalogue of the Permanent Collection of Pictures* (Liverpool, 1902), no. 179.

25   Morris 2005, pp. 35–6, 262–4.

26   City of Manchester Art Gallery, *Catalogue of the Permanent Collection of Pictures in Oil and Water Colours* (Manchester, 1894), p. 5.

27   [Leicester Art Gallery], *Annual Report of the Art Gallery Committee*, 1891.

28   Leicester Art Gallery maintained this educational brief into the twentieth century by appointing in 1926 a guide-lecturer, the first in any provincial museum, at least according to its own estimation.

29   Cole 1867, p. iii.

30   *Hand-book to the Pictures in the Fitzwilliam Museum, Cambridge* (Cambridge, 1853).

31   [Museum of Classical Archaeology, Cambridge], Charles Waldstein, *Catalogue of Casts in the Museum of Classical Archaeology* (Cambridge, 1889), p. iii.

32   *Report of the Library and Museum Committee to the Town Council, of the Borough of Liverpool*, 1885, p. 4.

33   Ibid., 1887, p. 3.

34   These were dispersed to schools in the 1920s.

35   E. Howarth, 'Aberdeen Art Gallery', *Museums Journal*, 4 (1904–5), pp. 368–71, at p. 370.

36   E.A. Gardner, *City of Birmingham Museum and Art Gallery, Catalogue of the Collection of Casts of Greek and Roman Sculpture* (Birmingham, 1921), p. i.

37   Ibid.

38   Alan Wallach, *Exhibiting Contradictions: Essays on the Art Museum in the United States* (Amherst, 1998), p. 70.

39   *The Freeman's Journal*, 9 March 1864.

40   Hill 2005, Chapter Seven, discusses rowdyism in museums, notably at the Mappin Gallery.

41   *Report of the Library and Museum Committee to the Town Council, of the Borough of Liverpool*, 1874, p. 7.

42   See, for example, Oswald Latter, 'The Equipment of a School Museum', *Museums Journal*, 6 (1906–7), pp. 164–72; Herbert Bolton, 'Museums of Elementary and Higher Grade Schools', *Museums Journal*, 7 (1907–8), pp. 299–302; E. Howarth, 'The School Museum System in Sheffield', *Museums Journal*, 7 (1907–8), pp. 339–43.

43   See Waterfield 1994.

44   Bradford Art Gallery, *Annual Report*, 1912.

45   City of Sheffield, *Report of the Public Museums*, 1908–10, and ibid., 1910–12.

46   *Museums Journal*, 4 (1904–5), pp. 275–83.

47   Letter from H.W. Vincent of H.M. Treasury to William Seguier, National Gallery archives, NG/3/1824.

48   Johnstone 1859, p. 5.

49   Birkett 1898, p. 3.

50   Dyall 1902.

51   The painting was then entitled *Venus Instructing Cupid* but also *Venus and Mercury Instructing Cupid*,

either name advocating companionate education and close family relationships.

52   *The National Gallery of Pictures by the Great Masters. Presented by Individuals or Purchased by Grant of Parliament* (two vols, London, 1838), vol. 2, p. 110.

53   Dyall 1902, no. 322.

54   Ibid., no. 281.

55   Though never published, the manuscript catalogue of the Royal Collection (Archives of the Surveyor of the Queen's Pictures) initiated in the late 1850s by Richard Redgrave, Surveyor of the Queen's Pictures, and continued by his successor, J.C. Robinson, showed a similar level of expertise, noting the history and condition of each picture and including a photograph.

56   F.R. Earp, *A Descriptive Catalogue of the Pictures in the Fitzwilliam Museum* (Cambridge, 1902), p. x.

57   Ibid., title page.

58   James Paton (ed.), *Catalogue Descriptive and Historical of the Pictures and Sculpture in the Corporation Galleries of Art, Glasgow* (Glasgow, 1892), pp. vi–vii.

59   See J.H. Hays, 'The London Lecturing Empire, 1800–50', in Inkster and Morrell 1983, pp. 91–119.

60   *Report of the Library and Museum Committee to the Town Council, of the Borough of Liverpool*, 1865, p. 7, and 1866, p. 6.

61   Quoted in Williams 1981, p. 60.

62   [City of Glasgow], *Report on the City Industrial Museum, Kelvingrove Park, and the Corporation Galleries of Art*, 1886, p. 4.

63   *Museums Journal*, 1 (1901–2), p. 116.

64   *Leeds Art Gallery Annual Report*, 1912–13, pp. 10–11.

65   Howarth and Platnauer 1911, p. 125.

66   *Fitzwilliam Museum Annual Report*, 1911.

67   See Lord Sudeley, *The Public Utility of Museums* (Kingston-on-Thames, 1911); archive in possession of the present Lord Sudeley; Philippa Heath, 'Lord Sudeley: A Great Pioneer: Museum Education in London, 1901–1922', MA dissertation, Courtauld Institute of Art, 2003.

68   It was supplemented in 1914 by the Geffrye Museum, intended as an exemplary museum for the furniture trade.

69   For a discussion of the Manchester parks, see Conway 1991, pp. 81–3 and 121–2.

70   Queen's Park Museum has been closed for many years, though it still stands. Wythenshawe Hall closed in 2010.

71   Crawford 1891, p. 8.

72   For a general history, see Waterfield 1994.

73   See Frances Borzello, *Civilising Caliban: The Misuse of Art 1875–1980* (London, 1987).

74   South London Gallery archives.

75   See T.C. Horsfall, *Art Gallery for Manchester* (Manchester, 1877) and *Handbook to the Manchester Art Museum* (Manchester, 1886); and Michael Harrison, 'Art

and Philanthropy: T.C. Horsfall and the Manchester Art Museum', in A. Kidd and K. Roberts (eds), *City, Class and Culture: Studies of Social Production and Social Policy in Victorian Manchester* (Manchester, 1985), pp. 120–47.

76 A similar enterprise was undertaken during the same period by the museum librarian and museum director J.C. Dana, notably in Newark, New Jersey. See Carol Duncan, *A Matter of Class: John Cotton Dana, Progressive Reform, and the Newark Museum* (Pittsburgh, 2009).

77 Correspondence in Manchester City Art Gallery, and see Leonée Ormond, 'A Leighton Memorial', in Waterfield 1994, pp. 19–29.

78 This example was widely followed, with some circulating collections, such as the Rutherston collection in Manchester, achieving high standards.

II: PATRONS, DONORS, COUNCILLORS, CURATORS, VISITORS

1 Hans Hess, 'The City Art Gallery', *Museums Journal*, 53 (1953), pp. 122–6, at p. 122.

2 Duncan 1995, Chapter Four, and Higonnet 2009. Higonnet is severe in her definitions, not including even Sir John Soane's Museum.

3 Duncan 1995, p. 95.

4 I am grateful to Charlotte Gere for her guidance on these collectors.

5 Hardy 1970, p. 177.

6 Duncan 1995, p. 74.

7 *A Record of the Collections in the Lady Lever Art Gallery, Port Sunlight, Cheshire, Formed by the first Viscount Leverhulme* (London, 1928), p. 14.

8 See John Harris, *Moving Rooms* (New Haven and London, 2007).

9 In Britain at least, the independent trust has proved a short-lived guarantor of financial viability: Dulwich College Picture Gallery (as Dulwich Picture Gallery was at first called), the Bowes, the Holburne and the Lady Lever all suffered financial agonies in the twentieth century before a more permanent solution was found.

10 Hardy 1970, p. 30.

11 The Wallaces did have a son (who had four illegitimate children himself), but he predeceased his father.

12 Barbara Lasic, '"Splendid Patriotism": Richard Wallace and the Construction of the Wallace Collection', *Journal of the History of Collections*, 21, no. 2 (2009), pp. 173–82, makes this case for the Wallace Collection.

13 See John Ingamells, *The 3rd Marquess of Hertford (1777–1842) as a Collector* (London, 1983); Howard Coutts and Sarah Medlam, 'John and Josephine Bowes' Purchases from the International Exhibitions of 1862,

1867 and 1871', *Journal of the Decorative Arts Society*, 16 (1992), pp. 50–61.

14 'Russell Cotes Art Gallery, Bournemouth', *Museums Journal*, 7 (1907–8), pp. 151–4, at p. 152. See Olding 1999.

15 'The Collection of Merton Russell Cotes, Esq., J.P.', *The Art Journal* (1895), pp. 81–4, at p. 82.

16 Russell-Cotes 1921, p. 316.

17 The collection has been extensively catalogued and discussed. See, for example, *Journal of the History of Collections*, 4, no. 2 (1992), an issue devoted to the Lady Lever Art Gallery.

18 *Report of the Library and Museum Committee to the Town Council, of the Borough of Liverpool*, 1869, pp. 5–6.

19 Dyall 1888, p. 3.

20 A.B. Chamberlain, *The Corporation Museum & Art Gallery* (Birmingham, 1913), p. 9.

21 'Burnley Art Gallery', *Museums Journal*, 2 (1902–3), pp. 358–61, at p. 358.

22 Edward Morris points out (written communication to the author) that whereas Birmingham, Nottingham and Manchester City Councils were generous to their art galleries, Leeds and Liverpool were strikingly ungenerous. The smaller Lancashire industrial towns were generally more willing to spend than their counterparts in Yorkshire and the Midlands, a pattern that is not easily explained.

23 Leeds City Art Gallery, *Catalogue of Loan Collection* (Leeds, 1888), p. 5.

24 *Leeds Art Gallery Annual Report*, 1899, p. 5.

25 *Leeds Art Gallery Annual Report*, 1900, p. 5.

26 Wallis in Muirhead 1911, p. 510.

27 T.C. Horsfall, *The Relation of Art to the Welfare of the Inhabitants of English Towns* (Manchester, 1894), p. 3.

28 George Moore, 'The Alderman in Art', in Moore 1898, pp. 160–74, at p. 169.

29 Rutter 1927, p. 201.

30 Ibid.

31 Hill 2005, pp. 53–6.

32 Edward Morris, *Public Art Collections in North-West England: A History and Guide* (Liverpool, 2001), p. 8.

33 Rowley 1911, p. 9.

34 Faucher 1844, p. 26.

35 Taylor 1999, pp. 61, develops the link between public health and museums.

36 Hartley Bateson, *A Centenary History of Oldham* (Oldham, 1949), p. 166.

37 Oldham Art Gallery, *Catalogue of the Permanent Collection of Pictures* (Oldham, 1910), Introduction.

38 Robert Morris, 'Citizens, Subscribers and Ratepayers of Leeds 1780–1914', *Leeds Museums and Galleries Review*, 2 (1999), pp. 11–18, at p. 14.

39 Jessop and Sinclair 1996, pp. 58–9.

40 Muspratt 1917, p. 255. Muspratt, a friend of

Rathbone, remarked of him that 'Anyone less "aldermanic" in appearance it is difficult to conceive'. For an account of collecting in Liverpool, particularly in relation to the Walker Art Gallery, see Morris 1996, pp. 1–24.

41 *Report of the Library and Museum Committee to the Town Council, of the Borough of Liverpool*, 1895, p. 4.

42 Roy Hartnell, *Pre-Raphaelite Birmingham* (Studley, 1996), p. 55.

43 Stephen Wildman, 'Opportunity and Philanthropy: The Pre-Raphaelites as Seen and Collected in Birmingham', in Wildman 1995, pp. 57–69. Kenrick commissioned a magnificent new house on being elected MP, in order to fit his new status.

44 See Richard Ormond, 'Victorian Paintings and Patronage in Birmingham', *Apollo*, 87 (April, 1968), pp. 240–51.

45 *Who's Who in Glasgow* (Glasgow, 1909).

46 Crawford 1891, p. 13.

47 Ibid., p. 14.

48 Ibid., p. 15.

49 Ibid., p. 17.

50 Ibid., p. 19.

51 Fowle 2010, p. 93 and *passim*. His relation W.A. Coats was an important collector, owning Vermeer's *Christ in the House of Martha and Mary* (National Gallery of Scotland) and major British portraits.

52 See Knox 1994, pp. 117–19.

53 *Report of the Library and Museum Committee to the Town Council, of the Borough of Liverpool*, 1873, p. 5.

54 Dyall 1888, p. 4.

55 See Morris and Stevens 2013, p. 13.

56 The Mappin Art Gallery was founded in 1887 with J.N. Mappin's nephew Sir Frederick Mappin playing an active role as legatee in carrying out his uncle's wishes.

57 Laing Art Gallery, *The Creation of an Art Gallery: The History of the Laing Art Gallery and the Creation of its Permanent Collections since the Opening in 1904* (Newcastle upon Tyne, 1956), p. 3.

58 'Memoir of Sir Joseph Whitworth, Bart.', *Minutes of Proceedings of the Institution of Civil Engineers*, 91 (1887–8), p. 5.

59 The first woman trustee of the National Gallery, Dame Veronica Wedgwood, was appointed in 1962; the first woman curator, Dillian Gordon, in 1978.

60 See Bailkin 2004, pp. 127–35, for the role of women in museums.

61 Ibid., p. 130.

62 Donisthorpe 1868.

63 See Thompson 1988, p. 160.

64 'Museum Guide: A Short History of the Hastings Museum' (typescript, n.d.), Hastings Museum and Art Gallery archives. The Durbar Hall was incorporated into the building in 1930.

65 *The Beaney Institute*, pamphlet (article reprinted

from *The Kentish Gazette and Canterbury Press*, 16 September 1899), p. 4.

66 Ibid.

67 Bernard Alderson, *Andrew Carnegie: From Telegraph Boy to Millionaire* (London, 1902), p. 20.

68 His career in business and as a patron is recorded in Edward Morris and Christopher Fifield, 'A.G. Kurtz: A Patron of Classical Art and Music in Victorian Liverpool', *Journal of the History of Collections*, 7, no. 1 (1995), pp. 103–14.

69 See John C. Eastberg and Eric Vogel, *Layton's Legacy: A Historic American Art Collection* (Madison, 2013).

70 Quoted in Robin Pearson, 'Thomas Robert Ferens (1847–1930)', *Oxford Dictionary of National Biography*.

71 Willett gave land near Abingdon to the Ashmolean Natural History Society of Oxford, to be kept for all time in its natural condition.

72 Jessica Rutherford, 'Henry Willett as a Collector', *Apollo*, 115 (March, 1982), pp. 176–81, at p. 181.

73 Ruskin, *Works*, vol. 17, pp. 309–464.

74 William Rossiter, one of the founders of the South London Art Gallery in Camberwell, offers a rare parallel, but in Rossiter's case a parallel fraught with social tensions.

75 Fletcher and Helmreich 2011, p. 1.

76 Lorente 1998, p. 34.

77 Macleod 1996, p. 100.

78 Bennett 2010, vol. 1, p. 282.

79 Escott 1897, p. 51.

80 The collection was bequeathed to the city of Liverpool by his daughter Emma in 1944.

81 Stanfield 1894, no. 31.

82 Bolton Museum and Art Gallery, *Presents from the Past: Gifts to Greater Manchester Galleries from Local Art Collectors* (Bolton, 1978), p. 33. Direct sales to museums were made largely to the three national galleries in the British Isles (though even those were rare) and to newly founded art museums in the British Empire, such as the Art Gallery of New South Wales.

83 Whitworth Art Gallery, Minutes of Council, 28 July 1899, Whitworth Art Gallery archives.

84 Fowle 2010.

85 Olding 1999, p. 11 and *passim*.

86 He had come from fifteen years at the Edinburgh Museum of Science and Art.

87 'English Provincial Museums – I', *The Burlington Magazine*, 10, no. 43 (October 1906), pp. 3–6, at p. 4.

88 Nancy Moss, *James Reeve 1833–1920*, Norwich Castle Museum broadsheet (Norwich, 2005).

89 Ibid. Ripps 2010 indicates that J.C. Robinson enjoyed a similarly close relationship with private collectors, as would Sydney Cockerell at the Fitzwilliam Museum later.

90 The transition was also exemplified by James Paton in Glasgow.

91 Mulvany was in office from 1862 to 1869; Johnstone from 1858 to 1868.

92 Ripps 2010, p. 17. Ripps is addressing expertise in Dutch art, but his comments may be more generally applied.

93 See Wilson 2002 for a detailed account of the museum's personnel.

94 Obituary, *Yorkshire Evening Post*, 7 June 1911.

95 R.A.M. Stevenson to J.M. Whistler, October 1891, in Glasgow University Library, MS Whistler 5240 (acc. no 05594), University of Glasgow, 'The Correspondence of James McNeill Whistler' (www.whistler.arts.gla.ac.uk, accessed 24 July 2011).

96 See Davies 1985.

97 *Birmingham Post*, 17 January 1927.

98 Flower 1898, p. 12.

99 Greenwood 1888, p. 12.

100 Frederic Kenyon, *Museums and National Life* (Oxford, 1927), p. 17. Thompson was the first Principal Librarian of the British Museum to be named Director.

101 For an account of the Museums Association, see Geoffrey Lewis, *For Instruction and Recreation: A Centenary History of the Museums Association* (London, 1989).

102 A. Capel Shaw, 'The Birmingham Free Libraries', in Muirhead 1911, pp. 399–443, at p. 403.

103 Kriegel 2007, p. 189.

104 Perry 2006, pp. 128–366, analyses the public, and particularly the female visitors, at the National Portrait Gallery in the nineteenth century.

105 J.G. Wood, 'The Dullness of Museums', *The Nineteenth Century*, 21 (1887), pp. 384–96, at p. 384.

106 E.R. Dibdin, 'The Pictures in the Oldham Art Gallery', *The Windsor Magazine*, 32 (1910), pp. 128, 126.

107 Ibid., p. 128.

108 Ibid., pp. 134–6.

109 'General Notes: A Novel Talk on Pictures', *Museums Journal*, 7 (1908), pp. 329–30, at p. 329.

110 Williams, 1981, p. 66.

111 Knox 1994, p.119. Not the least of their cultural contributions was being ancestors of Kenneth Clark.

112 Ibid., p. 84.

12: ADDRESSING THE PAST

1 Philippa Levine, *The Amateur and the Professional: Antiquarians, Historians and Archaeologists in Victorian England, 1838–1886* (Cambridge, 1986), p. 1.

2 See Graham Parry, *The Trophies of Time: English Antiquarians of the Seventeenth Century* (Oxford, 1995).

3 Ibid., p. 3.

4 Piggott 1976, p. 110.

5 Ibid., p. 12.

6 See Sam Smiles, *Image of Antiquity: Ancient Britain and the Romantic Imagination* (New Haven and London, 1994).

7 Ibid., p. 8.

8 Perry 2006, p. 37.

9 Duncan Thomson, *A History of the Scottish National Portrait Gallery* (Edinburgh, 2011).

10 Gaynor Kavanagh, 'History of Museums in Britain: A Brief Survey of Trends and Ideas', in David Fleming, Crispin Paine, John G. Rhodes (eds.), *Social History in Museums: A Handbook for Professionals* (London, 1993), pp. 13–24, at p. 14. The museum dedicated to the history of an individual city has never been common in Britain unlike, for example, Germany, where civic pride has created major city museums in Dresden, Hamburg and many other places.

11 Stephen Bann, *The Clothing of Clio: A Study of the Representation of History in Nineteenth-Century Britain and France* (Cambridge, 1984), p. 23.

12 Ibid., p. 30.

13 Manchester City Art Gallery, *Catalogue of the Permanent Collection of Pictures in Oil and Water Colours with Descriptive Notes and Illustrations, Compiled by William Stanfield, Curator, Under the Direction of the Art Gallery Committee* (Manchester, 1894), no. 82.

14 Flaxman 1838.

15 Select Committee Report, National Gallery 1853 (7657–80).

16 Officially, Sir Austen Henry Layard.

17 Quoted in Piggott 2004, p. 78.

18 Ibid.

19 See G.F. Mulvany, *Catalogue, Descriptive and Historical, of the Works of Art in the National Gallery of Ireland, With Biographical Notices of the Masters* (Dublin, 1867).

20 Ibid., p. 110, and see Somerville-Large 2004.

21 According to the museum's website, the casts are no longer extant, apart from Ghiberti's *Gates of Paradise*: www.harrismuseum.org.uk, accessed 17 August 2012.

22 For example, Paolo Giovio, *Vitae Illustrium virorum* (Florence, 1549) and Paulus Freherus, *Theatrum Virorum Eruditione Clarorum* (Nuremberg, 1683). The latter includes neatly categorised images of churchmen, lawyers, doctors and philosophers, emperors and kings, counts and barons, throughout Europe.

23 Notably James Granger, *A Biographical History of England, from Egbert the Great to the Revolution* (London, 1769); Edmund Lodge, *Portraits of Illustrious Personages of Great Britain* (first ed., four vols, London, 1821–34; new ed., twelve vols, London, 1835); Sylvester and Edward Harding, *The Biographical Mirror, Comprising a Series of Ancient and Modern English Portraits, of Eminent and Distinguished Persons, from Original Pictures and Drawings* (three vols, London, 1810).

24 Marcia Pointon, *Hanging the Head: Portraiture and Social Formation in Eighteenth-Century England* (New Haven and London, 1993).

25 Hoare 1813, p. 270.

26 For an extended recent analysis of this process, see Holger Hoock, *Empires of the Imagination: Politics, War and the Arts in the British World, 1750–1850* (London, 2010), Chapters Three and Four.

27 *Fine Arts Commissioners, Third Report*, 1844, p. 15.

28 *Fine Arts Commissioners, Fourth Report*, 1845, p. 9.

29 Alun Howkins, 'The Discovery of Rural England', in Robert Colls and Phillip Dodd, *Englishness – Politics and Culture 1880–1920* (London, 1986), pp. 62–78, at p. 70. On 'Olden Times', see Peter Mandler, *The Fall and Rise of the Stately Home* (New Haven and London, 1997).

30 Jameson 1842, Part 2, p. 11.

31 The Gallery had been mooted ten years earlier in Parliament.

32 Perry 2006, p. 97.

33 *Fine Arts Commissioners, First Report*, 1842, pp. 5, 7.

34 Ibid., p. 10.

35 Bennett 2010, vol. 0, p. 286.

36 Ibid., p. 282.

37 *Fine Arts Commissioners, Third Report*, 1844, Appendix No. 10, p. 26.

38 Benedict Read, *Victorian Sculpture* (New Haven and London, 1982), p. 112.

39 Birmingham Handbook 1885. Wellington was also represented in the collection by a portrait in oils.

40 Richard Altick, *Paintings from Books: Art and Literature in Britain, 1760–1900* (Columbus, 1985), p. 93.

41 Dyall 1902.

42 Stanfield 1894, catalogue entry 56.

43 Ibid., catalogue entry 149.

44 *Catalogue of the Collection of Objects, Selected from the Museum at South Kensington to be Contributed on Loan for Twelve Months (Until June 1873) to the Midland Counties Museum of Science and Art, Nottingham* (London, 1872), p. vi.

45 Ibid., pp. vii, x.

46 'Mr. Cole's Speech at the Distribution of Prizes to the Students of the Nottingham School of Art, 15th January, 1873', in Cole 1884, vol. 1, p. 345.

47 Ibid., p. 344.

48 Nottingham Castle Museum, *The Midlands Counties Art Museum – A Statement of the Objects of this Institution* (Nottingham, 1878), p. 7.

49 Nottingham Castle Museum, *First Annual Report of the Castle Museum Committee*, p. 9.

50 See John Beckett (ed.), *A Centenary History of Nottingham* (Manchester, 1997), p. 310.

51 The unusual character of Nottingham Castle Museum was reflected in the fact that one of the first gifts it received was a collection of classical antiquities excavated by Lord Savile at Lake Nemi – neither the donor nor the donation being at all typical.

52 Nottingham Castle Museum, *First Annual Report of the Castle Museum Committee*, p. 5.

53 Select Committee Report, Works of Art, 1848, p. v.

54 For an account of the restoration work, see Simon Thurley, *Hampton Court* (New Haven and London, 2003), pp. 294–303.

55 Margaret Aston, '"English Ruins and English History": The Dissolution and the Sense of the Past', *Journal of the Warburg and Courtauld Institutes*, 36 (1973), pp. 231–55, at p. 255.

56 John Soane (with Barbara Hofland), *Description of the House and Museum… The Residence of Sir John Soane* (London, 1835), p. 13.

57 Ibid., p. 67.

58 Waugh 2008, p. 14.

59 William IV tried unsuccessfully to persuade the Government to take the half-finished Buckingham Palace as a new National Gallery.

60 An evocation of the character of the medieval keep was attempted only early in the twenty-first century.

61 Quoted in Davies 1985, p. 46.

62 H.M. Cundall, 'Our Provincial Art Museums and Galleries: V – Birmingham City Museum and Art Gallery', *Art Journal* (1892), pp. 330–5, at pp. 333–4.

63 For example, Percy Macquoid, *A History of English Furniture* (four volumes, London, 1904–8).

64 Further such acquisitions followed in the 1920s, notably Temple Newsam House, near Leeds, sold by the future first Earl of Halifax to Leeds City Council in 1922.

65 'Museum Conference at Bolton, Lancashire', *Museums Journal*, 5 (1905–6), pp. 120–4, at pp. 120–1.

66 D.A. Farnie, 'Samuel Crompton (1753–1827)', in *Oxford Dictionary of National Biography*.

67 *Museums Journal*, 5 (1905–6), p. 121.

68 'Bolling Hall Museum, Bradford, Yorkshire', *Museums Journal*, 15 (1915–16), pp. 159–61, at p. 159.

69 Ibid.

13: A NEW ORDER

1 See Physick 1982, Chapter Fourteen.

2 Sir Charles Holmes, *Self and Partners: Mostly Self* (London, 1936), p. 290. This redecoration took place from 1910 to 1912.

3 Ibid., p. 242.

4 The official opening took place in 1927.

5 *Museums Journal*, 8 (1908–9), p. 291.

6 *The Studio*, 16 (1899), p. 196.

7 See Tickner 2000 for a discussion of the Whitechapel Exhibition of 1914.

8 See Bailkin 2004, where this theme runs through the book.

9 *Museums Journal*, 2 (1902–3), p. 76.

10 Bury, Public Library and Art Gallery, *Annual Report*, 1911.

11 'Notes and News: Mr John Burns on Museums', *Museums Journal*, 12 (1912), pp. 260–1.

12 See Black 2000, Chapter Four.

13 Rose 1986, p. 165.

14 *Report of the Library and Museum Committee to the Town Council, of the Borough of Liverpool*, 1912, p. 80.

15 Best 1971, pp. 200 and *passim*, and Thompson 1988, pp. 29 and *passim*.

16 Bailkin 2004, pp. 3–5 and *passim*.

17 James Jackson Jarves, 'The Proposed Reorganisation and Union of the Pitti, Uffizi, and other Galleries and Museums of Florence', *Art Journal* (1876), pp. 22–4.

18 Bailkin 2004, p. 19.

19 Sharp 1898, p. 360.

20 *Art Journal* (1898), p. 353. The name 'Carnegie Art Gallery' was used loosely to denote the art department of the Carnegie Institute, founded in 1895 by Andrew Carnegie. The art department had its own building and director but at this period was not officially an independent museum.

21 Frederic Kenyon, *Libraries and Museums* (London, 1930), p. 64.

22 Jeremy Warren, 'Bode and the British', *Jahrbuch der Berliner Museen*, 38 (1996), pp. 121–42.

23 For a recent history of the National Art-Collections Fund (now the Art Fund) and of the pressure on British collections, see Richard Verdi (ed.), *Saved! 100 Years of the National Art Collections Fund* (London, 2003).

24 By Arthur Balfour, when Conservative Leader of the House of Commons, quoted in Hynes 1968, p. 16.

25 Rose 1986, pp. 117–18.

26 Hynes 1968, p. 257.

27 Robert Ross, 'The Post-Impressionists at the Grafton', *The Morning Post*, 7 November 1910, reprinted in J.B. Bullen (ed.), *Post-Impressionists in England: The Critical Reception* (London, 1988), p. 104.

28 For a discussion of the Victorian art press, see Julie Codell, 'The Art Press and the Art Market: The Artist as "Economic Man"', in Fletcher and Helmreich 2011, pp. 128–50.

29 *The Connoisseur – An Illustrated Magazine for Collectors*, 1 (1901), p. 1.

30 See Michael Levey (ed.), *The Burlington Magazine: A Centenary Anthology* (New Haven and London, 2003), p. x.

31 'Editorial Article', *The Burlington Magazine*, vol. 1, no. 1 (March, 1903), pp. 3–5, at p. 3.

32 Bell 1949, p. 178.

33 Ibid., pp. 19–20.

34 Colvin served as Director of the Fitzwilliam Museum from 1876 to 1884 and then as a notable Keeper of Prints and Drawings at the British Museum until 1912.

35 Sidney Colvin, *Memories and Notes of Persons and Places, 1852–1912* (London, 1921), pp. 49

36 Roger Fry, 'Art and Socialism', in Fry 1920, pp. 36–51. The article had originally been published in Lady Warwick, H.G. Wells and C.R.S. Taylor (eds), *The Great State: Essays in Construction* (London and New York, 1912).

37 D.S. MacColl, 'The Greater and the Lesser Mirrors: English Art from Hogarth to our Time: Introduction to the Pictures in the Cartwright Gallery, Bradford, 1904', in MacColl, 1931, pp. 52–61, at p. 60.

38 Fry 1920, p. 64.

39 Ibid., p. 55.

40 Bell 1949, p. 170.

41 Ibid., p. 262.

42 Ibid., p. 263.

43 Ibid., p. 262.

44 Ibid., pp. 284–5.

45 Rowley 1911, p. 77.

46 Rothenstein 1965, p. 212.

47 The most important avant-garde exhibitions are listed in Tickner 2000, p. 221 (note 2).

48 Camille Pissarro, to Lucien Pissarro, 5 November 1891, in Camille Pissarro, *Letters to his Son Lucien*, ed. John Rewald (London, 1943), p. 185.

49 See Philip Vainker, 'Brighton's Early Art Exhibitions', in *The Royal Pavilion and Museums Review*, 2 (1988), p. 3.

50 *Museums Journal*, 10 (1910–11), p. 223; Henry Roberts, 'The Organisation of Exhibitions of Foreign Art in Great Britain', *Museums Journal*, 12 (1912–13), pp. 69–78.

51 Steele 1990, p. 4.

52 Ibid., p. 177

53 Leeds City Art Gallery, *Loan Exhibition of Post-Impressionist Pictures and Drawings* (Leeds, 1913).

54 Rutter 1927, p. 205.

55 Rutter 1933, p. 77.

56 Wolverhampton Art and Industrial Exhibition, *Official Catalogue of the Fine Art Section* (Wolverhampton, 1902), p. 10.

57 Rutter 1933, p. 85.

58 Leeds City Art Gallery, *Works By and After John Constable, R.A.* (Leeds, 1913). Rutter published a book on Constable in 1923.

59 Steele 1990, p. 190. Sadleir changed the spelling of his name to distinguish him from his father.

60 Rutter 1927, p. 207. This approach has re-emerged in various towns since the 1990s.

61 The Whitworth Art Gallery in 1924 and the Victoria Art Gallery in 1925. See Wendy Baron, *Sickert: Paintings and Drawings* (New Haven and London, 2006).

62 See Bradford Art Galleries and Museums, *The Connoisseur – Art Patrons and Collectors in Victorian Bradford* (Bradford, 1989).

63 *Catalogue of the Works of Art in the Cartwright Memorial Hall* (Bradford, 1904), p. 3.

64 Ibid., p. 4.

65 *Art Journal* (1905), p. 356, with illustrations, pp. 354–5.

66 *Cartwright Memorial Hall, Illustrated Catalogue* (Bradford, 1924).

14: THE AFTERMATH

1 Leeds City Art Gallery, *What German Invasion Means…An Exhibition of Photographs, Proclamations, Relics &c.* (Leeds, 1914), p. 2. The exhibition ran from 21 December 1914 to 16 January 1915.

2 City of Bradford, *Annual Report of the Libraries, Art Gallery and Museum Committee*, 1917.

3 Ashmolean Museum, *Keeper's Report*, 1915, p. 1 (internal publication).

4 For the Country Houses Scheme, see Merlin Waterson, *The National Trust: The First Hundred Years* (London, 1994), Chapter Five. The history of the development of the historic house in local government care remains to be written.

5 Inventories in Birmingham City Art Gallery archives: 'Birmingham Museums and Art Gallery – Master Inventory'; 'Applied Art/ Archaeology'; 'Fine Art/Social History'.

6 For an extended account of Cotton, see Morris and Stevens 2013, pp. 65–84.

7 Frank Lambert, 'The Walker Art Gallery: The Growth of a Policy – 2', in *Liverpool Libraries, Museums & Arts Committee Bulletin*, 1, no. 3 (February, 1952), pp. 3–17, at p. 9.

8 Ibid., p. 10.

9 Henry Miers, *A Report on the Public Museums of the British Isles (Other than the National Museums)* (Edinburgh, 1928), p. 46.

10 Ibid., p. 1.

11 Rothenstein 1965, p. 194.

12 Ibid., p. 196.

13 Hendy 1939, p. 387.

14 Quoted in Adam White, 'Curators and Directors at the Art Gallery through the Past Hundred Years', *Leeds Art Calendar*, 102 (1988), pp. 3–7, at p. 6, from which this account is taken.

15 Hendy 1939, p. 388.

16 The Burrell Collection had been bequeathed to the city many years before, but was not given a permanent building until 1983.

17 See, for example, Richard Altick, *Paintings from Books: Art and Literature in Britain, 1760–1900* (Columbus, 1985), p. 58.

18 A painting by Guercino sold for over £5 million at Christie's in 2010.

19 Birmingham City Art Gallery, inventories. Drawings by Bawden and Spencer were acquired for £20 each in 1947.

20 Walker Art Gallery, *John Moores Liverpool Exhibition* (Liverpool, 1957). The first exhibition ran from 10 November 1957 to 11 January 1958. The series continues in the form of the biennial John Moores Painting Prize and Exhibition.

21 Noël Annan, *Our Age: Portrait of a Generation* (London, 1990), p. 14.

22 This history is definitively told by Morris and Stevens 2013, Chapter Four, 'The Struggle for State Aid'.

23 A vivid account of this period is given in Morris and Stevens 2013.

24 The Mappin has been renamed the Weston Park Museum.

25 At Middlesborough, Milton Keynes, Gateshead, Dundee, Margate, Nottingham, Wakefield and elsewhere.

26 Objections to Jaffé's innovations were recalled orally to the present writer by Professor Jaffé.

27 Notably, at Manchester Art Gallery and the Whitworth Art Gallery, which now share a director.

BIBLIOGRAPHY

The literature on the history and theory of museums is already formidably large and is growing by the year. The writing of this book has been influenced by numerous important texts that do not feature in this bibliography since they do not allude specifically to the history of art museums in Victorian Britain, but their contribution is none the less notable.

Place of publication is London unless stated otherwise.

Ackermann et al. 1808–10 Rudolph Ackermann et al., *The Microcosm of London*, three vols

Altick 1978 Richard Altick, *The Shows of London*, Cambridge, MA

Archer 1985 John G. Archer (ed.), *Art and Architecture in Victorian Manchester: Ten Illustrations of Patronage and Practice*, Manchester

Armstrong 1895 Richard Armstrong, *Henry William Crosskey*, Birmingham

Atkins 1996 E.M. Atkins, 'The Genesis of the Laing Art Gallery, Newcastle upon Tyne', in T.E. Faulkner (ed.), *Northumbrian Panorama: Studies in the History and Culture of North East England* (Newcastle upon Tyne, 1996), pp. 195–219

Auerbach 1998 Jeffrey Auerbach, *The Great Exhibition of 1851: A Nation on Display*, New Haven and London

Bailey 1998 Peter Bailey, *Popular Culture and Performance in the Victorian City*, Cambridge

Bailkin 2004 Jordanna Bailkin, *The Culture of Property: The Crisis of Liberalism in Modern Britain*, Chicago

Baretti 1781 Joseph Baretti, *A Guide Through the Royal Academy*

Barker 1906 W.R. Barker, *The Bristol Museum and Art Gallery: The Development of the Institution during a Hundred and Thirty-Four Years, 1772–1906*, Bristol

Barlow and Trodd 2000 Paul Barlow and Colin Trodd (eds), *Governing Culture: Art Institutions in Victorian London*, Aldershot

Barringer 2005 Timothy Barringer, *Men at Work: Art and Labour in Mid-Victorian Britain*, New Haven and London

Barry 1799 James Barry, *A Letter to the Dilettanti Society Respecting the Obtention of Certain Matters Essentially Necessary for the Improvement of Public Taste, and for Accomplishing the Original Views of the Royal Academy of Great Britain*, 2nd ed.

Bell 1949 Clive Bell, *Art*, 1914, repr. 1949

Bell and Paton 1896 Sir James Bell and James Paton, *Glasgow: Its Municipal Organization and Administration*, Glasgow

Bennett 1995 Tony Bennett, *The Birth of the Museum: History, Theory, Politics*

Bennett 2010 Mary Bennett, *Ford Madox Brown: A Catalogue Raisonné*, two vols, New Haven and London

Best 1971 Geoffrey Best, *Mid-Victorian Britain*

Birkett 1898 [Leeds City Art Gallery], George Birkett, *Catalogue of Paintings and Drawings in the Permanent Collection, with Notes, Descriptive and Biographical*, Leeds

Birmingham Handbook 1885 Birmingham Museum and Art Gallery, *Handbook to the Art Exhibition of the Inauguration of the Museum and Art Gallery*, Birmingham

Black 2000 Barbara J. Black, *On Exhibit: Victorians and their Museums*, Charlottesville

Brears and Davies 1989 Peter Brears and Stuart Davies, *Treasures for the People: The Story of Museums and Galleries in Yorkshire and Humberside*, Hull

Brewer 1997 John Brewer, *The Pleasures of the Imagination: English Culture in the Eighteenth Century*, New York

British Institution 1805 *An Account of the British Institution for Promoting the Fine Arts in the United Kingdom*

British Institution 1814 *Catalogue of Pictures by the Late William Hogarth, Richard Wilson, Thomas Gainsborough, and J. Zoffani [sic]*

Carey 1810 William Carey, *Cursory Thoughts on the Present State of the Fine Arts; Occasioned by the Founding of the Liverpool Academy*, Liverpool

Carey 1829 William Carey, *Observations on the Primary Object of the British Institution and of the Provincial Institutions for the Promotion of the Fine Arts...*

Carlyle 2005 Thomas Carlyle, *Past and Present* (1843), ed. Chris R. Vanden Bossche, Berkeley

Casteras and Parkinson 1988 Susan P. Casteras and Ronald Parkinson (eds), *Richard Redgrave 1804–88*, New Haven and London

Chapel and Gere 1985 Jeannie Chapel and Charlotte Gere, *The Fine and Decorative Art Collections of Britain and Ireland*, New York

Chesneau 1885 Ernest Chesneau, *The English School of Painting*

Church and Lawson 1987 Dorian Church and Paul Lawson, *Cartwright Hall*, Bradford

Cole 1867 Henry Cole (ed.), *Notes for a Universal Art Inventory of Works of Fine Art which may be Found throughout the Continent of Europe, for the Most Part…in Connexion with Architecture*

Cole 1884 A.S. and H. Cole (eds), *Fifty Years of Public Work of Sir Henry Cole K.C.B., Accounted for in his Deeds, Speeches and Writings*, two vols

Conlin 2006 Jonathan Conlin, *The Nation's Mantelpiece: A History of the National Gallery*

Conn 1998 Steven Conn, *Museums and American Intellectual Life*, Chicago

Conway 1991 Hazel Conway, *People's Parks: The Design and Development of Victorian Parks in Britain*, Cambridge

Crane 1983 M. Crane, 'A Present from the Past: the City of Bristol Museum and Art Gallery', 1983, unpublished typescript, Bristol Museum and Art Gallery archives

Crawford 1891 Robert Crawford, *The People's Palace of the Arts for the City of Glasgow*, Glasgow

Cunningham 1879–80 Allan Cunningham, *The Lives of the Most Eminent British Painters*, revised ed., three vols

Cuno 2004 James Cuno (ed.), *Whose Muse?: Art Museums and the Public Trust*, Princeton

Davies 1985 Stuart Davies, *By the Gains of Industry: Birmingham Museums and Art Gallery 1885–1985*, Birmingham

Davis 1999 John Davis, *The Great Exhibition*, Stroud

Donisthorpe 1868 George Donisthorpe, *An Account of the Origin and Progress of the Devon and Exeter Albert Memorial Museums*, Exeter

Duncan 1995 Carol Duncan, *Civilizing Rituals: Inside Public Art Museums*, London and New York

Dyall 1888 Charles Dyall, *First Decade of the Walker Art Gallery: A Report on Its Operations from 1877 to 1887*, Liverpool

Dyall 1902 Charles Dyall, *Descriptive Catalogue of the Permanent Collection of Pictures*, Liverpool

Edwards 1877 Eliezer Edwards, *Personal Rec-ollections of Birmingham and Birmingham Men*, Birmingham

Engels 1958 Friedrich Engels, *The Condition of the Working Class in England* (1844), ed. W.O. Henderson and W.H. Chaloner, Oxford

Eyre-Todd 1934 George Eyre-Todd, *Leaves from the Life of A Scottish Man of Letters*, Glasgow

Farington 1978–98 Kenneth Garlick and Kathryn Cave (eds), *The Diary of Joseph Farington*, seventeen vols, New Haven and London

Faucher 1844 Léon Faucher, *Manchester in 1844; Its Present Condition and Future Prospects*

Fawcett 1974 Trevor Fawcett, *The Rise of Provincial Art: Artists, Patrons, and Institutions outside London, 1800–1830*, Oxford

Flaxman 1838 John Flaxman, *Lectures on Sculpture*

Fletcher and Helmreich 2011 Pamela Fletcher and Anne Helmreich, *The Rise of the Modern Art Market in London, 1850–1939*, Manchester

Flower 1898 W.H. Flower, *Essays on Museums and Other Subjects Connected with Natural History*

Forgan 1994 Sophie Forgan, 'The Architecture of Display: Museums, Universities and Objects in Nineteenth-Century Britain', *History of Science*, 32 (1994), pp. 139–62

Fowle 2010 Frances Fowle, *Van Gogh's Twin: The Scottish Art Dealer Alexander Reid 1854–1928*, Edinburgh

Fox 2009 Celina Fox, *The Arts of Industry in the Age of Enlightenment*, New Haven and London

Fry 1920 Roger Fry, *Vision and Design*

Gibbs 1887 'H.S.G.' [Henry Gibbs], *Autobiography of a Manchester Cotton Manufacturer: or, Thirty Years' Experience of Manchester*, Manchester

Gill and Grant Robertson 1938 Conrad Gill and Charles Grant Robertson, *A Short History of Birmingham from its Origin to the Present Day*, Birmingham

Greenhalgh 1988 Paul Greenhalgh, *Ephemeral Vistas: The Expositions Universelles, Great Exhibitions and World's Fairs, 1851–1939*, Manchester

Greenwood 1888 Thomas Greenwood, *Museums and Art Galleries*

Gunn 2000 Simon Gunn, *The Public Culture of the Victorian Middle Class: Ritual and Authority and the English Industrial City, 1840–1914*, Manchester

Hamlyn 1993 Robin Hamlyn, *Robert Vernon's Gift: British Art for the Nation, 1847*

Hardy 1970 Charles E. Hardy, *John Bowes and the Bowes Museum*, Newcastle upon Tyne

Hartnell 1996 Roy Hartnell, *Pre-Raphaelite Birmingham*, Studley

Haskell 2000 Francis Haskell, *The Ephemeral Museum: Old Master Paintings and the Rise of the Art Exhibition*, New Haven and London

Hawthorne 1941 Nathaniel Hawthorne, *The English Notebooks*, ed. Randall Stewart, New York and London

Haydon 1844–6 B.R. Haydon, *Lectures on Painting and Design*, two vols

Haydon 1960–3 *The Diary of Benjamin Robert Haydon*, ed. W.B. Pope, five vols, Cambridge, Mass.

Hazlitt 1856 William Hazlitt, *Criticisms on Art: and Sketches of the Picture Galleries of England*, 2nd ed.

Helps 1862 Arthur Helps (ed.), *The Principal Speeches and Addresses of…The Prince Consort*

Hendy 1939 Philip Hendy, 'The Leeds Art Collections at Temple Newsam', *Museums Journal*, 39 (1939), pp. 387–8

Higonnet 2009 Anne Higonnet, *A Museum of One's Own: Private Collecting, Public Gift*, Pittsburgh

Hill 2005 Kate Hill, *Culture and Class in English Public Museums, 1850–1914*, Aldershot

Hoare 1813 Prince Hoare, *Epochs of the Arts: Including Hints on the Use and Progress of Painting and Sculpture in Great Britain*

Hobbes 1849 James R. Hobbes, *The Picture Collector's Manual*

Holmes 1903 C.H. Holmes, *Pictures and Picture Collecting*

Howarth and Platnauer 1911 E. Howarth and H.M. Platnauer, *Directory of Museums in Great Britain and Ireland*

Hudson 1851 J.W. Hudson, *The History of Adult Education: In Which is Comprised a Full and Complete History of the Mechanics and Literary Institutions, Athenaeums, Philosophical, Mental and Christian Improvement Societies, Literary Unions, Schools of Design, etc., of Great Britain, Ireland, America, etc, etc*

Hunt 2004 Tristram Hunt, *Building Jerusalem: The Rise and Fall of the Victorian City*

Hynes 1968 Samuel Hynes, *The Edwardian Turn of Mind*, Princeton and London

Illustrated Exhibitor 1851 *The Illustrated Exhibitor, A Tribute to the World's Industrial Jubilee: Comprising Sketches, by Pen and Pencil, of the Principal Objects in the Great Exhibition of the Industry of All Nations, 1851*

Inkster and Morrell 1983 Ian Inkster and Jack Morrell, *Metropolis and Province: Science in British Culture, 1780–1850*

Jameson 1842 Anna Jameson, *A Handbook to the Public Galleries of Art In and Near London*, two parts

Jessop and Sinclair 1996 L. Jessop and N.T. Sinclair, *Sunderland Museum: The People's Palace in the Park*, Sunderland

Johnstone 1859 W.B. Johnstone, *Catalogue, Descriptive and Historical of the National Gallery of Scotland*, Edinburgh

Kay 1832 Sir James Kay, *The Moral and Physical Condition of the Working Classes Employed in the Cotton Manufacture in Manchester*, 2nd ed.

Kay 1911 Thomas Kay, *Catalogue of Pictures in the Art Gallery of the Technical School at Heywood*, Heywood

Kennedy 1960 Michael Kennedy, *The Hallé Tradition*, Manchester

Kinchin 1988 Perilla Kinchin and Juliet Kinchin, *Glasgow's Great Exhibitions: 1888, 1901, 1911, 1938, 1988*, Wendlebury

Knox 1994 W.W. Knox, *Hanging by a Thread: The Scottish Cotton Industry c. 1850–1914*, Preston

Kriegel 2007 Lara Kriegel, *Grand Designs: Labor, Empire, and the Museum in Victorian Culture*, Durham, N.C.

Law 1881 Ernest Law, *Historical Catalogue of the Pictures in the Royal Collection at Hampton Court*

Leigh 1818 *Leigh's New Picture of London…Presenting a Luminous Guide to the Stranger, on All Subjects Connected with General Information, Business, or Amusement*

Liscombe 1980 R.W. Liscombe, *William Wilkins 1778–1859*, Cambridge

Lorente 1998 J. Pedro Lorente, *Cathedrals of Urban Modernity: The First Museums of Contemporary Art, 1800–1930*, Aldershot

Luckhurst 1951 Kenneth Luckhurst, *The Story of Exhibitions*, London and New York

MacColl 1931 D.S. MacColl, *Confessions of a Keeper*

Macleod 1989 D.S. Macleod, 'Avant-Garde Patronage in the North East', in [Laing Art Gallery], Brian Vickers (ed.), *Pre-Raphaelites: Painters and Patrons in the North East* (Newcastle upon Tyne, 1989), pp. 9–37

Macleod 1996 Dianne Sachko Macleod, *Art and the Victorian Middle Class*, Cambridge

Mainardi 1987 Patricia Mainardi, *Art and Politics of the Second Empire*, New Haven and London

Mainardi 1993 Patricia Mainardi, *The End of*

the Salon: Art and the State in the Early Third Republic*, Cambridge

Manchester 1859 *Exhibition of Art Treasures of the United Kingdom – Held at Manchester in 1857, Report of the Executive Committee*, Manchester

Mayhew 1851 Henry Mayhew, *1851: or The Adventures of Mr. and Mrs. Cursty Sandboys and Family Who Came up to London To "Enjoy Themselves", and To See the Great Exhibition*, illustrated by George Cruikshank

McClellan 2008 Andrew McClellan, *The Art Museum from Boullée to Bilbao*, Berkeley

McGibbon 1901 Alexander McGibbon, 'The Glasgow International Exhibition, 1901', *Art Journal* (1901), pp. 129–32

Minihan 1977 Janet Minihan, *The Nationalization of Culture: The Development of State Subsidies to the Arts in Great Britain*, New York

Moore 1898 George Moore, *Modern Painting*, 2nd ed.

Morris 1986 Barbara Morris, *Inspiration for Design: The Influence of the Victoria and Albert Museum*

Morris 1996 Edward Morris, *Victorian and Edwardian Paintings in the Walker Art Gallery and at Sudley House: British Artists Born After 1810 But Before 1861*, Liverpool

Morris 2005 Edward Morris, *French Art in Nineteenth-Century Britain*, New Haven and London

Morris and Stevens 2013 Edward Morris and Timothy Stevens, *The Walker Art Gallery Liverpool 1873–2000*, Bristol

Muirhead 1911 J.H. Muirhead (ed.), *Birmingham Institutions: Lectures given at the University*, Birmingham

Murray 1904 David Murray, *Museums, their History and their Use*, three vols, Glasgow

Musgrave 1995 Michael Musgrave, *The Musical Life of the Crystal Palace*, Cambridge

Muspratt 1917 E.K. Muspratt, *My Life and Work*, London and New York

Nottingham Castle 1878 *Nottingham Castle: A Statement of the Objects of this Institution, and the Adaptation of Nottingham Castle as its Permanent Location by the Town Council of Nottingham*, Nottingham

Olding 1999 Simon Olding (ed.), *A Victorian Salon: Paintings from the Russell-Cotes Art Gallery and Museum*, Bournemouth

Palgrave 1862 F.T. Palgrave, *Handbook to the Fine Art Collections in the International Exhibition of 1862*

Palgrave 1869 F.T. Palgrave, *Gems of English Art of This Century*, London and New York

Paul 2012 Carole Paul, 'Capitoline Museum, Rome: Civic Identity and Personal Cultivation', in Carole Paul (ed.), *The First Modern Museums of Art: The Birth of an Institution in 18th- and Early-19th-Century Europe* (Los Angeles, 2012), pp. 21–45

Pergam 2011 Elizabeth Pergam, *The Manchester Art-Treasures Exhibition of 1857: Entrepreneurs, Connoisseurs and the Public*, Farnham

Perry 2006 Lara Perry, *History's Beauties: Women in the National Portrait Gallery*, Aldershot

Physick 1982 John Physick, *The Victoria and Albert Museum: The History of its Building*, Oxford

Piggott 1976 Stuart Piggott, *Ruins in a Landscape: Essays in Antiquarianism*, Edinburgh

Piggott 2004 J.R. Piggott, *Palace of the People: The Crystal Palace at Sydenham 1854–1936*

Plagemann 1967 Volker Plagemann, *Das deutsche Kunstmuseum 1790–1870*, Munich

Priestley 1902–3 'Museums Association: Bradford Conference, 1902: Address by the President, W.E.B. Priestley, J.P.', *Museums Journal*, 2 (1902–3), pp. 5–13

Quilter 1892 Harry Quilter, *Preferences in Art, Life, and Literature*

Reach 1972 A.B. Reach, *Manchester and the Textile Districts in 1849*, ed. C. Aspin, [Rossendale]

Redgrave 1857 Richard Redgrave, *On the Gift of the Sheepshanks Collection: With a View to the Formation of a National Gallery of British Art*, no. 2 in the series *Introductory Addresses on the Science and Art Department and the South Kensington Museum*

Redgrave 1947 Richard and Samuel Redgrave, *A Century of Painters of the English School*, 1866, repr. 1947

Reynolds 1975 Sir Joshua Reynolds, *Discourses on Art*, ed. Robert R. Wark, New Haven and London

Richards 1990 Thomas Richards, *The Commodity Culture of Victorian England: Advertising and Spectacle, 1851–1914*, Stanford

Richardson 1719 Jonathan Richardson, *Two Discourses*

Ripps 2010 M.J. Ripps, 'Bond Street Picture Dealers and the International Trade in Dutch Old Masters, 1882–1914', D.Phil. thesis, University of Oxford

Robertson 1978 David Robertson, *Sir Charles*

Eastlake and the Victorian Art World, Princeton

Robinson 1880 J.C. Robinson, 'Our National Art Collections and Provincial Art Museums', in *The Nineteenth Century*, 8 (1880), pp. 249–65

Rose 1986 Jonathan Rose, *The Edwardian Temperament, 1895–1919*, Athens, Ohio

Rothenstein 1965 John Rothenstein, *Summer's Lease: Autobiography 1901–1938*

Rouquet 1755 Jean André Rouquet, *The Present State of the Arts in England*

Rowley 1911 Charles Rowley, *Fifty Years of Work Without Wages: (Laborare est Orare)*

Royal Academy of Arts 1998 *Art Treasures of England: The Regional Collections*

Ruskin 1880 John Ruskin, 'A Museum or Picture Gallery: Its Functions and Its Formation', *Art Journal* (1880), pp. 161–3

Ruskin, *Works* E.T. Cook and A. Wedderburn, *The Works of John Ruskin*, thirty-nine vols, London and New York, 1904–9

Russell-Cotes 1921 Merton Russell-Cotes, *Home and Abroad: Autobiography of an Octogenerian*, Bournemouth

Rutter 1927 Frank Rutter, *Since I was Twenty-Five*

Rutter 1933 Frank Rutter, *Art in My Time*

Saint 2007 Andrew Saint, *Architect and Engineer: A Study in Sibling Rivalry*, New Haven and London

Seed 1982 John Seed, 'Unitarianism, Political Economy and the Antinomies of Liberal Culture in Manchester, 1830–50', *Social History*, 7, no. 1 (January 1982), pp. 1–25

Select Committee Report, Arts and Manufactures 1836 *Report from the Select Committee on Arts and their Connexion with Manufactures; With the Minutes of Evidence, Appendix and Index*

Select Committee Report, National Gallery 1850 *Report from the Select Committee on the National Gallery: Together with the Minutes of Evidence, Appendix and Index*

Select Committee Report, National Gallery 1853 *Report of Select Committee appointed to Inquire into the Management of the National Gallery…1853*

Select Committee Report, Works of Art 1848 *Report, Proceedings and Minutes of Evidence of the Select Committee Appointed to Consider the Best Mode of Providing Additional Room for Works of Art given to the Public, or Purchased by Means of Parliamentary Grants*

Shaffner and Owen 1862 Colonel Taliaferro P. Shaffner and the Revd William Owen, *The Illustrated Record of the International Exhibition of the Industrial Arts and Manufactures, and the Fine Arts, of All Nations, in 1862*, London and New York

Sharp 1898 William Sharp, 'The Art Treasures of America', *The Nineteenth Century*, 44 (1898), pp. 359–72

Sheehan 2000 James Sheehan, *Museums in the German Art World from the End of the Old Regime to the Rise of Modernism*, Oxford

Sherman 1989 Daniel Sherman, *Worthy Monuments: Art Museums and the Politics of Culture in Nineteenth-Century France*, Cambridge, Mass.

Simond 1815 Louis Simond, *Journal of a Tour and Residence in Great Britain, during…1810 and 1811, by a French Traveller*, two vols, Edinburgh

Somerville-Large 2004 Peter Somerville-Large, *1854 –2004: The Story of the National Gallery of Ireland*, Dublin

Sparke 1907 Archibald Sparke, *The Bury Art Gallery and the Wrigley Collection*, Bury

Stanfield 1894 William Stanfield, *Manchester City Art Gallery, Catalogue of the Permanent Collection of Pictures in Oil and Water Colours with Descriptive Notes and Illustrations*, Manchester

Steele 1990 Tom Steele, *Alfred Orage and the Leeds Art Club 1893–1923*, Mitcham

Summerson 1955 John Summerson, 'Museums as Architecture', *Museums Journal* (December 1955), pp. 31–8

Summerson 1985 John Summerson, 'The Architecture of British Museums and Art Galleries', in Jeannie Chapel and Charlotte Gere (eds), *The Fine and Decorative Art Collections of Britain and Ireland*

Taylor 1999 Brandon Taylor *Art for the Nation: Exhibitions and the London Public 1747–2001*, Manchester

Thompson 1988 F.M.L. Thompson, *The Rise of Respectable Society: A Social History of Victorian Britain 1830–1900*, Cambridge, Mass.

Thornbury 1861 Walter Thornbury, *British Artists from Hogarth to Turner: Being a Series of Biographical Sketches*, two vols

Tickner 2000 Lisa Tickner, *Modern Life and Modern Subjects: British Art in the Early Twentieth Century*, New Haven and London

Tocqueville 1958 Alexis de Tocqueville, *Journey to England*, 1835, repr. 1958

Treuherz 1993 Julian Treuherz, *Pre-Raphaelite Paintings from Manchester City Art Galleries*, Manchester

Usherwood 1984 Paul Usherwood, *Art for Newcastle – Thomas Miles Richardson and the Newcastle Exhibitions 1822–1843*, Newcastle upon Tyne

Waagen 1853 Gustav Waagen, 'Thoughts on the New Building to be Erected for the National Gallery of England and on the Arrangement, Preservation, and Enlargement of the Collection', *Art Journal* (1853), pp. 101–3 and 121–5

Waagen 1854–7 Gustav Waagen, *Treasures of Art in Great Britain*, three vols

Wallis 1911 Whitworth Wallis, 'The Museum and Art Gallery' in Muirhead 1911, pp. 475–521

Wallis and St Johnston 1885 Whitworth Wallis and Alfred St Johnston, *Official Catalogue of the Contents of the Birmingham Museum and Art Gallery*, Birmingham

Waterfield 1991 Giles Waterfield (ed.), *Palaces of Art: Art Galleries in Britain 1790–1990*

Waterfield 1994 Giles Waterfield (ed.), *Art for the People: Culture in the Slums of Late Victorian Britain*

Waugh 2008 Edwin Waugh *The Diary of Edwin Waugh: Life in Victorian Manchester and Rochdale, 1847–1851*, ed. Brian Hollingworth, Lancaster

Wey 1935 Francis Wey, *A Frenchman Sees the English in the '50s*, trans. Valérie Pirie

What to See 1857 *What to See, and Where to See It!*

Whitehead 2005 Christopher Whitehead, *The Public Art Museum in Nineteenth Century Britain: The Development of the National Gallery*, Aldershot

Whitehead 2005a Christopher Whitehead in 'Architectures of Display at the National Gallery', *Journal of the History of Collections*, 17, no. 2 (2005), pp. 189–211

Whiteley 1997 J.J.L. Whiteley, 'The University Galleries', in M.G. Brock and M.C. Curthoys (eds), *The History of the University of Oxford*, VI, *Nineteenth-Century Oxford*, Part I, Oxford, pp. 611–30

Wildman 1995 Stephen Wildman (ed.), *Visions of Love and Life: Pre-Raphaelite Art from the Birmingham Collection, England*, Alexandria, VA

Williams 1981 Heather Williams, 'The Lives and Works of Nottingham Artists from 1750 to 1914', D.Phil. thesis, University of Nottingham

Wilson 1851 C.H. Wilson, 'Some Remarks upon Lighting Picture and Sculpture Galleries', *Art Journal* (1851), pp. 205–7

Wilson 2002 David M. Wilson, *The British Museum – A History*

Woodson-Boulton 2012 Amy Woodson-Boulton, *Transformative Beauty: Art Museums in Industrial Britain*, Stanford

Wornum 1848 Ralph Wornum (ed.), *Lectures on Painting by the Royal Academician*

Yanni 1999 Carla Yanni, *Nature's Museums: Victorian Science and the Architecture of Display*

ILLUSTRATION CREDITS

INDEX